BLACK+DECKER

THE BOOK OF HOME HOW-TO

UPDATED 3RD EDITION

MW01155343

BLACK+DECKER™

THE BOOK OF

HOME HOW-TO

UPDATED 3RD EDITION

COMPLETE PHOTO GUIDE TO HOME REPAIR + IMPROVEMENT

The Editors of Cool Springs Press

COOL
SPRINGS
PRESS

Quarto.com

© 2025 Quarto Publishing Group USA Inc.
Text © 2014, 2020, 2025 Quarto Publishing Group USA Inc.

Second edition published in 2020
First Published in 2014 by Cool Springs Press, an imprint of The Quarto Group,
100 Cummings Center, Suite 265-D, Beverly, MA 01915, USA.
T (978) 282-9590 F (978) 283-2742

All rights reserved. No part of this book may be reproduced in any form without written permission of the copyright owners. All images in this book have been reproduced with the knowledge and prior consent of the artists concerned, and no responsibility is accepted by producer, publisher, or printer for any infringement of copyright or otherwise, arising from the contents of this publication. Every effort has been made to ensure that credits accurately comply with the information supplied. We apologize for any inaccuracies that may have occurred and will resolve inaccurate or missing information in a subsequent reprinting of the book.

Cool Springs Press titles are also available at discount for retail, wholesale, promotional, and bulk purchase. For details, contact the Special Sales Manager by email at specialsales@quarto.com or by mail at The Quarto Group, Attn: Special Sales Manager, 100 Cummings Center, Suite 265-D, Beverly, MA 01915, USA.

29 28 27 26 25   1 2 3 4 5

ISBN: 978-0-7603-9547-9

Digital edition published in 2025
eISBN: 978-0-7603-9548-6

Library of Congress Cataloging-in-Publication Data available

Page Layout: *tabula rasa* graphic design

Printed in China

BLACK+DECKER The Book of Home How-to, Updated 3rd Edition
Created by: The Editors of Cool Springs Press, in cooperation with BLACK+DECKER.

BLACK+DECKER and the BLACK+DECKER logo are trademarks of The Black+Decker Corporation and are used under license. All rights reserved.

NOTICE TO READERS

For safety, use caution, care, and good judgment when following the procedures described in this book. The publisher and BLACK+DECKER cannot assume responsibility for any damage to property or injury to persons as a result of misuse of the information provided.

The techniques shown in this book are general techniques for various applications. In some instances, additional techniques not shown in this book may be required. Always follow manufacturers' instructions included with products, since deviating from the directions may void warranties. The projects in this book vary widely as to skill levels required: some may not be appropriate for all do-it-yourselfers, and some may require professional help.

Consult your local building department for information on building permits, codes, and other laws as they apply to your project.

CONTENTS

INTRODUCTION

Being the master of your own castle means getting on top of the myriad DIY tasks any home requires over time due to exposure to the elements and basic wear and tear. Systems age and develop problems. Paint wears thin, floors crack as the building settles, and clogs happen to the best of us. The good news? Take the initiative to fix and maintain your home and you can save a lot of money. The better news? Along the way, you develop a sense of pride and the uniquely reassuring confidence that you can handle whatever goes wrong inside your walls (or even outside them).

Those skills will also allow to upgrade your home even when nothing is wrong with it. After all, styles change. Globe lights give way to track lights that give way to modern recessed cans (and now, "canless" recessed lighting). The ability to wire one of those, is the ability to wire and install any of them.

You'll find that kind of skill-building throughout this new edition of *BLACK + DECKER The Book of Home How-To*. We updated the book to include timely insightful information from the professionals at a DIY brand founded on trust and quality. The information here has been thoroughly vetted and carefully curated to make it as accessible and usable as possible. Even if you struggle to figure out which screwdriver to use. This new edition has been updated with information that complies with the latest codes and the current best standards and practices.

This book is literally an A–Z guide. The structure is organized to make it easy to find exactly what you want to know, when you need to know it. There's also a handy, in-depth index in the back that will lead you right to the topic at hand. The entire book has been developed for ease of use, so you never need to struggle to find exactly the information you want and need.

Each step along the way, you'll be building skills and improving the value of the home. Given the financial benefits, it's likely this book will pay for itself in the first project you tackle (and the cost savings from the first professional you don't need to hire). The pride and satisfaction of doing a job well? That part is priceless.

ANATOMY OF A HOUSE

Before you start a do-it-yourself project, you should familiarize yourself with a few basic elements of home construction and remodeling. Take some time to get comfortable with the terminology shown on the next few pages. The understanding you will gain in this section will make it easier to plan your project, buy the right materials, and clear up any confusion you might have about the internal design of your home.

If your project includes modifying exterior or load-bearing walls, you must determine if your house was built using platform- or balloon-style framing. The framing style of your home determines what kind of temporary supports you will need to install while the work is in progress. If you have trouble determining what type of framing was used in your home, refer to the original blueprints, if you have them, or consult a building contractor or licensed home inspector.

ANATOMY OF A HOUSE WITH PLATFORM FRAMING

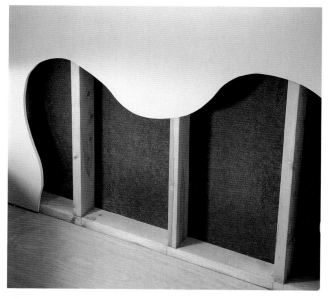

Platform framing (photos right and above) is identified by the floor-level sole plates and ceiling-level top plates to which the wall studs are attached. Most houses built after 1930 use platform framing. If you do not have access to unfinished areas, you can remove the wall surface at the bottom of a wall to determine what kind of framing was used in your home.

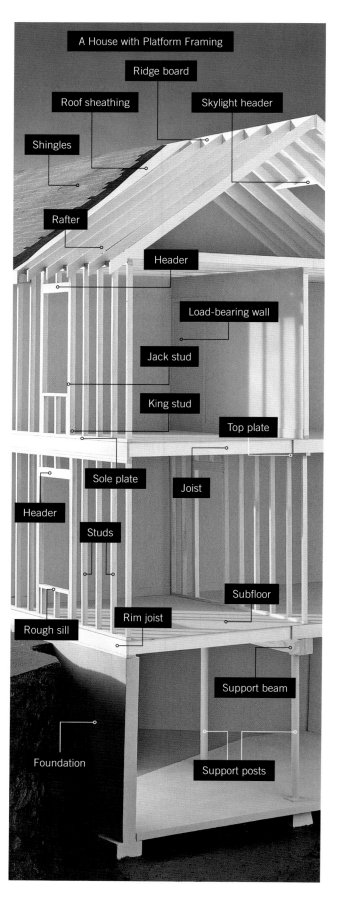

A House with Platform Framing
Ridge board
Roof sheathing
Skylight header
Shingles
Rafter
Header
Load-bearing wall
Jack stud
King stud
Top plate
Sole plate
Joist
Header
Studs
Subfloor
Rough sill
Rim joist
Support beam
Foundation
Support posts

Framing in a new door or window on an exterior wall normally requires installing a header. Make sure that the header you install meets the requirements of your local building code, and always install cripple studs where necessary.

Floors and ceilings consist of sheet materials, joists, and support beams. All floors used as living areas must have joists with at least 2 × 8 construction.

There are two types of walls: load-bearing and partition. Load-bearing walls require temporary supports during wall removal or framing of a door or window. Partition walls carry no structural load and do not require temporary supports.

ANATOMY OF A HOUSE WITH BALLOON FRAMING

Balloon framing (photos right and above) is identified by wall studs that run uninterrupted from the roof to a sill plate on the foundation, without the sole plates and top plates found in platform-framed walls (opposite page). Balloon framing was used in houses built before 1930, and it is still used in some new home styles, especially those with high vaulted ceilings.

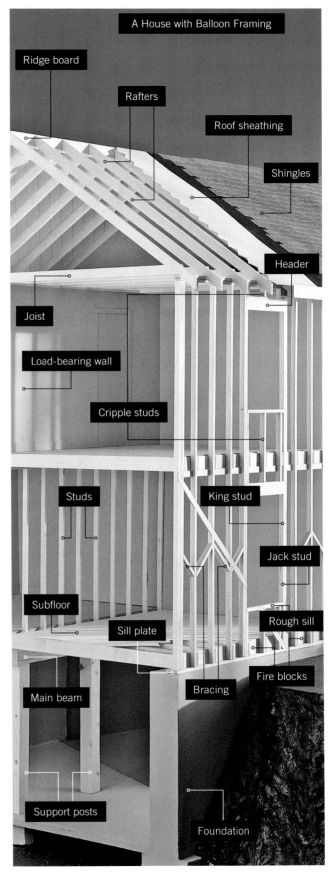

A House with Balloon Framing

Ridge board

Rafters

Roof sheathing

Shingles

Header

Joist

Load-bearing wall

Cripple studs

Studs

King stud

Jack stud

Subfloor

Rough sill

Sill plate

Fire blocks

Main beam

Bracing

Support posts

Foundation

ANATOMY DETAILS

Many remodeling projects, like adding new doors or windows, require that you remove one or more studs in a load-bearing wall to create an opening. When planning your project, remember that new openings require a permanent support beam called a header, above the removed studs, to carry the structural load directly.

The required size for the header is set by local building codes and varies according to the width of the rough opening. For a window or door opening, a header can be built from two pieces of 2-inch dimensional lumber sandwiched around ½-inch plywood (chart, right). When a large portion of a load-bearing wall (or an entire wall) is removed, a laminated beam product can be used to make the new header.

If you will be removing more than one wall stud, make temporary supports to carry the structural load until the header is installed.

Recommended Header Sizes

ROUGH OPENING WIDTH	RECOMMENDED HEADER CONSTRUCTION
Up to 3'	½" plywood between two 2 × 4s
3 to 5'	½" plywood between two 2 × 6s
5 to 7'	½" plywood between two 2 × 8s
7 to 8'	½" plywood between two 2 × 10s

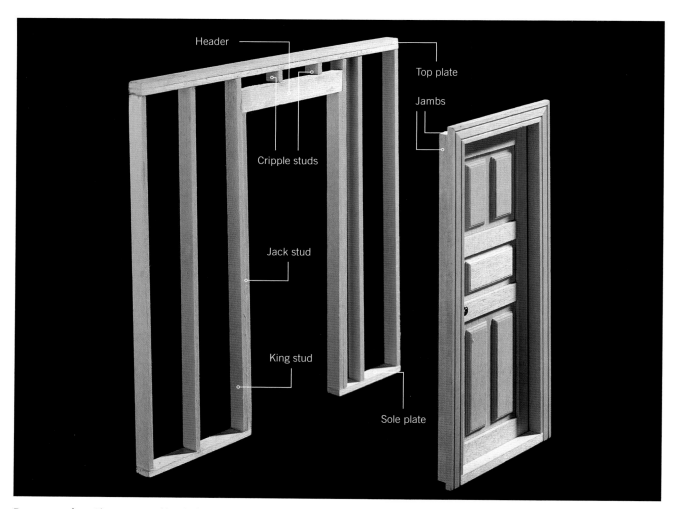

Door opening: The structural load above the door is carried by cripple studs that rest on a header. The ends of the header are supported by jack studs (also known as trimmer studs) and king studs that transfer the load to the sole plate and the foundation of the house. The rough opening for a door should be 1" wider and ½" taller than the dimensions of the door unit, including the jambs. This extra space lets you adjust the door unit during installation.

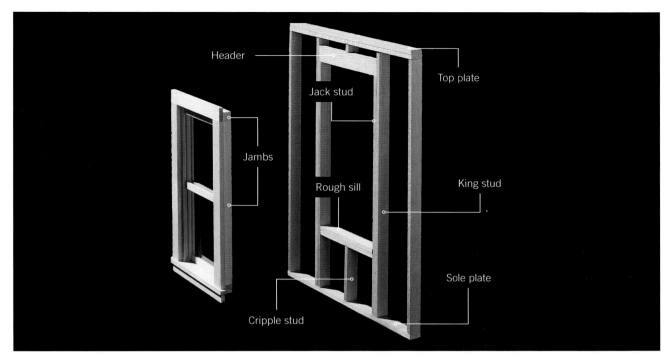

Window opening: The structural load above the window is carried by cripple studs resting on a header. The ends of the header are supported by jack studs and king studs, which transfer the load to the sole plate and the foundation of the house. The rough sill, which helps anchor the window unit but carries no structural weight, is supported by cripple studs. To provide room for adjustments during installation, the rough opening for a window should be 1" wider and ½" taller than the window unit, including the jambs.

FRAMING OPTIONS FOR WINDOW + DOOR OPENINGS (NEW LUMBER SHOWN IN YELLOW)

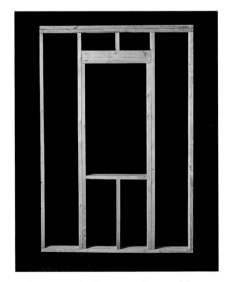
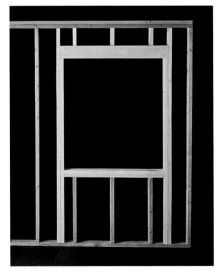

Using an existing opening avoids the need for new framing. This is a good option in homes with masonry exteriors, which are difficult to alter. Order a replacement unit that is 1" narrower and ½" shorter than the rough opening.

Framing a new opening is the only solution when you're installing a window or door where none existed or when you're replacing a unit with one that is much larger.

Enlarging an existing opening simplifies the framing. In many cases, you can use an existing king stud and jack stud to form one side of the new opening.

BASEMENTS: WET WALLS

Basement moisture can destroy your efforts to create functional living space. Over time, even small amounts of moisture can rot framing, turn wallboard to mush, and promote the growth of mold and mildew. Before proceeding with your basement project, you must deal with any moisture issues. The good news is that moisture problems can be resolved, often very easily.

Basement moisture appears in two forms: condensation and seepage. Condensation comes from airborne water vapor that turns to water when it contacts cold surfaces. Vapor sources include humid outdoor air, poorly ventilated appliances, damp walls, and water released from concrete. Seepage is water that enters the basement by infiltrating cracks in the foundation or by leeching through masonry, which is naturally porous. Often caused by ineffective exterior drainage, seepage comes from rain or groundwater that collects around the foundation or from a rising water table.

If you have a wet basement, you'll see evidence of moisture problems. Typical signs include peeling paint, white residue on masonry (called efflorescence), mildew stains, sweaty windows and pipes, rusted appliance feet, rotted wood near the floor, buckled floor tile, and strong mildew odor.

To reduce condensation, run a high-capacity dehumidifier in the basement. Insulate cold-water pipes to prevent condensate drippage, and make sure your dryer and other appliances have vents running to the outside. Extending central air conditioning service to the basement can help reduce vapor during warm, humid months.

Crawlspaces can also promote condensation, as warm, moist air enters through vents and meets cooler interior air. Crawlspace ventilation is a source of ongoing debate, and there's no universal method that applies to all climates. It's best to ask the local building department for advice on this matter.

Solutions for preventing seepage range from simple do-it-yourself projects to expensive, professional jobs requiring excavation and foundation work. Since it's often difficult to determine the source of seeping water, it makes sense to try some common cures before calling in professional help. If the simple measures outlined here don't correct your moisture problems, you must consider more

Repairing cracks restores the integrity of concrete foundation walls that leak, but it is often only a temporary fix. Selecting an appropriate repair product and doing careful preparation will make the repair more long lasting. A hydraulic concrete repair product like the one seen here is perfect for basement wall repair because it actually hardens from contact with water.

extensive action. Serious water problems are typically handled by installing footing drains or sump pump systems. Footing drains are installed around the foundation's perimeter, near the footing, and they drain out to a distant area of the yard. These usually work in conjunction with waterproof coatings on the exterior side of the foundation walls. Sump systems use an interior underslab drainpipe to collect water in a pit, and water is discharged outside by an electric sump pump.

Installing a new drainage system is expensive and must be done properly. Adding a sump system involves breaking up the concrete floor along the basement's perimeter, digging a trench, and laying a perforated drainpipe in a bed of gravel. After the sump pit is installed, the floor is patched with new concrete. Installing a footing drain is far more complicated. This involves digging out the foundation, installing gravel and drainpipe, and waterproofing the foundation walls. A footing drain is considered a last-resort measure.

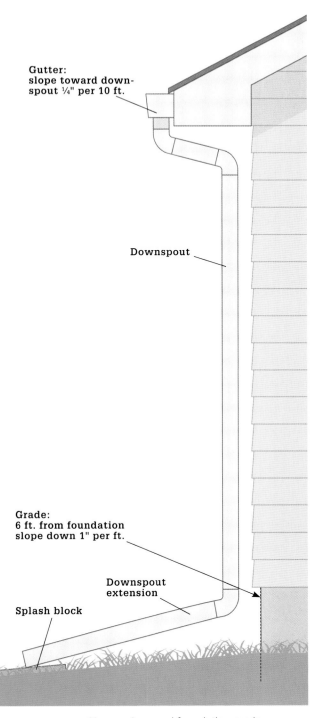

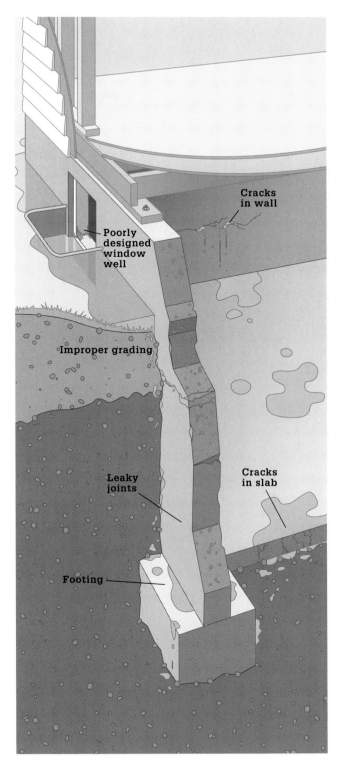

Gutter:
slope toward down-
spout ¼" per 10 ft.

Downspout

Grade:
6 ft. from foundation
slope down 1" per ft.

Downspout
extension

Splash block

Cracks
in wall

Poorly
designed
window
well

Improper grading

Leaky
joints

Cracks
in slab

Footing

Improve your gutter system and foundation grade to prevent rainwater and snowmelt from flooding your basement. Keep gutters clean and straight. Make sure there's a downspout for every 50 ft. of roof eave, and extend downspouts at least 8 ft. from the foundation. Build up the grade around the foundation so that it carries water away from the house.

Common causes of basement moisture include improper grading around the foundation, inadequate or faulty gutter systems, condensation, cracks in foundation walls, leaky joints between structural elements, and poorly designed window wells. More extensive problems include large cracks in the foundation, damaged or missing drain tiles, a high water table, or the presence of underground streams. Often, a combination of factors is at fault.

HOW TO SEAL CRACKS IN A FOUNDATION WALL

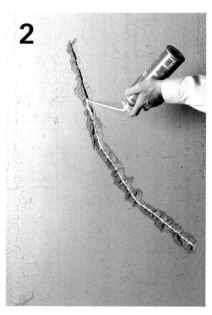

To repair a stable crack, chisel cut a keyhole cut that's wider at the base then at the surface, and no more than ½" deep. Clean out the crack with a wire brush.

To help seal against moisture, fill the crack with expanding insulating foam, working from bottom to top.

Mix hydraulic cement according to the manufacturer's instructions, then trowel it into the crack, working from the bottom to top. Apply cement in layers no more than ¼" thick, until the patch is slightly higher than the surrounding area. Feather cement with the trowel until it's even with the surface. Allow to dry thoroughly.

HOW TO SKIM-COAT A FOUNDATION WALL

Resurface heavily cracked masonry walls with a water-resistant masonry coating such as surface bonding cement. Clean and dampen the walls according to the coating manufacturer's instructions, then fill large cracks and holes with the coating. Finally, plaster a ¼" layer of the coating on the walls using a square-end trowel. Specially formulated heavy-duty masonry coatings are available for very damp conditions.

Scratch the surface with a paintbrush cleaner or a homemade scratching tool after the coating has set up for several hours. After 24 hours, apply a second, smooth coat. Mist the wall twice a day for three days as the coating cures.

Brush-on Waterproofing Sealant ▸

Epoxy waterproofing sealers are thick, paint-like materials that are brushed onto surfaces like basement foundation walls to make them watertight. First used on water tanks, ponds and pools, these products are self-curing, easy to use, and designed to resist hydrostatic pressure. This makes them a good choice to coat basement walls in which large or small cracks have been repaired. Most epoxy sealers are available with a variety of tints. This allows you to color an exposed foundation wall to match the rest of the house. When not tinted, the material cures clear.

Waterproofing paint is less effective than epoxy coatings, but is a decorative option that will keep a wall relatively water resistant. If you choose this option, make sure the label specifies that the product is meant for use on basement walls.

Clean your gutters and patch any holes. Make sure the gutters slope toward the downspouts at ¹⁄₁₆" per ft. or more. Add downspout extensions and splash blocks to keep roof runoff at least 8 ft. away from the foundation.

Cover window wells that will otherwise allow water into a basement. Covering them with removable plastic is the easiest way to keep them dry. Covers on egress window wells must be easily removed from inside. If you prefer to leave wells uncovered, add a gravel layer and a drain to the bottom of the well. Clean the well regularly to remove moisture-heavy debris.

HOW TO REPAIR CONCRETE FLOOR CRACKS

Prepare the crack for the repair materials by knocking away any loose or deteriorating material and beveling the edges down and outward with a cold chisel. Sweep or vacuum the debris and thoroughly dampen the repair area. Do not allow any water to pool, however.

Mix the repair product to fill the crack according to the manufacturer's instructions. Here, a fast-setting cement repair product with acrylic fortifier is being used. Trowel the product into the crack, overfilling slightly. With the edge of the trowel, trim the excess material and feather it so it is smooth and the texture matches the surrounding surface.

HOW TO PATCH A SMALL HOLE

Cut out around the damaged area with a masonry-grinding disc mounted on a portable drill (or use a hammer and stone chisel). The cuts should bevel about 15° away from the center of the damaged area. Chisel out any loose concrete within the repair area. Always wear gloves and eye protection.

Dampen the repair area with clean water and then fill it with vinyl concrete patcher. Pack the material in with a trowel, allowing it to crown slightly above the surrounding surface. Then, feather the edges so the repair is smooth and flat. Protect the repair from foot traffic for at least one day and from vehicle traffic for three days.

HOW TO PATCH A LARGE HOLE

Use a hammer and chisel or a heavy floor scraper to remove all material that is loose or shows any deterioration. Thoroughly clean the area with a hose and nozzle or a pressure washer.

OPTION: Make beveled cuts around the perimeter of the repair area with a circular saw and masonry-cutting blade. The bevels should slant down and away from the damage to create a "key" for the repair material.

Mix concrete patching compound according to the manufacturer's instructions, and then trowel it neatly into the damage area, which should be dampened before the patching material is placed. Overfill the damage area slightly.

Smooth and feather the repair with a steel trowel so it is even with the surrounding concrete surface. Finish the surface of the repair material to blend with the existing surface. For example, use a whisk broom to re-create a broomed finish. Protect the repair from foot traffic for at least one day and from vehicle traffic for three days.

DRAINAGE SOLUTION: HOW TO INSTALL A SUMP PUMP

If water continues to accumulate in your basement despite all your efforts at sealing your basement walls, installing a sump pump may be your only option. Permanently located in a pit beneath your basement floor, the sump pump turns on whenever enough water accumulates in the pit to trigger the pump float. The water is then pumped out of the basement through a pipe that runs through the rim joist of the house.

Because you'll be digging well beneath the basement floor, make certain there is no sewer pipe or water supply pipe in the digging area. Contact a plumber if you aren't sure if the area is clear.

The purpose of a sump pump is to collect and remove water that accumulates beneath your basement floor (usually due to a high water table) before it can be drawn or forced up into the basement. The most effective installations have drain tile around the entire perimeter of the house and channeling water to the pump pit. This system can be created as a retrofit job, but it is a major undertaking best left to a pro.

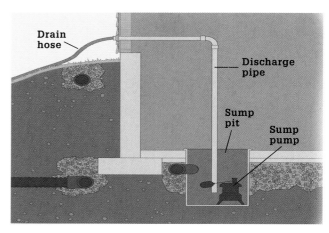

A submersible sump pump is installed in a pit beneath a basement floor to pump water out before it seeps up into the basement.

HOW TO INSTALL A SUMP PUMP

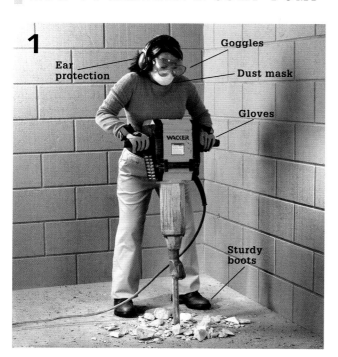

Dig the sump pit. Start by finding the lowest point of the floor (or the spot where water typically accumulates) that is at least 8" from a foundation wall. Outline an area that's about 6" wider than the pit liner all around. Remove the concrete in this area. Basement floors are typically 3" to 4" thick, so renting an electric jackhammer is a good idea.

Install the pit liner after digging a hole for it in the granular material under the floor. The hole should be a few inches wider than the liner. Remove the excavated material right away. Add gravel to the bottom of the hole as needed to bring the liner level with the top of its rim at floor level.

Pack the liner in place by pouring ½" gravel around it. Add a 1" base of gravel and then mix concrete to patch the floor. Trowel the concrete around the rim with a float so the patch is level and smooth.

Prepare the sump pump for installation. Thread a PVC adapter fitting onto the pump outlet, and then cement a PVC standpipe to the adapter. The standpipe should be long enough to extend about 1 ft. past the liner rim when the pump is set on the bottom of the liner.

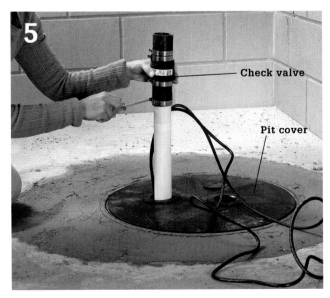

Check valve

Pit cover

Attach a check valve to the top of the standpipe to prevent the backflow of water into the pump pit. Cement another riser to fit into the top of the check valve and run upward to a point level with the rim joist, where the discharge tube will exit the basement.

Drill a hole in the rim joist for the discharge tube and finish routing the drainpipe out through the rim joist. Caulk around the tube on both the interior and exterior sides. On the exterior, attach an elbow fitting to the discharge tube and run drainpipe down from the elbow. Place a splash block beneath the drainpipe to direct water away from the house. Plug the pump in to a GFCI-protected receptacle.

RESURFACING A CONCRETE FLOOR

Badly degraded concrete basement floors can be restored by applying a topcoat of floor resurfacer. This cement-based product is designed to be poured on as a thick liquid so it can use gravity to find and fill in the low areas. After the resurfacer has set up, you will have a surface that's flat and smooth enough for installing just about any floorcovering you choose, including padded carpet and floating floors with underlayment pads.

Concrete resurfacer typically should not be applied in layers thicker than ½". If your floor has lower areas than this, fill them with sand-mix concrete first to get the low spots close to level, and then top with resurfacer over the whole floor.

Tools + Materials ▸

Pressure washer
Steel concrete
    finishing trowel
Long-handled
    squeegee
5-gallon bucket

½" drill with paddle
    mixer
Duct tape or backer rod
Stiff-bristle brush
Concrete resurfacer

BEFORE **AFTER**

Concrete resurfacer offers an easy, inexpensive solution for renewing concrete surfaces in basements.

HOW TO RESURFACE A CONCRETE FLOOR

1

Thoroughly clean the entire project area. If necessary, remove all oil and greasy or waxy residue using a concrete cleaner and scrub brush. Water beading on the surface indicates residue that could prevent proper adhesion with the resurfacer; clean these areas again as needed.

2

Wash the concrete with a pressure washer. Hold the fan-spray tip about 3" from the surface or as recommended by the washer manufacturer. Remove standing water.

Fill sizeable pits and spalled areas using a small batch of concrete resurfacer—mix about 5 pints of water per 40-lb. bag of resurfacer for a trowelable consistency. Repair cracks as shown on page 16. Smooth the repairs level with the surrounding surface, and let them harden.

Section off the slab on a large project into areas no larger than 100 sq. ft. It's easiest to delineate sections along existing control joints. On all projects, cover or seal off all control joints with duct tape, foam backer rod, or weatherstripping to prevent resurfacer from spilling into the joints.

Mix the desired quantity of concrete resurfacer with water, following the mixing instructions. Work the mix with a ½" drill and a mixing paddle for 5 minutes to achieve a smooth, pourable consistency. If necessary, add water sparingly until the mix will pour easily and spread well with a squeegee.

Saturate the work area with water, then use a squeegee to remove any standing water. Pour the mix of concrete resurfacer onto the center of the repair area or first repair section.

Spread the resurfacer with the squeegee, using a scrubbing motion to make sure all depressions are filled. Then spread it into a smooth, consistent layer. If desired, broom the surface for a nonslip finish. You can also tool the slab edges with a concrete edger within 20 minutes of application. Let the resurfacer cure.

CREATING DECORATIVE CONCRETE FINISHES

Most people are accustomed to thinking of concrete primarily as a utilitarian substance, but it can also mimic a variety of flooring types and be a colorful and beautiful addition to your basement room.

Concrete is a hard and durable building material, but it is also porous—so it is susceptible to staining. Many stains can be removed with the proper cleaner, but sealing and painting prevents oil, grease, and other stains from penetrating the surface in the first place; and cleanup is a whole lot easier.

Even after degreasing a concrete floor, residual grease or oils can create serious adhesion problems for coatings of sealant or paint. To check whether your floor has been adequately cleaned, pour a glass of water on the concrete. If it is ready for sealing, the water will soak into the surface quickly and evenly. If the water beads, you have to clean it again. Detergent used in combination with a steam cleaner can remove stubborn stains better than a cleaner alone.

There are four important reasons to seal your concrete floor: to protect the floor from dirt, oil, grease, chemicals, and stains; to dust-proof the surface; to protect the floor from abrasion and sunlight exposure; and to repel water and protect the floor from freeze-thaw damage.

Tools + Materials ▸

Acid-tolerant pump sprayer	Garden hose with nozzle
Alkaline-base neutralizer	Paint roller frame
Sealant	Paint
Rubber boots	Soft-woven roller cover
Rubber gloves	High-pressure washer
Roller tray	Paintbrush
Wet vacuum	Respirator
Acid-tolerant bucket	Stiff-bristle broom
Eye protection	Extension handle

HOW TO SEAL CONCRETE BASEMENT FLOORS

Clean and prepare the surface by first sweeping up all debris. Next, remove all surface mud, wax, and grease. Finally, remove existing paints or coatings.

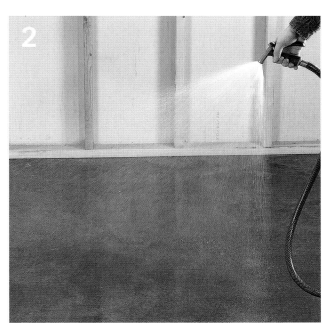

Saturate the surface with clean water. The surface needs to be wet before acid etching. Use this opportunity to check for any areas where water beads up. If water beads on the surface, contaminants still need to be cleaned off with a suitable cleaner or chemical stripper.

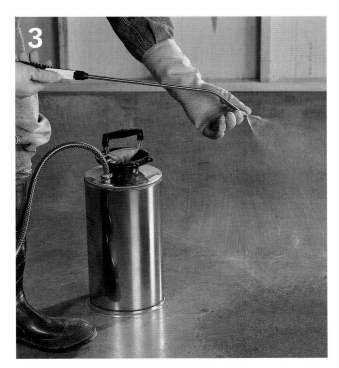

Test your acid-tolerant pump sprayer with water to make sure it releases a wide, even mist. Once you have the spray nozzle set, check the manufacturer's instructions for the etching solution and fill the pump sprayer (or sprinkling can) with the recommended amount of water.

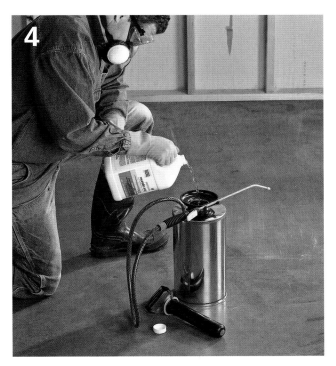

Add the acid etching contents to the water in the acid-tolerant pump sprayer. Follow the directions (and mixing proportions) specified by the manufacturer. Use caution and wear safety equipment.

(continued)

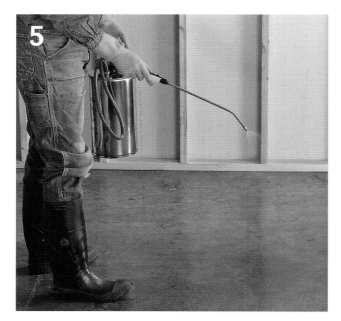

Apply the acid solution. Using the sprinkling can or acid-tolerant pump spray unit, evenly apply the diluted acid solution over the concrete floor. Do not allow the acid solution to dry at any time during the etching and cleaning process. Etch small areas at a time, 10 × 10 ft. or smaller. If there is a slope, begin on the low side of the slope and work upward.

Use a stiff-bristle broom or scrubber to work the acid solution into the concrete. Let the acid sit for 5 to 10 minutes, or as indicated by the manufacturer's directions. A mild foaming action indicates that the product is working. If no bubbling or fizzing occurs, it means there is still grease, oil, or a concrete treatment on the surface that is interfering. If this occurs, follow steps 7 to 12 and then clean the floor again.

Once the fizzing has stopped, the acid has finished reacting with the alkaline concrete surface and formed pH-neutral salts. Neutralize any remaining acid with an alkaline-base solution. Put 1 gal. of water in a 5-gal. bucket and then stir in an alkaline-base neutralizer. Using a stiff-bristle broom, make sure the concrete surface is completely covered with the solution. Continue to sweep until the fizzing stops.

Use a garden hose with a pressure nozzle or, ideally, a pressure washer in conjunction with a stiff-bristle broom to thoroughly rinse the concrete surface. Rinse the surface two to three times. Reapply the acid (repeat steps 5, 6, 7, and 8).

If you have any leftover acid, you can make it safe for your septic system by mixing more alkaline solution in the 5-gal. bucket and carefully pouring the acid from the spray unit into the bucket until all of the fizzing stops.

Use a wet/dry vacuum to clean up the mess. Some sitting acids and cleaning solutions can harm local vegetation, damage your drainage system, and are just plain environmentally unfriendly. Check your local disposal regulations for proper disposal of the neutralized spent acid.

To check for residue, rub a dark cloth over a small area of concrete. If any white residue appears, continue the rinsing process. Check for residue again.

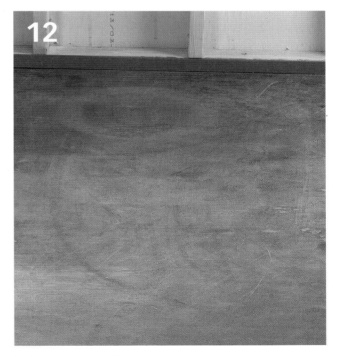

Let the concrete dry for at least 24 hours and sweep up dust, dirt, and particles leftover from the acid etching process. Your concrete should now have the consistency of 120-grit sandpaper and be able to accept concrete sealants.

INSTALLING RAISED SUBFLOOR PANELS

Raised subfloor panels are an excellent choice as a base layer when installing wood or laminate floors over concrete slabs, such as in a basement. The raised panels do an even better job of protecting against moisture than simple plastic vapor barriers.

Do not expect a raised subfloor to eliminate problems in a basement with severe water problems, however. The system works very well for combatting the normal moisture that is always present in an otherwise water-secure basement, but a basement that frequently has puddled water must be corrected in a more aggressive way before flooring can be laid over the slab.

The raised subfloor panels fit together securely with simple tongue-and-groove edges, and for best results the concrete slab must first be examined for dips or cracks, and leveled out before laying the subfloor panels.

Tools + Materials ▸

Long board
Floor leveler and trowel (if needed)
Tape measure
Circular saw
Jigsaw
Carpenter's square
Tapping block and pull bar
Hammer
¼" wall spacers
Particle mask
Eye protection
Work gloves

HOW TO INSTALL RAISED SUBFLOOR PANELS OVER A CONCRETE SLAB

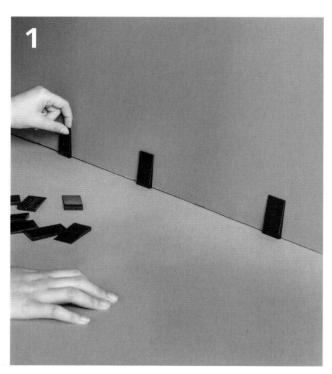

Clean the concrete floor and install temporary ¼" spacers along all walls. Starting with the longest wall, measure the length of the wall, and calculate the number of panels needed by dividing this length by the width of the panel (most products are 2 × 2'). If necessary, trim the starting panel to ensure that the last panel in the first row will be at least 3" in width.

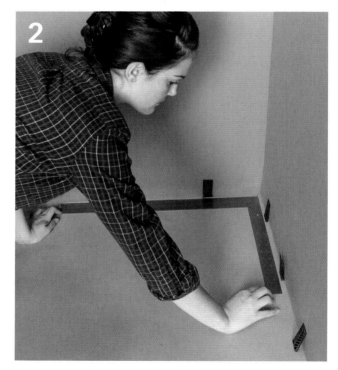

Check the first corner for square, using a carpenter's square. If it is not square, the first panel will need to be angled in the back corner to ensure the first row will fit flush against the wall along its entire length.

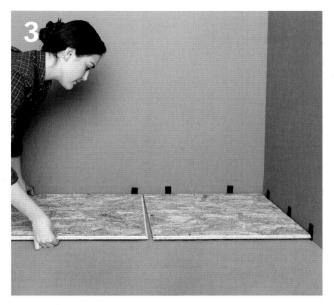

Lay the first panel with the tongue side flat against the wall spacers. Slide the next panel into place by connecting its tongue into the groove of the preceding panel. Using a tapping block, snug up the tongue-and-groove joint. For the last panel in the first row, measure the gap between the last installed panel and the wall spacer, and cut the last panel to this measurement. Install by inserting the tongue of the cut panel into the groove of the preceding panel, and levering it down into place. Pull it into place so the joint is secure, using a pull bar.

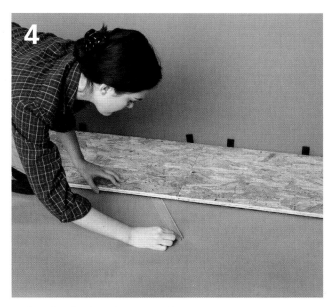

Before beginning the second row, check the first row for flatness, and if there are any areas with "give" or bounce, adjust them with leveling shims inserted under the panels.

As you start the second row, cut the first panel in half, so that seams will be staggered between rows. Begin with the half panel, and install the second row as you did the first, sliding the tongues into the grooves of the preceding row, and snugging them up with the tapping block. Install the subsequent rows, so that the first panels alternate, with odd number rows matching the pattern of the first row, even numbered rows matching the pattern of the second row.

At the last row, trim the wall side of the panels to fit the space between the previous row and the wall spacers, and snug up their joints with the pull bar. Remove all spacers.

INSULATION SOLUTION FOR DRY WALLS: INTERIOR WALL INSULATION

As a general rule, it is best to leave breathing space for the concrete or block so moisture that enters through the walls is not trapped. If your exterior basement walls meet the definition of a dry wall however, adding some interior insulation can increase the comfort level in your basement. If you are building a stud wall for hanging wallcovering materials, you can insulate between the studs with rigid foam—do not use fiberglass batts and do not install a vapor barrier. If you are building a stud wall, it's a good idea to keep the wall away from the basement wall so there is an air channel between the two. Basements and soil conditions can be unique to the home. If you have any doubts about how to correctly insulate, contact a basement-remodeling contractor.

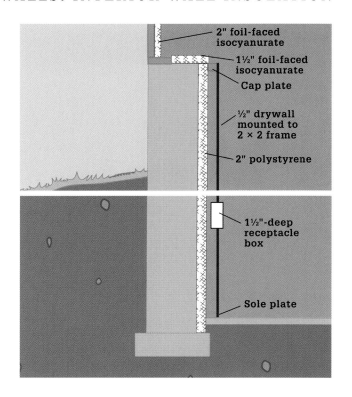

Interior insulation can be installed if your foundation walls meet the conditions for dry walls. It is important to keep the framed wall isolated from the basement wall with a seamless layer of rigid insulation board.

HOW TO INSULATE AN INTERIOR BASEMENT WALL

Begin on the exterior wall by digging a trench and installing a 2"-thick rigid foam insulation board up to the bottom of the siding and down at least 6" below grade. The main purpose of this insulation is to inhibit convection and air transfer in the wall above grade.

Insulate the rim joist with strips of 2"-thick isocyanurate rigid insulation with foil facing. Be sure the insulation you purchase is rated for interior exposure (exterior products can produce harmful vapors). Use adhesive to bond the insulation to the rim joist, and then caulk around all the edges with acoustic sealant.

Seal and insulate the top of the foundation wall, if it is exposed, with strips of 1½"-thick, foil-faced isocyanurate insulation. Install the strips using the same type of adhesive and caulk you used for the rim joist insulation.

Attach sheets of 2"-thick extruded polystyrene insulation to the wall from the floor to the top of the wall. Make sure to clean the wall thoroughly and let it dry completely before installing the insulation.

Seal the gaps between the insulation boards with insulation vapor barrier tape. Do not caulk gaps between the insulation boards and the floor.

Install a stud wall by fastening the cap plate to the ceiling joists and the sole plate to the floor. If you have space, allow an air channel between the studs and the insulation. Do not install a vapor barrier.

REPLACING BASEMENT WINDOWS

Replacing an old and underperforming basement window can accomplish much in conjunction with your basement remodeling project. Newer windows can allow more light in while keeping drafts out. They may have ventilation capabilities that older fixed windows lack. They can offer better security, especially if you install a window that does not let people see inside but still allows light into the room.

Most home centers sell basement windows in standard 32-inch-wide sizes (standard heights are 13, 15, 17, 19, and 23 inches). The main types are awning windows that are hinged on top, hopper windows that are hinged on the bottom, and fixed windows. Some glass block or acrylic block fixed windows include a ventilation opening in lieu of one of the blocks.

If your basement window opening is not a standard size, you have three options. You can have a window custom-made (not as expensive as it sounds), you can remove the old window and enlarge the opening, or you can shrink the opening by using thicker lumber for the rough frame.

Basement windows are the only source of natural light, but they also can allow cold air or even intruders to enter. If you are remodeling your basement, it makes sense to update old windows with new ones that offer better energy efficiency and security.

HOW TO REPLACE A BASEMENT WINDOW

Remove the old window and inspect the rough frame. If it shows signs of rot, remove the frame by cutting the sill and header in half and prying the halves out. Cut new frame members from pressure-treated dimension lumber.

Install the new rough frame using a powder-actuated tool to drive masonry nails. Apply several thick beads of caulk to the concrete surfaces first to create a good seal. The header and sill should run the full width of the opening and be installed before the side members. Caulk around the frame edges and paint the frame with exterior primer.

Position the new window unit in the opening and check for plumb and level. Use shims to raise it so it is not resting on the sill. Adjust it so the gaps are even on the sides. *TIP: You may find it easier to adjust and install the window frame if you remove the glass sash first.*

Attach the window frame to the rough frame opening with screws driven through the jambs. Often, the screw is accessed through a hole in the inner jamb layer. Arrange shims so the screws will pass through them. Do not overdrive screws—it can pull the window frame out of square.

Fill gaps between the rough window frame and the new window unit with minimal-expanding spray foam. Do not spray in too much—it can distort the frame when it dries.

Install stop molding on both sides of the window to cover gaps between the window and the rough frame. Paint the stop molding and frame to match your trim color.

WINDOWS: INSTALLING AN EGRESS WINDOW

Any living space measuring more than 200 square feet in a basement must have at least one means of egress (escape). There must also be an egress in any bedroom. More is always better. The egress can be either a walk-out doorway, or a window large enough for an adult to escape through—or an emergency responder to enter.

The diagram below shows the minimum measurement requirements for an egress window. An acceptable basement egress window also requires an oversized window well that is at least 36 inches wide, and projects 36 inches out from the foundation. Wells deeper than 44 inches must have a fixed ladder. The egress must open onto an area that leads to a public space—not an enclosed courtyard or similar area. Always consult local codes, which often require at least two egress openings in any below-ground dwelling.

Tools + Materials ▸

Tape measure
4-ft. level
Stakes and string line
Shovel
Colored tape
Hammer drill and ½" × 12–16" masonry bit
Masonry saw
Hand maul
Cold chisel
Trowel
Miter saw
Hammer
Drill and bits
Exterior silicone caulk
Caulk gun
Gloves
New window
Pea gravel
Plastic sheeting
Self-tapping masonry screws
2× pressure-treated lumber
Wood shims
Insulation
Concrete sleeve anchors
Quick-curing concrete
3½" deck screws
Foam backer rod
Window well
Tamper
Mask or respirator
Eye and ear protection

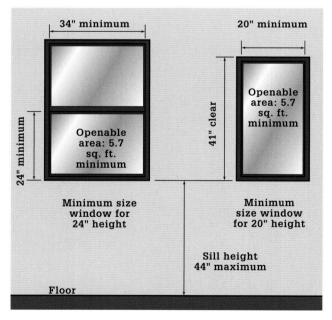

In order to satisfy building codes for egress, a basement window must have a minimum opening of 5.7 sq. ft. through one sash, with at least 20" of clear width and 24" of clear height. Casement, double-hung, and sliding window styles can be used, as long as their dimensions for width and height meet these minimum requirements.

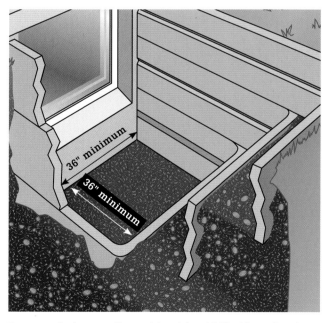

Egress window wells must be at least 36" wide and project 36" from the foundation. Those deeper than 44" must have a means of escape, such as a tiered design that forms steps or an attached ladder. Drainage at the bottom of the well should extend down to the foundation footing drain, with pea gravel used as the drainage material.

HOW TO INSTALL AN EGRESS WINDOW + WINDOW WELL

Lay out the border of the window well area with stakes and string. Plan the length and width of the excavation to be several feet larger than the window well's overall size to provide extra room for installation and adjustment.

Excavate the well to a depth 6 to 12" deeper than the well's overall height to allow room for drainage gravel. Make sure to have your local public utilities company inspect the well excavation area and okay it for digging before you start.

Measure and mark the foundation wall with brightly colored masking tape to establish the overall size of the window's rough opening (here, we're replacing an existing window). Be sure to take into account the window's rough opening dimensions, the thickness of the rough framing (usually 2x stock), and the width of the structural header you may need to build. Remember also that sill height must be within 44" of the floor. Remove existing wall coverings inside the layout area.

If the floor joists run perpendicular to your project wall, build a temporary support wall parallel to the foundation wall and 6 to 8 ft. from it. Staple sheet plastic to the wall and floor joists to form a work tent that will help control concrete dust.

(continued)

5

Drill reference holes at each bottom corner with a hammer drill and long masonry bit. These holes will provide reference points for cutting from both sides, ensuring clean breaks.

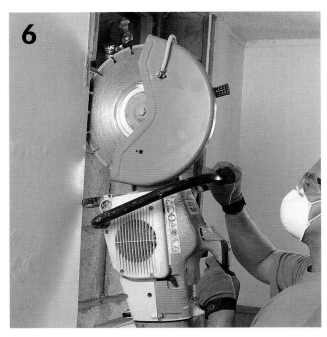

6

Equip a masonry cutting saw (or large angle grinder) with a diamond blade and set it for a ½" cut to score the blocks first. Then reset the saw to full depth and make the final bottom and side cuts through the blocks. Wear a tight-fitting particle mask, ear and eye protection, and gloves for all of this cutting work; the saw will generate a tremendous amount of thick dust. Feed the saw slowly and steadily. Stop and rest periodically so the dust can settle.

7

On the outside foundation wall, score the cuts, then make full-depth cuts.

8

Strike the blocks with a hand maul to break or loosen the block sections. When all the blocks are removed, carefully chip away remaining debris with a cold chisel to create flat surfaces.

9

Fill the hollow voids in concrete block walls, with broken pieces of block, then level and smooth the voids by trowelling on a fresh layer of quick-curing concrete. Flatten the surfaces, and allow the concrete to dry overnight.

10

If your project requires a new header above the new window, build it from pieces of 2× lumber sandwiching ½" plywood and fastened together with construction adhesive and 10d nails. Slip it into place and tack it temporarily to the mudsill with 3½" deck screws driven toenail style.

11

Cut the sill plate for the window's rough frame from 2× treated lumber that's the same width as the thickness of the foundation wall. Fasten the sill to the foundation with ³⁄₁₆ × 3¼" countersunk masonry screws. Drill pilot holes for the screws first with a hammer drill.

12

Cut two pieces of treated lumber just slightly longer than the opening so they'll fit tightly between the new header and sill. Tap them into place with a maul. Adjust them for plumb and fasten them to the foundation with countersunk masonry screws or powder-actuated fasteners.

(continued)

13

Apply a thick bead of silicone caulk around the outside edges of the rough frame and set the window in its opening, seating the nailing flanges into the caulk. Shim the window so the frame is level and plumb. Test the action of the window to make sure the shims aren't bowing the frame.

14

Attach the window's nailing flanges to the rough frame with screws or nails, as specified by the manufacturer. Check the window action periodically as you fasten it to ensure that it still operates smoothly.

15

Seal gaps between the rough frame and the foundation with a bead of exterior silicone or polyurethane caulk. If the gaps are wider than ¼", insert a piece of backer rod first, then cover it with caulk. On the interior, fill gaps around the window shims with strips of foam backer rod, fiberglass insulation, or a bead of minimally expanding spray foam. Do not distort the window frame.

16

Fill the well excavation with 6 to 12" of pea gravel. This will serve as the window's drain system. Follow the egress well kit instructions to determine the exact depth required; you may need to add more gravel so the top of the well will be above the new window. *NOTE: We added a drain down to the foundation's perimeter tile for improved drainage.*

17

Set the bottom section of the well into the hole, and position it evenly from left to right relative to the window. Adjust the gravel surface to level the well section carefully.

18

Stack the second well section on top of the first, and connect the two with the appropriate fasteners.

19

Fasten the window well sections to the foundation wall with concrete sleeve anchors driven into prebored pilot holes. You could also use masonry nails driven with a powder-actuated tool.

20

When all the well sections are assembled and secured, nail pieces of trim around the window frame to hide the nailing flange. Complete the well installation by using excavated dirt to backfill around the outside of the well. Pack the soil with a tamper, creating a slope for good drainage. If you are installing a window well cover, set it in place and fasten it according to the manufacturer's instructions. The cover must be removable.

PLANNING + PREPARATION

An important early step in your remodeling project is to carefully measure the windows and doors that you wish to replace. You will use these measurements to purchase the new unit, and you must be sure it will fit in the opening.

To finalize your project ideas and make sure they will really work, the next step is to put all the information down on paper. There are two basic types of construction drawings: floor plans and elevation drawings. These drawings may be required if your project needs a building permit. (There are several user-friendly computer-aided design [CAD] programs on the market for homeowners and DIYers to use in creating drawings. Many can produce permit-compliant blueprints, plans, and elevation sketches.)

Floor plans show a room as seen from above. These are useful for showing overall room dimensions, layouts, and the relationship between neighboring rooms. Elevation drawings show a side view of a room, usually with one wall per drawing. Elevations are made for both the interior and exterior of a house and generally show more architectural detail than floor plans.

Both floor plans and elevation drawings provide you with a method for planning and recording structural and mechanical systems for your project. They also help the local building department to ensure your project meets code requirements.

If you will be doing several projects in a short time, you may want to draw a plan of each complete floor of the home. If you're doing one isolated project, you may want to draw the plan of just that room.

To create floor plans, draw one story at a time. First, measure each room from wall to wall. Transfer the room's dimensions onto ¼-inch grid paper, using a scale of ¼ inch = 1 foot. Label each room for its use and note its overall dimensions. Include wall thicknesses, which you can determine by measuring the widths of window and door jambs—do not include the trim.

Next, add these elements to your drawings:

- Windows and doors; note which way the doors swing.
- Stairs and their direction as it relates to each story.
- Permanent features such as plumbing fixtures, major appliances, countertops, built-in furniture, and fireplaces.
- Overhead features such as exposed beams or wall cabinets—use dashed lines.
- Plumbing, electrical, and HVAC elements. You may want a separate set of drawings for these mechanical elements and service lines.
- Overall dimensions measured from outside the home. Use these to check the accuracy of interior dimensions.

To create elevation drawings, use the same ¼ inch = 1 foot scale, and draw everything you see on one wall (each room has four elevations). Include:

- Ceiling heights and the heights of significant features such as soffits and exposed beams.
- Windows, including the height and width of the sills and tops of the openings.
- Doors, including the heights (from the floor to the top of the opening) and widths.
- Trim and other decorative elements.

When your initial floor plans and elevations are done, use them to sketch your remodeling layout options. Use tissue overlays to show hidden elements or proposed changes to a plan. Photographs of your home's interior and exterior may also be helpful. Think creatively and draw many different sketches; the more design options you consider, the better your final plans will be.

When you have completed your remodeling plans, draft your final drawings and create a materials list for the project.

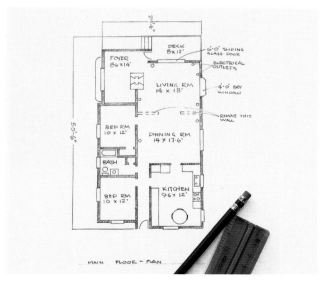

A floor plan can help you envision how a new door or window will impact the living space and traffic patterns.

MEASURING WINDOWS + DOORS

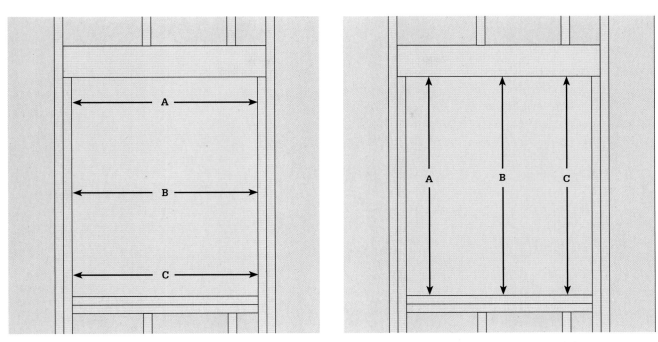

Determine the exact size of your new window or door by measuring the opening carefully. For the width (left), measure between the jack studs in three places: near the top, at the middle, and near the bottom of the opening. Use the same procedure for the height (right), measuring from the header to the sill near the left edge, at the middle, and near the right edge of the opening. Use the smallest measurement of each dimension for ordering the unit.

WORKING WITH PLANS

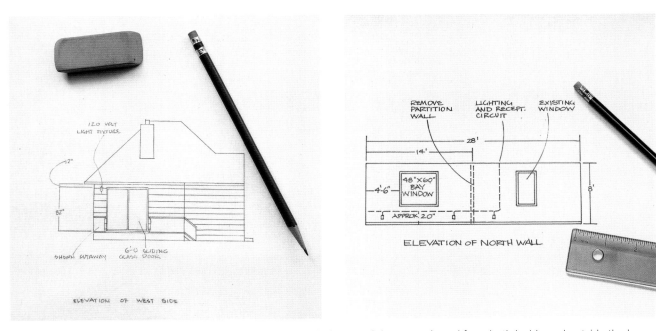

Create elevation drawings showing a side view layout of windows and doors, as viewed from both inside and outside the home. Indicate the size of windows and doors, ceiling heights, and the location of wiring and plumbing fixtures. Creating these drawings will often be easier, quicker, and more precise if you use one of the inexpensive CAD programs on the market.

HOW TO INSTALL A WINDOW

Installing the right windows for your home and region can instantly reduce your energy usage. That's why, when choosing windows for an addition, you should always look for the Energy Star label. A designation given by the U.S. Department of Energy, the Energy Star label ensures a window meets or exceeds federal guidelines for home energy efficiency. An even more important gauge than simply looking for an Energy Star label is to read the NFRC label on the window. Specifically, note the U-factor and Solar Heat Gain Coefficient (SHGC) ratings for the window. If you live in a fairly cold region of the country, you want the lowest U-factor you can find, with a moderate to high SHGC. If your home is located in a temperate area with consistently warm temperatures, the SHGC number is the most important one to you, and it should be as low as possible.

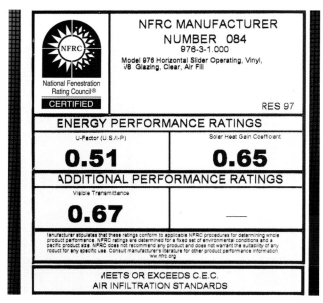

Look for and evaluate energy rating labels, usually attached directly to the glass on new windows.

Flash the rough sill. Apply 9"-wide self-adhesive flashing tape to the rough sill to prevent moisture infiltration below the window. Install the flashing tape so it wraps completely over the sill and extends 10 to 12" up the jack studs. Fold the rest of the tape over the housewrap to create a 3" overlap. Peel off the backing and press the tape firmly in place. Install tape on the side jambs butting up to the header, and then flash the header.

Caulk the opening. Apply a ½"-wide bead of caulk around the outside edges of the jack studs and header to seal the window flange in the opening. Leave the rough sill uncaulked to allow any water that may penetrate the flashing to drain out.

Position the window. Set the window unit into the rough opening, and center it side to side. Check the sill for level.

Tack the top corners. Drive a roofing nail through each top corner hole of the top window flange to tack it in place. Do not drive the rest of the nails into the top flange yet.

Plumb the window. Have a helper hold the window in place from outside while you work inside. Check the window jamb for square by measuring from corner to corner. If the measurements are the same, the jamb is square. Insert shims between the side jambs and rough opening near the top corners to hold the jambs in position. Use additional shims as needed to bring the jamb into square. Recheck the diagonals after shimming.

Nail the flanges. Drive 2" roofing nails through the flange nailing holes and into the rough sill to secure it. Handnail this flange, being careful not to damage the flange or window cladding.

(continued)

7

Flash the side flanges. Seal the side flanges with flashing tape, starting 4 to 6" below the sill flashing and ending 4 to 6" above the top flange. Press the tape firmly in place.

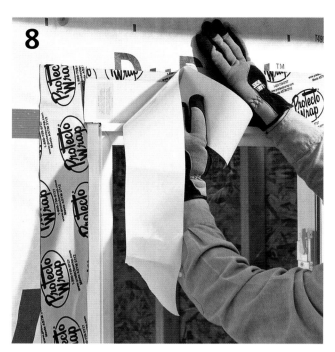

8

Install the drip cap. Cut a piece of metal drip edge to fit over the top window jamb. This is particularly important if your new window has an unclad wooden jamb with preinstalled brickmold. Set the drip edge in place on the top jamb, and secure the flange with a strip of wide flashing tape. Do not nail it. Overlap the side flashing tape by 6". NOTE: *If you plan to trim the window with wood brickmold or other moldings, install the drip edge above that trim instead.*

9

Finish the installation. Cut the shim ends so they are flush with the inside of the wall using a utility knife or handsaw.

10

Spray minimal-expanding foam insulation for windows and doors around the perimeter of the window on the interior side.

HOW TO LUBRICATE CASEMENT WINDOW CRANKS

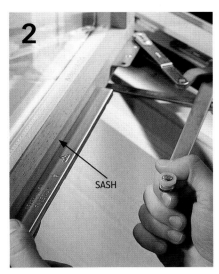

If a casement window is hard to crank, clean the accessible parts. Open the window until the roller at the end of the extension arm is aligned with the access slot in the window track.

Disengage the extension arm by pulling it down and out of the track. Clean the track with a stiff brush, and wipe the pivoting arms and hinges with a rag.

Lubricate the track and hinges with spray lubricant or household oil. Wipe off excess lubricant with a cloth, then reattach the extension arm. If that doesn't solve the problem, repair or replace the crank assembly.

HOW TO REPAIR A CASEMENT WINDOW CRANK ASSEMBLY

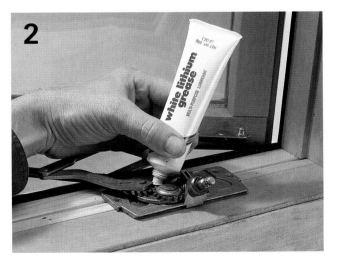

Disengage the extension arm from the window track, then remove the molding or cap concealing the crank mechanism. Unhinge any pivot arms connected to the window. Remove the screws securing the crank assembly, then remove the assembly and clean it thoroughly. If the gears are badly worn, replace the assembly. Check a home center or contact the manufacturer for new parts. Note which way the window opens—to the right or left—when ordering replacement parts.

Apply an all-purpose grease to the gears, and reinstall the assembly. Connect the pivot arms, and attach the extension arm to the window. Test the window operation before installing the cap and molding.

HOW TO REPLACE WINDOW GLASS

Wearing heavy leather gloves, remove the broken pieces of glass. Then, soften the old glazing compound using a heat gun or a hair dryer (carefully). Scrape out softened putty with a putty knife. If a section is difficult to scrape clean, reheat it.

Apply a thin bed of glazing compound to the wood frame opening and smooth it in place with your thumb. If you are having trouble getting the glazing compound to stick, make sure the product is not too old and dried out—fresh compound always works better. You can also try applying a coat of shellac on the wood in the recess if the wood frame is very old.

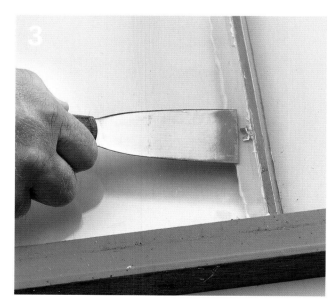

Press the new pane into the opening, making sure to achieve a tight seal with the compound on all sides. Do not press all the compound out. Drive glazier's points into the wood frame to hold the pane in place. Use the tip of a putty knife to slide the point against the surface of the glass. Install at least two points on each side of the pane.

Make a rope of glazing compound (about ½" dia.) by rolling it between your hands. Then press it against the pane and the wood frame. Smooth it in place by drawing a putty knife, held at a 45° angle, across its surface. Scrape off excess. Let the glazing compound dry for at least one week, and then prime and paint it to match the rest of the sash. When the paint is dry, scrape off the extra with a razor blade paint scraper.

STORM WINDOWS + DOORS: REPAIRING

Compared to removable wood storm windows and screens, repairing combination storm windows is a little more complex. But there are several repairs you can make without too much difficulty, as long as you find the right parts. Take the old corner keys, gaskets, or other original parts to a hardware store that repairs storm windows so the clerk can help you find the correct replacement parts. If you cannot find the right parts, have a new sash built.

Tools + Materials ▸

Tape measure
Screwdriver
Scissors
Drill
Utility knife
Spline roller
Nail set
Puncture-proof
   work gloves
Eye protection
Hammer
Spline cord
Screening
Rubber gasket
Replacement glass
Replacement hardware

Remove the metal storm window sash by pressing in the release hardware in the lower rail then lifting the sash out. Sash hangers on the corners of the top rail should be aligned with the notches in the side channels before removal.

HOW TO REPLACE SCREENING IN A METAL STORM WINDOW

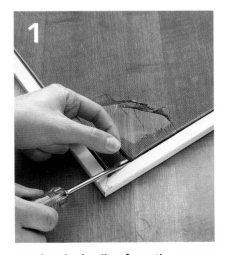

Pry the vinyl spline from the groove around the edge of the frame with a screwdriver. Retain the old spline if it is still flexible, or replace it with a new spline.

Stretch the new screen tightly over the frame so that it overlaps the edges of the frame. Keeping the screen taut, use the convex side of a spline roller to press the screen into the retaining grooves.

Use the concave side of the spline roller to press the spline into the groove (it helps to have a partner for this). Cut away excess screen using a utility knife.

HOW TO REPLACE GLASS IN A METAL STORM WINDOW

Remove the sash frame from the window, then completely remove the broken glass from the sash. Remove the rubber gasket that framed the old glass pane and remove any glass remnants. Find the dimensions for the replacement glass by measuring between the inside edges of the frame opening, then adding twice the thickness of the rubber gasket to each measurement.

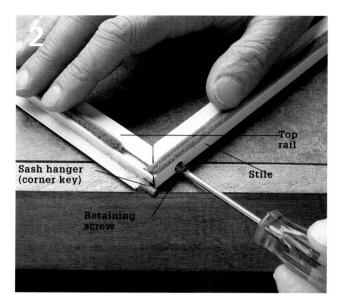

Top rail

Sash hanger (corner key)

Stile

Retaining screw

Set the frame on a flat surface, and disconnect the top rail. Remove the retaining screws in the sides of the frame stiles where they join the top rail. After unscrewing the retaining screws, pull the top rail loose, pulling gently in a downward motion to avoid damaging the L-shaped corner keys that join the rail and the stiles. For glass replacement, you need only disconnect the top rail.

Fit the rubber gasket (buy a replacement if the original is in poor condition) around one edge of the replacement glass pane. At the corners, cut the spine of the gasket partway so it will bend around the corner. Continue fitting the gasket around the pane, cutting at the corners, until all four edges are covered. Trim off any excess gasket material.

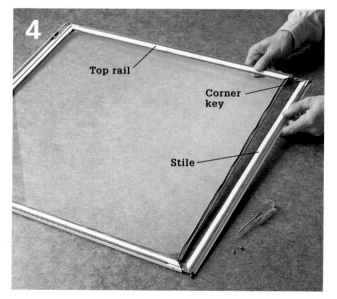

Top rail

Corner key

Stile

Slide the glass pane into the channels in the stiles and bottom rail of the sash frame. Insert corner keys into the top rail, then slip the other ends of the keys into the frame stiles. Press down on the top rail until the mitered corners are flush with the stiles. Drive the retaining screws back through the stiles and into the top rail to join the frame together. Reinsert the frame into the window.

HOW TO DISASSEMBLE + REPAIR A METAL SASH FRAME

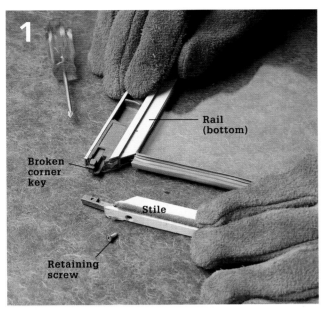

Metal window sash are held together at the corner joints by L-shaped pieces of hardware that fit into grooves in the sash frame pieces. To disassemble a broken joint, start by disconnecting the stile and rail at the broken joint—there is usually a retaining screw driven through the stile that must be removed.

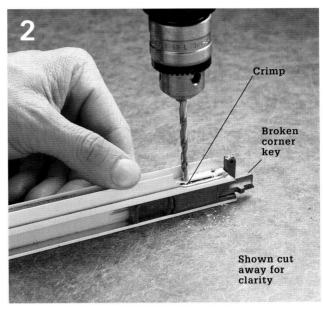

Corner keys are secured in the rail slots with crimps that are punched into the metal over the key. To remove keys, drill through the metal in the crimped area using a drill bit the same diameter as the crimp. Carefully knock the broken key pieces from the frame slots with a screwdriver and hammer.

Locate matching replacement parts for the broken corner key, which is usually an assembly of two or three pieces. There are dozens of different types, so it is important that you save the old parts for reference.

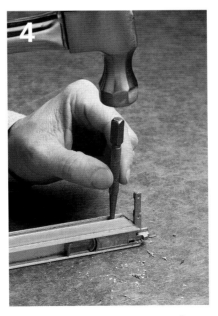

Insert the replacement corner key assembly into the slot in the rail. Use a nail set as a punch, and rap it into the metal over the corner key, creating a new crimp to hold the key in place.

Insert the glass and gasket into the frame slots, then reassemble the frame and drive in retainer screws (for screen windows, replace the screening).

INSTALLING PREHUNG INTERIOR DOORS

Install prehung interior doors after the framing work is complete and the drywall has been installed. If the rough opening for the door has been framed accurately, installing the door takes about an hour.

Standard prehung doors have 4½-inch-wide jambs and are sized to fit walls with 2 × 4 construction and ½-inch wallboard. If you have 2 × 6 construction or thicker wall surface material, you can special order a door to match, or you can add jamb extensions to a standard-sized door (photo, below).

Tools + Materials ▸

Level
Hammer
Handsaw
Prehung interior door
Wood shims

8d casing nails
Glue
Eye and ear
  protection
Work gloves

Tip: Jamb Extensions ▸

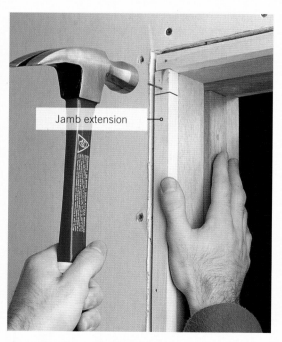

Jamb extension

If your walls are built with 2 × 6 studs, you'll need to extend the jambs by attaching wood strips to the edges of the jamb before the door is installed. Use glue and 4d casing nails when attaching jamb extensions.

HOW TO INSTALL A PREHUNG INTERIOR DOOR

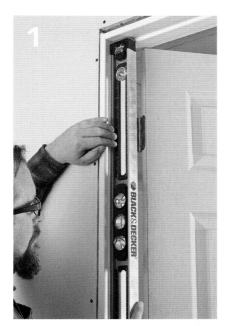

Slide the door unit into the framed opening so the edges of the jambs are flush with the wall surface and the hinge-side jamb is plumb.

Insert pairs of wood shims driven from opposite directions into the gap between the framing members and the hinge-side jamb, spaced every 12". Check the hinge-side jamb to make sure it is still plumb and does not bow.

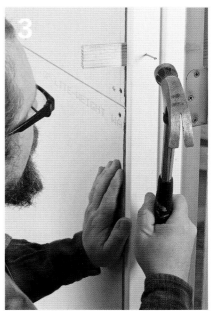

Anchor the hinge-side jamb with 8d casing nails driven through the jamb and shims and into the jack stud.

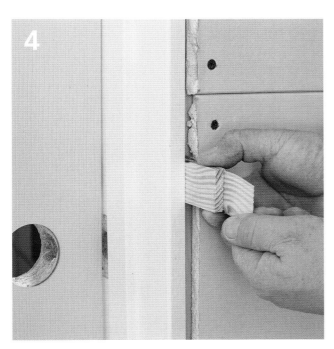

Insert pairs of shims in the gap between the framing members and the latch-side jamb and top jamb, spaced every 12". With the door closed, adjust the shims so the gap between door edge and jamb is ⅛" wide. Drive 8d casing nails through the jambs and shims, into the framing members.

Cut the shims flush with the wall surface, using a handsaw. Hold the saw vertically to prevent damage to the door jamb or wall. Finish the door and install the lockset as directed by the manufacturer. Install trim around the door.

ENTRY DOORS

Few parts of a house have a more dramatic effect on the way your home is perceived than the main entry door. A lovely, well-maintained entryway that is tastefully matched architecturally to the house can utterly transform a home's appearance. In fact, industry studies have suggested that upgrading a plain entry door to a higher-end entry door system can pay back multiple times in the resale of your house. But perhaps more importantly, depending on your priorities, it makes a great improvement in how you feel about your home. Plus, it usually pays benefits in home security and energy efficiency as well.

If you are replacing a single entry door with a double door or a door with a sidelight or sidelights, you will need to enlarge the door opening. Be sure to file your plans with your local building department and obtain a permit. You'll need to provide temporary support from the time you remove the wall studs in the new opening until you've installed and secured a new door header that's approved for the new span distance.

The American Craftsman style door with sidelights) installed in this project has the look and texture of a classic wood door, but it is actually created from fiberglass. Today's fiberglass doors are quite convincing in their ability to replicate wood grain, while still offering the durability and low-maintenance of fiberglass.

Tools + Materials ▸

Tape measure	Circular saw
Level	Framing nails
Reciprocating saw	Finish nails
Hammer	Nail set
Shims	Finishing materials
Exterior silicone caulk	Eye and ear protection
Caulk gun	

After

Before

Replacing an ordinary entry door with a beautiful new upgrade has an exceptionally high payback in increased curb appeal and in perceived home value, according to industry studies.

HOW TO REPLACE AN ENTRY DOOR

Remove the old entry door by cutting through the fasteners driven into the jamb with a reciprocating saw. If the new door or door system is wider, mark the edges of the larger rough opening onto the wall surface. If possible, try to locate the new opening so one edge will be against an existing wall stud. Be sure to include the thickness of the new framing you'll need to add when removing the wall coverings.

Frame in the new rough opening for the replacement door. The instructions that come with the door will recommend a rough opening size, which is usually sized to create a ½" gap between the door and the studs and header. Patch the wall surfaces.

Cut metal door dripcap molding to fit the width of the opening and tuck the back edge up behind the wallcovering at the top of the door opening. Attach the dripcap with caulk only–do not use nails or screws.

Unpack the door unit and set it in the rough opening to make sure it fits correctly. Remove it. Make sure the subfloor is clean and in good repair, and then apply heavy beads of caulk to the underside of the door sill and to the subfloor in the sill installation area. Use plenty of caulk.

(continued)

5

Set the door sill in the threshold and raise the unit up so it fits cleanly in the opening, with the exterior trim flush against the wall sheathing. Press down on the sill to seat it in the caulk and wipe up any squeeze-out with a damp rag.

6

Use a 6' level to make sure the unit is plumb and then tack it to the rough opening stud on the hinge side, using pairs of 10d nails driven partway through the casing on the weatherstripped side of the door (or the sidelight). On single, hinged doors, drive the nails just above the hinge locations. *NOTE: Many door installers prefer deck screws over nails when attaching the jambs. Screws offer more gripping strength and are easier to adjust, but covering the screw heads is more difficult than filling nail holes.*

7

Drive wood shims between the jamb and the wall studs to create an even gap. Locate the shims directly above the pairs of nails you drove. Double check the door with the level to make sure it is still plumb.

8

Drive shims between the jamb on the latch side of the unit and into the wall stud. Only drive the nails part way. Test for plumb again and then add shims at nail locations (you may need to double-up the shims, as this gap is often wider than the one on the hinge side). Check to make sure the door jamb is not bowed.

9

Drive finish nails at all remaining locations, following the nailing schedule in the manufacturer's installation instructions.

10

Use a nail set to drive the nail heads below the wood surface. Fill the nail holes with wood putty (you'll get the best match if you apply putty that's tinted to match the stained wood after the finish is applied). The presence of the wood shims at the nail locations should prevent the jamb from bowing as you nail.

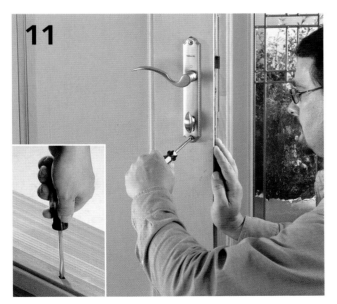

11

Install the lockset, strikeplates, deadbolts or multipoint locks, and any other door hardware. If the door finish has not been applied, you may want to do so first, but generally it makes more sense to install the hardware right away so the door can be operated and locked. Attach the door sill to the threshold and adjust it as needed, normally using the adjustment screws (inset).

12

Apply your door finish if it has not yet been applied. Read the manufacturer's suggestions for finishing very closely and follow the suggested sequences. Some manufacturers offer finish kits that are designed to be perfectly compatible with their doors. Install interior case molding and caulk all the exterior gaps after the finish dries.

DOORS: BIFOLD

Bifold doors provide easy access to a closet without requiring much clearance for opening. Most home centers stock kits that include two pairs of prehinged doors, a head track, and all the necessary hardware and fasteners. Typically, the doors in these kits have predrilled holes for the pivot and guide posts. Hardware kits are also sold separately for custom projects. There are many types of bifold door styles, so read and follow the manufacturer's instructions for the product you use.

Tools + Materials ▶

Tape measure
Level
Straightedge
  (optional)
Drill
Screwdriver
Prehinged bifold doors

Head track
Mounting hardware
Panhead screws
Flathead screws
Protective
  equipment

A variety of designer bifold doors are available for installation between rooms and closets. They provide the same attractive appearance as French doors but require much less floor space.

HOW TO INSTALL BIFOLD DOORS

1

Cut the head track to the width of the opening using a hacksaw. Insert the roller mounts into the track, then position the track in the opening. Fasten it to the header using panhead screws.

2

Measure and mark each side jamb at the floor for the anchor bracket so the center of the bracket aligns exactly with the center of the head track. Fasten the brackets in place with flathead screws.

3

Check the height of the doors in the opening, and trim if necessary. Insert pivot posts into predrilled holes at the bottoms and tops of the doors. Insert guide posts at the tops of the leading doors. Make sure all posts fit snugly.

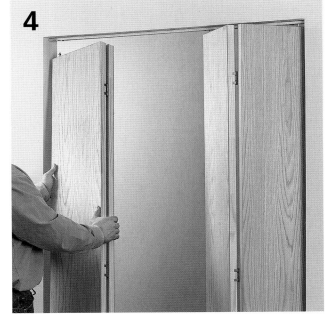

4

Fold one pair of doors closed and lift into position, inserting the pivot and guide posts into the head track. Slip the bottom pivot post into the anchor bracket. Repeat for the other pair of doors. Close the doors and check alignment along the side jambs and down the center. If necessary, adjust the top and bottom pivots following the manufacturer's instructions.

HANDLESETS + DEADBOLTS

Installing a handleset (door knob) is easy if your interior or exterior doors are predrilled with holes. In fact, it is relatively difficult to find any doors these days that are pure slabs without predrilled lockset and bolt holes. Pretty much all exterior doors and many interior doors also have a predrilled hole for a deadbolt. If you are adding these to a new door or replacing them on an old one, the main thing to know when you go shopping is the backset distance. This is measured from the edge of the door to the centerpoint of the predrilled hole. In almost all cases it is either 2⅜" or 2¾". The holes themselves are a standard 2⅛" in diameter. In addition to your desired finish, other questions to answer include whether you want a lever or a knob and whether you want the knob or lever to be keyed. If you are buying both a handleset and a deadbolt, it is best and easiest to buy a packaged matched set, where both are keyed the same. You can also buy programmable handlesets that use punch codes rather than keys.

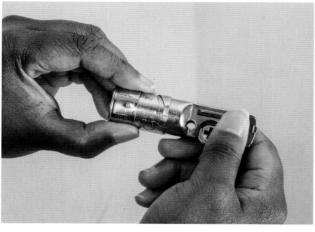

TIP: Many handlesets and deadbolts can be adjusted to either a 2⅜" or 2¾" backset by twisting a fitting on the strikebolt or latchbolt to make it shorter or longer.

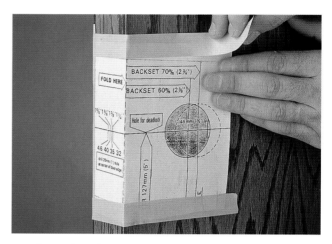

TIP: If your door does not come with predrilled handleset or deadbolt holes, use the template provided by the manufacturer to locate the correct position for drilling your own hole with a hole saw.

HOW TO INSTALL A HANDLESET IN A PREDRILLED DOOR

Insert the latch bolt into the 1" -dia. hole in the door edge. The latch bolt can be installed simply by setting the round housing at the end into the door edge by rapping with a piece of scrapwood or mallet. If your door edge has a pre-cut mortise around the latch hole, use the optional, rectangular mounting plate that can be attached to the end of the bolt and then screwed into the mortise. Make sure the latchbolt is oriented so the beveled edge faces the closing direction.

Insert the flat spindle from the outside handle (on exterior doors) into the matching slotted hole in the latchbolt. If you are installing a lever type, the lever should be horizontal and pointing away from the door edge.

Insert the other door handle into the hole so that its screw mounting holes align with the predrilled holes in the latch mechanism. Use the long screws provided by the manufacturer. Tighten both screws, making sure you hit the mounting holes inside, drawing the two handle cylinders together securely.

Attach the latch strike plate to the door jamb. If you have a prehung door, the mortise for the latch plate is probably precut. Otherwise, smear some chalk on the end of the latchbolt, close the door to mark where it hits the jamb, and cut a mortise to fit with a 1" wood chisel. Test the closing action and make adjustments to the strike plate position as needed.

HOW TO INSTALL A DEADBOLT

Set the strike bolt length to 2⅜" or 2¾" (see previous page) and then drive the round bolt into the door edge; or use the optional mounting plate if your door has a precut deadbolt mortise in the edge.

Insert the flat spindle from the outer deadbolt cylinder into the bolt mechanism slot. The key slot should be vertical, with the brand name on the cylinder reading normally.

With the thumblatch vertical and the bolt withdrawn, use long screws (provided with the deadbolt) to draw the two deadbolt cylinders together tightly. Test the thumblatch to make sure the bolt extends and retracts smoothly and completely. If not, try removing the thumblatch cylinder, flipping it 180°, and then reattaching.

Screw the strike plate into the mortise around the hole for the bolt in the door jamb (see step 4 above). For security reasons, at least one of the screws used to attach the strike plate should be 3" to 4" long so it extends past the jamb and into the framing member in the door rough opening.

STORM DOORS

Storm doors protect the entry door from driving rain or snow. They create a dead air buffer between the two doors that acts like insulation. When the screen panels are in place, the door provides great ventilation on a hot day. And, they deliver added security, especially when outfitted with a lockset and a deadbolt lock.

If you want to install a new storm door or replace an old one that's seen better days, your first job is to go shopping. Storm doors come in many different styles to suit just about anyone's design needs. And they come in different materials, including aluminum, vinyl, and even fiberglass. (Wood storm doors are still available but not in preassembled form.) All these units feature a prehung door in a frame that is mounted on the entry door casing boards.

Depending on the model you buy, installation instructions can vary. Be sure to check the directions that come with your door before starting the job.

Tools + Materials ▸

Drill/driver	Masking tape
Tape measure	Hacksaw
Finish nails	Level
Screwdriver	Primer
Paintbrush	Paint
Hammer	Eye protection

A quality storm door helps seal out cold drafts, keeps rain and snow off your entry door, and lets a bug-free breeze into your home when you want one.

HOW TO INSTALL A STORM DOOR

1

Test-fit the door in the opening. If it is loose, add a shim to the hinge side of the door. Cut the piece with a circular saw and nail it to the side of the jamb, flush with the front of the casing.

2

Install the drip edge molding at the top of the door opening. The directions for the door will explain exactly how to do this. Sometimes it's the first step, like we show here; otherwise it's installed after the door is in place.

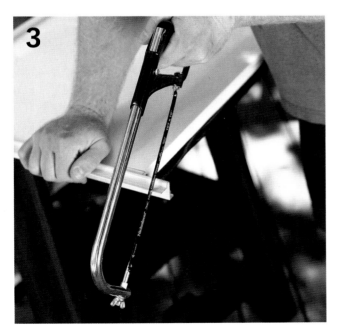

3

Measure the height of the opening and cut the hinge flange to match this measurement. Use a hacksaw and work slowly so the saw won't hop out of the cut and scratch a visible area of the hinge.

4

Lift the door and push it tightly into the opening. Partially drive one mounting screw near the bottom and another near the top. Check the door for plumb, and when satisfied, drive all the mounting screws tight to the flange.

(continued)

5

Measure from the doorway sill to the rain cap to establish the length of the latch-side mounting flange.

6

Cut the latch-side flange with a hacksaw. Work carefully so you don't pull out the weatherstripping from the flange channel as you cut. Install the flange with screws.

7

To install the door sweep, slide it over the bottom of the door and install its mounting screws loosely. Make sure the sweep forms a tight seal with the sill, then tighten the screws.

8

Mount the lockset on the door. Tape can help hold the outside hardware in place while you position the inner latch and tighten the screws.

Install the strike plates for both the lockset (shown here) and the deadbolt locks. These plates are just screwed to the door jamb where the lock bolt and deadbolt fall. Install the deadbolt.

Begin installing the door closer by screwing the jamb bracket in place. Most of these brackets have slotted screw holes so you can make minor adjustments without taking off the bracket.

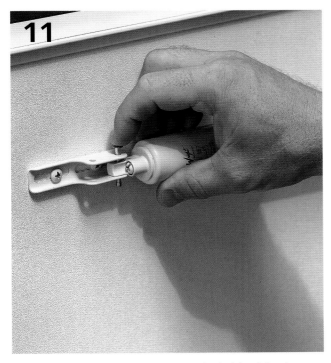

Install the door closer bracket on the inside of the door. Then mount the closer on the jamb bracket and the door bracket. Usually the closer is attached to these with some form of short locking pin.

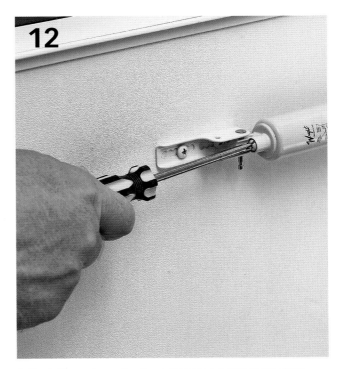

Adjust the automatic door closer so it closes the door completely without slamming it. The adjustment is usually made by turning a set screw in and out with a screwdriver.

FIXING COMMON DOOR PROBLEMS

Many door problems are caused by loose hinges. When hinges are loose, the door won't hang right, causing it to rub, stick and throw off the latch mechanism.

The first thing to do is check the hinge screws. If the holes for the hinge screws are worn and won't hold the screws, try the repair on the next page. If the hinges are tight but the door still rubs against the frame, sand or plane down the door's edge.

Door latch problems can occur for a number of other reasons, including door warpage, swollen wood, sticking latchbolts, and paint buildup. If you've addressed those issues and the door still won't stay shut, it's probably because the door frame is out of square. This happens as a house settles with age; you can make minor adjustments by filing the strike plate on the door frame. If there's some room between the frame and the door, you can align the latchbolt and strike plate by shimming the hinges. Or, drive a couple of extra-long screws to pull the frame into adjustment.

Common closet doors, such as sliding and bifold types, usually need only some minor adjustments and lubrication to stay in working order.

Door locksets tend to be very reliable, but they do need to be cleaned and lubricated occasionally. One simple way to keep an entry door lockset working smoothly is to spray a light lubricant into the keyhole, then move the key in and out a few times. Don't use graphite in locksets, because it can abrade some metals with repeated use.

Sticking doors usually leave a mark where they rub against the door frame. Warped doors may resist closing and feel springy when you apply pressure. Check for warpage with a straightedge. Draw pencil lines across the wear areas and sand until the marks disappear. Recheck and repeat if necessary.

Tools + Materials ▸

Tape measure
Pencil or grease pencil
Utility knife
Hammer
Screwdrivers
Drill and bits

Golf tees or wood dowels (optional)
Replacement hardware (optional)
Metal lubricant
Rag
3" wood screws
Cardboard shims
Sanding block

Plane (optional)
Cardboard protection
Heavy weights
Paintbrush
Clear wood sealer
Work gloves

HOW TO REMOVE A DOOR

Drive the lower hinge pin out using a screwdriver and hammer. Have a helper hold the door in place, then drive out the upper (and center, if applicable) hinge pins. Once you have the hinge pin started, you may find it easier to extract it with pliers.

Remove the door and set it aside. Clean and lubricate the hinge pins before reinstalling the door.

HOW TO TIGHTEN A LOOSE HINGE PLATE

Remove the door from the hinges. Tighten any loose screws on the door jamb or the door itself. If the wood won't hold the screws tightly, remove all the hinge plate screws to access the screw holes.

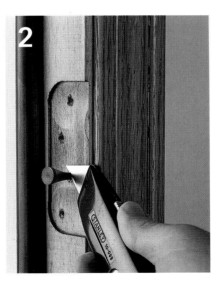

Coat wooden golf tees or wood dowels with wood glue, and drive them into the worn screw holes. If necessary, drill out the screw holes to accept dowels—it's better than pounding too hard on the dee or dowels and splitting the jamb wood. Let the glue dry, then cut off excess wood with a sharp utility knife.

Drill small pilot holes in the new wood patch, and reinstall the hinge.

TIPS FOR ALIGNING A LATCHBOLT + STRIKE PLATE

Install a thin cardboard shim behind the bottom hinge to raise the position of the latchbolt. To lower the latchbolt, shim behind the top hinge. Reinstall the hinge plate.

Remove two hinge screws from the top or bottom hinge, and drive a 3" wood screw into each hole. The screws will reach the framing studs in the wall and pull the door jamb, changing the angle of the door. Add long screws to the top hinge to raise the latchbolt or to the bottom hinge to lower it.

TIPS FOR STRAIGHTENING A WARPED DOOR

STOP

Adjust the door trim to follow the door. You can do this by removing or loosening the doorstop molding and reattaching it to conform to the door's warped profile. You likely will have some touch-up work to do on the door jamb where the doorstop edge has moved.

If the warpage is slight, you may be able to straighten it by removing it and placing heavy weights on the convex side of the warpage. Leave the weights on the door for several days, and check it periodically with a straightedge. This has a relatively low chance of success but may be worth a try.

TIPS FOR FREEING A STICKING DOOR

Tighten all of the hinge screws. If the door still sticks, use light pencil lines to mark the areas where the door rubs against the door jamb. Remove the door and sand the sticking points. You may be able to get away with sanding the door while it is still hanging. Replace the door and test the fit. If the sanding has not fixed the sticking, remove it again and go to the next step.

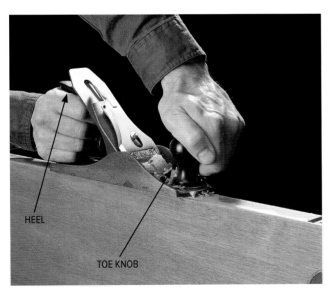

HEEL

TOE KNOB

Secure the door on-edge. If the door has veneered surfaces, sand back the veneer edges slightly so they do not catch the plane blade and splinter. Grip the toe knob and handle firmly, and plane with long, smooth strokes. You could also use a belt sander or a power planer for this step if you are not good with a hand plane—it is an acquired skill. Check the door's fit, then sand the planed area smooth.

Apply clear sealer or paint to the sanded or planed area and any other exposed surfaces of the door. This will prevent moisture from entering the wood and is especially important for entry doors.

WEATHERIZING DOORS + WINDOWS

No matter whether you live in a hot or a cold climate, weatherizing your home's windows and doors can pay off handsomely. Heating and cooling costs may account for over half of the total household energy bill. Since most weatherizing projects are relatively inexpensive, you can recover your investment quickly. In fact, in some climates, you can pay back the cost of a weatherproofing project in one season.

If you live in a cold climate, you probably already understand the importance of weatherizing. The value of keeping warm air inside the house during a cold winter is obvious. From the standpoint of energy efficiency, it's equally important to prevent warm air from entering the house during summer.

Weatherizing your home is an ideal do-it-yourself project, because it can be done a little at a time, according to your schedule. In cold climates, the best time of the year to weatherize is the fall, before it turns too cold to work outdoors.

Generally, metal and metal-reinforced weather stripping is more durable than products made of plastic, rubber, or foam. However, even plastic, rubber, and foam weather stripping products have a wide range of quality. The best rubber products are those made from neoprene rubber—use this whenever it's available.

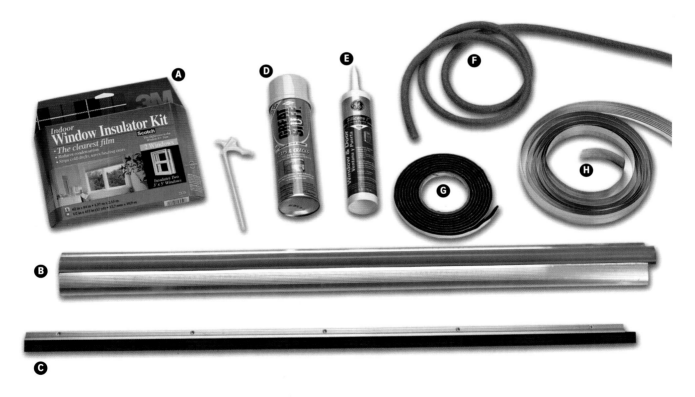

Weatherizing products commonly found in home centers include clear film, heat-shrink window insulator kit (A); an aluminum door threshold with vinyl weather stripping insert (B); a nail-on, rubber door sweep (C); minima-expanding spray foam (D); silicone window and door caulk (E); open-cell foam caulk-backer rod (F); self-adhesive, closed-cell foam weather stripping coil (G); flexible brass weather stripping coil, also called V-channel, (H).

TIPS FOR WEATHERIZING WINDOWS + DOORS

Install a storm door to decrease drafts and energy loss through entry doors. Look for an insulated storm door with a continuous hinge and seamless exterior surface.

Caulking is a simple and inexpensive way to fill narrow gaps, indoors or out. One primary spot for heat loss is the gap between the window brickmold and the exterior wall.

A felt, bristle, or rubber door sweep seals out drafts, even if you have an uneven floor or a low threshold.

(continued)

Patio door: Use rubber compression strips to seal the channels in patio door jambs, where movable panels fit when closed. Also install a patio door insulator kit (plastic sheeting installed similarly to plastic sheeting for windows) on the interior side of the door.

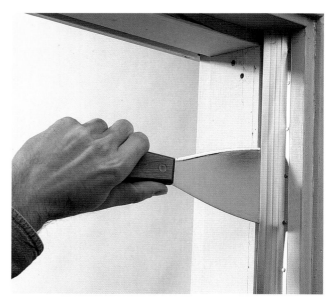

Cut two pieces of metal tension strip or V-channel the full height of the door opening, and cut another to full width. Use wire brads to tack the strips to the door jambs and door header on the interior side of the doorstops. Attach metal weather stripping from the top down to help prevent buckling. Flare out the tension strips with a putty knife to fill the gaps between the jambs and the door when the door is in the closed position (do not pry too far at a time).

Add reinforced felt strips to the edge of the doorstop on the exterior side. The felt edge should form a close seal with the door when closed. Drive fasteners only until they are flush with the surface of the reinforcing spine—overdriving will cause damage and buckling.

Sliding windows: Treat side-by-side sliding windows as if they were double-hung windows turned 90°. For greater durability, use metal tension strips, rather than self-adhesive compressible foam, in the sash track that fit against the edge of the sash when the window is closed.

Casement windows: Attach self-adhesive foam or rubber compression strips on the outside edges of the window stops.

Storm windows: Create a tight seal by attaching foam compression strips to the outside of storm window stops. After installing the storm window, fill any gaps between the exterior window trim and the storm window with caulk backer rope.

Lower sash of a double-hung window. Wipe down the underside of the bottom window sash with a damp rag, and let it dry; then attach self-adhesive compressible foam or rubber to the underside of the sash. Use high-quality hollow neoprene strips, if available. This will create an airtight seal when the window is locked in position.

BOTTOM SASH (RAISED)

TOP SASH (LOWERED)

Upper sash of a double-hung window. Seal the gap between the top sash and the bottom sash on double-hung windows. Lift the bottom sash and lower the top sash to improve access, and tack metal V-channel to the bottom rail of the top sash using wire brads. The open end of the "V" should be pointed downward so moisture cannot collect in the channel. Flare out the V-channel with a putty knife to fit the gap between the sash.

LAMINATE FLOORING

These samples of laminates sold at major home improvement centers show the enormous variety of looks that are available. Today's laminate floors require close inspection to distinguish them from genuine wood.

Tools + Materials ▸

Eye and ear protection	Jigsaw	Hammer
Work gloves	Hole saw	Level
Utility knife	Pull bar	Liquid floor leveler (if necessary)
Tape measure	Tapping block	Nails (as needed)
Miter saw	Rubber mallet	Sheet underlayment kit with clear tape
Circular saw	Rubber gloves	Laminate flooring
Pry bar	Compass	Flooring spacers

HOW TO PREPARE THE FLOOR FOR LAMINATE FLOORING

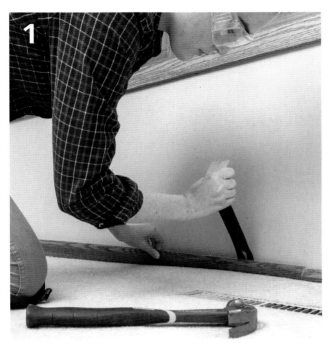

Remove baseboard shoe moldings using a small pry bar. If your trim style does not include shoe moldings, as is the case if you have ranch-style moldings, remove the entire baseboard molding. Carefully removed baseboards can be easily reinstalled.

Remove the old flooring, if necessary. Before continuing with preparation, unpack the new flooring and stack it in the room for 8 to 24 hours to acclimate the flooring.

Using a long level or other straightedge, check the floor for dips or crowns, and if necessary correct these. Loose underlayment can be nailed down, and small dips can be leveled out with liquid floor leveler. On concrete, install a DRIcore subfloor to raise the new floor slightly above the slab.

Using a prybar and hammer, loosen and pry up the tackstrip that held the carpet in place. The tackstrip may break apart as you work; use care to avoid injuring yourself on the sharp tacks.

(continued)

Plan the layout. Measure the width of the room and subtract ¾" to accommodate the ⅜" gap needed along each wall. Now, divide this number by the width of the flooring planks to arrive at the number of rows of flooring you will need. If the resulting number of rows gives you a partial fraction that is more than ½ the plank width, rip planks for the first row to this measurement. But if the partial fraction is less than ½ the plank width, then divide this measurement by 2, and plan to rip both the first and the last rows to this measurement. The goal is to avoid a very narrow strip on one side of the room only.

Install the required sheet underlayment. Cut the underlayment sheets to fit using a utility knife, then tape sheets together to cover the floor using clear tape. (Some underlayment products unfold, with self-adhesive edges.) Follow manufacturer's recommendation for overlap between sheets. *NOTE: On concrete floors, you will need to install a 6-mil sheet plastic vapor barrier, then the sheet underlayment; or install a DRIcore raised underlayment.*

Install ⅜"-thick spacers around each wall, spaced every 2'. A flooring installation kit specified by your manufacturer may have these spacers included; or, you can trim wood shims to this thickness and use them as spacers.

HOW TO INSTALL A FLOATING LAMINATE FLOOR

Inspect each plank, and reject any that are scarred or that have damaged tongues or grooves. For the first row of planks along the wall, remove the tongues along the long sides of the planks using a circular saw or table saw. If you are ripping the first row down to accommodate a partial plank, cut away the tongue side of the plank.

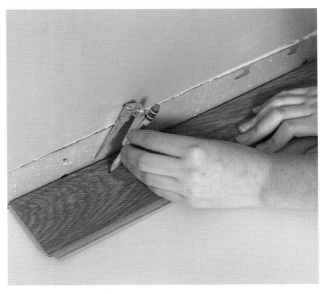

VARIATION: If your wall is irregular, use a compass to trace the wall outline on the plank, then use a jigsaw to cut the plank to conform to the wall's contours.

Cross-cut a plank into ⅓- and ⅔-length segments. These pieces will be used to start the second and third rows, respectively.

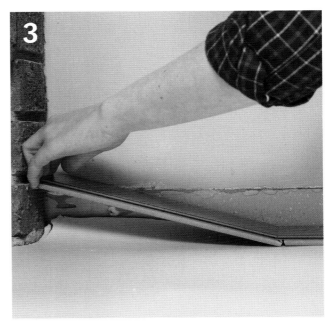

Begin laying the first row using the planks with the tongues cut away, beginning with a full-length piece in the corner. Maintain a ⅜" gap along both walls. For the second piece, align the end tongue-and-groove, and snap into place. At the last plank in the row, cut the plank to fit with a miter saw, maintaining the ⅜" gap to the wall.

(continued)

Install the subsequent rows of planks, alternating full plank, ⅔-length plank, and ⅓-length plank, so that joints are staggered in a repeating pattern. To fit each plank, first insert the tongue into the edge groove of the previous row of planks, then slide it laterally until the new plank butts up to the end of the preceding piece. Snap downward to lock into place.

If necessary, tap on the opposite end of the plank with a tapping block to snug up the joint. Take care not to damage the plank.

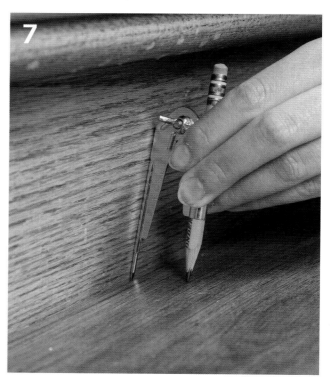

At the last piece in the row, cut length to size, then fit the piece into the edge groove, and use the pull bar and hammer to lightly draw the piece back to secure the end joint.

As you install the last row, lay each full piece against the wall on top of the last installed piece, with a scrap plank positioned vertically against the wall as a spacer. Trace the wall contour onto the plank.

Cut along the traced lines of the last planks using a jigsaw. Saw on the face of the board with a fine-toothed blade.

To install the pieces of the final row, slide the long-side tongue into the groove of the previous row, with the ends aligned. Use the pull bar and hammer to work along the length of the plank, pulling toward you to gently secure the joint.

Reinstall the trim moldings that were removed, covering the gaps between the flooring and the wall. Remember: the floating floor needs to expand and contract, so drive finish nails at an angle into the wall, not into the flooring.

VINYL TILE: INSTALLING

As with any tile installation, resilient tile requires carefully positioned layout lines. Before committing to any layout and applying tile, conduct a dry run to identify potential problems.

Keep in mind the difference between reference lines (see opposite page) and layout lines. Reference lines mark the center of the room and divide it into quadrants. If the tiles don't lay out symmetrically along these lines, you'll need to adjust them slightly, creating layout lines. Once layout lines are established,

installing the tile is a fairly quick process. Be sure to keep joints between the tiles tight and lay the tiles square.

Tiles with an obvious grain pattern can be laid so the grain of each tile is oriented identically throughout the installation. You can also use the quarter-turn method, in which each tile has its pattern grain running perpendicular to that of adjacent tiles. Whichever method you choose, be sure to be consistent throughout the project.

Tools + Materials ▸

Tape measure	Heat gun	Flooring adhesive (for dry-back tile)	Work gloves
Chalk line	Resilient tile	⅛" spacer	1⁄16" notched trowel
Framing square	Pencil	Threshold material (if necessary)	Ceramic tile cutter
Utility knife	Cardboard	Knee pads	

Resilient tiles have a pattern layer that is bonded to a vinyl base and coated with a transparent wear layer. Some come with adhesive preapplied and covered by a paper backing, others have dry backs and are designed to be set into flooring adhesive.

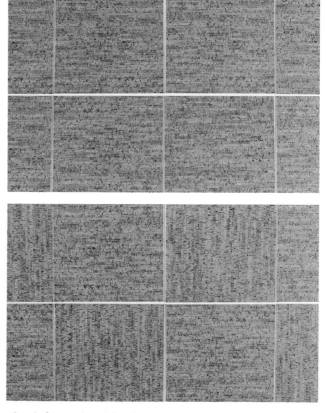

Check for noticeable directional features, like the grain of the vinyl particles. You can set the tiles in a running pattern so the directional feature runs in the same direction (top), or in a checkerboard pattern using the quarter-turn method (bottom).

HOW TO MAKE REFERENCE LINES FOR TILE INSTALLATION

Position a reference line (X) by measuring along opposite sides of the room and marking the center of each side. Snap a chalk line between these marks.

Measure and mark the centerpoint of the chalk line. From this point, use a framing square to establish a second reference line perpendicular to the first one. Snap the second line (Y) across the room.

Check the reference lines for squareness using the 3-4-5 triangle method. Measure along reference line X and make a mark 3 ft. from the centerpoint. Measure from the centerpoint along reference line Y and make a mark at 4 ft.

Measure the distance between the marks. If the reference lines are perpendicular, the distance will measure exactly 5 ft. If not, adjust the reference lines until they're exactly perpendicular to each other.

HOW TO INSTALL DRY-BACKED RESILIENT TILE

Snap perpendicular reference lines with a chalk line (see previous page). Dry-fit tiles along layout line Y so a joint falls along reference line X. If necessary, shift the layout to make the layout symmetrical or to reduce the number of tiles that need to be cut.

If you shift the tile layout, create a new line that is parallel to reference line X and runs through a tile joint near line X. The new line, X1, is the line you'll use when installing the tile. Use a different colored chalk to distinguish between lines.

Dry-fit tiles along the new line, X1. If necessary, adjust the layout line as in steps 1 and 2. Check and adjust the direction of each tile if you're accommodating grain patterns or other variations.

If you adjusted the layout along X1, measure and make a new layout line, Y1, that's parallel to reference line Y and runs through a tile joint. Y1 will form the second layout line you'll use during installation.

5

Apply adhesive around the intersection of the layout lines using a trowel with ¼₆" V-shaped notches. Hold the trowel at a 45° angle and spread adhesive evenly over the surface.

6

Spread adhesive over most of the installation area, covering three quadrants. Allow the adhesive to set according to the manufacturer's instructions, then begin to install the tile at the intersection of the layout lines. You can kneel on installed tiles to lay additional tiles.

7

When the first three quadrants are completely tiled, spread adhesive over the remaining quadrant, then finish setting the tile.

8

To cut tiles to fit along the walls, place the tile to be cut (A) face up on top of the last full tile you installed. Position a ⅛"-thick spacer against the wall, then set a marker tile (B) on top of the tile to be cut. Trace along the edge of the marker tile to draw a cutting line.

(continued)

Outside Corners ▸

To mark tiles for cutting around outside corners, make a cardboard template to match the space, keeping a ⅛" gap along the walls. After cutting the template, check to make sure it fits. Place the template on a tile and trace its outline.

9

Cut tile to fit using a ceramic-tile cutter to make straight cuts. You may use a straightedge guide and utility knife instead.

10

Install cut tiles next to the walls. If you're precutting all tiles before installing them, measure the distance between the wall and install tiles at various points in case the distance changes.

11

Check the entire floor. If you find loose areas, press down on the tiles to bond them to the underlayment. Install metal threshold bars at room borders where the new floor joins another floor covering. It's wise to roll the floor with a metal roller to ensure bonding of the adhesive.

HOW TO INSTALL SELF-ADHESIVE RESILIENT TILE

Once your reference lines are established, peel off the paper backing and install the first tile in one of the corners formed by the intersecting layout lines. Lay three or more tiles along each layout line in the quadrant.

Rub the entire surface of each tile to thoroughly bond the adhesive to the underlayment. Begin installing tiles in the interior area of the quadrant. Keep the joints tight between tiles.

Finish setting full tiles in the first quadrant, then set the full tiles in an adjacent quadrant. Set the tiles along the layout lines first, then fill in the interior tiles.

Continue installing the tile in the remaining quadrants until the room is completely covered. Check the entire floor. If you find loose areas, press down on the tiles to bond them to the underlayment. Install metal threshold strips at room borders where the new floor joins another floor covering.

CERAMIC FLOOR TILE

Although the floor tiles shown in the steps that follow are porcelain, this process would be the same if you were installing ceramic or stone tiles.

In all cases, a successfully tiled floor relies on proper preparation. That starts with laying down a stable, secure surface for the tile. But the most important step for the look of the finished floor is snapping the chalk lines and dry fitting to determine the most visually pleasing tile placement.

Beyond that, work carefully and steadily, using spacers throughout to maintain proper spacing, and be careful never to walk on a newly tiled floor. This means planning so that you never tile yourself into a corner. Plan carefully, pay attention when laying the tiles, and work within your own abilities and capacity, and you'll wind up with a long-lasting, beautiful tile floor.

Tools + Materials ▶

¼" square-notched trowel
Rubber mallet
Tile cutter
Tile nippers
Handheld tile cutter
Needlenose pliers
Grout float
Grout sponge
Soft cloth
Thinset mortar
Tile
Tile spacers
Grout
Latex grout additive
Wall adhesive
2 × 4 lumber
Grout sealer
Tile caulk
Sponge brush
Cementboard
Chalk line
Tape measure
Drill and bits
Paddle bit
Caulk gun
1¼" cementboard screws
Fiberglass-mesh wallboard tape
Utility knife or grout knife
Threshold material
Jigsaw or circular saw
    with a tungsten-carbide blade
Rounded bullnose tile
Work gloves
Knee pads
Eye protection

HOW TO INSTALL CERAMIC FLOOR TILE

Screw the tile backer board down to the subfloor with 1¼" self-piloting screws driven every 2" around the edge. Tape the seams with fiberglass mesh tape and finish the backer board surface.

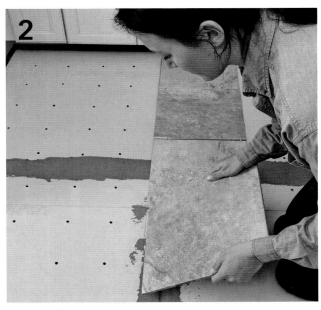

Draw reference lines and establish the tile layout. Check that the lines are square to each other using the 3-4-5 method. Dry-lay 2 half rows of tiles in place, running from the center in 2 directions out to the wall. Determine if the layout leaves less than ⅓ of a tile at either wall, and adjust your reference lines if it does.

OPTION: Build a grid system of chalk lines based on the actual dimensions of your tiles, including the grout lines. A grid system ensures that you will stay on track and it helps you divide the project into small sections so you can apply the correct amount of thinset without guessing.

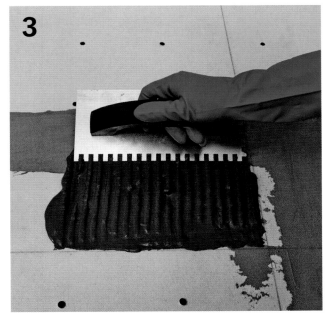

Mix a batch of thinset mortar and spread it evenly across a square along both reference lines of the quadrant. Use the notched edge to create furrows, being careful not to press down all the way to the backer board.

(continued)

Press the first tile down into the mortar at the corner of the quadrant where the reference lines intersect. Twist it slightly and press down. Use a putty knife to pull the tile up to check that the mortar consistency is correct and coating all areas on the bottom of the tile. Press the tile back into position. Use a rubber mallet to gently tap the center area of the tile to set it properly.

VARIATION: For 16 × 16" or larger tiles or uneven stone, use a larger trowel with notches that are at least ½" deep.

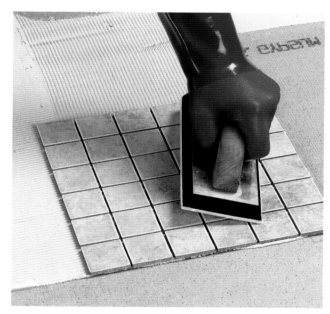

Continue laying tiles along one row, using spacers to maintain spacing between tiles. Use the appropriate spacers for the size tile you are laying, and stand them upright; do not lay spacers flat at tile intersections because they will be impossible to remove from the mortar and can compromise the integrity of the grout lines.

VARIATION: For mosaic sheets, use a ³⁄₁₆" V-notched trowel to spread the mortar and a grout float to press the sheets into the mortar. Apply pressure gently to avoid creating an uneven surface.

6

To make sure tiles are level with one another, place a straight 2 × 4 across several tiles in a row and tap the top of the board with a rubber mallet.

7

As you work, clean up any mortar on the top of the tiles as soon as you detect it. Use a damp sponge to wipe up the mortar completely, to ensure it doesn't dry on the surface of the tile.

8

Lay the rest of the tile in the remaining area of the quadrant, repeating steps 2 through 7. Be careful to plan tile placement so that you don't tile yourself into a corner. Avoid stepping or kneeling on the laid tiles.

(continued)

In corners and against walls, leave a gap of at least
¼" between the tiles and the walls or cabinets. Make sure
the gap is still narrow enough that your base shoe molding
or trim will cover it.

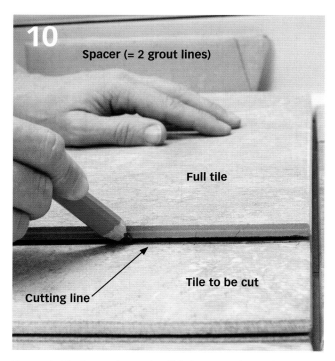

Spacer (= 2 grout lines)

Full tile

Tile to be cut

Cutting line

To mark tile for cutting so it will fit between the end or edge
of a row and the wall, lay the tile to be cut directly on top
of the full tile it will sit next to. Stand one or two tiles up flat
against the wall as spacers (this will account for an expansion
and the grout space between tiles) and lay another tile on top
of the tile to be marked, with the edge butted against the tiles
on the wall. Mark the second tile for cutting. Check the dry fit
and then apply mortar for two partial tiles at a time and set
them in place, leaving an expansion gap between the tile edge
and the wall or obstruction.

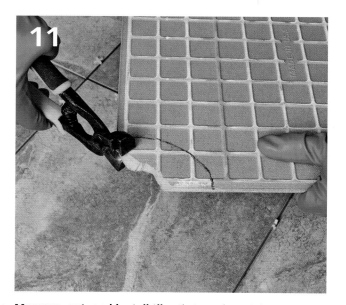

Measure, cut, and install tiles that require notches or curves
to fit around obstacles, such as exposed pipes or toilet drains.

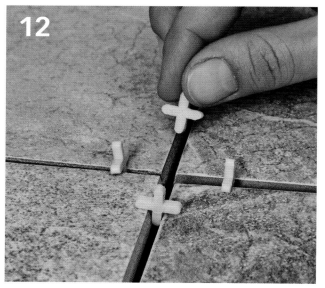

Continue laying tiles until the floor is complete. Allow
24 hours for the mortar to dry and then remove the spacers.
To prepare for grouting, use painter's tape to protect any trim
that abuts the tiled surface.

Mix the grout using the drill and paddle bit. Follow the instructions for the grout you're using. *NOTE: When mixing grout for porous tile, such as unsealed quarry or natural stone, include an additive with a release agent to prevent the grout from bonding to the tile surfaces.*

Start in a corner and pour a small amount of grout onto the tiles. Use the float to spread the grout out from the corner, working in smooth arcs and pressing the grout into the spaces between tiles. Hold the float at about a 60° angle and work in a figure-eight motion. Work on 4-tile sections.

As you finish one small quadrant of tile, use the float and a small trowel to clean the excess grout off the surface of the tiles. Continue applying the grout at a 45° angle to the joints until you've finished about 25 sq. ft. of the floor.

Wipe a damp grout sponge diagonally over about 2 sq. ft. of the floor to remove grout residue. Rinse the sponge in cool water between passes. Be careful not to press so hard you pull grout out of the joints, but use as many passes as necessary to clean the surface of the tiles. Change the rinse water frequently.

STRIP + PLANK FLOORS

Installing tongue-and-groove hardwood strips or planks is straightforward. They can be fastened with mechanical fasteners such as nails or staples, or they can be glued down or fully bonded. Regardless of installation methods, strips, planks, or engineered planks must run perpendicular to the joists unless additional underlayment has been installed. Be sure to measure and cut boards at the appropriate ends to ensure the tongue-and-groove joints fit together for end matches.

To fasten with mechanical fasteners, the first and last boards are facenailed, while the other boards are blind-nailed through the tongue. Once the first few rows are installed, use a power nailer—either manual or pneumatic. The power nailer positions the fastener at exactly the right angle through the tongue, the body of the board, and into the floor. It is critical that the nail depth is set correctly. The fastener should be set slightly below the surface of the tongue. If it is set above or flush with the surface, it may cause dimpling in the finished floor. If the staple or nail penetrates more than halfway through the tongue, the board will creak or squeak. To set the fastener depth correctly, fasten a sample board to the subfloor/underlayment. Once you have adjusted the depth, fasten a second board to check for consistency. Once set, remove the sample boards and destroy.

A fully bonded wood floor is attached to the subfloor with adhesive, much like a tile floor. A bonded wood floor can be installed over concrete

and tile, and is typically used over radiant heating systems so the heating elements are not punctured by fasteners. The flooring product, adhesive, and subfloor and underlayment must all be compatible. The instructions that come with your floor cover all the appropriate combinations.

Tools + Materials ▶

Jigsaw
Circular saw
Stapler
Utility knife
Tape measure
Chalk line
Drill
Flooring pull bar
Rubber mallet

Hammer
Pry bar
Power nailer
Rosin paper
Wood floor strips or planks
Nails or staples
Reducer strip or transition strip
Nail set
Wood putty

Knee pads
Work gloves

For bonded floor:
Notched trowel
Flooring adhesive
Wood glue
Cardboard
Floor roller

HOW TO INSTALL A HARDWOOD PLANK FLOOR

Acclimate the flooring by stacking planks in the installation room. Separate the rows of flooring with wood scraps. Allow the material to rest in the space for several days, or as directed by the manufacturer's instructions. *NOTE: Inspect the wood flooring as soon as it arrives. Look for any major defects such as knots, cracks, and damaged, warped, or bowed boards. It's easier to replace inadequate boards during the acclimation period than in mid-installation.*

Install a layer of rosin paper over the entire subfloor, stapling it down and overlapping the edges by 4". The purpose of this layer is mostly to eliminate noise caused by the floorboards scraping or pressing on the wood subfloor or underlayment (if required), which should be installed and leveled before the flooring installation begins.

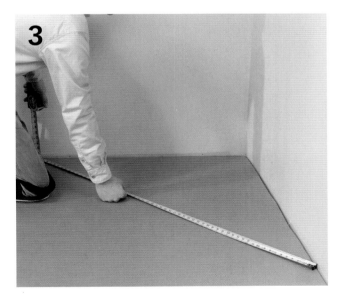

Check that the room is square using the 3-4-5 rule: measure out 3' from a corner in one direction and 4' in the other direction—the distance between the marks should be exactly 5'. If the room is out of square, you'll have to decide which wall (usually the longest) to follow as a baseline for laying the flooring.

Determine the location of the floor joist and drive a nail in at each end, centered on the joists. Snap chalk lines along the centerlines of each joist, connecting the nails. Use these as a reference for installing floorboards.

(continued)

FLOORS

5

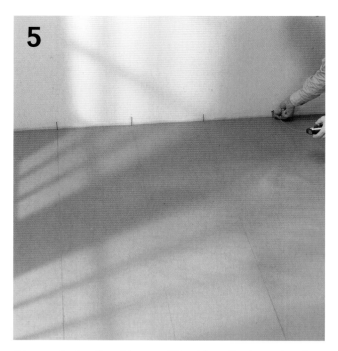

Snap a starter line. Measure ¾" out from the longest wall, perpendicular to the floor joists, to allow for an expansion gap. Drive a nail at each end, and snap a chalk line parallel to the wall.

6

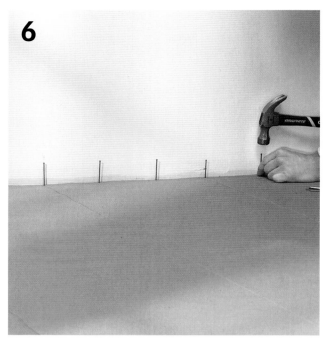

Drive spacer nails, such as 8d finish nails, every 4 to 5" along the chalk line, as a guide for placement of the first row of planks. Drive the nails in far enough to be stable, but with enough of the nail protruding to serve as a bumper for the flooring (and to make the nail easier to remove later).

7

Lay down a dry run for the first two or three rows to determine plank positions for best appearance. Mark the backs of planks with a pencil to keep them in your preferred order and remove them from the work area. Make sure the end joints are staggered by more than 6" apart on adjoining planks. Create a lay out that has perimeter pieces that are longer than 6".

VARIATION: Some manufacturers recommend that you apply a bead of flooring adhesive to the backs of wider planks prior to nailing them. Use the recommended adhesive and lay beads across the width of the plank; keep adhesive at least ½" from the edges and 1½" from the ends.

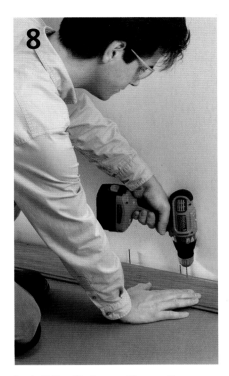

Install the first row. Choose the longest planks available for this row. Lay the planks in place and drill holes every 8" for facenailing along the wall edge. Locate the holes ¼ to ½" in from the edge, where they'll be covered up by the base molding and shoe.

Attach the first floorboards by facenailing 8d finish nails into the pilot holes along the wall edge. Sink the nail heads with a nail set.

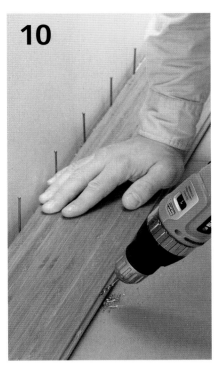

Predrill pilot holes through the tongues of the first row planks and blind-nail 8d finish or flooring nails. Make sure the heads of the nails do not stick up through the tops of the tongues, where they would interfere with the tongue-and-groove joint.

(continued)

Plugging Counterbores ▸

Wider plank floors frequently require that you fasten the ends of floorboards by screwing down through the board and into the subfloor. This is most commonly needed when you are installing wood flooring that does not have tongue-and-groove ends. In such cases, drill counterbored pilot holes for the screws, making sure the counterbores are deep enough to accept a wood plug. After the floorboards are installed, check to make sure the screws are tight (but be careful not to overdrive them) and then glue a wood plug into each counterbore. Wood plugs should be the same species as the flooring or, if that's not available, make them a contrasting species. Sand the plugs so the tops are even with surrounding floor and finish them at the same time.

NOTE: If you are using matching plugs, orient them in the counterbores with the wood grain running parallel to the floorboards; if you are using contrasting plugs, position the grains perpendicular.

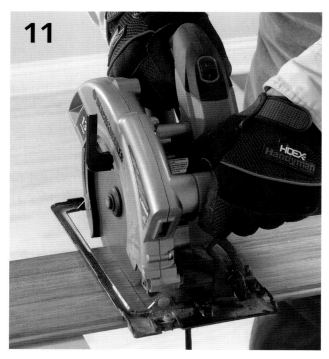

11

Cut the end planks for each row to length, so that the butt end faces the wall. In other words, try and preserve the tongue-and-groove profiles if your flooring has them on the ends. Saw the planks with a fine-tooth blade, making sure to orient the workpiece so you'll be cutting into the face, minimizing tearout on the surface.

12

After the second row, use a flooring nailer to blind-nail the tongues of each plank. Flooring nailers are struck with a mallet to drive and set the flooring nails through the floorboard tongues. They can be rented at most home centers or rental centers. *NOTE: You can continue to hand-nail if you choose, but it is difficult to get the same consistency, and it is certainly more painstaking. Be sure to continue pre-drilling pilot holes as well to avoid damaging the tongues.*

13

Keep joints tight. As you install each successive plank in a row, use a flooring pull bar at the open end of the plank. Drive the end of the board toward the joint by rapping on the pull bar with a mallet.

14

At the end of rows and along walls, use a pull bar to seat the boards. For the last row, rip the planks as necessary, use the pull bar to seat them, and facenail along the edge as you did with the first row.

15

If a plank is slightly bowed, cut fitting wedges to force the wayward board into position before nailing it. Make wedges by cutting two triangles from a 1' or longer scrap of flooring (inset). Attach one half of the wedge pair with the outside edge parallel to the bowed plank. Slide the groove of the other wedge piece onto the tongue of the bowed plank, and hammer until the plank sits flush against its neighbor. Nail the plank into place. Remove the wedge parts.

16

Install a reducer strip or other transition as needed between the plank floor and adjoining rooms. Cut the strip to size and fit the strip's groove over the plank's tongue. Drill pilot holes and facenail the strip with 8d finishing nails. Sink the nails with a nail set, putty, and sand smooth.

17

Install a quarter-round shoe molding to cover all the expansion gaps between the floor and walls at the edge of the floor. Paint, stain, or finish the molding before installing.

18

To reverse the direction of the tongue and groove at doorways or other openings, glue a spline into the groove of the plank. Fit the groove of the following board onto the spline and nail into place as before.

REFINISHING HARDWOOD FLOORS

There are two ways a hardwood floor can be renovated and before deciding what approach to take, carefully evaluate your floor, because one method is considerably more involved and should be done only if necessary.

The first method is called screening—a process that involves fitting an upright floor buffer with a metal screen pad that roughens up the glossy surface finish of your floor without sanding down into the hardwood. After the floor is screened and all dust removed, a new top finish layer is applied to the floor. Where appropriate, screening and applying a new top coat is a very efficient and relatively easy means to transform a hardwood floor. Screening is appropriate where the wear and damage to a floor is confined to the surface finish, and where the top layer is a standard polyurethane or varnish finish.

But be aware that there are instances where screening and refinishing is not possible. For example, if the floor has been maintained by waxing, or

The timeless beauty of a refinished hardwood floor enlivens the whole room.

finished with a modern aluminum oxide coat, new polyurethane simply will not bond to the underlying layer, and your only option will be to completely sand down into the wood layer.

The second method for refinishing hardwood is a complete sanding and refinishing project, in which a rented upright drum sander or upright orbital sander grinds down a thin layer of the actual hardwood in preparation for applying a new top coat finish. This is the option if the wood itself shows damage or if the original top coat is wax or a super-hard aluminum oxide coat. In this method, after the major floor area is sanded with the upright sander, the corners and edges are sanded with a handheld rented edge sander. Historically, this is a difficult project for DIYers, because drum sanders are hard to control and small errors in handling the tool can badly gouge a floor. Careful DIYers can do this successfully.

This project will show you how to evaluate your floor and then give you both options for refinishing: screening to remove just the top surface finish, or complete sanding to remove a thin layer of the actual wood.

BEFORE

AFTER

HOW TO SCREEN + REFINISH A HARDWOOD FLOOR

Tools and materials for screening and refinishing a hardwood floor include: upright floor buffer (A); handheld random-orbit sander (B); sanding screens for rental sander (C); paint scraper (D); brad puller (E); hammer (F); nail set (G); pry bar (H); shop vacuum (I); mop (J); rags (K); polyurethane finish (L) painting pad (M); paintbrushes (N); paint tray (O); vinegar (P); detail sander (Q); tape measure (R); ear protection (S); particle mask; and eye protection (T).

1

Remove shoe moldings using a pry bar. Your results will be best if you screen and refinish all the way to the walls.

2

Vacuum floor and damp mop with a solution of vinegar in water. Make sure to let the floor dry completely, and don't allow standing water to sit on the floor.

3

Fit a sanding screen on the pad of an upright floor buffer. Buff over the entire floor until the finish is dull.

4

Screen edges and corners with a handheld power sander. In the very back of corners, and under obstacles such as radiators, use a piece of sanding screen to remove the finish by hand. Thoroughly vacuum the floor, then wipe it down with a slightly moistened cloth.

5

Apply polyurethane finish as directed by the manufacturer using a painting pad on a pole, and a paintbrush for small corners. If necessary, a second coat can be applied after the first coat dries completely. Lightly buff the previous coat with a fiber pad between coats.

6

Reinstall the baseboard moldings. If the moldings were old and brittle, cutting and installing new pieces may give your floor a nice finishing touch.

HOW TO SAND A HARDWOOD FLOOR

Tools and materials for sanding a hardwood floor include: hammer (A); nail set (B); sheet plastic (C); painter's tape (D); ear protection (E); drum sander [rented] (F); floor sander/edger (G); under-radiator sander [rented, if needed] (H); shop vacuum (I); wood filler (J); putty knife (K); clean cloths (L); pre-stain conditioner (M); wood stain (N); latex gloves (O); detail sander/mouse (P); eye protection (Q); and respirator (R).

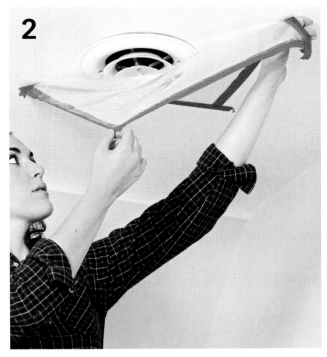

Examine the floor and remove any protruding tacks or staples. Drive down any nail heads that can be felt by hand. Scrape away any paint splatters from the floor. Vacuum the floor thoroughly. Damp-mop the floor and let it dry completely. Remove shoe moldings with a prybar or claw hammer.

Cover doorways, HVAC vents, and other openings with sheets of plastic secured with painter's tape. Shelves holding books or other decorative items can also be covered with plastic. Power sanding a floor is a messy business, and dust can infiltrate any opening.

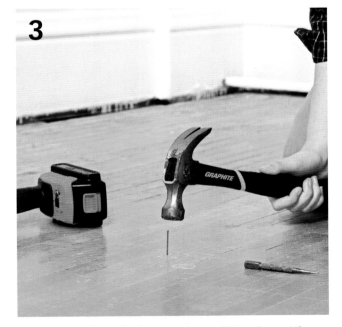

SAFETY TIP

Even with proper ventilation, inhaling sawdust is a health risk. We recommend getting a respirator for a project like this. If you don't use one, you must at least wear a dust mask. Eye protection is also a must; and you'll thank yourself for buying a good pair of strong work gloves—they make the sander vibrations a little more bearable.

IMPORTANT! Always unplug the sander whenever loading or unloading sandpaper.

Examine the floor for loose or bowed boards, and if necessary, nail them down. Badly damaged floorboards should be replaced. Examine any stained areas. Surface stains will probably sand out, but deep stains, such as where water damage has soaked in, may require that the floorboards be replaced.

(continued)

4

Practice with the drum sander turned off. Move forward and backward. Tilt or raise it off the floor a couple of times. A drum sander is heavy, bulky, and awkward. Once it touches the floor, it walks forward; if you stop it, it gouges the floor. For the initial pass with the drum sander, sand with the grain using 40- or 60-grit paper. Start two-thirds down the room length on the right side; work your way to the left. Raise drum. Start motor. Slowly lower the drum to the floor and move forward. Lift the sander off the floor when you reach the wall. Move to the left 2" to 4" and then walk it backward the same distance you just walked forward. Repeat.

5

6

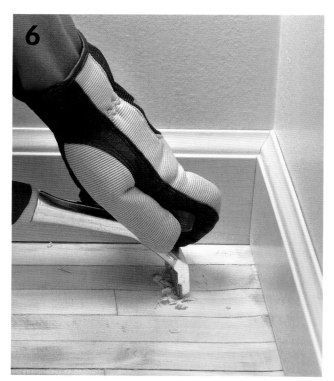

In small corners, you may need to sand by hand, or with a handheld detail sander. After sanding is complete, completely vacuum the floor with a brush attachment.

Use a paint scraper to get into corners and hard-to-reach nooks and crannies. Pull the scraper toward you with a steady downward pressure. Pull with the grain. Next, sand with a sanding block.

7

Prepare the room for finish by sweeping and vacuuming. Sweep and vacuum again. Wipe up fine particles with a tack cloth.

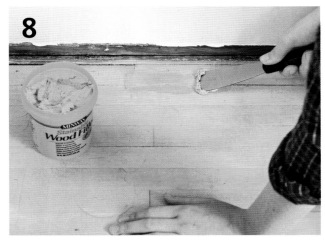

8

Examine the floor carefully. Nicks, knots, holes, or wide cracks between floorboards can be filled with wood filler that color matches the wood. Let the wood filler dry completely. Repeat steps 4 to 6, first with medium-grit sandpaper, then fine-grit sandpaper. Vacuum thoroughly after each sanding, and after last sanding thoroughly wipe the floor clean with slightly damp (not wet) cloths.

9

To stain, apply the liquid stain to the floor with a brush or clean cloth, in a motion parallel to the wood grain. Allow the stain to soak in for 5 to 15 minutes, then wipe away excess with a clean cloth. If you wish to darken the color, wait about 6 hours, then apply a second coat of stain. You can also choose to simply finish the floor with two or more coats of polyurethane, using the process described in the screening project on page 97.

Sandpapers for Drum Sanders + Edgers ▸

Grits	Grade	Use
20, 30, 40, 60	Coarse	To level uneven boards
100, 120	Medium	To minimize scratches from coarse grits
150, 180	Fine	To eliminate scratches from medium grits

Sandpaper becomes less effective over time; it may even rip. Buy three to five sheets of every grade for each room you want to refinish. You won't use them all, but most rentals allow you to return what you don't use. It's far better to have too many than to find yourself unable to continue until the next day because you ran out and the hardware store is closed.

Reminder: Before you leave the rental shop, have an employee show you how to load the paper. Every machine is a little different.

CARPET SQUARES: INSTALLING

Most carpeting has a single design and is stretched from wall to wall. It covers more square feet of American homes than any other material. You can install it yourself, but if you want a soft floor covering that gives you more options, carpet squares are an excellent choice.

Manufacturers have found ways to create attractive new carpet using recycled fibers. This not only reuses material that would otherwise become landfill, it reduces waste in manufacturing as well. So, instead of adding to problems of resource consumption and pollution, carpet squares made from recycled materials help reduce them.

The squares are attached to each other and to the floor with adhesive dots. They can be installed on most clean, level, dry underlayment or onto an existing floor. If the surface underneath is waxed or varnished, check with the manufacturer before you use any adhesives on it.

Tools + Materials ▸

Adhesive (optional)	Marking pen or pencil
Carpenter's square	Straightedge
Chalk line	Carpet squares
Cleaning supplies	Scrap plywood
Craft/utility knife	Knee pads
Measuring tape	Work gloves

HOW TO INSTALL CARPET SQUARES

Take the squares out of the package. Usually, you want to keep new flooring out of the way until you're ready to install it. But some materials, such as carpet or sheet vinyl, should be at room temperature for at least 12 hours before you lay them down.

Check the requirements for the recommended adhesive. You can install carpet squares over many other flooring materials, including hardwood, laminates, and resilient sheets or tiles. The carpet squares shown here are fastened with adhesive dots, so almost any existing floor will provide a usable surface.

Make sure the existing floor is clean, smooth, stable, and dry. Use floor leveler if necessary to eliminate any hills or valleys. If any part of the floor is loose, secure it to the subfloor or underlayment before you install the carpet squares. Vacuum the surface and wipe it with a damp cloth.

Snap chalk lines between diagonally opposite corners to find the center point for the room. In rooms with unusual shapes, determine the visual center and mark it. Next, snap chalk lines across the center and perpendicular to the walls. This set of guidelines will show you where to start.

(continued)

5

Lay a base row of carpet squares on each side of the two guidelines. When you reach the walls, make note of how much you will need to cut. You should have the same amount to cut on each side. If not, adjust the center point and realign the squares.

6

Check the backs of the squares before you apply any adhesive. They should indicate a direction, using arrows or other marks, so that the finished pile has a consistent appearance. If you plan to mix colors, this is the time to establish your pattern.

7

Fasten the base rows in place using the manufacturer's recommended adhesive. This installation calls for two adhesive dots per square. As you place each square, make sure it is aligned with the guidelines and fits tightly against the next square.

8

When you reach a wall, flip the last square over. Push it against the wall until it is snug. If you are planning a continuous pattern, align the arrows with the existing squares. If you are creating a parquet pattern, turn the new square 90 degrees before marking it.

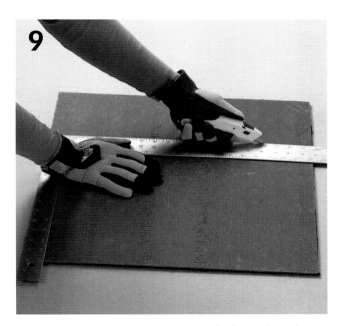

9

Mark notches or draw a line across the back where the new square overlaps the next-to-last one. Using a sharp utility knife, a carpenter's square, and a tough work surface, cut along this line. The cut square should fit neatly in the remaining space.

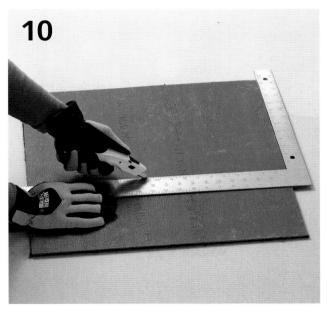

10

At a door jamb, place a square face up where it will go. Lean the square against the jamb and mark the point where they meet. Move the square to find the other cutline, and mark that as well. Flip the square over, mark the two lines using a carpenter's square, and cut out the corner.

11

Finish all four base rows before you fill in the rest of the room. As you work, check the alignment of each row. If you notice a row going out of line, find the point where the direction changed, then remove squares back to that point and start again.

12

Work outward from the center so that you have a known reference for keeping rows straight. Save the cut pieces from the ends. They may be useful for patching odd spaces around doorways, heat registers, radiator pipes, and when you reach the corners.

BUILDING WALLS

Partition walls are constructed between load-bearing walls to divide space. Building a partition wall is less technically demanding than building a load-bearing surface, and these walls allow you to customize interior floor plans and even radically transform rooms and living spaces. They should be strong and well made, but their main job is to house doors and to support wall coverings.

ANCHORING NEW PARTITION WALLS

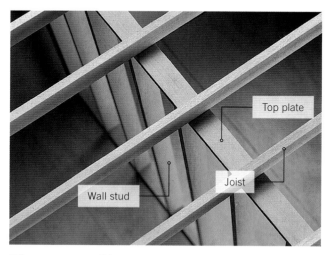

When a new wall is perpendicular to the ceiling or floor joists above, attach the top plate directly to the joists, using 16d nails.

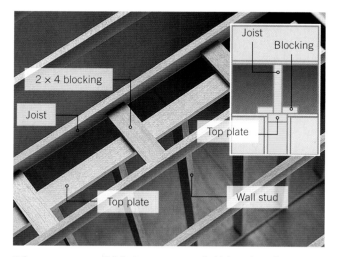

When a new wall falls between parallel joists, install 2 × 4 blocking between the joists every 24". If the new wall is aligned with a parallel joist, install blocks on both sides of the wall, and attach the top plate to the joist (inset).

WALL ANATOMY

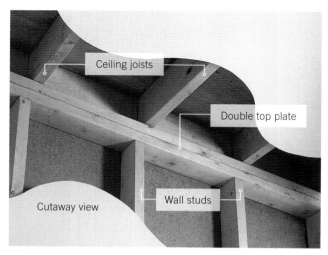

Load-bearing walls carry the structural weight of your home. In platform-framed houses, load-bearing walls can be identified by double top plates made from two layers of framing lumber. Load-bearing walls include all exterior walls and any interior walls that are aligned above support beams.

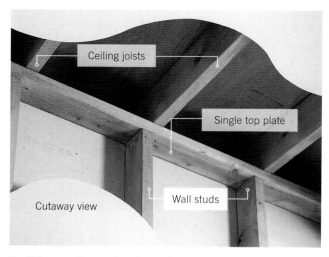

Partition walls are interior walls that do not carry the structural weight of the house. They have a single top plate and can be perpendicular to the floor and ceiling joists but are not aligned above support beams. Any interior wall that is parallel to floor and ceiling joists is a partition wall.

HOW TO BUILD A NON-LOAD-BEARING PARTITION WALL

Mark the location of the new wall on the ceiling, then snap two chalk lines or use a scrap piece of 2× lumber as a template to mark layout lines for the top plate. Use a stud finder to locate floor joists or roof framing above the ceiling, and mark these locations with tick marks or tape outside the layout lines.

Cut the top and sole plates to length and lay them side by side. Use a speed square or framing square to draw pairs of lines across both plates to mark the stud locations. Space the studs at 16" intervals, on center.

Mark the location of any door framing on the top and sole plates. Refer to the door's rough opening specifications when marking the layout. Draw lines for both the king and jack studs.

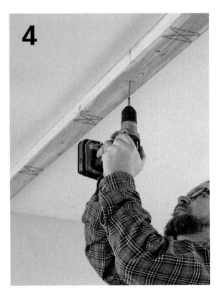

Fasten the top plate to the ceiling using 3" deck screws or 10d nails. Be sure to orient the plate so the stud layout faces down.

OPTION: Rather than toenailing the studs to the sole plate, some builders prefer to attach them by face-nailing through the underside of the sole plate and into the bottom ends of the walls studs. Then, after the cap plate is installed on the ceiling, they tip the wall up, nail the sole plate in position, and then toenail or toe-screw the studs to the cap plate.

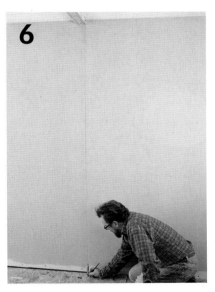

Hang a plumb bob from the edge of the top plate at several points along its length to find the sole plate location on the floor. The tip of the plumb bob should almost touch the floor. Wait until it stops moving before marking the sole plate reference point. Connect the points with a line to establish one edge of the sole plate. Use a piece of scrap 2× material as a template for marking the other edge.

(continued)

7

Drive the fasteners into the floor framing. For concrete floors, attach the sole plate with a powder-actuated nail gun or with hardened masonry screws. Cut out and remove a section of sole plate in the door opening or openings, if any.

8

Measure the distance between the top and sole plates at several places along the wall to determine the stud lengths. The stud length distance may vary, depending on structural settling or an uneven floor. Add ⅛" to the stud length(s), and cut them to size. The extra length will ensure a snug fit between the wall plates.

9

Fasten the end wall studs to adjoining walls. If the new studs do not fall at stud locations, you'll need to install blocking in the old walls.

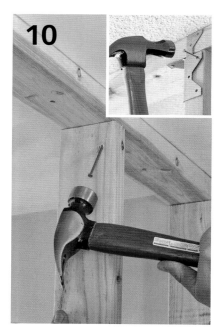

10

Nail the king studs, jack studs, a header, and a cripple stud in place to complete the rough door framing. An option for attaching wall studs to plates is to use metal connectors and 4d nails (Inset).

11

If building codes in your area require fire blocking, install 2× cutoff scraps between the studs, 4' from the floor, to serve this purpose. Stagger the blocks so you can endnail each piece.

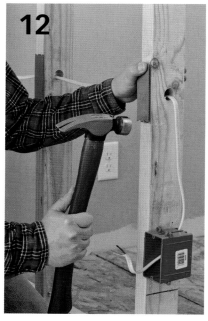

12

Drill holes through the studs to create guide holes for wiring and plumbing. When this work is completed, fasten metal protector plates over these areas to prevent drilling or nailing through wiring and pipes later. Have your work inspected before proceeding with drywall.

Joining Sections Using Steel Studs ▸

Steel studs and tracks have the same basic structure—a web that spans two flanged sides—but, studs also contain a ¼" lip to improve their rigidity.

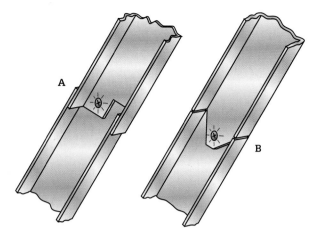

Join sections with a spliced joint (A) or notched joint (B). Make a spliced joint by cutting a 2" slit in the web of one track. Slip the other track into the slit and secure with a screw. For a notched joint, cut back the flanges of one track and taper the web so it fits into the other track; secure with a screw.

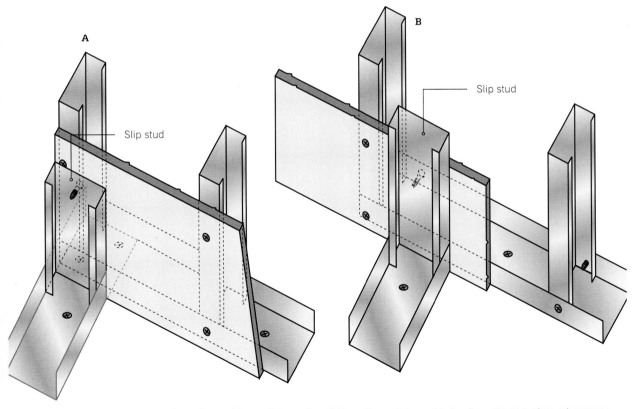

Build corners using a slip stud: A slip stud is not fastened until the adjacent drywall is in place. Form L-shaped corners (A) by overlapping the tracks. Cut off the flange on one side of one track, removing enough to allow room for the overlapping track and drywall. Form a T-shaped corner (B) by leaving a gap between the tracks for the drywall. Secure each slip stud by screwing through the stud into the tracks of the adjacent wall. Also screw through the back side of the drywall into the slip stud, if possible. Where there's no backing behind the slip stud, drive screws at a 45° angle through the back corners of the slip stud and into the drywall.

MAKING A LAYOUT PLAN

Planning the layout of drywall panels prior to installation makes it a lot easier to create a materials list, minimize seams, and solve potential problems before they crop up. Take careful measurements and sketch each wall and ceiling to be covered. Note the center-to-center (O.C.) spacing of the framing members, which can determine the thickness of drywall you install as well as how you install it (either parallel or perpendicular to the framing). See the chart on the opposite page for maximum framing spacing allowances.

Standard drywall is commonly available in widths of 4 feet and lengths of 8, 10, 12, 14, and 16 feet. It's in your best interest to use the longest drywall panels you can: It'll save you a lot of work during the finishing phase. Home centers and lumberyards always have 4 × 8 foot panels in stock and usually carry smaller quantities of the other sizes, or you can special order them.

The goal of planning the optimal drywall layout is to minimize seams. Seams require joint tape, compound, and sanding, which means the fewer of them there are, the less work you have ahead of you. For wall or ceiling surfaces 48 inches wide or less, cover the entire area using a single drywall panel. With no seams to tape, you'll only have to cover the screw heads with a few thin coats of compound.

Walls that are wider than 48 inches will require at least two panels. While there are a number of ways you can hang them, some possibilities yield better results than others. For example, for a wall that is 8 feet high and 12 feet long (as shown in first two plans at the top right), three panels could be installed vertically (Plan A), resulting in only tapered seams and no butt joints. However, this plan requires 16 linear feet of vertical taping, working from floor to ceiling, which is more difficult than taping a horizontal seam. Using two 4 × 12 foot panels (Plan B) reduces the amount of taping by 25 percent and places the seam about waist high, easing the finishing process. While a reduction of 25 percent of the finish work may not mean much on a small project, on a large remodel or new construction it can save you a lot of time and money.

Avoid butt joints where possible, but if they are necessary, locate them as far from the center of the wall as possible to help mask the seam. While it is best to use full panels, do not butt a tapered edge to panel ends (Plan C). This configuration produces an 8-foot long butt seam that will be difficult to finish. The best solution is to stagger the long panels and fill in with

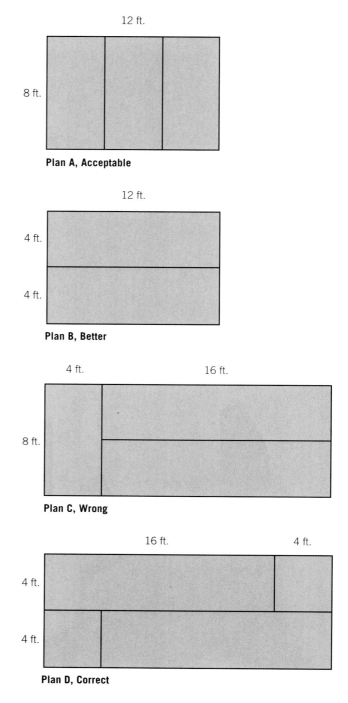

Plan A, Acceptable

Plan B, Better

Plan C, Wrong

Plan D, Correct

pieces cut from another (Plan D). For all butt joints, panel ends must break on a framing member unless you plan to use back blocking to recess the seam.

In rooms with ceilings over 8 feet in height, use 54-inch-wide panels. If ceilings are taller than 9 feet, consider using longer panels installed vertically.

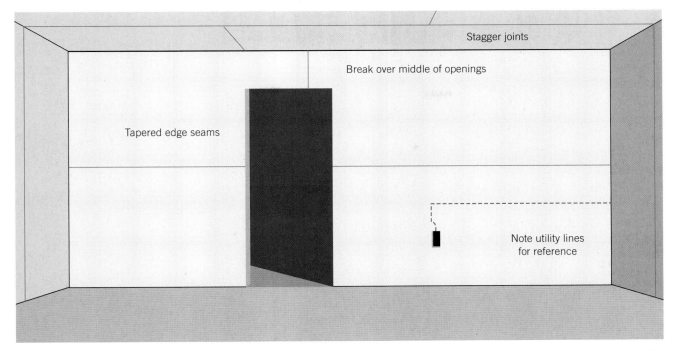

Drywall seams must fall on the centers of framing members, so measure and mark the framing when planning your layout. Use long sheets horizontally to span an entire wall. Avoid butted end joints whenever possible; where they do occur, stagger them between rows so they don't fall on the same framing member. Don't place seams over the corners of doors, windows, or other openings; joints there often crack or cause bulges that interfere with trim. Where framing contains utility lines, draw a map for future reference, noting locations of wiring, pipes, and shutoff valves.

Maximum Framing Spacing ▸

PANEL THICKNESS	INSTALLATION	MAXIMUM FRAMING SPACING
⅜"	Ceilings, perpendicular to framing walls	16" O.C.
		16" O.C.
½"	Ceilings, parallel to framing	16" O.C.
	Ceilings, perpendicular to framing walls	24" O.C.
		24" O.C.
⅝"	Ceilings, parallel to framing	16" O.C.
	Ceilings, perpendicular to framing walls	24" O.C.
		24" O.C.

ESTIMATING MATERIALS

To estimate the number of drywall panels you'll need, simply count the number used in your layout sketch. For larger projects, you can do a quick estimation for 4 × 8 foot panels by measuring the length of the walls and dividing the total by 4. For each window, subtract a quarter panel; for doors, half a panel. Keep in mind that panels are sold in pairs, so round odd numbered totals up to an even number.

The number of screws you'll need depends on the spacing of your framing and the fastener spacing schedule required. For a rough estimate, calculate the square footage of the wall and ceiling surfaces, and multiply by one fastener per square foot. Drywall screws are sold in pounds; one pound of screws equals roughly 320 screws. Construction adhesive is available in tubes. Check the manufacturer's specifications on the tube for coverage.

MEASURING + CUTTING DRYWALL

WALLS + CEILINGS

Drywall is one of the easiest building materials to install, partly because it allows for minor errors. Most professionals measure and cut to the nearest ⅛ inch, and it's perfectly acceptable to trim off a little extra from a panel to make it easier to get into a tight space. The exceptions to this are cutouts for electrical boxes and recessed light fixtures, which must be accurate because the coverplates usually hide less than you think they will.

Make sure your utility knife is sharp. A sharp blade ensures clean, accurate cuts that slice through the face paper and score the gypsum core in one pass. A dull blade can slip from the cutting line to snag and rip the face paper and is more likely to cause injury.

With a sharp utility knife, you can make cuts from either side of panels. But when using drywall and keyhole saws, make all cuts from the front side to prevent tearing the face paper. For projects that require a number of cutouts, use a spiral saw. This tool makes short work of large openings and electrical boxes, though it generates a lot of dust; make sure to wear a dust mask. Inexpensive spiral saws are available at home centers, or you can use a standard router outfitted with a piloted drywall bit.

Tools + Materials ▸

Work gloves
Eye protection
Tape measure
T-square
Pencil
Chalk line
Utility knife
Drywall rasp
Drywall saw

Keyhole saw
Compass or
    drywall compass
Spiral saw
Drywall panels
Clamps
Straightedge
Chalk

HOW TO MAKE STRAIGHT CUTS

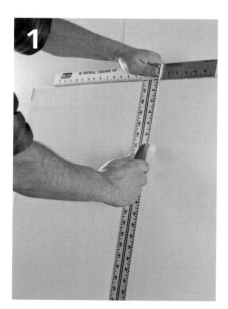

Mark the length on the face of the panel, then set a T-square at the mark. Hold the square in place with your hand and foot, and cut through the face paper using a utility knife with sharp blade.

Bend the scored section backward with both hands to snap the gypsum core.

Fold back the waste piece and cut through the back paper with the utility knife. This process is also called the snap cut method.

HOW TO MAKE ANGLED CUTS

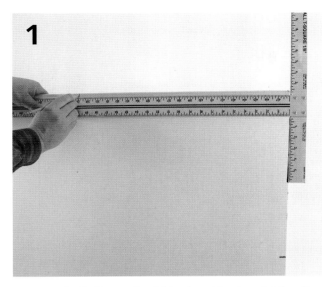

Measure both the vertical "rise" and horizontal "run" of the area, and mark the dimensions along the corresponding edges of the panel.

TIP: Making Rough Cuts ▸

Make horizontal cuts using a tape measure and utility knife. With one hand, hold the knife blade at the end of the tape. With the other hand, grip the tape at the desired measurement; slide this hand along the panel edge as you make the cut.

Connect the marks with a T-square, hold down firmly, and score the drywall from point to point. Finish the cut using the snap cut method on the opposite page. Be careful not to damage the pointed ends.

Smooth rough edges with a drywall rasp. One or two passes with the rasp should be sufficient. To help fit a piece into a tight space, bevel the edge slightly toward the back of the panel.

HOW TO CUT NOTCHES

Using a full-size drywall saw, cut the vertical sides of the notch. (These saws are also handy for cutting out door and window openings after the drywall is installed.)

Cut the face paper along the bottom of the notch using a utility knife. Snap the waste piece backward to break the core, then cut through the back paper.

HOW TO CUT LARGE OPENINGS

Measure the location of the cutout and transfer the dimensions to the backside of the panel. Score along the line that represents the header of the opening using a straightedge and utility knife.

Install the panel over the opening. The scored line should fall at the header. Cut the drywall along the jambs and up to the header using a drywall saw. Snap forward the waste piece to break the core, then cut through the face paper and remove.

HOW TO CUT AN ELECTRICAL BOX OPENING: COORDINATE METHOD

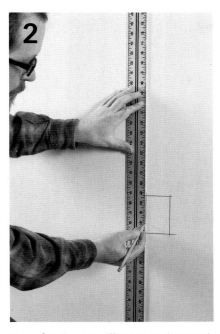

Locate the four corners of the box by measuring from the nearest fixed edge—a corner, the ceiling, or the edge of an installed panel—to the outside edges of the box.

Transfer the coordinates to the panel and connect the points, using a T-square. Measure from the panel edge that will abut the fixed edge you measured from. If the panel has been cut short for a better fit, make sure to account for this in your measurements.

Drill a pilot hole in one corner of the outline, then make the cutout with a keyhole or drywall saw.

HOW TO CUT AN ELECTRICAL BOX OPENING: CHALK METHOD

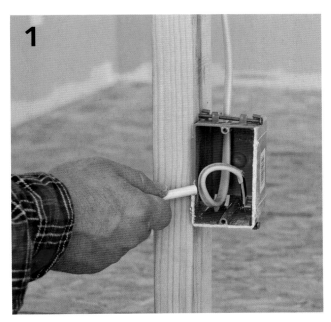

Rub the face of the electrical box with chalk or lipstick, position the panel where it will be installed, and press it against the box.

Pull the panel back from the wall; a chalk outline of the box is on the back of the panel. Drill a pilot hole in one corner of the outline, then make the cut with a keyhole or drywall saw.

HOW TO CUT ROUND HOLES IN DRYWALL

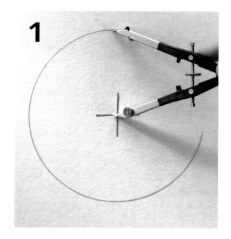

To make round cutouts, measure to the center of the object, then transfer the centerpoint to the drywall panel. Use a compass set to half the diameter of the cutout to mark the circle on the panel face.

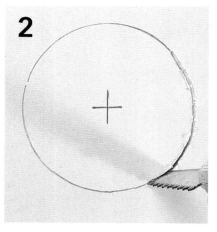

Force the pointed end of a drywall saw through the panel from the face side, then saw along the marked line. (These saws work well for all internal cuts.)

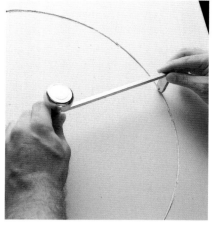

VARIATION: Drive the point of a drywall compass into the center marking, then rotate the compass wheel to cut the face paper. Tap a nail through the centerpoint, score the back paper, then knock out the hole through the face.

HOW TO MAKE A CUTOUT FOR A ROUND FIXTURE BOX

Locate the four outermost edges of the round box by measuring from the nearest fixed edge—a corner, the ceiling, or the edge of an installed panel—to the outermost edges of the box.

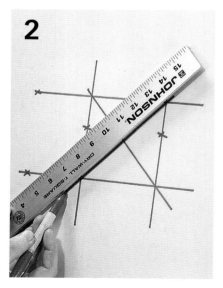

Transfer the coordinates to the panel, measuring from the panel edge that will abut the fixed edge you measured from, then connect the points using a T-square. The point where the lines intersect is the centerpoint of the circle. If the panel has been cut short for a better fit, make sure to account for this in your measurements.

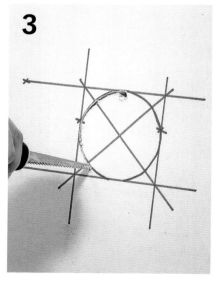

Use a compass to draw the outline of the round box on the panel (see above). Drill a pilot hole at one point of the outline, then make the cutout with a keyhole saw. *NOTE: To avoid the need for stainblocking primer, substitute a pencil for a permanent marker.*

MAKING CUTS WITH A COMPASS

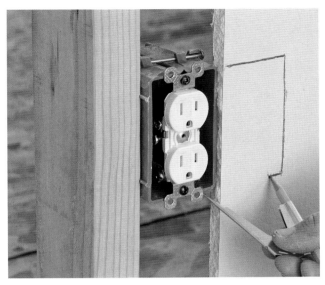

For out-of-square corners, cut the panel 1" longer than necessary, then hold it in position so it is plumb. Set a compass at 1¼", then run it along the wall to scribe the corner onto the face of the panel. Snap cut along the line using a utility knife.

Irregular surfaces can be scribed onto panels using the same method. Cut along the scribe line with a keyhole saw, then test fit the piece and make adjustments as necessary.

CUTTING DRYWALL WITH A SPIRAL SAW

Spiral saws (or drywall routers) are handy for cutting holes for electrical boxes and openings. You can use a spiral saw made for the purpose or outfit a standard router by removing the router base and installing a piloted drywall bit.

For electrical boxes, mark the floor at the locations of the box centers. Hang the drywall, fastening only at the top edge. Plunge the bit into the box center, move the bit sideways to the edge, then carefully work the bit to the outside. Follow the outside of the box, cutting counterclockwise.

For doorways and other openings, install the drywall over the opening. Moving clockwise, let the bit follow the inside of the frame to make the cutout. Always work clockwise when cutting along the inside of a frame; counterclockwise when following the outside of an object, like an electrical box.

FASTENING DRYWALL

The key to fastening drywall is to countersink screwheads to create a slight recess, or "dimple," without breaking the face paper. The best tool for the job is a screwgun, which has an adjustable clutch that can be set to stop screws at a preset depth. A variable speed drill/driver and a light touch will also get the job done.

When driving screws, hold the screwgun or drill at a right angle to the framing, placing the fastener ⅜ inch from the panel edge. Space screws evenly along the perimeter and across the field of the panel, following the chart on the opposite page. Do not fasten the entire perimeter and then fasten the field; work along the length or width of the panel, moving across to the sides as you push the drywall tight against the framing. Construction adhesive can be used in addition to screws to create a stronger bond between panel and framing.

Pre-drive fasteners near the edges of panels at the location of each framing member to help facilitate installation. Drive fasteners deep enough to hold their place but not enough to penetrate the backside of the panel. This lets you hold the panel in place as you finish driving the screws one-handed.

Tools + Materials ▸

Work gloves	Drywall
Eye protection	Drywall nails
Screwgun or ⅜" drill	Drywall screws
Caulk gun	Construction adhesive

Fastening Drywall ▸

Adhesives create stronger bonds than fasteners and reduce the number of screws needed for panel installation. Apply a ⅜" bead along framing members, stopping 6" from panel edges (left). At butt joints, apply beads to both sides of the joint (right). Panels are then fastened along the perimeter.

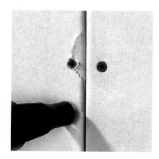

At panel edges, drive fasteners ⅜" from the edges, making sure to hit the framing squarely. If the fastener tears the paper or crumbles the edge, drive another about 2" away from the first.

Recess all screws to provide a space, called a "dimple," for the joint compound. However, driving a screw too far and breaking the paper renders it useless.

Maximum Fastener Spacing ▸

FRAMING	O.C. SPACING	INSTALLATION STYLE	MAXIMUM SCREW SPACING
Wood joists	16" O.C.	Single panel w/screws	12" O.C.
		Single panel w/adhesive & screws	16" O.C.
		Multiple layers w/screws	
		Base layer:	24" O.C.
		Face layer:	12" O.C.
		Multiple layers w/adhesive & screws:	
		Base layer:	12" O.C.
		Face layer:	12" O.C. (perimeter)
			16" O.C. (field)
	24" O.C.	Single panel w/screws	12" O.C.
		Single panel w/adhesive & screws	16" O.C.
		Multiple layers w/screws	12" O.C.
		Multiple layers w/adhesive & screws:	
		Base layer:	12" O.C.
		Face layer:	12" O.C. (perimeter)
			16" O.C. (field)
Wood studs	16" O.C.	Single panel w/screws	16" O.C.
		Single panel w/adhesive & screws:	
		Load-bearing partitions	24" O.C.
		Nonload-bearing partitions	24" O.C.
		Multiple layers w/screws	
		Base layer:	24" O.C.
		Face layer:	16" O.C.
		Multiple layers w/adhesive & screws:	
		Base layer:	16" O.C.
		Face layer:	16" O.C. (at top & bottom only)
	24" O.C.	Single panel w/screws	12" O.C.
		Single panel w/adhesive & screws:	
		Load-bearing partitions	16" O.C.
		Nonload-bearing partitions	24" O.C.
		Multiple layers w/screws	
		Base layer:	24" O.C.
		Face layer:	12" O.C.

FRAMING	O.C. SPACING	INSTALLATION STYLE	MAXIMUM SCREW SPACING
Wood studs (cont.)	24" O.C.	Multiple layers w/adhesive & screws:	
		Base layer:	12" O.C.
		Face layer:	16" O.C. (at top & bottom only)
Steel studs	16" O.C.	Single panel w/screws	16" O.C.
		Multiple layers w/screws:	
		Base layer:	
		Parallel panels	24" O.C.
		Perpendicular	*(see below)
		Face layer:	16" O.C.
		Multiple layers w/adhesive & screws:	
		Base layer:	24" O.C.
		Face layer:	12" O.C. (perimeter)
			16" O.C. (field)
Steel studs & resilient channel walls	24" O.C.	Single panel w/screws	12" O.C.
		Multiple layers w/screws:	
		Base layer:	
		Parallel panels	24" O.C.
		Perpendicular	*(see below)
		Face layer:	12" O.C.
		Multiple layers w/adhesive & screws:	
		Base layer:	24" O.C.
		Face layer:	12" O.C. (perimeter)
			16" O.C. (field)
Resilient channel ceilings	24" O.C.	Single panel w/screws	12" O.C.
		Multiple layers w/screws:	
		Base layer:	
		Parallel panels	24" O.C.
		Perpendicular	*(see below)
		Face layer:	12" O.C.
		Multiple layers w/adhesive & screws:	
		Base layer:	24" O.C.
		Face layer:	12" O.C. (perimeter)
			16" O.C. (field)

*1 screw at each end and 1 screw centered in the field, at each fastener location.
NOTE: The above information is subject to manufacturer installation specifications.

HANGING DRYWALL

Hanging drywall is a project that can be completed quickly and easily with a little preplanning and a helping hand.

If you're installing drywall on both the ceilings and the walls, do the ceilings first so the wall panels add extra support for the ceiling panels. When it comes time to install the walls, hang all full panels first, then measure and cut the remaining pieces about ⅛ inch too small to allow for easy fit.

In nearly every installation, you'll deal with corners. For standard 90° corners, panels most often can butt against one another. But other corners, such as those lacking adequate nailing surfaces or ones that are prone to cracking, may require the use of drywall clips or specialty beads.

Drywall is heavy. While it's possible to hang drywall by yourself, work with a helper whenever possible. A panel lift is also a time and back saver, simplifying installation to ceilings and the upper portion of walls. If you don't want to rent a panel lift, you can make a pair of T-braces, called "deadmen" to hold ceiling panels tight against framing for fastening.

Use a panel lifter to position drywall for fastening. Slide the front end of the lifter beneath the panel edge, then rock backward with your foot to raise the panel into place.

Tip ▸

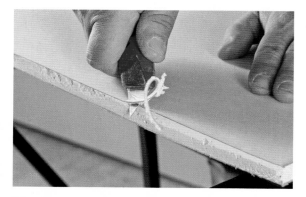

Where untapered panel ends will be butted together, bevel-cut the outside edges of each panel at 45°, removing about ⅛" of material. This helps prevent the paper from creating a ridge along the seam. Peel off any loose paper from the edge.

Tools + Materials ▸

Work gloves	Drywall screws
Eye protection	Deadmen
T-square	Ladders
Utility knife	Metal flashing
Screwgun or drill	Self-tapping
Panel lift	steel screws
Chalk line	Drywall clips
Drywall panels	

HOW TO INSTALL DRYWALL ON FLAT CEILINGS

1

Snap a chalk line perpendicular to the joists, 48⅛" from the starting wall. Measure to make sure the first panel will break on the center of a joist. If necessary, cut the panel on the end that abuts the side wall so the panel breaks on the next farthest joist.

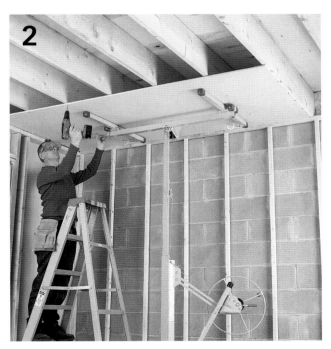

2

Load the panel onto a rented panel lift, or use a helper, and lift the panel flat against the joists. Position the panel with the leading edge on the chalk line and the end centered on a joist.

3

After the first row of panels is installed, begin the next row with a half-panel. This ensures that the butted end joints will be staggered between rows.

T-braces ▸

A pair of T-braces or "deadmen" that are 1" taller than the ceiling height can help hold drywall against the framing during ceiling installations. Cut a straight 2 × 4 so it's ½" shorter than the ceiling height, then fasten a 36"-long 2 × 4 to the end for the bracing arm.

HOW TO INSTALL CEILING PANELS USING DEADMEN

Construct two 2 × 4 deadmen. Lean one against the wall where the panel will be installed, with the top arm a couple inches below the joists. Have a helper assist in lifting the panel and placing the lead edge on the arm. Angle the deadman to pin the panel flush against the joists, but don't use so much pressure you risk damage to the panel.

Use the other deadman to hoist the panel against the joists 24" from the back end. Place ladders at each deadman location and adjust the panel's position by loosening the braces with one hand and moving the panel with the other. Replace the braces and fasten the panel to the framing.

Setting Your Clutch ▸

Professional drywallers drive hundreds, even thousands, of screws per day. Consequently, they invest in pro-quality screwdriving equipment, often with self-feeding coils of screws for rapid-fire work. For DIYers, this equipment can be rented—and may be worth the investment for a very large project. But in most cases, a decent quality cordless drill/driver will do nicely. If the drill/driver has a clutch (and most do these days), so much the better. Essentially, a clutch stops the drill's chuck from spinning when the screw encounters a specific amount of resistance. This prevents overdriving of the screw, which is especially important when drywalling (you want to avoid driving the screw far enough into the drywall to break the surface paper). But for the clutch to work properly you need to make sure it is set to the appropriate level of sensitivity. A drill/driver normally has several settings indicated on a shroud or ring near the drill chuck. The highest setting is used for drilling. Basically, the clutch won't disengage the chuck unless it encounters so much resistance that the drill could be damaged. On the lowest setting, the drill will disengage when it encounters only very slight resistance, as when completing driving a screw into drywall. Before you

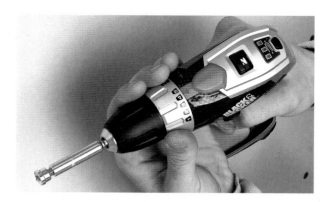

start driving any drywall screws, test your clutch setting by driving a screw into a piece of scrap drywall and a 2 × 4. Re-set the clutch as needed until it stops driving the moment the screwhead becomes countersunk, creating a very slight dimple. Having the clutch set correctly ensures that your fasteners will have maximum holding power with just enough of a surrounding dimple to give the joint compound a place to go.

INSTALLING FLOATING CEILING JOINTS

 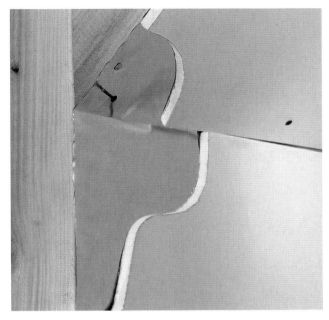

Use metal flashing to prevent cracks along the peak of pitched and cathedral ceilings (left) and the angle between pitched ceilings and sidewalls (right). For both applications, cut metal flashing 16" wide and to the length of the joint, then bend it lengthwise to match the angle of the peak or corner. Fasten flashing to the framing on one side only, then fasten the panels on that side to the framing. However, fasten the panels at the unfastened side to the flashing only, using self-tapping steel screws. Drive the first row of screws into the framing not less than 12" from the "floating" edge of the panels.

Bending Flashing ▸

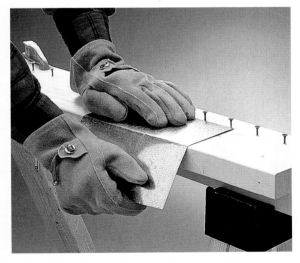 

To bend flashing, make a bending jig by driving screws into a piece of wood, creating a space one-half the width of the flashing when measured from the edge of the board. Clamp the bending jig to a work surface. Lay a piece of flashing flat on the board, and bend it over the edge.

For a ceiling with trusses, use drywall clips to eliminate cracks caused by "truss uplift," the seasonal shifting caused by weather changes. Slip clips on the edge of the panel prior to installation, then fasten the clips to the top plate. Fasten the panel to the trusses not less than 18" from the edge of the panel.

HOW TO INSTALL DRYWALL ON WOOD-FRAMED WALLS

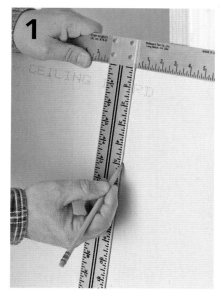

Measure from the wall end or corner to make sure the first panel will break on the center of the stud. If necessary, trim the sheet on the side or end that will be placed in the corner. Mark the stud centers on the panel face, and pre-drive screws at each location along the top edge to facilitate fastening. Apply adhesive to the studs, if necessary.

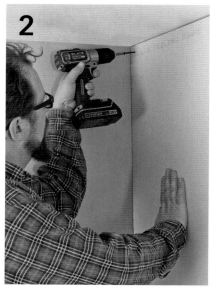

With a helper or a drywall lifter, hoist the first panel tight against the ceiling, making sure the side edge is centered on a stud. Push the panel flat against the framing, and drive the starter screws to secure the panel. Make any cutouts, then fasten the field of the panel, following the screw spacing on page 119.

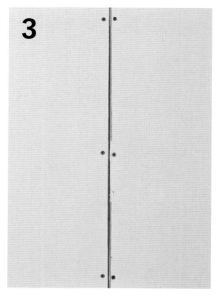

Measure, cut, and install the remaining panels along the upper wall. Bevel panel ends slightly, leaving a ⅛" gap between them at the joint. Butt joints can also be installed using back blocking to create a recess.

Measure, cut, and install the bottom row, butting the panels tight to the upper row and leaving a ½" gap at the floor. Secure to the framing along the top edge using the starter screws, then make all cutouts before fastening the rest of the panel.

VARIATION: When installing drywall vertically, cut each panel so it's ½" shorter than the ceiling height to allow for expansion. (The gap will be covered by base molding.)

INSTALLING DRYWALL AT INSIDE CORNERS

Flashing panel with no fasteners to corner stud.

Secured panel pins floating panel in place.

Standard 90° inside corners are installed with the first panel butted against the framing and the adjacent panel butted against the first. The screw spacing remains the same as on a flat wall. If the corner is out of plumb or the adjacent wall has an irregular surface, see page 112 for cutting instructions.

Use a "floating corner" to reduce the chances of popped fasteners and cracks. Install the first panel, fastening only to within one stud bay of the corner. Push the leading edge of the adjacent panel against the first to support the unfastened edge. Fasten the second panel normally, including the corner.

Drywall clips can be used at corners that lack an adequate nailing surface, allowing two panels to be secured to the same stud. Slide clips onto the leading edge of the first panel, with the metal nailing flange outward. Install the panel, fastening the flange to the stud on the adjacent wall with drywall screws. Install the adjacent panel normally.

For off-angle corners do not overlap panel ends. Install so the panel ends meet at the corner with a ⅛" gap between them.

DRYWALL: TAPING

Finishing drywall is the more difficult phase of surfacing walls and ceilings, but it's a project well within the ability of any homeowner. Armed with a basic understanding of the variety of finish materials available, you'll be able to walk out of your local home center with the exact supplies you need to cover all joints, corners, and fasteners for a successful wallboard finish project.

Corner bead is the angle strip, usually made of metal or vinyl, that covers a wallboard corner, creating a straight, durable edge where walls intersect. Most corner beads are installed over the wallboard and are finished with compound. In addition to standard 90° outside-corner bead, there's an ever-growing variety of bead types designed for specific situations and easy application. There are beads for inside corners, flexible beads for off-angles and curves, J-beads and L-beads for flat panel edges, and bullnose beads for creating rounded inside and outside corners. While metal beads are installed with fasteners, vinyl beads can be installed with vinyl adhesive and staples, or be embedded in joint compound using the same techniques for installing paper-faced beads.

A selection of taping knives is required to handle different parts of the process of applying joint tape and compound. A 6" knife is used for the initial compound application of tape beds and to set tape into the beds. A 12" knife is used for the final coat, and a knife with an L-shaped blade gets into corners.

Achieving a smooth wall surface depends completely on how well you manage the taping, "mudding," and sanding tasks in your project.

Joint tape is combined with joint compound to create a permanent layer that covers the wallboard seams, as well as small holes and gaps. Without tape, thick applications of compound are highly prone to cracking. There are two types of joint tape—paper and self-adhesive fiberglass mesh.

Joint compound, commonly called mud, seals and levels all seams, corners, and depressions in a wallboard installation. It's also used for skim-coating and some texturing treatments. There are several types of compounds with important differences among them, but the two main forms are setting-type and drying-type.

Setting-type compound is sold in dry powder form that is mixed with water before application. Because it dries through chemical reaction, setting compound dries quickly and is virtually unaffected by humidity and temperature. Setting compounds generally shrink less, bond better, and become harder than drying types, but they're more difficult to sand, a characteristic that makes them a better choice for the taping coat than for the filler and final coats. Drying-type compounds dry through evaporation and usually take about 24 hours to dry completely. Available in dry powder and convenient premixed forms in resealable one- and five-gallon buckets, drying compounds are highly workable and consistent.

HOW TO INSTALL METAL CORNER BEAD

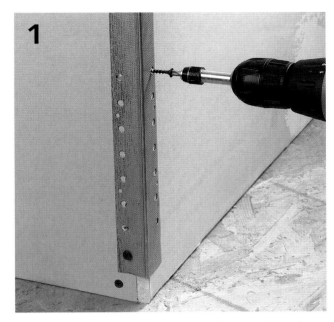

Starting at the top, fasten the bead flanges with 1¼" drywall screws driven every 9" and about ¼" from the edge. Alternate sides with each screw to keep the bead centered. The screws must not project beyond the raised spine.

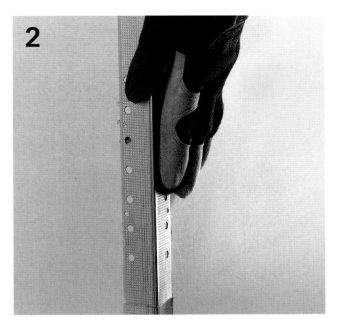

Use full lengths of corner bead where possible. If you must join two lengths, cut the two pieces to size, then butt together the finished ends. Make sure the ends are perfectly aligned and the spine is straight along the length of the corner. File ends, if necessary.

HOW TO INSTALL VINYL CORNER BEAD

Cut vinyl bead to length and test fit over corner. Spray vinyl adhesive evenly along the entire length of the corner, then along the bead.

Quickly install the bead, pressing the flanges into the adhesive. Fasten the bead in place with ½" staples every 8".

The Finishing Sequence ▶

Finishing newly installed drywall is satisfying work that requires patience and some basic skill, but it's easier than most people think. Beginners make their biggest, and most lasting, mistakes by rushing the job and applying too much compound in an attempt to eliminate coats. But even for professionals, drywall finishing involves three steps, and sometimes more, plus the final sanding. The first step is the taping coat, when you tape the seams between the drywall panels. If you're using standard metal corner bead on the outside corners, install it before starting the taping coat; paper-faced beads go on after the tape. The screw heads get covered with compound at the beginning of each coat. After the taping comes the second, or filler, coat. This is when you leave the most compound on the wall, filling in the majority of each depression. With the filler coat, the walls start to look pretty good, but they don't have to be perfect; the third coat will take care of minor imperfections. Lightly sand the second coat, then apply the final coat.

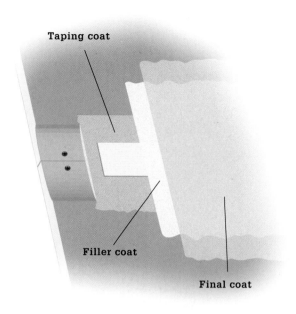

Taping coat

Filler coat

Final coat

HOW TO MIX JOINT COMPOUND

Mix powdered setting-type compound with cool, potable water in a clean 5-gal. bucket, following the manufacturer's directions. All tools and materials must be clean—dirty water, old compound, and other contaminants will affect compound set time and quality.

Use a heavy-duty drill with a mixing paddle to thoroughly mix the compound to a stiff yet workable consistency. Use a low speed to avoid whipping air into the compound. Do not overwork setting-type compound, as it will begin setup. For powdered drying-type compound, remix after 15 minutes. Clean tools thoroughly immediately after use.

Use a hand masher to loosen premixed compound. If the compound has been around a while and is stiff, add a little water and mix to an even consistency.

WALLS + CEILINGS

HOW TO TAPE + MUD

1

Using a 4 or 6" taping knife, apply compound over each screw head, forcing it into the depression. Firmly drag the knife in the opposite direction, removing excess compound from the panel surface.

2

Apply an even bed layer of setting-type compound about ⅛" thick and 6" wide over tapered seams using a 6" taping knife. *NOTE: With paper tape, you can also use premixed taping or all-purpose compound.*

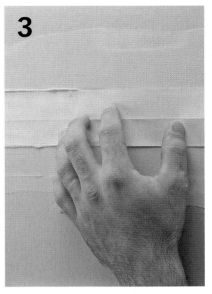

3

Center the tape over the seam and lightly embed it in the compound, making sure the tape is smooth and straight. At the end of the seam, tear off the tape so it extends all the way into the inside corners and up to the corner bead at outside corners.

4

Smooth the tape with the taping knife, working out from the center. Apply enough pressure to force compound from underneath the tape, so the tape is flat and has a thin layer beneath it.

5

At inside corners, smooth the final bit of tape by reversing the knife and carefully pushing it toward the corner. Carefully remove excess compound along the edges of the bed layer with the taping knife.

6

Cover vertical butt seams with a ⅛"-thick layer of joint compound. You should try and avoid this kind of joint, but in some cases there is no way around it. Cover the compound with seam tape and more compound. Make the taped area extra wide so you can feather it back gradually.

(continued)

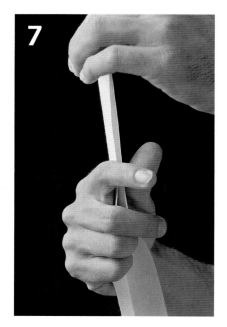

7

Fold precreased paper tape in half to create a 90° angle to tape inside corners.

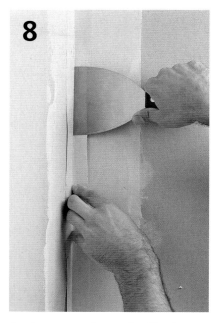

8

Apply an even layer of setting-type compound about ⅛" thick and 3" wide, to both sides of the corner, using a 4" taping knife. Embed the tape into the compound using your fingers and a taping knife.

9

Carefully smooth and flatten both sides of the tape, removing excess compound to leave only a thin layer beneath. Make sure the center of the tape is aligned straight with the corner.

Tip ▸

An inside corner knife can embed both sides of the tape in one pass—draw the knife along the tape, applying enough pressure to leave a thin layer of compound beneath. Feather each side using a straight 6" taping knife, if necessary.

10

Finish outside corner bead with a 6" knife. Apply the compound while dragging the knife along the raised spine of the bead. Make a second pass to feather the outside edge of the compound, then a third dragging along the bead again. Smooth any areas where the corner bead meets taped corners or seams.

11

Scrape off any remaining ridges and chunks after the taping coat has dried completely, then second-coat the screw heads, using a 6" taping knife and all-purpose compound. *NOTE: Setting-type compound and drying-type topping compound are also acceptable.*

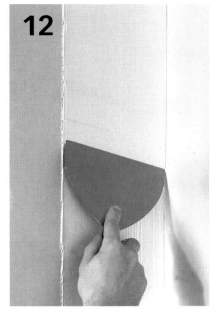

12

Apply an even layer of compound to both sides of each inside corner using a 6" taping knife. Smooth one side at a time, holding the blade about 15° from horizontal and lightly dragging the point along the corner. Make a second pass to remove excess compound along the outer edges. Repeat, if necessary.

13

Coat tapered seams with an even layer of all-purpose compound using a 12" taping knife. Whenever possible, apply the coat in one direction and smooth it in the opposite. Feather the sides of the compound first, holding the blade almost flat and applying pressure to the outside of the blade so the blade just skims over the center of the seam.

14

After feathering both side edges of the compound, make a pass down the center of the seam, applying even pressure to the blade. This pass should leave the seam smooth and even, with the edges feathered out to nothing. The joint tape should be completely covered.

15

Second-coat the outside corners, one side at a time, using a 12" knife. Apply an even layer of compound, then feather the outside edge by applying pressure to the outside of the knife— enough so that the blade flexes and removes most of the compound along the edge but leaves the corner intact. Make a second pass with the blade riding along the raised spine, applying even pressure.

16

After the filler coat has dried, lightly sand all of the joints, then third-coat the screws. Apply the final coat, following the same steps used for the filler coat but do the seams first, then the outside corners, followed by the inside corners. Use a 12" knife and spread the compound a few inches wider than the joints in the filler coat. Remove most of the compound, filling scratches and low spots but leaving only traces elsewhere. Make several passes, if necessary, until the surface is smooth and there are no knife tracks or other imperfections. Carefully blend intersecting joints so there's no visible transition.

HOW TO SAND JOINT COMPOUND

1

Use sheet plastic and 2" masking tape to help confine dust to the work area. Cover all doorways, cabinets, built-ins, and any gaps or other openings with plastic, sealing all four edges with tape; otherwise the fine dust produced by sanding can find its way through.

2

Knock down any ridges, chunks, or tool marks prior to sanding, using a 6" taping knife. Do not apply too much pressure—you don't want to dig into the compound, only remove the excess.

Tip ▸

As you work, if you oversand or discover low spots that require another coat of compound, mark the area with a piece of tape for repair after you finish sanding. Make sure to wipe away dust so the tape sticks to the surface.

3

Lightly sand all seams and outside corners using a pole sander with 220-grit sanding screen or 150-grit sandpaper. Work in the direction of the joints, applying even pressure to smooth transitions and high areas. Don't sand out depressions; fill them with compound and resand. Be careful not to over-sand or expose joint tape.

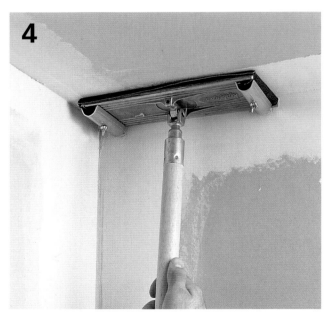

4

Inside corners often are finished with only one or two thin coats of compound over the tape. Sand the inside edge of joints only lightly and smooth the outside edge carefully; inside corners will be sanded by hand later.

WALLS + CEILINGS

5

Fine-sand the seams, outside corners, and fastener heads using a sanding block with 150- to 220-grit sanding screen or sandpaper. As you work, use your hand to feel for defects along the compound. A bright work light angled to highlight seams can help reveal problem areas.

6

To avoid damage from oversanding, use a 150-grit dry sanding sponge to sand inside corners. The sides of sanding sponges also contain grit, allowing you to sand both sides of a corner at once to help prevent oversanding.

7

For tight or hard-to-reach corners, fold a piece of sanding screen or sandpaper in thirds and sand the area carefully. Rather than using just your fingertips, try to flatten your hand as much as possible to spread out the pressure to avoid sanding too deep.

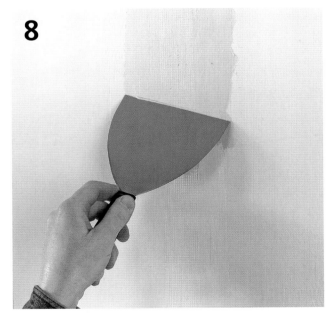

8

Repair depressions, scratches, or exposed tape due to oversanding after final sanding is complete. Wipe the area with a dry cloth to remove dust, then apply a thin coat of all-purpose compound. Allow to dry thoroughly, then resand.

9

With sanding complete, remove dust from the panels with a dry towel or soft broom. Use a wet-dry vacuum to clean out all electrical boxes and around floors, windows, and doors, then carefully roll up sheet plastic and discard. Finally, damp mop the floor to remove any remaining dust.

CEMENTBOARD

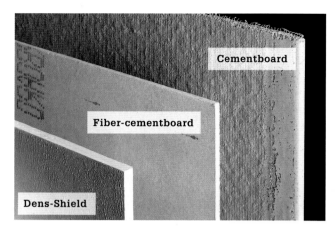

Use tile backer board as the substrate for tile walls in wet areas. Unlike drywall, tile backer won't break down and cause damage if water gets behind the tile. The three basic types of tile backer are cementboard, fiber-cementboard, and Dens-Shield.

Though water cannot damage either cementboard or fiber-cementboard, it can pass through them. To protect the framing members, install a water barrier of 4-mil plastic or 15# building paper behind the backer.

Dens-Shield has a waterproof acrylic facing that provides the water barrier. It cuts and installs much like drywall, but requires galvanized screws to prevent corrosion and must be sealed with caulk at all untaped joints and penetrations.

Common tile backers are cementboard, fiber-cementboard, and Dens-Shield. Cementboard is made from Portland cement and sand reinforced by an outer layer of fiberglass mesh. Fiber-cementboard is made similarly, but with a fiber reinforcement integrated throughout the panel. Dens-Shield is a water-resistant gypsum board with a waterproof acrylic facing.

Tools + Materials ▶

Work gloves	Hammer	Cementboard	Spacers
Eye protection	Jigsaw with a carbide	1¼" cementboard screws	Screwgun or drill
Utility knife or carbide-tipped cutter	grit blade	Cementboard joint tape	Ceramic tile adhesive
T-square	Taping knives	Latex-Portland cement mortar	Paper joint tape
Small masonry bits	Staple gun	15# building paper	Drywall joint compound
	4-mil plastic sheeting		

HOW TO HANG CEMENTBOARD

Staple a water barrier of 4-mil plastic sheeting or 15# building paper over the framing. Overlap seams by several inches, and leave the sheets long at the perimeter. *NOTE: Framing for cementboard must be 16" on center; steel studs must be 20-gauge.*

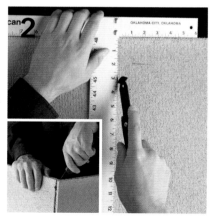

Cut cementboard by scoring through the mesh just below the surface with a utility knife or carbide-tipped cutter. Snap the panel back, then cut through the back-side mesh (inset). *NOTE: For tile applications, the rough face of the board is the front.*

Make cutouts for pipes and other penetrations by drilling a series of holes through the board, using a small masonry bit. Tap the hole out with a hammer or a scrap of pipe. Cut holes along edges with a jigsaw and carbide grit blade.

4

Install the sheets horizontally. Where possible, use full pieces to avoid butted seams, which are difficult to fasten. If there are vertical seams, stagger them between rows. Leave a ⅛" gap between sheets at vertical seams and corners. Use spacers to set the bottom row of panels ¼" above the tub or shower base. Fasten the sheets with 1¼" cementboard screws, driven every 8" for walls and every 6" for ceilings. Drive the screws at least ½" from the edges to prevent crumbling. If the studs are steel, don't fasten within 1" of the top track.

5

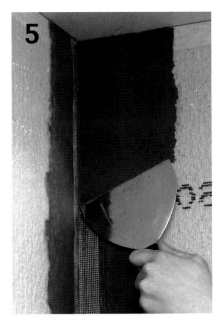

Cover the joints and corners with cementboard joint tape (alkali-resistant fiberglass mesh) and latex-Portland cement mortar (thin-set). Apply a layer of mortar with a taping knife, embed the tape into the mortar, then smooth and level the mortar.

FINISHING CEMENTBOARD

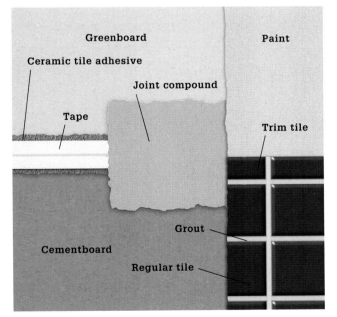

To finish a joint between cementboard and greenboard, seal the joint and exposed cementboard with ceramic tile adhesive, a mixture of four parts adhesive to one part water. Embed paper joint tape into the adhesive, smoothing the tape with a taping knife. Allow the adhesive to dry, then finish the joint with at least two coats of all-purpose drywall joint compound.

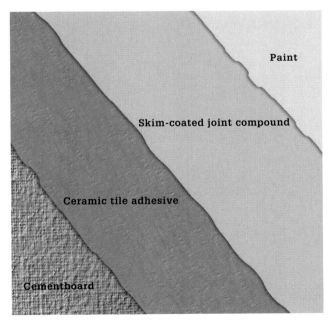

To finish small areas of cementboard that will not be tiled, seal the cementboard with ceramic tile adhesive, a mixture of four parts adhesive to one part water, then apply a skim-coat of all-purpose drywall joint compound using a 12" drywall knife. Then prime and paint the wall.

ACOUSTIC TILE

Easy-to-install ceiling tile can lend character to a plain ceiling or help turn an unfinished basement or attic into beautiful living space. Made of pressed mineral and fiberboard, ceiling tiles are available in a variety of styles. They also provide moderate noise reduction.

Ceiling tiles typically can be attached directly to a drywall or plaster ceiling with adhesive. If your ceiling is damaged or uneven, or if you have an unfinished joist ceiling, install 1 × 2 furring strips as a base for the tiles, as shown in this project. Some systems include metal tracks for clip-on installation.

Unless your ceiling measures in even feet, you won't be able to install the 12-inch tiles without some cutting. To prevent an unattractive installation with small, irregular tiles along two sides, include a course of border tiles along the perimeter of the installation. Plan so that tiles at opposite ends of the room are cut to the same width and are at least half the width of a full tile.

Most ceiling tile comes prefinished, but it can be painted to match any decor. For best results, apply two coats of paint using a roller with a ¼-inch nap, and wait 24 hours between coats.

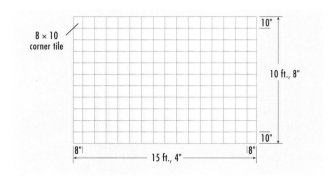

Measure the ceiling and devise a layout. If the length (or width) doesn't measure in even feet, use this formula to determine the width of the border tiles: add 12 to the number of inches remaining and divide by 2. The result is the width of the border tile. (For example, if the room length is 15 ft., 4", add 12 to the 4, then divide 16 by 2, which results in an 8" border tile.)

An acoustic tile ceiling differs from a suspended ceiling primarily in that the support structure for the tiles is attached directly to the ceiling instead of hung by wires. This maximizes the headspace in a room. Some systems, like the one shown here, use lightweight plastic tracks to support lightweight PVS panels. Others employ traditional (and thicker) fibrous panels that are stapled to wood furring strips attached to the ceiling.

HOW TO INSTALL DIRECT-MOUNTED CEILING PANELS

Plan your ceiling tile layout to minimize cutting but ensure that cut panels are limited to the room borders and are even (see previous page). Snap square chalklines on the ceiling joists or ceiling to indicate the locations of the hangers.

Attach wall brackets around the perimeter of the room using 1" coarse-thread drywall screws spaced 16" to 24" apart. The screws can be driven into the ceiling joists or the wall framing members. Try not to overdrive them and kink the brackets.

Use aviator snips or good scissors to cut the plastic tracking. At corners, miter cut the bracket material to make a cleaner joint (the bottoms of brackets and hangers will be visible when installation is complete so be as neat as possible).

Fit the final corners together to complete the perimeter layout.

(continued)

5

Attach the first top hanger track to the ceiling along your layout lines. Center the strips on the lines, with the broad, flat surface of the track against the ceiling. Use drywall screws and alternate which side of the track strip the screws are driven on. The end of the hanger track should fit into the channels in the wall brackets and any seams should fall at joist locations.

6

Fit one of the 2-ft. cross tees into the end notch of the first top hanger. Use the cross tee as a spacer to make sure the next top hanger is the correct distance from the first. Snap the free end of the cross bracket into the matching notch on the second bracket. Make any adjustments necessary to the second bracket and then secure the bracket to the ceiling joists with screws. Work your way down to the other end of the brackets, using the cross tees as spacers.

7

Install the rest of the top brackets and cross tees in the manner as the first pair, working in sequence. Wait to install the last cross tee along each border.

8

Measure the border tiles and cut to fit. The cut sides should be against the wall brackets. Aviator snips or good scissors can be used to cut the tiles. You can also use a straightedge and sharp utility knife. Either way, be very careful as the ceiling panels are a bit fragile and can crack easily.

9

Fit the cut ceiling panels into the track system by lifting them, lowering, and letting them rest flat on the track ledges. Fill in the borders up to the point where the last tee has not been installed.

10

When you reach a corner, cut the last cross tee to use it to help raise the last panel into position. Snap the tee into the notch in the last top hanger to lock the panel into place.

11

Cut runner strips to fit into the snaps in the top hangers, locking everything together and giving the installation a more finished appearance. Simply press upward to the bottoms of the runners until they snap in with a click.

OPTION: The more traditional and true "acoustic tile" ceiling (so called because it has sound-canceling properties) is installed using fibrous tiles with hanger ledges at the edges through which they are stapled to a grid of wood furring strips mounted to the ceiling or ceiling joists.

SUSPENDED CEILING

Suspended ceilings are traditionally popular ceiling finishes for basements because they hang below pipes and other mechanicals, providing easy access to them. Manufacturers offer a wide array of ceiling tiles to choose from. Popular styles mimic historical tin tiles and add depth to the ceiling while minimizing sound and vibration noise.

A suspended ceiling is a grid framework made of lightweight metal brackets hung on wires attached to ceiling or floor joists. The frame consists of T-shaped main beams (mains), cross tees (tees), and L-shaped wall angles. The grid supports ceiling panels, which rest on the flanges of the framing pieces. Panels are available in 2 × 2-ft. or 2 × 4-ft., in a variety of styles. Special options include insulated panels, acoustical panels that absorb sound, and light-diffuser screens for use with fluorescent lights. Generally, metal-frame ceiling systems are more durable than ones made of plastic.

To begin your ceiling project, devise the panel layout based on the size of the room, placing equally sized trimmed panels on opposite sides to create a balanced look. Your ceiling must also be level.

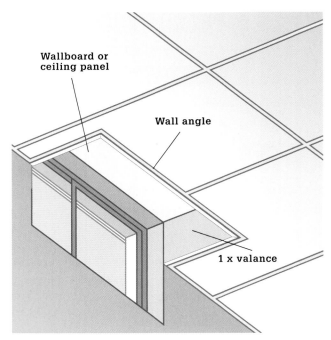

Build a valance around basement awning windows so they can be opened fully. Attach 1× lumber of an appropriate width to joists or blocking. Install drywall (or a suspended-ceiling panel trimmed to fit) to the joists inside the valance.

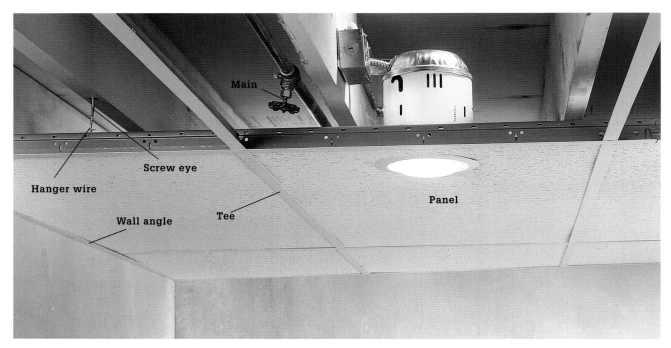

Suspended ceilings are very practical in basement rooms, and you can find them in many more design choices than you might expect. As shown here, they can easily accommodate traditional "can" recessed lighting fixtures or even newer canless versions. Cut the hole for each fixture in the tile and finish with the supplied trim kit.

HOW TO INSTALL A SUSPENDED CEILING

1

Establish your ceiling layout plan, limiting cut ceiling tiles to the border rows. Mark the finished ceiling height onto a wall—it needs to be at least 3" down from the joists or ceiling you are building on. Extend level lines all around the room and snap chalklines for reference. This is a great opportunity to use a laser level if you have one. Install the wall angle at stud locations with 1½" drywall screws or nails. The bottom of the wall angle should be flush with your reference lines. Cut the metal track sections with aviator snips and back-cut the mating pieces at the corners so you can overlap the lower flanges.

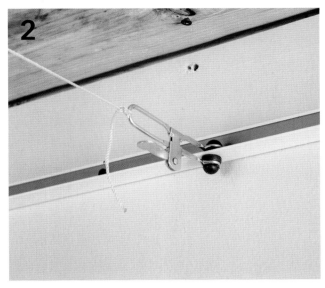

2

Once all of the wall angle is installed, use the angle to mark the locations for the main beams. These should be installed perpendicular to the ceiling joists and establish a grid with opening matched to the panel sizes and configurations. Run taut mason's string reference lines between the wall channels to set both the grid and the ceiling height. *TIP: Use lock clamps on the lower flanges to secure the string so you can run lines that are exactly level.*

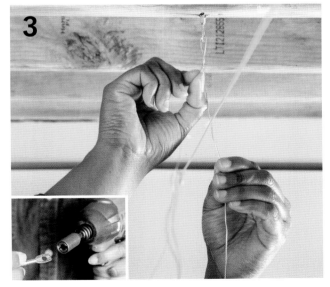

3

Attach the hanger wires that support the main beams. The wires should be positioned directly above the hanger holes in the beams. For smaller, light-duty ceilings you can use drywall screws to anchor 12-guages wires with preattached eye hooks. For heavier ceilings, use screw eyes designed for use with a suspended ceiling. These can be driven easier with a special bit driver mounted in an impact gun (inset photo).

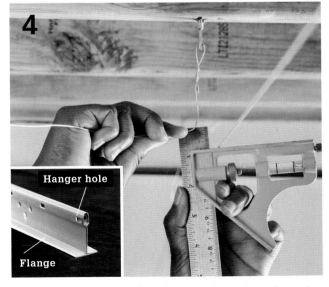

4

Hanger hole

Flange

Measure the distance from the mounting holes in the main beam to the bottom ledges—usually around 1" (inset photo). Set the handle of a combination square set to that distance and use it and the string lines as guides for bending the hanger wires so the bend will match the mounting holes relative to the ceiling height.

(continued)

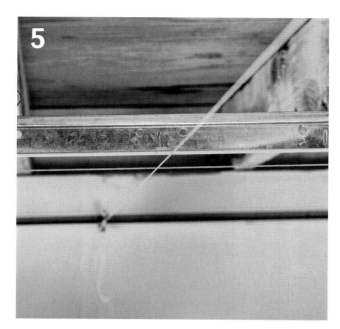

5

It is important that the tee slots in the main beam (these accept the cross tees tabs) be lined up exactly with the planned cross tee location. This very likely will mean that you have to cut the main beam so it fits against the wall with the tee slot in position.

6

Hang the first main beam, which will be multiple pieces if the run is longer than 12 feet. Insert hanger wires into the hanger holes at their bend point and then twist the wires multiple times around themselves to secure them. If you are confident in your layout, you can hang all the main beams at the same time, but it is a good idea to attach the tees in the first course to confirm that they fit and are parallel—it is easier to make adjustments at this point.

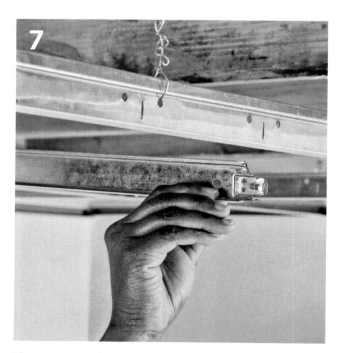

7

The cross tees for the border panels rest on the wall channel ledge. The other ends have tabs that snap into the tee slots in the main beams. Begin installing the cross tees.

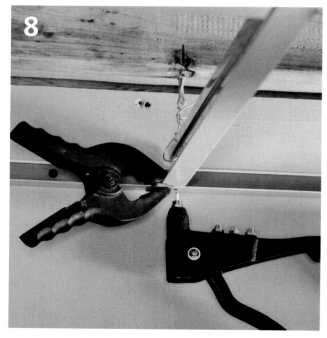

8

Make sure the cross tees are perpendicular to the wall channels and parallel to one another. With the parts clamped together, drill guide holes through the bottoms of the wall channels and then through the cross tees. Secure them in place with a pop rivet. White pop rivets that match the ceiling grid are sold with most suspended ceiling accessories. Complete the grid of main beams and cross tees.

9

Cut the suspended ceiling tiles for the border rows using a sharp utility knife and a straightedge (a drywall framing square works very well for this). Score each tile deeply and then snap them as you would drywall.

10

At the cut edge of tiles that will rest on the wall channel, you need to re-create the recessed ledge that was cut off when you trimmed the tile. Do this by making a ½"-deep cut ½" from the cut edge, through the tile top. Then, from the side, make a shoulder cut with your utility knife and remove the waste material. Keep your cut lines as straight and clean as possible—they will be visible if you look closely after installation.

11

Begin installing the ceiling tiles by lifting them into their opening in the grid and then lowering onto the support ledges. Don't press down too hard. Fill in all of the field tiles.

12

Install the border tiles last—if you have to make any adjustments, they should be done on the borders. If necessary, push up on the adjoining tiles to create space to reach your hand in and press down on the border tiles.

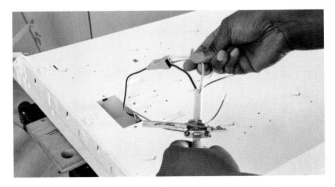

OPTION: PANEL LIGHTS Lightweight ceiling panel lights are designed to fit into and be supported by the suspended ceiling grid. New LED types are very lightweight, are long-lasting, and can be purchased for $50 to $100 for a 2 × 2 ft. light. You'll need to provide power service above the suspended ceiling, of course, but the light panels can be hooked up pretty easily before being mounted in the track grid.

PAINTING INTERIOR WALLS

Paints are either latex (water based) or alkyd (oil based). Latex paint is easy to apply and clean up, and the improved chemistry of today's latexes makes them suitable for nearly every application. Some painters feel that alkyd paint provides a smoother finish, but local regulations may restrict the use of alkyd products.

Paints come in various sheens, from high gloss to flat. Gloss enamels dry to a shiny finish and are used for surfaces that need to be washed often, such as walls in bathrooms and kitchens and woodwork. Flat paints are used for most wall and ceiling applications.

Paint prices are typically an accurate reflection of quality. As a general rule, buy the best paint your budget can afford. High-quality paints are easier to use, look better, last longer, cover better, and because they often require fewer coats they are usually less expensive in the long run. More expensive brands also typically offer a wider palette of more subtle and sophisticated colors.

Before applying the finish paint, prime all of the surfaces with a good-quality primer. Primer bonds well to all surfaces and provides a durable base that keeps the paint from cracking and peeling. Priming is particularly important when using a high-gloss paint on walls and ceilings, because the paint alone might not completely hide finished drywall joints and other variations in the surface. To avoid the need for additional coats of expensive finish paint, tint the primer to match the new color.

How to Estimate Paint ▸

1) **Length of** wall or ceiling (linear feet)	×
2) **Height of** wall, or width of ceiling	=
3) **Surface area** (square feet)	÷
4) **Coverage per** gallon of chosen paint	=
5) **Gallons of** paint needed	

For large jobs, mix paint together (called "boxing") in a large bucket to eliminate slight color variations between cans. Stir the paint thoroughly with a wooden stick or paddle drill attachment.

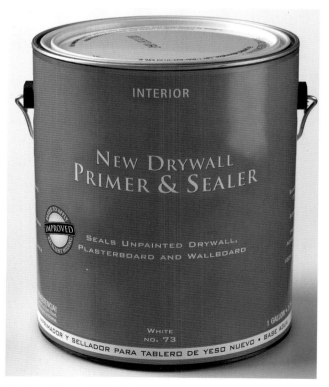

Latex-based drywall primer and sealer equalizes the absorption rates between the dried joint compound and the drywall paper facing, allowing the paint to go on evenly with no blotching.

SELECTING A QUALITY PAINT

Paint coverage (listed on can labels) of quality paint should be about 400 sq. ft. per gallon. Bargain paints (left) may require two or even three coats to cover the same area as quality paints (right).

High washability is a feature of quality paint. The pigments in bargain paints (right) may "chalk" and wash away with mild scrubbing.

PAINT SHEENS

Paint comes in a variety of surface finishes, or sheens. Gloss enamel (A) provides a highly reflective finish for areas where high washability is important. All gloss paints tend to show surface flaws. Alkyd-base enamels have the highest gloss. Medium-gloss (or "satin") latex enamel (B) creates a highly washable surface with a slightly less reflective finish. Like gloss enamels, medium-gloss paints tend to show surface flaws. Eggshell enamel (C) combines a soft finish with the washability of enamel. Flat latex (D) is an all-purpose paint with a matte finish that hides surface irregularities.

PAINTING TOOLS

Most painting jobs can be completed with a few quality tools. Purchase two or three premium brushes, a sturdy paint pan that can be attached to a stepladder, and one or two good rollers. With proper cleanup, these tools will last for years. See the following pages for tips on how to use paintbrushes and rollers.

CHOOSING A PAINTBRUSH

A quality brush (left), has a shaped hardwood handle and a reinforced ferrule made of noncorrosive metal. Multiple spacer plugs separate the bristles. A quality brush has flagged (split) bristles and a chiseled end for precise edging. A cheaper brush (right) will have a blunt end, unflagged bristles, and a cardboard spacer plug that may soften when wet.

There's a proper brush for every job. A 4" straight-edged brush (bottom) is good for cutting in along ceilings and corners. For woodwork, a 2" trim brush (middle) works well. A tapered sash brush (top) helps with corners. Use brushes made of natural bristles only with alkyd paints. All-purpose brushes, suitable for all paints, are made with a blend of polyester, nylon, and sometimes natural bristles.

CHOOSING PAINT ROLLERS

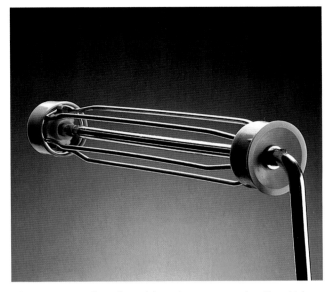

Choose a sturdy roller with a wire cage construction. Nylon bearings should roll smoothly and easily when you spin the cage. The handle end should be threaded for attaching an extension handle.

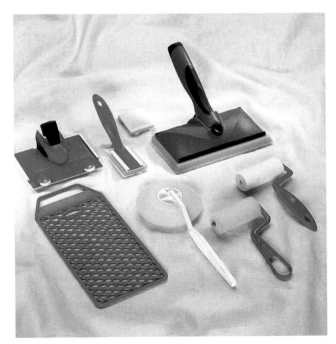

Paint pads and specialty rollers come in a wide range of sizes and shapes to fit different painting needs.

Select the proper roller cover for the surface you intend to paint. A ¼"-nap cover is used for enamel paints and very flat surfaces. A ⅜"-nap cover will hide the small flaws found in most flat walls and ceilings. A 1"-nap cover is for rough surfaces like concrete blocks or stucco. Foam rollers fit into small spaces and work well when painting furniture or doing touch-ups. Corner rollers have nap on the ends and make it easy to paint corners without cutting in the edges. Synthetic covers are good with most paints, especially latexes. Wool or mohair roller covers give an even finish with alkyd products. Always choose good-quality roller covers, which will be less likely to shed lint.

HOW TO USE A PAINT ROLLER

1

Wet the roller cover with water (for latex paint) or mineral spirits (for alkyd enamel), to remove lint and prime the cover. Squeeze out excess liquid. Dip the roller fully into the paint pan reservoir and roll it over the textured ramp to distribute the paint evenly. The roller should be full, but not dripping. Make an upward diagonal sweep about 4 ft. long on the surface, using a slow stroke to avoid splattering.

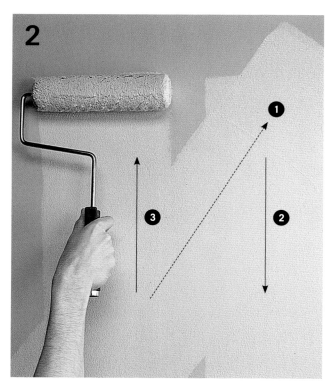

2

Draw the roller straight down (2) from the top of the diagonal sweep made in step 1. Lift and move the roller to the beginning of the diagonal sweep and roll up (3) to complete the unloading of the roller.

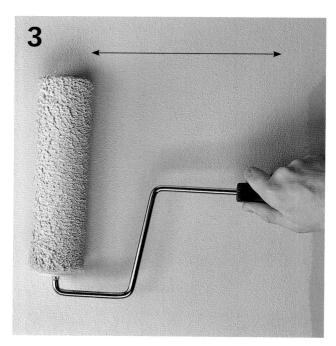

3

Distribute the paint over the rest of the section with horizontal and diagonal back-and-forth strokes.

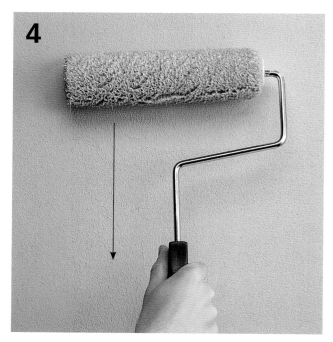

4

Smooth the area by lightly drawing the roller vertically from the top to the bottom of the painted area. Lift the roller and return it to the top of the area after each stroke.

PAINT + TRIM

HOW TO USE A PAINTBRUSH

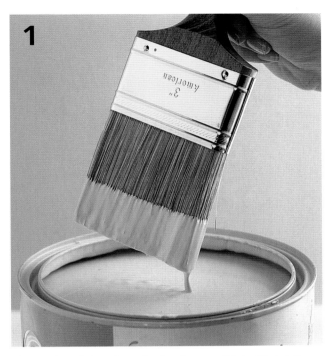

Dip the brush into the paint, loading one-third of its bristle length. Tap the bristles against the side of the can to remove excess paint, but do not drag the bristles against the lip of the can.

Paint along the edges (called "cutting in") using the narrow edge of the brush, pressing just enough to flex the bristles. Keep an eye on the paint edge, and paint with long, slow strokes. Always paint from a dry area back into wet paint to avoid lap marks.

Brush wall corners using the wide edge of the brush. Paint open areas with a brush or roller before the brushed paint dries.

To paint large areas with a brush, apply the paint with 2 or 3 diagonal strokes. Hold the brush at a 45° angle to the work surface, pressing just enough to flex the bristles. Distribute the paint evenly with horizontal strokes.

Smooth the surface by drawing the brush vertically from the top to the bottom of the painted area. Use light strokes and lift the brush from the surface at the end of each stroke. This method is best for slow-drying alkyd enamels.

PAINTING WALLS + CEILINGS

For a smooth finish on large wall and ceiling areas, paint in small sections. First use a paintbrush to cut in the edges, then immediately roll the section before moving on. If brushed edges are left to dry before the large surfaces are rolled, visible lap marks will be left on the finished wall. Working in natural light makes it easier to see missed areas.

Spread the paint evenly onto the work surface without letting it run, drip, or lap onto other areas. Excess paint will run on the surface and can drip onto woodwork and floors. Conversely, stretching paint too far leaves lap marks and results in patchy coverage.

For fast, mess-free painting, shield any surfaces that could get splattered. If you are painting only the ceiling, drape the walls and woodwork to prevent splatters. When painting walls, mask the baseboards and the window and door casings. (See top of opposite page.)

While the tried-and-true method of aligning painter's tape with the edge of moldings and casings is perfectly adequate, the job goes much faster and smoother with a tape applicator. Similarly, painter's tape can be used to cover door hinges and window glass, but hinge masks and corner masks simplify the job enormously. Evaluate the available choices and the project at hand: there are many new, easy-to-use options available.

Use an adjustable extension handle to paint ceilings and tall walls easily without a ladder.

Cut in around doors and window casing with a paintbrush and then finish painting the wall with a roller.

HOW TO TAPE + DRAPE FOR WALLS AND CEILINGS

Align wide masking tape with the inside edge of the molding; press in place. Run the tip of a putty knife along the inside edge of the tape to seal it against seeping paint. After painting, remove the tape as soon as the paint is too dry to run.

Press the top half of 2" masking tape along the joint between the ceiling and the wall, leaving the bottom half of the tape loose. Hang sheet plastic under the tape, draping the walls and baseboards. After painting, remove the tape as soon as the paint is too dry to run.

Specialized Roller Techniques ▸

Using a corner roller makes it unnecessary to cut in inside corners. It also matches the rolled texture of the rest of the wall better than most paintbrushes.

Minimize brush marks. Slide the roller cover slightly off of the roller cage when rolling near wall corners or a ceiling line. Brushed areas dry to a different finish than rolled paint.

HOW TO PAINT CEILINGS

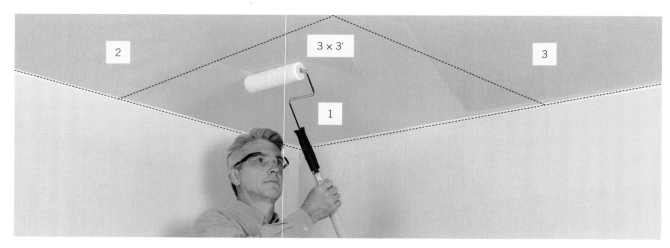

Paint ceilings with a roller handle extension. Use eye protection while painting overhead. Start at the corner farthest from the entry door. Paint the ceiling along the narrow end in 3 × 3-ft. sections, cutting in the edges with a brush before rolling. Apply the paint with a diagonal stroke. Distribute the paint evenly with back-and-forth strokes. For the final smoothing strokes, roll each section toward the wall containing the entry door, lifting the roller at the end of each sweep.

HOW TO PAINT WALLS

Paint walls in 2 × 4-ft. sections. Start in an upper corner, cutting in the ceiling and wall corners with a brush, then rolling the section. Make the initial diagonal roller stroke from the bottom of the section upward, to avoid dripping paint. Distribute the paint evenly with horizontal strokes, then finish with downward sweeps of the roller. Next, cut in and roll the section directly underneath. Continue with adjacent areas, cutting in and rolling the top sections before the bottom sections. Roll all finish strokes toward the floor.

PAINTING EXTERIORS: PREPARING

The key to an even exterior paint job is to work on a smooth, clean, dry surface—so preparing the surface is essential. Generally, the more preparation work you do, the smoother the final finish will be and the longer it will last.

For the smoothest finish, sand all the way down to the bare wood with a power sander. For a less time-consuming (but rougher) finish, scrape off any loose paint, then spot-sand rough areas. You can use pressure washing to remove some of the flaking paint, but by itself, pressure washing won't create a smooth surface for painting.

Tools + Materials ▶

Pressure washer	Heat gun
Scrapers	Coarse abrasive pad
Siding sander	Wire-wheel attachment
Finishing sander	N95 dust mask
Sanding block	Sandpaper (80-, 120-, 150-grit)
Putty knife	Wood putty
Stiff-bristle brush	Paintable siliconized caulk
Wire brush	Muriatic acid
Steel wool	Sealant
Drill	Colored push pins or tape
Caulk gun	Eye protection

Sanded to bare wood

Scraped and spot-sanded

Pressure washed only

The amount of surface preparation you do will largely determine the final appearance and durability of your paint job. Decide how much sanding and scraping you're willing to do to obtain a finish you'll be happy with.

HOW TO REMOVE PAINT

Use a heat gun to loosen thick layers of old paint. Aim the gun at the surface, warm the paint until it starts to bubble, then scrape the paint as soon as it releases.

To remove large areas of paint on wood lap siding, use a siding sander with a disk that's as wide as the reveal on your siding.

HOW TO PREPARE SURFACES FOR PAINT

Clean the surface and remove loose paint by pressure washing the house. As you work, direct the water stream downward, and don't get too close to the surface with the sprayer head. Allow all surfaces to dry thoroughly before continuing.

Scrape off loose paint using a paint scraper. Be careful not to damage the surface by scraping too hard.

Smooth out rough paint with a finishing sander and 80-grit sandpaper. Use sanding blocks and 80- to 120-grit sandpaper to sand hard-to-reach areas of trim. *TIP: You can make sanding blocks from dowels, wood scraps, or garden hoses.*

Use detail scrapers to remove loose paint in hard-to-reach areas. Some of these scrapers have interchangeable heads that match common trim profiles.

Inspect all surfaces for cracks, rot, and other damage. Mark affected areas with colored pushpins or tape. Fill the holes and cracks with epoxy wood filler.

Use a finishing sander with 120-grit sandpaper to sand down repaired areas, ridges, and hard edges left from the scraping process, creating a smooth surface.

HOW TO PREPARE WINDOW + DOOR TRIM FOR PAINT

Scuff-sand glossy surfaces on doors, window casings, and all surfaces painted with enamel paint. Use a coarse abrasive pad or 150-grit sandpaper.

Fill cracks in siding and gaps around window and door trim with paintable siliconized acrylic caulk.

HOW TO REMOVE CLEAR FINISHES

Pressure wash stained or unpainted surfaces that have been treated with a wood preservative or protectant before recoating them with fresh sealant.

Use a stiff-bristle brush to dislodge any flakes of loosened surface coating that weren't removed by pressure washing. Don't use a wire brush on wood surfaces.

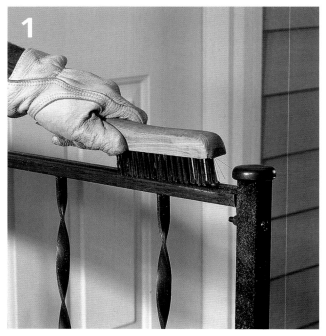

Remove rust and loose paint from metal hardware, such as railings and ornate trim, using a wire brush. Cover the surface with metal primer immediately after brushing to prevent the formation of new rust.

Scuff-sand metal siding and trim with medium-coarse steel wool or a coarse abrasive pad. Wash the surface and let dry before priming and painting.

Remove loose mortar, mineral deposits, or paint from mortar lines in masonry surfaces with a drill and wire-wheel attachment. Clean broad, flat masonry surfaces with a wire brush. Correct any minor damage before repainting.

Dissolve rust on metal hardware with diluted muriatic acid solution. When working with muriatic acid, it's important to wear safety equipment, work in a well-ventilated area, and follow all manufacturer's directions and precautions.

HOW TO PAINT FASCIA, SOFFITS + TRIM

Prime all surfaces to be painted, and allow ample drying time. Paint the face of the fascia first, then cut in paint at the bottom edges of the soffit panels. *TIP: Fascia and soffits are usually painted the same color as the trim.*

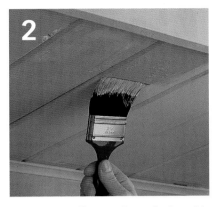

Paint the soffit panels and trim with a 4" brush. Start by cutting in around the edges of the panels using the narrow edge of the brush, then feather in the broad surfaces of the soffit panels with full loads of paint. Be sure to get good coverage in the grooves.

Paint any decorative trim near the top of the house at the same time you paint the soffits and fascia. Use a 2½" or 3" paintbrush for broader surfaces, and a sash brush for more intricate trim areas.

HOW TO PAINT SIDING

Paint the bottom edges of lap siding by holding the paintbrush flat against the wall. Paint the bottom edges of several siding pieces before returning to paint the faces of the same boards.

Paint the broad faces of the siding boards with a 4" brush using the painting technique shown on page 149. Working down from the top of the house, paint as much surface as you can reach without leaning beyond the sides of the ladder.

Paint the siding all the way down to the foundation, working from top to bottom. Shift the ladder or scaffolding, then paint the next section. *TIP: Paint up to the edges of end caps and window or door trim that will be painted later.*

On board and batten or vertical panel siding, paint the edges of the battens, or top boards, first. Paint the faces of the battens before the sides dry, then use a roller with a ⅝"-nap sleeve to paint the large, broad surfaces between the battens.

BASIC CASING

Stock wood casings provide an attractive border around window and door openings while covering the gaps between the wall surface and the window jamb. Install casings with a consistent reveal between the inside edges of the jambs and the edges of the casings.

In order to fit casings properly, the jambs and wall surfaces must be in the same plane. If one of them protrudes, the casing will not lie flush. To solve this problem, you may need to shave the edges of the jambs down with a block plane. Or you may need to attach jamb extensions to the window or door to match the plane of the wall. For small differences where a drywall surface is too high, you can sometimes use a hammer to compress the drywall around the jambs to allow the casings to lie flush.

Although wood casings are shown here, extruded acrylic casings are often less expensive and easier to work with. They are also available in a vast variety of profiles. That can be useful if you're trying to match existing cases in other rooms of an older home, or just want a distinctive look.

Tools + Materials ▶

Tape measure	Miter saw
Drill	Casing material
Pencil	Baseboard molding
Nail set	and corner blocks
Hammer or	(optional)
pneumatic nailer	4d and 6d finish nails
Level	Wood putty
Combination square	Eye protection
Straightedge	Work gloves

Simple case molding installed with mitered corners is a very common approach to trimming windows and doors. While it lacks visual interest, it is easy to install and relatively inexpensive.

HOW TO INSTALL MITERED CASING ON WINDOWS + DOORS

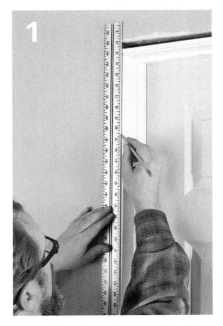

On each jamb, mark a reveal line ³⁄₁₆ to ¼" from the inside edge. The casings will be installed flush with these lines.

Place a length of casing along one side jamb, flush with the reveal line. At the top and bottom of the molding, mark the points where horizontal and vertical reveal lines meet. (When working with doors, mark the molding at the top only.)

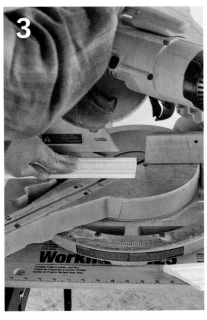

Make 45° miter cuts on the ends of the moldings. Measure and cut the other vertical molding piece, using the same method.

Drill pilot holes spaced every 12" to prevent splitting, and attach the vertical casings with 4d finish nails driven through the casings and into the jambs. Drive 6d finish nails into the framing members near the outside edge of the casings.

Measure the distance between the side casings and cut top and bottom casings to fit, with ends mitered at 45°. If the window or door unit is not perfectly square, make test cuts on scrap pieces to find the correct angle of the joints. Drill pilot holes and attach with 4d and 6d finish nails.

Locknail the corner joints by drilling pilot holes and driving 4d finish nails through each corner, as shown. Drive all nail heads below the wood surface, using a nail set, then fill the nail holes with wood putty.

BUILT-UP BASE MOLDING

Built-up base molding is made up of several strips of wood (usually three) that are combined for a particular effect. It is installed in two common scenarios: (1) to match existing trim in other rooms of a house or (2) to match a stock one-piece molding that is not available.

Installing a built-up base molding is no more difficult than a standard one-piece molding, because the same installation techniques are used. However, built-up base molding offers a few advantages over standard stock moldings. Wavy floors and walls are easier to conceal, and the height of the molding is completely up to you, making heat registers and other obstructions easier to deal with.

In this project, the base molding is made of high-grade plywood rather than solid stock lumber. Plywood is more economical and dimensionally stable than solid lumber and can be built up to any depth, as well as cut down to any height. Keep in mind that plywood molding is less durable than solid wood and is only available in 8- and 10-foot lengths, making joints more frequent.

Tools + Materials ›

Pneumatic finish nail gun	Tape measure
Air compressor	Sandpaper
Air hose	Power sander
Miter saw	¾" finish-grade oak plywood
Hammer	Base shoe molding
Nail set	Cap molding
Tablesaw or straightedge guide and circular saw	1¼" brad nails
	2" finish nails
Pencil	Wood putty
	Eye and ear protection

Built-up base trim is made by combining baseboard, base shoe, and another molding type, typically cap molding.

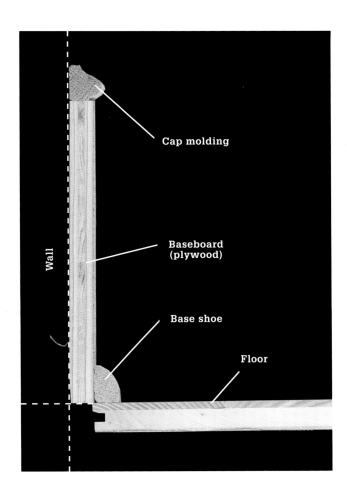

Cap molding

Baseboard (plywood)

Base shoe

Wall

Floor

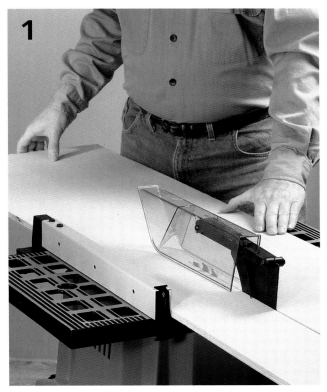

1

Cut the plywood panel into 6" strips with a tablesaw or a straightedge guide and a circular saw. Lightly sand the strips, removing any splinters left from the saw. Then apply the finish of your choice to the moldings and the plywood strips.

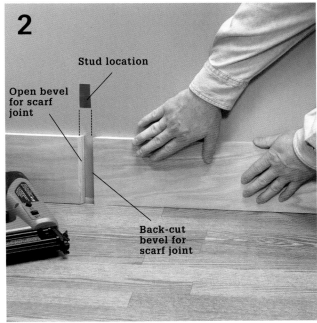

2

Stud location

Open bevel for scarf joint

Back-cut bevel for scarf joint

Install the plywood strips with 2" finish nails driven at stud locations. Use scarf joints on continuous runs, driving pairs of fasteners into the joints. Cut and install moldings so that all scarf joints fall at stud locations.

Base Trim Spacers ▸

Baseboard can be built up on the back with spacer strips so it will project farther out from the wall. This can allow you to match existing casings or to create the impression of a thicker molding. However, the cap rail needs to be thick enough to cover the plywood edge completely or the core of the panel may be visible.

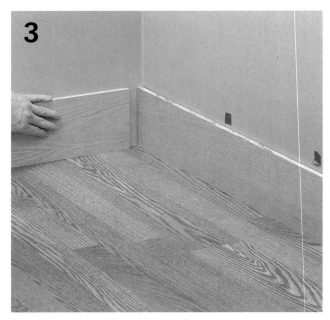

3

Test-fit inside corner butt joints before cutting a workpiece. If the walls are not square or straight, angle or bevel the end cut a few degrees to fit the profile of the adjoining piece. The cap molding will cover any gaps at the top of the joint.

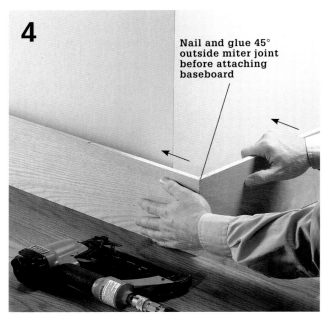

4

Nail and glue 45° outside miter joint before attaching baseboard

Miter outside corners squarely at 45°. Use wood glue and 1¼" brad nails to pull the mitered pieces tight, and then nail the base to the wall at stud locations with 2" finish nails. Small gaps at the bottom or top of the base molding will be covered with cap or base shoe.

5

Use a brad nailer with 18-gauge, ⅝" brads to install the cap and base shoe moldings along the edges of the plywood base. Fit scarf joints on longer lengths, coped joints on inside corners, and miter joints on outside corners. Stagger the seams so that they do not line up with the base molding seams. Set any protruding nails with a nail set and fill all nail holes with putty.

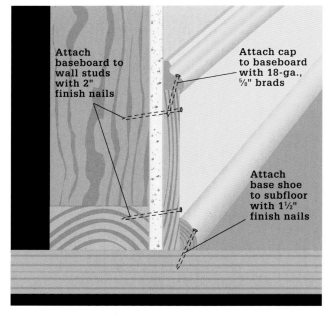

Attach baseboard to wall studs with 2" finish nails

Attach cap to baseboard with 18-ga., ⅝" brads

Attach base shoe to subfloor with 1½" finish nails

Built-up baseboard requires more attention to the nailing schedule than simple one-piece baseboards. The most important consideration (other than making sure your nails are all driven into studs or other solid wood), is that the base shoe must be attached to the floor, while the baseboard is attached to the wall. This way, as the gap between the wall and floor changes, the parts of the built-up molding can change with them.

CROWN MOLDING

Simply put, crown molding is angled trim that bridges the joint between the ceiling and the wall. To cover this joint effectively, crown moldings are "sprung." This means that the top and bottom edges of the molding are beveled, so when the molding is tilted away from the wall at an angle, the tops and bottoms are flush on the wall and ceiling surfaces. Some crown moldings have a 45-degree angle at both the top and the bottom edges; another common style ("38-degree crown") has a 38-degree angle on one edge and a 52-degree angle on the other edge.

Installing crown molding can be a challenging and sometimes confusing process. Joints may be difficult for you to visualize before cutting, and wall and ceiling irregularities can be hard to overcome. If you have not worked on crown molding joints before, start with paint-grade materials. Stain-grade crown is commonly made of solid hardwood stock, which makes for expensive cutting errors and difficulty concealing irregularities in joints.

Inside corner joints should be cope-cut, not mitered, except in the case of very intricate profile crown that is virtually impossible to cope. While mitering inside corners may appear to save time and produce adequate results, after a few changing seasons the joints will open up and be even more difficult to conceal.

In most houses that have been around for more than a couple of seasons, walls have bulges caused by warped studs or improper stud placement causing the drywall to push out. Ceilings have issues caused by warped joists or drywall that has loosened or pulled away from the joists. Corners may be best finished with extra-thick layers of joint compound, causing an outside corner piece to sit further away from the corner bead. These are just a few of the issues that can work against you and cause even an experienced carpenter to become frustrated.

Tools + Materials ▸

Tape measure	Painter's tape
Drill and bits	Finish nails
Miter saw	Molding
Coping saw	Wood putty
Sandpaper	Putty knife
Fine wood file	Paintable caulk
Pencil	Caulk gun

Basic crown molding softens the transitions between walls and ceilings. If it is made from quality hardwood, crown molding can be quite beautiful when installed and finished with a clear top coat. But historically, it is most often painted, either the same color as the ceiling (your eye tends to see it as a ceiling molding, not a wall molding) or with highly elaborate painted-and-carved details.

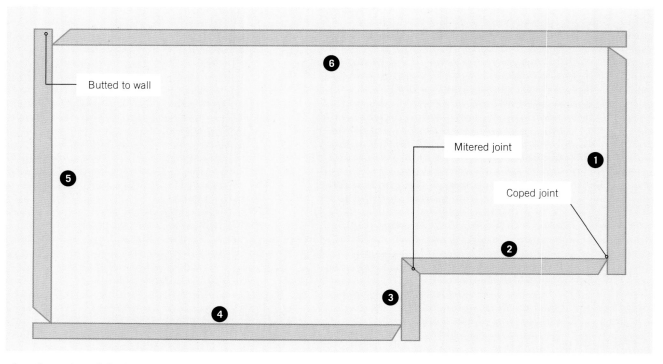

Plan the order of the installation to minimize the number of difficult joints on each piece, and use the longest pieces for the most visible sections of wall. Notice that the left end of first piece is cope-cut rather than butted into the wall. Cope-cutting the first end eliminates the need to cope-cut both ends of the final piece and places the cuts in the same direction. This simplifies your installation, making the method to cut each piece similar.

HOW TO INSTALL BASIC CROWN MOLDING

Cut a piece of crown molding about 1' long with square ends. Temporarily install the piece in the corner of the last installation wall with two screws driven into the blocking. This piece serves as a template for the first cope cut on the first piece of molding.

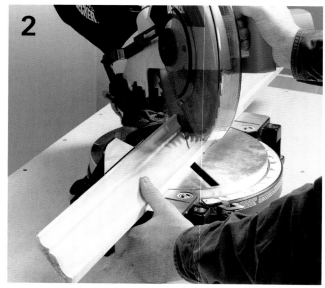

Place the first piece of molding upside down and sprung against the fence of the miter saw. Mark a reference line on the fence for placement of future moldings, and cut the first coped end with an inside miter cut to reveal the profile of the piece.

PAINT + TRIM

3

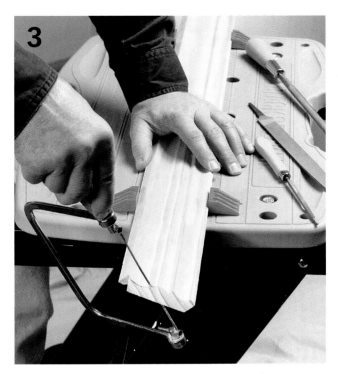

Cope-cut the end of the first piece with a coping saw. Carefully cut along the profile, angling the saw as you cut to back-bevel the cope. Test-fit the coped cut against the temporary scrap from step 1. Fine-tune the cut with files and fine-grit sandpaper.

4

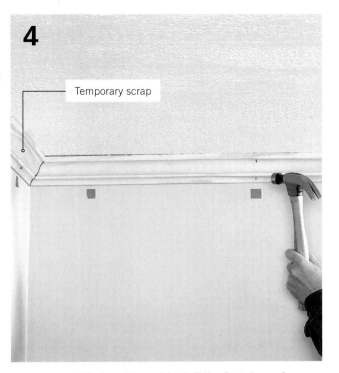

Temporary scrap

Measure, cut to length, and install the first piece of crown molding, leaving the end near the temporary scrap loose for final fitting of the last piece. Nail the molding at the top and bottom of each stud location.

5

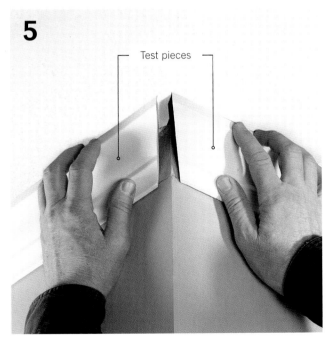

Test pieces

Cut two test pieces to check the fit of outside corners. Start with each molding cut at 45°, adjusting the angles larger or smaller until the joints are tight. Make sure the test moldings are properly aligned and are flush with the ceiling and walls. Make a note of your saw settings once the joint fits tightly.

6

Position the actual stock so a cut end is flush against the wall at one end and, at the other end, mark the outside corner on the back edge of the molding. Miter-cut the piece at the mark, according to the angles you noted on the test pieces.

(continued)

7

Measure and cut the third piece with an outside corner miter to match the angle of your test pieces. Cut the other end squarely, butting it into the corner. Install the piece with nails driven at stud locations. Install the subsequent pieces of crown molding, coping the front end and butting the other as you work around the room.

8

Temporary spacer removed

To fit the final piece, cope the end and cut it to length. Remove the temporary scrap piece from step 3, and slide the last molding into position. Nail the last piece at the stud locations when the joints fit well, and finish nailing the first piece.

9

Fill all nail holes. Use spackling compound if painting; wait until the finish is applied, and fill with tinted putty for clear finishes. Use a putty knife to force spackling compound or tinted wood putty into loose joints, and caulk gaps ⅛" or smaller between the molding and the wall or ceiling with flexible, paintable, latex caulk.

10

Lightly sand the filled nail holes and joint gaps with fine sandpaper. Sand the nail holes flush with the surface of the moldings, and apply a final coat of paint to the entire project.

HOW TO INSTALL A BUILT-UP CROWN

1

Remove any old crown molding in the cornice area. Use a utility knife to cut through old paint and caulk between the molding and the wall or ceiling. Then use a pry bar to work the crown molding loose in small sections. Be sure to brace the end of the pry bar on the inside of the crown and pull downward. Do not pry upwards; this can damage the ceiling.

2

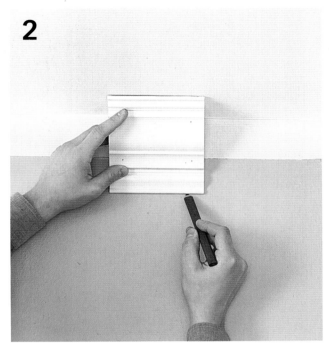

Use a mock-up of the built-up molding as a marking gauge to establish a baseline for the bottom of the assembly on the wall. Start in the corners and work your way around the room. This will allow you to see how the ceiling rises and falls so you know where to install the first piece.

3

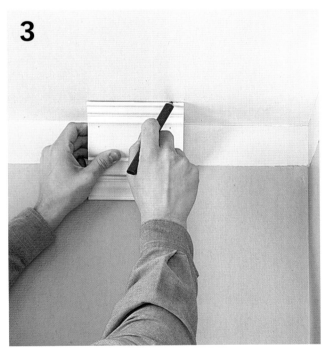

Make a reference line for the top of the built-up assembly, using the mock-up as a gauge.

Tip ▶

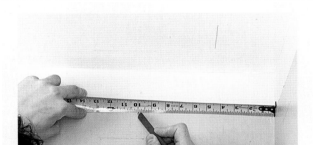

To measure a wall when working alone, first make a mark on the wall or ceiling exactly 10" out from one corner. Then, press the tab against the wall at the other end, measure to the marked line, and add 10" to the measurement.

KITCHEN CABINETS

1

Position a corner upper cabinet on a ledger and hold it in place, making sure it is resting cleanly on the ledger. Drill ³⁄₁₆" pilot holes into the wall studs through the hanging strips at the top rear of the cabinet. Attach the cabinet to the wall with 2½" screws. Do not tighten fully until all cabinets are hung.

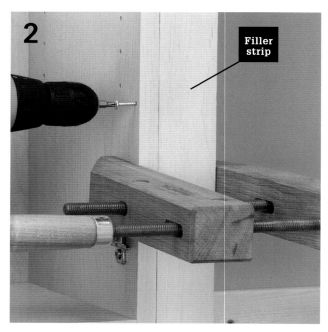

2

Filler strip

Attach a filler strip to the front edge of the cabinet, if needed. Clamp the filler in place and drill counterbored pilot holes through the cabinet face frame near hinge locations. Attach filler to cabinet with 2½" cabinet screws or flathead wood screws.

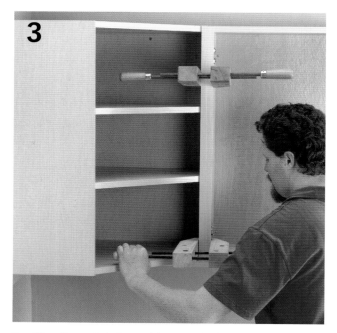

3

Position the adjoining cabinet on the ledger, tight against the corner cabinet or filler strip. Clamp the corner cabinet and the adjoining cabinet together at the top and bottom. Handscrew clamps will not damage wood face frames.

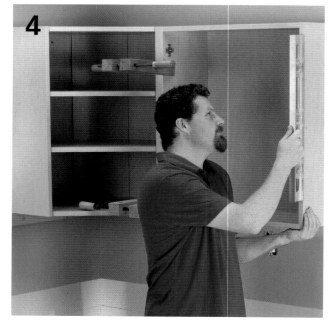

4

Check the front cabinet edges or face frames for plumb. Drill ³⁄₁₆" pilot holes into the wall studs through the hanging strips in the rear of the cabinet. Attach the cabinet with 2½" screws. Do not tighten the wall screws fully until all the cabinets are hung.

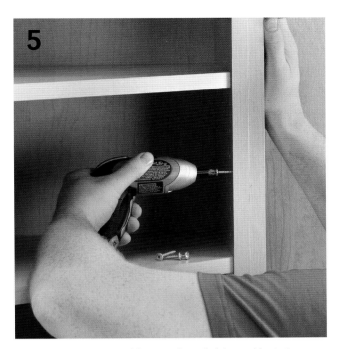

Attach the corner cabinet to the adjoining cabinet. From the inside corner cabinet, drill pilot holes through the face frame. Join the cabinets with sheet-metal screws.

Position and attach each additional cabinet. Clamp frames together, and drill counterbored pilot holes through the side of the face frame. Join the cabinets with wood screws. Drill ³⁄₁₆" pilot holes in the hanging strips, and attach the cabinet to the studs with wood screws.

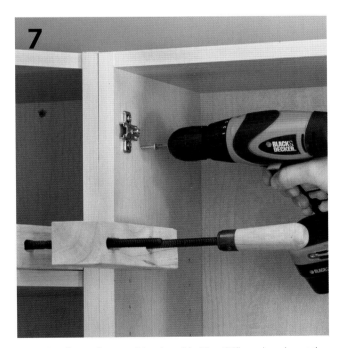

Join the frameless cabinets with #8 × 1¼" panhead wood screws or wood screws with decorative washers. Each pair of cabinets should be joined by at least four screws.

Fill the gaps between the cabinet and wall or neighboring appliance with a filler strip. Cut the filler strip to fit the space, then wedge wood shims between the filler and the wall to create a friction fit that holds it in place temporarily. Drill counterbored pilot holes through the side of the cabinet (or the edge of the face frame) and attach filler with screws.

(continued)

9

Remove the temporary ledger. Check the cabinet run for plumb, and adjust if necessary by placing wood shims behind the cabinet, near the stud locations. Tighten the wall screws completely. Cut off the shims with a utility knife.

10

Use trim moldings to cover any gaps between the cabinets and the walls. Stain the moldings to match the cabinet finish.

11

Attach decorative valance above the sink. Clamp the valance to the edge of cabinet frames and drill counterbored pilot holes through the cabinet frames and into the end of the valance. Attach with sheet-metal screws.

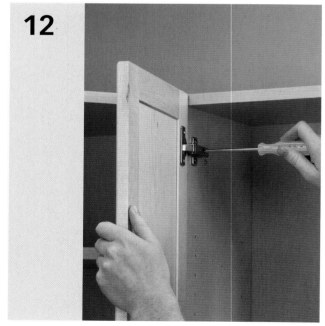

12

Install the cabinet doors. If necessary, adjust the hinges so that the doors are straight and plumb.

CABINETS + COUNTERS

HOW TO INSTALL BASE CABINETS

Begin the installation with a corner cabinet. Draw plumb lines that intersect the 34½" reference line (measured from the high point of the floor) at the locations for the cabinet sides.

Place the cabinet in the corner. Make sure the cabinet is plumb and level. If necessary, adjust by driving wood shims under the cabinet base. Be careful not to damage the flooring. Drill ³⁄₁₆" pilot holes through the hanging strip and into the wall studs. Tack the cabinet to the wall with wood screws or wallboard screws.

Clamp the adjoining cabinet to the corner cabinet. Make sure the new cabinet is plumb, then drill counterbored pilot holes through the cabinet sides or the face frame and filler strip. Screw the cabinets together. Drill ³⁄₁₆" pilot holes through the hanging strips and into the wall studs. Tack the cabinets loosely to the wall studs with wood screws or wallboard screws.

Use a jigsaw to cut any cabinet openings needed in the cabinet backs (for example, in the sink base seen here) for plumbing, wiring, or heating ducts.

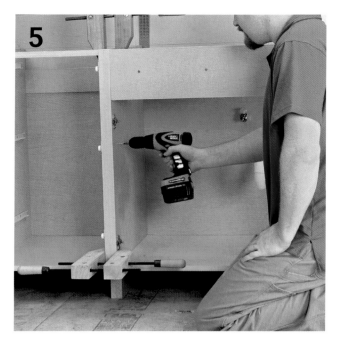

5

Position and attach additional cabinets, making sure the frames are aligned and the cabinet tops are level. Clamp cabinets together, then attach the face frames or cabinet sides with screws driven into pilot holes. Tack the cabinets to the wall studs, but don't drive screws too tight—you may need to make adjustments once the entire bank is installed.

6

Make sure all the cabinets are level. If necessary, adjust by driving shims underneath the cabinets. Place the shims behind the cabinets near the stud locations to fill any gaps. Tighten the wall screws. Cut off the shims with a utility knife.

7

Toe-kick molding

Use trim moldings to cover gaps between the cabinets and the wall or floor. The toe-kick area is often covered with a strip of wood finished to match the cabinets or painted black.

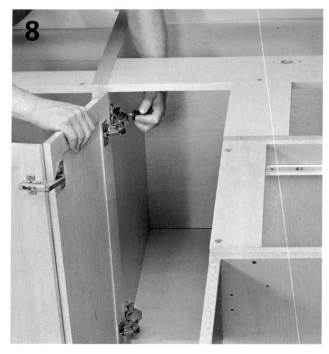

8

Hang the cabinet doors and mount the drawer fronts, then test to make sure they close smoothly and the doors fit evenly and flush. Self-closing cabinet hinges (by far the most common type installed today) have adjustment screws that allow you to make minor changes to the hardware to correct any problems.

VARIATION: INSTALLING FACE-FRAME CABINETS

The more traditional-looking face-frame cabinets differ only slightly from frameless cabinets in terms of installation. The opening of the cabinet is surrounded by vertical and horizontal frames constructed of "stiles" and "rails." The face frame typically overhangs the cabinet case on the outside by $\frac{1}{16}$" to $\frac{1}{8}$". Because of this overhang, the frames must be the connection point rather than the cabinet case. Use $2\frac{1}{2}$" No.10 wood screws to connect the frames (or use special $2\frac{1}{2}$"- or 3"-long cabinet screws). Do not screw the cabinet sides together at any other point than the face frame, because this will skew the cabinets and create structural stress.

Most face-frame cabinets use overlay doors. The hinges for these doors simply attach to the back of the door and to the side or face of the cabinet face-frame with screws. They are called "overlay wrap" or "partial wrap" hinges if they attach to the side of the face frame, and they are called "semi-concealed" if they attach to the front of the face-frame. Cup or Euro-style hinges are available for face-frame cabinets, but are somewhat more difficult to install if the doors have not been predrilled for this hinge style. The best way to attach the door hardware uniformly is to use a drilling template. You can usually purchase one where you purchase the cabinets or hardware.

Tools + Materials ▸

Drill	Filler strip (if needed)
No. 10 counterbore bit	¾" finish-grade plywood
⁵⁄₆₄" self-centering vix bit	Finish materials
Cabinet screws	Drilling template
(or 2½" No. 10 screws)	

To join face-frame cabinets, set the cabinets in position, aligned with the frame faces flush and the frame tops flush. Clamp the frames together at the top and bottom. Using a drill with a No.10 counterbore bit, drill two pilot holes through the sides of the frame into the adjoining frame. Attach the frames with cabinet screws or 2½" No. 10 screws.

Start at the corner when installing a bank of cabinets that includes a blind corner cabinet. Attach the cabinet adjoining the corner by driving screws through the face frame (see photo at the top of this page). If a filler strip is necessary to fill a gap between the two cabinets, attach the filler strip to the base cabinet first and then run screws through the corner cabinet face frame and into the filler strip only after the adjoining cabinet is positioned and shimmed.

To install partial wrap overlay hinges, use a template to mark the hinge locations on the back of the door. Drill ⁵⁄₆₄"-dia. pilot holes no more than ⅜" deep using a self-centering vix bit. Screw the hinge to the door back. Place the hinge against the face frame and mark the screw holes. Drill ⁵⁄₆₄" pilot holes. Drive all the screws for both hinges partially, then tighten all.

TRADITIONAL VANITY

Simple vanity bases are stages upon which much of the drama in a bathroom can play out. Because there are now so many sink and counter styles and materials, and ways of incorporating the two, a stable base that can be attractive in its own right is more important than ever.

Although vanity cabinet styles vary, the basic structure—such as incorporating a toe-kick—is common to the majority of them. The process outlined here covers the basic way that most vanities are secured in place to provide ample storage and sturdy foundation for sinks and countertops.

Tools + Materials ▸

Pencil	Stud finder
Electronic level	Tub and tile caulk
Screwdriver	4' level
Basin wrench	Shims
Cardboard	3" drywall screws
Masking tape	Drill
Plumber's putty	Work gloves
Lag screws	Eye and ear protection

A traditional bathroom base cabinet serves to support an integral sink-countertop unit. It also adds useful storage in a space that is often underutilized in the bathroom.

HOW TO INSTALL A VANITY CABINET

1

Measure and mark the top edge of the vanity cabinet on the wall, then use an electronic level/stud finder to mark the stud locations and a level line.

2

Slide the vanity into position so that the back rail of the cabinet can later be fastened to studs at both corners and in the center. The back of the cabinet should also be flush against the wall. (If the wall surface is uneven, position the vanity so it contacts the wall in at least one spot and the back cabinet rail is parallel with the wall.)

VARIATION: To install two or more cabinets, set the cabinets in position against the wall, and align the cabinet fronts. If one cabinet is higher than the other, shim under the lower cabinet until the two are even. Clamp the cabinet faces together, then drill countersunk pilot holes spaced 12" apart through the face frames so they go at least halfway into the face frame of the second cabinet. Drive wood screws through the pilot holes to join the cabinets together.

Using a level as a guide, shim below the vanity cabinet until the unit is level.

At the stud locations marked on the wall, drive 3" drywall screws through the rail on the cabinet back and into the framing members. The screws should be driven at both corners and in the center of the back rail.

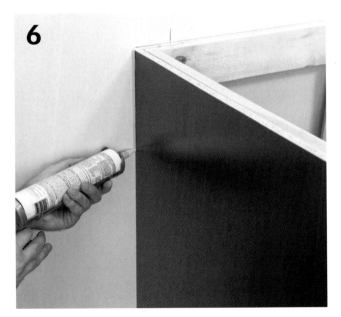

Run a bead of caulk along small gaps between the vanity and wall and between the vanity and floor. For larger gaps, use ¼-round molding between the vanity and wall. Between the vanity and floor, install the same baseboard material used to cover the gap between the wall and floor.

VANITY TOP WITH INTEGRAL SINK

Perhaps the easiest sink of all to install is one in which the countertop and sink are a single integrated unit that simply is attached to a standard vanity cabinet. These integrated sinks now come in hundreds of different styles and in a variety of materials, including premium solid-surface materials or synthetic stones. Gone are the days when integrated sinks were those plastic faux-marble units that looked as cheap as they were. Today's integrated bathroom sinks can be quite attractive as a design statement and are available in lots of different shapes and configurations.

What hasn't changed, though, is the ease with which they can be installed—a feature that makes them very attractive to DIYers. Since integral sinks are predrilled for faucet and drain hookups, installing one is really just a matter of laying the unit on the vanity cabinet, leveling and attaching it, and making the plumbing connections. Keep in mind that most integral sinks and vanity tops are predrilled with faucet holes. The configuration in the unit you choose may limit the types of faucets that you can install. This is most important if you want to reuse an existing faucet.

An integral sink-countertop is the traditional match to a stock bathroom base cabinet.

Tools + Materials ▶

Level
Shims
Faucet and drain
   fittings
Wrenches

Plumber's putty
Silicone caulk
Caulk gun
Eye protection
Work gloves

HOW TO INSTALL A VANITY TOP WITH INTEGRAL SINK

Check the vanity cabinet to make sure it is level. If not, you can place a shim under the base of the cabinet to bring it to level.

Test-fit the countertop-sink unit to make sure it fits solidly on the vanity. If it wobbles, or if the cabinet itself could not be leveled, you can level the countertop by placing shims between the bottom of the countertop and the top edge of the vanity cabinet.

3

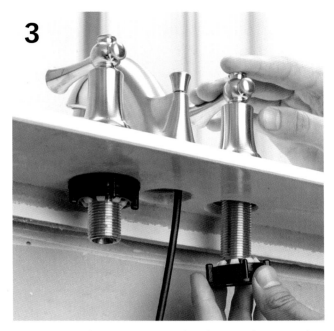

Remove the sink-countertop, place it on sawhorses, and then attach the faucet unit using the predrilled cutouts in the countertop. This is an easy matter of threading the mounting nuts onto the faucet tailpieces from below, but always make sure to follow the faucet manufacturer's directions. If you wish, you can also preattach the water-supply tubes to the bottom of the faucet tailpieces.

4

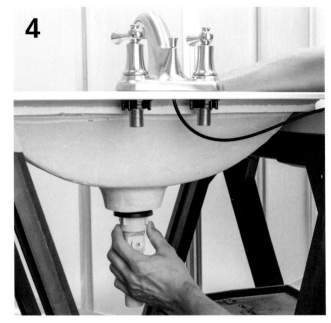

Begin installing the drain unit, again following the package instructions. Make sure to use plumber's putty between the sink surface and the bottom of the drain flange.

5

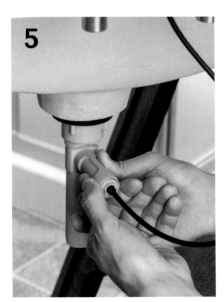

Finish up the drain installation by connecting the drain-stopper cable or lever to the pop-up drain fitting on the drain tailpiece.

6

Apply a bead of silicone caulk around the top lip of the vanity cabinet. Silicone caulk has good adhesive properties, and no other fasteners are required. Set the sink-countertop unit onto the cabinet, and press down firmly to bond it to the cabinet. Let the caulk dry completely before completing the plumbing hookups.

7

Complete the drain hookups by connecting the drain trap to the sink tailpiece at the drain-arm pipe. Connect the water-supply tubes from the faucet tailpieces to the shutoff valves inside the cabinet.

MEDICINE CABINETS

Medicine cabinets were traditionally just shallow containers for pill bottles, with a mirrored door on the front. We've come a long way since then. Today, you can buy a medicine cabinet that includes power outlets for recharging your electric toothbrush, adjustable shelves, built-in LED lighting, and more. Whether you're ready to purchase a deluxe unit or just want to replace a flat mirror with some small-item storage, you'll choose between a surface-mounted unit and the more difficult-to-install recessed cabinet. The instructions for both are outlined here.

Tools + Materials ▸

Electronic stud finder	Framing square
Level	Duplex nails
Pry bar	10d common nails
Hammer	Finish nails
Screwdriver	1 × 4 lumber
Drill and bits	2½" wood screws
Circular saw	Wood shims
Reciprocating saw	Cabinet
Pencil	Eye protection
Bar clamp	Work gloves

Medicine cabinets don't have to be frumpy. This sleek version has a simple knob handle and a sleek aesthetic.

HOW TO INSTALL A SURFACE-MOUNTED MEDICINE CABINET

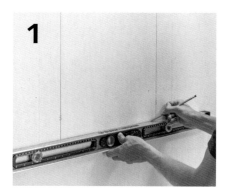

1

Locate the wall studs and mark them clearly on the wall surface. Draw a level line at the desired top height of the cabinet body, then measure and mark a second line to indicate the bottom of the cabinet.

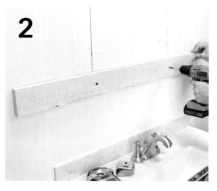

2

Attach a temporary ledger board (usually 1 × 4) just below the lower level line using duplex nails. Rest the base of the cabinet on the ledger and hold it in place or brace it with 2 × 4s.

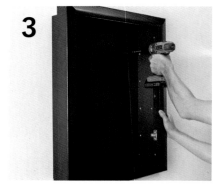

3

Attach the cabinet to the wall at the stud locations by drilling pilot holes and driving wood screws. Remove the ledger when finished, and patch the nail holes with drywall compound.

HOW TO INSTALL A RECESSED CABINET

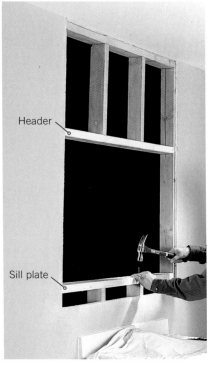

OPTION: Most recessed medicine cabinets sold today are sized in width to fit into the stud bay between standard studs that are 16" or 24" on center. If this lands the cabinet where you want it, you have a very easy job in front of you. But if you want the cabinet centered over a permanent furnishing, you may need to frame a new opening for the cabinet.

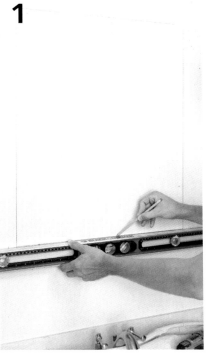

Use a stud finder to locate the wall-framing members and then draw an outline for the new cabinet, with the sides of the outline at the edges of the stud bay. (If you need to adjust the cabinet position or the cabinet you are installing is wider than the stud bay, see the option at left).

Shut off power at the main circuit panel in case there are any live wires in the stud cavity. Cut out the marked opening in the wall covering. A hand drywall saw will make neat work of this job.

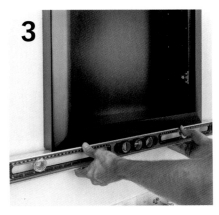

Remove the door/mirror from the cabinet and position the cabinet carcass in the opening. The opening should be slightly taller and wider than the cabinet. Set the height by resting the cabinet on a level and raising or lowering it. Tack the cabinet to a wall stud on one side with a nail driven through one of the screw access holes in the cabinet side.

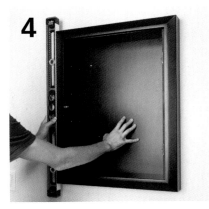

Move the level to the cabinet side and adjust the cabinet until it is plumb. Tack it to the wall stud on the side opposite the first nail.

Drive a 2" drywall screw through one of the screw access holes on each side of the cabinet. Do not overdrive. Double-check for level and plumb, then add additional screws on each side until the cabinet is secure. Reattach the door/mirror.

COUNTERTOPS: INSTALLING

Post-form laminate countertops are available in stock and custom colors. Pre-mitered sections are available for two- or three-piece countertops that continue around corners. If the countertop has an exposed end, you will need an endcap kit that contains a pre-shaped strip of matching laminate. Post-form countertops have either a waterfall edge or a no-drip edge. Stock colors are typically available in 4-, 6-, 8-, 10-, and 12-foot straight lengths and 6- and 8-foot mitered lengths.

Tools + Materials ▸

Tape measure
Framing square
Pencil
Straightedge
C-clamps
Hammer
Level
Caulking gun
Jigsaw with
    downstroke blade
Compass
Adjustable wrench
Belt sander
Drill and spade bit
Cordless screwdriver

Post-form countertop
Wood shims
Take-up bolts
Drywall screws
Wire brads
Endcap laminate
Silicone caulk
Wood glue
Household iron
Fasteners
Sealer
File
Eye protection
Work gloves

Post-form countertops are among the easiest and cheapest to install. They are a good choice for beginning DIYers, but the design and color options are fairly limited.

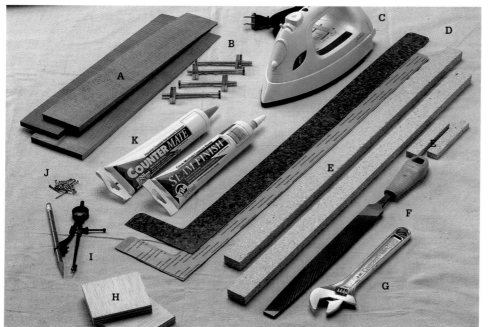

The following tools and materials will be used in this project: wood for shimming (A); take-up bolts for drawing miters together (B); household iron (C); endcap laminate to match countertop (D); endcap battens (E); file (F); adjustable wrench (G); buildup blocks (H); compass (I); fasteners (J); silicone caulk and sealer (K). You will also need a set of sturdy sawhorses (not pictured).

CABINETS + COUNTERS

HOW TO INSTALL A POST-FORM COUNTERTOP

OPTION: Use a jigsaw fitted with a downstroke blade to cut post-form. If you are unable to locate a downstroke blade, you can try applying tape over the cutting lines, but you are still likely to get tear-out from a normal upstroke jigsaw blade.

Use a framing square to mark a cutting line on the bottom surface of the countertop. Cut off the countertop with a jigsaw using a clamped straightedge as a guide.

Attach the battens from the endcap kit to the edge of the countertop using wood glue and small brads. Sand out any unevenness with a belt sander.

(continued)

4

Hold the endcap laminate against the end, slightly overlapping the edges. Activate adhesive by pressing an iron set at medium heat against the endcap. Cool with a wet cloth, then file the endcap laminate flush with the edges of the countertop.

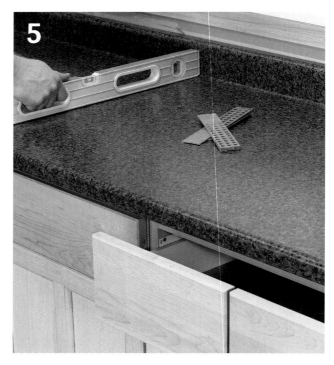

5

Position the countertop on the base cabinets. Make sure the front edge of the countertop is parallel to the cabinet faces. Check the countertop for level. Make sure that drawers and doors open and close freely. If needed, adjust the countertop with shims.

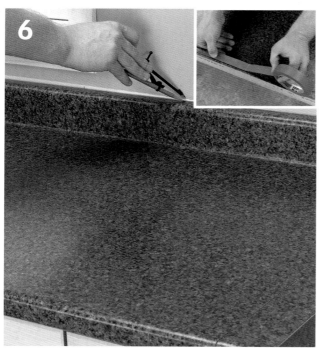

6

Because walls are usually uneven, use a compass to trace the wall outline onto the backsplash. Set the compass arms to match the widest gap, then move the compass along the length of the wall to transfer the outline to the top of the backsplash. Apply painter's tape to the top edge of the backsplash, following the scribe line (inset).

7

Remove the countertop. Use a belt sander to grind the backsplash to the scribe line. Work slowly and steadily to avoid oversanding any one spot.

Mark cutout for self-rimming sink.
Position the sink upside down on
the countertop and trace its outline.
Remove the sink and draw a cutting line
⅝" inside the sink outline.

Drill a starter hole just inside the
cutting line. Make sink cutouts with a
jigsaw. Support the cutout area from
below so that the falling cutout does
not damage the cabinet.

Apply a bead of silicone caulk to
the edges of the mitered countertop
sections. Force the countertop pieces
tightly together.

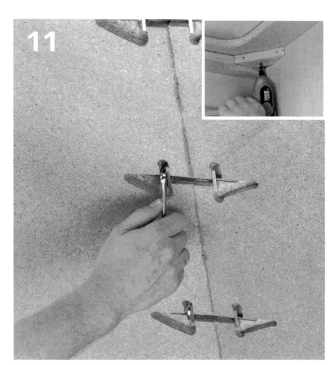

From underneath the countertop, install and tighten miter
take-up bolts. Position the countertop tightly against the wall
and fasten it to the cabinets by driving wallboard screws up
through the corner brackets and into the countertop (inset).
Screws should be long enough to provide maximum holding
power, but not long enough to puncture the laminate surface.

Seal the seam between the backsplash and the wall with
silicone caulk. Smooth the bead with a wet fingertip. Wipe
away excess caulk.

TILING: COUNTERTOP

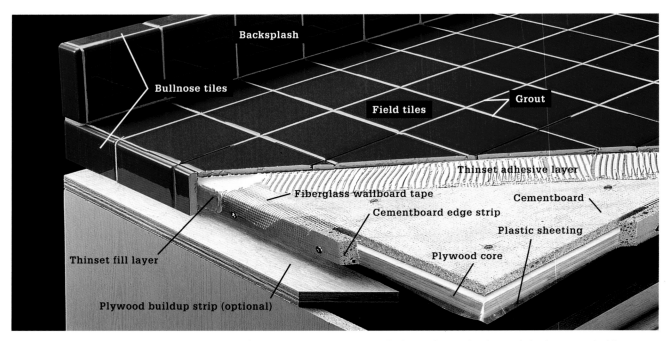

Backsplash

Bullnose tiles

Field tiles

Grout

Thinset adhesive layer

Fiberglass wallboard tape

Cementboard

Cementboard edge strip

Plastic sheeting

Thinset fill layer

Plywood core

Plywood buildup strip (optional)

A ceramic tile countertop made with wall or floor tile starts with a core of ¾" exterior-grade plywood that's covered with a moisture barrier of 4-mil polyethylene sheeting. Half-inch cementboard is screwed to the plywood, and the edges are capped with cementboard and finished with fiberglass mesh tape and thinset mortar. Tiles for edging and backsplashes may be bullnose or trimmed from the factory edges of field tiles.

OPTIONS FOR BACKSPLASHES + COUNTERTOP EDGES

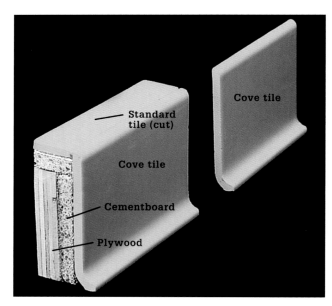

Standard tile (cut)

Cove tile

Cove tile

Cementboard

Plywood

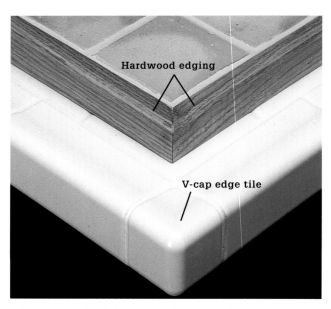

Hardwood edging

V-cap edge tile

Backsplashes can be made from cove tile attached to the wall at the back of the countertop. You can use the tile alone or build a shelf-type backsplash using the same construction as for the countertop. Attach the plywood backsplash to the plywood core of the countertop. Wrap the front face and all edges of the plywood backsplash with cementboard before laying tile.

Edge options include V-cap edge tile and hardwood strip edging. V-cap tiles have raised and rounded corners that create a ridge around the countertop perimeter—good for containing spills and water. V-cap tiles must be cut with a wet saw. Hardwood strips should be prefinished with at least three coats of polyurethane finish. Attach the strips to the plywood core so the top of the wood will be flush with the faces of the tiles.

HOW TO BUILD A TILE COUNTERTOP

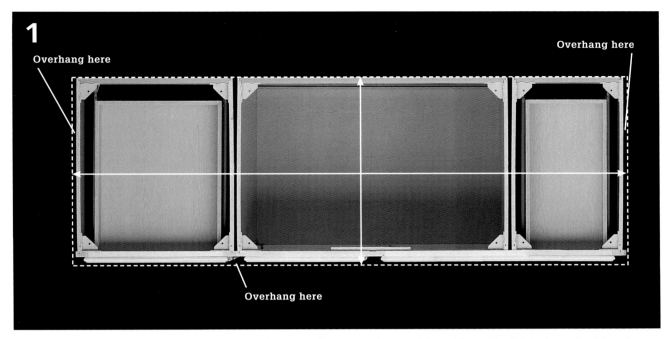

1

Overhang here

Overhang here

Overhang here

Determine the size of the plywood substrate by measuring across the top of the cabinets. The finished top should overhang the drawer fronts by at least ¼". Be sure to account for the thickness of the cementboard, adhesive, and tile when deciding how large to make the overhang. Cut the substrate to size from ¾" plywood using a circular saw. Also make any cutouts for sinks and other fixtures.

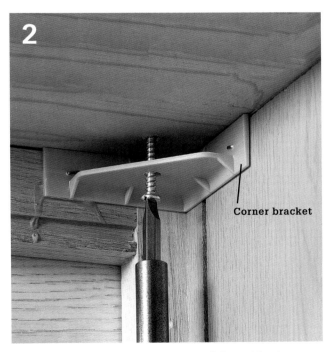

2

Corner bracket

Set the plywood substrate on top of the cabinets, and attach it with screws driven through the cabinet corner brackets. The screws should not be long enough to go through the top of the substrate.

3

Cut pieces of cementboard to size, then mark and make the cutout for the sink. Dry-fit them on the plywood core with the rough sides of the panels facing up. Leave a ⅛" gap between the cementboard sheets and a ¼" gap along the perimeter.

(continued)

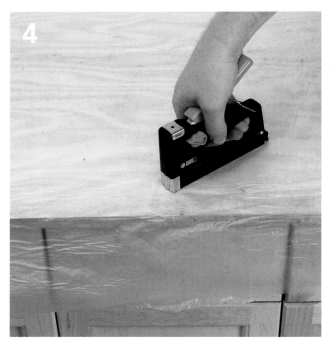

Lay the plastic moisture barrier over the plywood substrate, draping it over the edges. Tack it in place with a few staples. Overlap seams in the plastic by 6", and seal them with packing tape.

OPTION: Cut cementboard using a straightedge and utility knife or a cementboard cutter with a carbide tip. Hold the straightedge along the cutting line, and score the board several times with the knife. Bend the piece backward to break it along the scored line. Back-cut to finish.

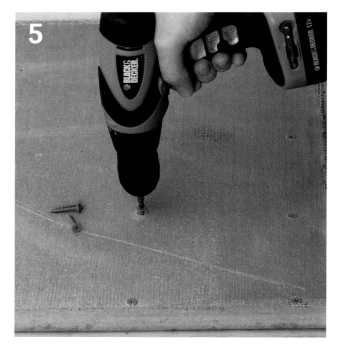

Lay the cementboard pieces rough-side up on top of the moisture barrier and attach them with cementboard screws driven every 6". Drill pilot holes using a masonry bit, and make sure all screw heads are flush with the surface. Wrap the countertop edges with 1¼"-wide cementboard strips, and attach them to the core with cementboard screws.

Tape all cementboard joints with fiberglass mesh tape. Apply three layers of tape along the front edge where the horizontal cementboard sheets meet the cementboard edging.

Fill all the gaps and cover all of the tape with a layer of thinset mortar. Feather out the mortar with a drywall knife to create a smooth, flat surface.

Determine the required width of the edge tiles. Lay a field tile onto the tile base so it overhangs the front edge by ½". Hold a metal ruler up to the underside of the tile and measure the distance from it to the bottom of the subbase. The edge tiles should be cut to this width (the gap for the grout line causes the edge tile to extend the subbase that conceals it completely).

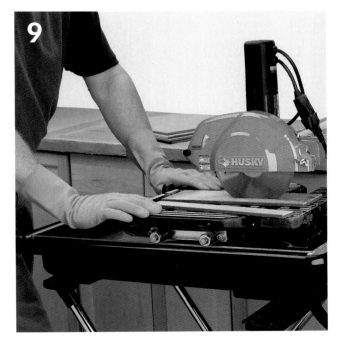

Cut edge tiles to the determined width using a wet saw. It's worth renting a quality wet saw for tile if you don't own one. Floor tile is thick and difficult to cut with a hand cutter (especially porcelain tiles).

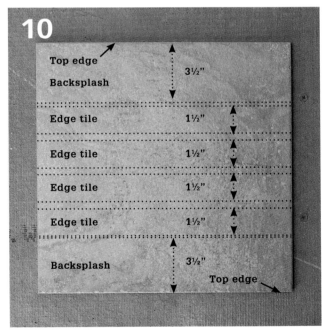

Cut tiles for the backsplash. The backsplash tiles (3½" wide in our project) should be cut with a factory edge on each tile that will be oriented upward when they're installed. You can make efficient use of your tiles by cutting edge tiles from the center area of the tiles you cut to make the backsplash.

(continued)

11

Sink cutout area

Dry-fit tiles on the countertop to find the layout that works best. Once the layout is established, make marks along the vertical and horizontal rows. Draw reference lines through the marks and use a framing square to make sure the lines are perpendicular.

Small Floor Tiles + Bullnose Edging ▶

Lay out tiles and spacers in a dry run. Adjust the starting lines, if necessary. If using battens, lay the field tile flush with the battens, then apply the edge tile. Otherwise, install the edging first. If the countertop has an inside corner, start there by installing a ready-made inside corner or by cutting a 45° miter in the edge tile to make your own inside corner.

Place the first row of field tile against the edge tile, separating the tile with spacers. Lay out the remaining rows of tile. Adjust the starting lines if necessary to create a layout using the smallest number of cut tiles.

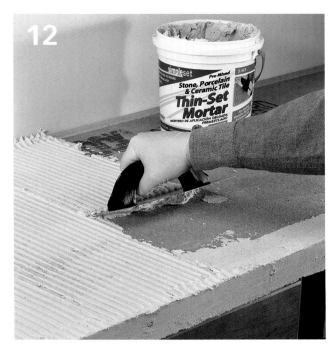

Use a ⅜" square notched trowel to apply a layer of thinset mortar to the cementboard. Apply enough for two or three tiles, starting at one end. Hold the trowel at roughly a 30° angle and try not to overwork the mortar or remove too much.

Set the first tile into the mortar. Hold a piece of the edge against the countertop edge as a guide to show you exactly how much the tile should overhang the edge.

Cut all the back tiles for the layout to fit (you'll need to remove about 1" of a 13 × 13" tile) before you begin the actual installation. Set the back tiles into the thinset, maintaining the gap for grout lines created by the small spacer nubs cast into the tiles. If your tiles have no spacer nubs, see the option.

OPTION: To maintain even grout lines, some beginning tilers insert plus-sign-shaped plastic spacers at the joints. This is less likely to be useful with large tiles like those shown here, but it is effective. Many tiles today feature built-in spacing lugs, so the spacers are of no use. Make sure to remove the spacers before the thinset sets. If you leave them in place they will corrupt your grout lines.

(continued)

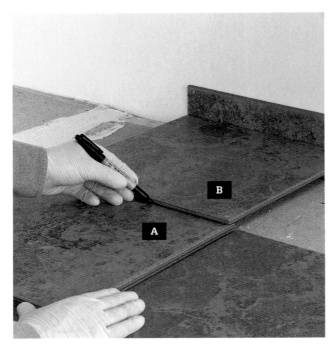

TIP: To mark border tiles for cutting, allow space for the backsplash tiles, grout, and mortar by placing a tile against the back wall. Set another tile (A) on top of the last full tile in the field, then place a third tile (B) over tile (A) and hold it against the upright tile. Mark and cut tile (A) and install it with the cut edge toward the wall. Finish filling in your field tiles.

To create a support ledge for the edge tiles, prop pieces of 2 × 4 underneath the front edge of the substrate overhang using wood scraps to prop the ledge tightly up against the substrate.

Apply a thick layer of thinset to the backside of the edge tile with your trowel. This is called "buttering" and it is easier and neater than attempting to trowel adhesive onto the countertop edge. Press the tiles into position so they are flush with the leading edges of the field tiles.

Butter each backsplash tile and press it into place, doing your best to keep all of the grout lines aligned. Allow the mortar to set according to the manufacturer's recommendations.

18

Mix a batch of grout to complement the tile (keeping in mind that darker grout won't look dirty as quickly as lighter grout). Apply the grout with a grout float.

19

Let the grout dry until a light film is created on the countertop surface, then wipe the excess grout off with a sponge and warm, clean water. See the grout manufacturer's instructions on drying tiles and polishing.

20

Run a bead of clear silicone caulk along the joint between the backsplash and the wall. Install your sink and faucet after the grout has dried.

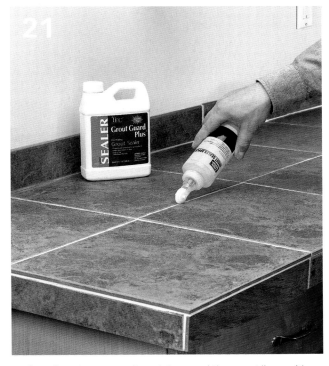

21

Wait at least one week and then seal the grout lines with a penetrating grout sealer. This is important to do. Sealing the tiles themselves is not a good idea unless you are using unglazed tiles (a poor choice for countertops, however).

RECYCLED PAPER COUNTERTOP

If you're on the hunt for a handsome, distinctive, durable, and eco-friendly countertop, you're not likely to do better than a recycled paper surface. Countertops like the PaperStone® product used in this project are 100 percent post-consumer recycled paper, emitting no volatile organic compounds (VOCs) and certified "food safe" by the National Safety Foundation (NSF).

You might not think that paper would make for effective countertop surface—especially in water-prone rooms such as kitchens and bathrooms. But fortunately, you'd be wrong. This material is non-porous and stain resistant. It can withstand heat up to 350°F (although many finishes used to seal the surface cannot), and scratches can be buffed or sanded out.

There are a few restrictions with this type of countertop. You should never use a bleach cleanser, and although cuts can be buffed out, it's best to use a cutting board rather than cutting directly on the countertop. You should also be aware that the counter comes in different thicknesses—we've used the thickest version here to show the fabrication and installation steps more clearly; a thinner panel (with a built-up edge) would be easier for the home DIYer to work with.

Tools + Materials ▸

Circular saw with fine-tooth carbide blade
Biscuit joiner
Router with carbide bits
Hole saw (1³⁄₈")
Jigsaw
Take-up bolts
Measuring tape
Drill and bits
Carpenter's level
Caulk gun
Painter's tape
2-part epoxy
Silicone adhesive
Silicone caulk
Orbital sander with an assortment of grits (80 to 240)
Maroon nonwoven pads
Straight edge and radius guides
Recycled paper countertop panels
Sink/stove templates (included with sink/stove or available online)
Speed square
Bar clamps
Acetone
Dust mask
Eye protection
Heavy-duty, rubber grip work gloves

HOW TO INSTALL A RECYCLED PAPER COUNTERTOP

Check that the cabinets are secure and level. Fabricate the template for the countertop using cardboard. Set the cardboard on top of the base cabinets and trace the outline on the underside. Note overhangs, appropriate anchor screw locations, and other features. Scribe the template to the wall on the backside (the fit can be less accurate if you are installing a backsplash).

Position the template over the panel and clamp it in place. Trace the template outline on the panel top face, and mark the position of fixtures such as sinks. We used a silver marker on this product, which can be removed later with acetone.

Remove the cardboard and position any sink, faucet, and fixture templates on the panel. Trace outlines for fixtures, checking the number and diameter of faucet holes (normally 1" diameter). Recheck all measurements against the master drawing, before cutting the panel.

Cut the material to length using a circular saw equipped with an 80- to 100-tooth, triple-chip carbide blade. Cut approximately 1/8" outside of the marked line. Also use the circular saw to make straight portions of the sink cutout (for the sink, cut 1/8" inside the cutting line).

Use a jigsaw and fine-tooth carbide blade to make curved cuts. Drill faucet holes with a hole saw. Use a router with a guide to make clean-up cuts precisely to the traced line. Use a radius guide with the router on inside radius corners. Use an random orbit sander to smooth out the cuts, sanding up to the cutting line as needed.

Test-fit the countertop on the cabinet bases and check for appropriate and correct alignment. Specifically, check that all cutouts are in the correct positions, that any overhangs are consistent, and that the surface is level across its span.

Rout exposed countertop edges to the preferred profile, using the appropriate router bit and a guide. Move the router steadily along the edge and avoid sitting too long at any one spot, which can lead to burn marks.

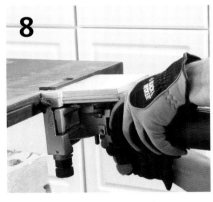

Dry-fit the countertop sections to ensure a tight fit. To help with alignment, mark and cut matching biscuit slots in the edge of each countertop, using a biscuit joiner.

Turn the countertops over and mark T channels for the take-up bolts. Rout the channels using a plunge router set to a depth half of the panel's thickness. Set the biscuits in the slots, coat the countertop seam edges with the adhesive recommended by the manufacturer (normally a two-part epoxy), and secure the countertops tightly with bar clamps. Install the take-up bolts.

Install an undermount sink before installing the counter. (Drop-in sinks are installed after.) Mark the edges of the sink and the edges of the sink cutout with centerline marks. With the countertop upside down, align the sink over the opening mark for the mounting screw guide holes.

Drill guide holes for the sleeves that will hold the sink-mounting clips. Insert the sleeves into the holes.

Apply a bead of silicone caulk to the sink flange. Set the sink into position in the underside of the countertop. Install the sink clips to secure the sink in place.

(continued)

Remove all clamps. With several helpers, carefully invert the countertop so it is rightside-up. Apply beads of silicone caulk to the tops of the cabinets and then lower the countertop in place.

Locate the anchor screw locations on the cabinet top frames and drill pilot holes using a carbide bit and a drill stop. Secure the countertop in place with screws driven into the pilot holes. Tap the sink if needed to adjust its position, and then finish tightening the mounting screws. Wipe away any squeeze out or excess adhesive from around the sink, underside edges of the counter, and along any seams.

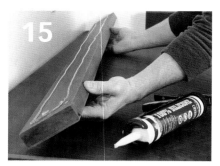

Measure, mark, and cut the backsplash sections from the leftover panel segments. (Sections should be joined with 90° butt seams.) Test-fit the backsplash sections in place. Lay a thin bead of silicone adhesive on the back and bottom of the backsplash sections. Carefully press the backsplash pieces into place and wipe away any squeezeout or excess adhesive. Allow the adhesive to cure according to the manufacturer's directions.

TILING: BACKSPLASH

There are few spaces in your home with as much potential for creativity and visual impact as the space between your kitchen countertop and your cupboards. A well-designed backsplash can transform the ordinary into the extraordinary. Tiles for the backsplash can be attached directly to wallboard or plaster and do not require backerboard. When purchasing the tile, order 10 percent extra to cover breakage and cutting. Remove the switch and receptacle coverplates and install box extenders to make up for the extra thickness of the tile. Protect the countertop from scratches by covering it with a drop cloth during the installation.

Contemporary glass mosaic sheets create a counter-to-cabinet backsplash for a waterproof, splash-proof wall with high visual impact.

Tools + Materials ▸

Level	Mastic adhesive
Tape measure	Masking tape
Pencil	Grout
Tile cutter	Caulk
Notched trowel	Drop cloth
Rubber grout float	Caulk gun
Rubber mallet	Scrap 2 × 4
Sponge	Carpet scrap
Story stick	Buff cloth
Tile spacers (if needed)	Eye protection
Wall tile	Work gloves

Break tiles into fragments and make a mosaic backsplash. Always use sanded grout for joints wider than ⅛".

HOW TO INSTALL A TILE BACKSPLASH

Make a story stick by marking a board at least half as long as the backsplash area to match the tile spacing. Story sticks are used to accurately transfer measurements from one surface to another.

Starting at the midpoint of the installation area, use the story stick to make layout marks along the wall. If an end piece is too small (less than half a tile), adjust the midpoint to give you larger, more attractive end pieces. Use a level to mark this point with a vertical reference line.

While it may appear straight, your countertop may not be level and therefore is not a reliable reference line. Run a level along the counter to find the lowest point on the countertop. Mark a point two tiles up from the low point and extend a level line across the entire work area.

VARIATION: Diagonal Layout. Mark vertical and horizontal reference lines, making sure the angle is 90°. To establish diagonal layout lines, measure out equal distances from the crosspoint, and then connect the points with a line. Additional layout lines can be extended from these as needed.

(continued)

4

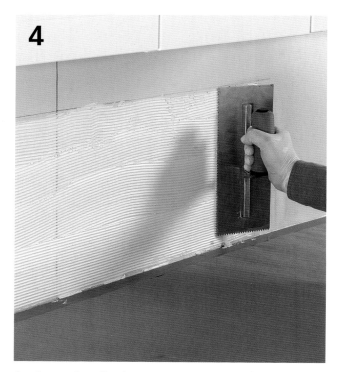

Apply mastic adhesive evenly to the area beneath the horizontal reference line using a notched trowel. Comb the adhesive horizontally with the notched edge.

5

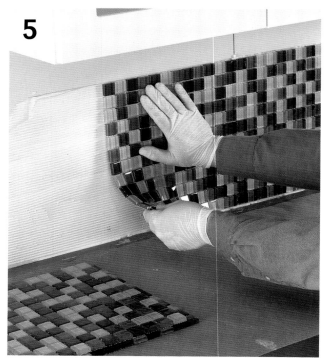

Press tiles into the adhesive with a slight twisting motion. If the tiles are not self-spacing, use plastic spacers to maintain even grout lines. If the tiles do not hang in place, use masking tape to hold them in place until the adhesive sets.

6

Install a whole row along the reference line, checking occasionally to make sure the tiles are level. Continue installing tiles below the first row, trimming tiles that butt against the countertop as needed.

7

Install an edge border if it is needed in your layout. Mosaic sheets normally do not have bullnose tiles on the edges, so if you don't wish to see the cut edges of the outer tiles, install a vertical column of edge tiles at the end of the backsplash area.

When the tiles are in place, make sure they are flat and firmly embedded by laying a beating block against the tile and rapping it lightly with a mallet. Remove the spacers. Allow the mastic to dry for at least 24 hours, or as directed by the manufacturer.

Mix the grout and apply it with a rubber grout float. Spread it over the tiles, keeping the float at a low 30° angle, pressing the grout deep into the joints. *NOTE: For grout joints ⅛" and smaller, use a nonsanded grout.*

Wipe off excess grout, holding the float at a right angle to the tile, working diagonally so as not to remove grout from the joints.

Clean excess grout with a damp sponge. When the grout has dried to a haze, buff the tile clean with a soft cloth. Apply a bead of caulk between the countertop and the tiles.

DROP-IN SINK

Most drop-in, self-rimming kitchen sinks are easy to install. Drop-in sinks for do-it-yourself installation are made from cast iron coated with enamel, stainless steel, enameled steel, acrylic, fiberglass, or resin composites. Because cast-iron sinks are heavy, their weight holds them in place, and they require no mounting hardware.

Stainless steel and enameled-steel sinks weigh less than cast-iron, and most require mounting brackets on the underside of the countertop. Some acrylic and resin sinks rely on silicone caulk to hold them in place. If you are replacing a sink, but not the countertop, make sure the new sink is the same size or larger than the old sink. All old silicone caulk residue must be removed with acetone or denatured alcohol, or the new caulk will not stick.

Shopping Tips ▸

- When purchasing a sink, you also need to buy strainer bodies and baskets, sink clips, and a drain trap kit.
- Look for basin dividers that are lower than the sink rim—this reduces splashing.
- Drain holes in the back or to the side make for more usable space under the sink.
- When choosing a sink, make sure the predrilled openings will fit your faucet.

Tools + Materials ▸

Caulk gun	Drill and bits
Spud wrench	Mounting clips
Screwdriver	Jigsaw
Sink	Pen or pencil
Sink frame	Wrench
Plumber's putty or	Eye protection
silicone caulk	Work gloves

Drop-in sinks, also known as self-rimming sinks, have a wide sink flange that extends beyond the edges of the sink cutout. They have a wide back flange to which the faucet is mounted directly.

HOW TO INSTALL A SELF-RIMMING SINK

Invert the sink and trace around the edges as a reference for making the sink cutout cutting lines, which should be parallel to the outlines, but about 1" inside of them to create a 1" ledge. If the sink comes with a template for the cutout, use it.

Drill a starter hole and cut out the sink opening with a jigsaw. Cut right up to the line. Because the sink flange fits over the edges of the cutout, the opening doesn't need to be perfect, but, as always, you should try to do a nice, neat job.

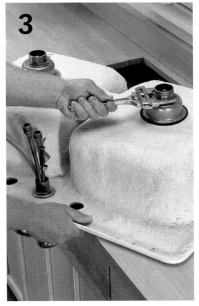

Attach as much of the plumbing as makes sense to install prior to setting the sink into the opening. Having access to the underside of the flange is a great help when it comes to attaching the faucet body, sprayer, and strainer, in particular.

Apply a bead of silicone caulk around the edges of the sink opening. The sink flange most likely is not flat, so apply the caulk in the area that will make contact with the flange.

Place the sink in the opening. Try to get the sink centered right away so you don't need to move it around and disturb the caulk, which can break the seal. If you are installing a heavy cast-iron sink, it's best to leave the strainers off so you can grab onto the sink at the drain openings.

For sinks with mounting clips, tighten the clips from below using a screwdriver or wrench (depending on the type of clip your sink has). There should be at least three clips on every side. Don't overtighten the clips—this can cause the sink flange to flatten or become warped.

APRON SINK

Despite their vintage look, apron sinks are relative newcomers in modern kitchen design. Also known as farmer's sinks or farmhouse sinks, they are notable for having an exposed front apron that usually projects past the cabinets. Although they can be double-bowl fixtures, most apron sinks are single bowl, and most are made from fireclay (a durable enameled porcelain). Other materials sometimes used for apron sinks include enameled cast iron, copper, stainless steel, and composite. The model seen here, made by Kohler, is a fireclay sink.

Apron sinks typically are not suspended from above as other undermount sinks are: they're just too heavy. Instead, you either attach wood ledgers to the cabinet sides to support a board that bears the sink from below, or you build a support platform that rests on the floor. Either way, the sink is not actually connected to the countertop except with caulk at the seams. As kitchen sinks go, apron sinks are definitely on the high-end side, with most models costing over $1,000. But they create a focal point that makes them rather unique. Plus, they have a warm, comforting appearance that people who own them find appealing.

Apron sinks, also called farmer's sinks or farmhouse sinks, can be nestled into a tiled countertop (called a tile-in) or pressed up against the underside of a solid countertop. Either way, they can be gorgeous.

Tools + Materials ▸

Countertop material	Level	Various screws	Silicone adhesive
Shims	Belt sander	Wood finish	Strainer
Carpenter's square	Pad sander	Brush	Drain tailpiece
Straightedge	Spindle sander	Framing lumber	¾" plywood or MDF
Jigsaw	Router or laminate trimmer	Sheet stock	Eye and ear protection
Tape measure	Drill/driver	Caulk gun	Work gloves

HOW TO INSTALL AN APRON SINK IN A BUTCHER BLOCK COUNTERTOP

1

If you are undermounting the sink, outline the sink opening in your countertop material. Plan the opening to create an equal reveal of approximately ½" on all three sides (which basically means making the opening 1" smaller than the overall sink dimensions). For the 22 × 25" sink seen here, the opening cut into the butcher block is 24" wide and 21" deep (½" reveal in the back plus ½" projection of the sink in front).

Mount a downstroke blade in a jigsaw (read up on working with butcherblock if that is your countertop surface). Cut out the waste to form the sink opening, cutting just inside the cutting lines. Support the waste wood from below so it does not break out prematurely.

Sand up to the cutting lines with a belt sander after the waste is removed. The goal is to create a smooth, even edge. Use steady, even pressure and work slowly to avoid oversanding and creating a noticeable indent.

Sand into the corners of the cutout with a detail sander or, if you own one, a spindle sander (you can mount a small-diameter sanding drum bit in an electric drill, but be sure to practice first on some scrap wood).

Flip the countertop and sand the cutout along the bottom edges of the opening to prevent any splintering.

Round over the top edges of the cutout with a piloted roundover bit mounted in a small router or a laminate trimmer.

(continued)

Apply several coats of urethane varnish to the exposed wood around the opening. This wood will have a high level of water exposure, so take care to get a good, even coat. Where possible, match the finish of the countertop (if any).

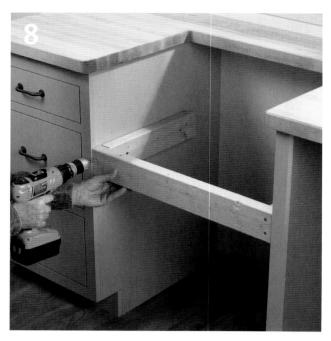

Measure and draw layout lines for a wood support frame to be attached to the adjoining cabinet walls. Attach the frame members (2 × 4) to the cabinet sides first and then face-screw through the front frame member and into the ends of side members.

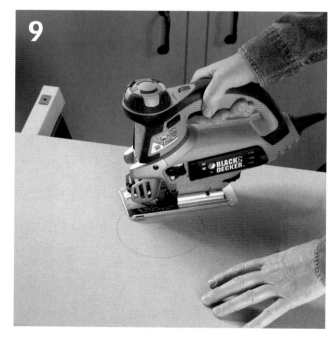

Cut a support platform to size from ¾" plywood or MDF, then layout and cut a drain clearance hole (if your drain will include a garbage disposer, make the hole large enough to accommodate the disposer easily). Also cut holes for the water supply lines if they come up through the floor and there is not enough room between the platform and the wall for the lines to fit.

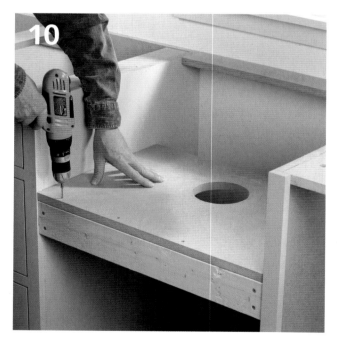

Remove the countertop section containing the sink cutout, if feasible (if you can't remove the countertop, see sidebar next page). Then, screw the platform to the frame.

Set the sink on the platform and confirm that it is level with the cabinet tops by setting a straightedge so it spans the sink opening. If necessary, shim under the sink to bring it to level (if the sink is too high you'll need to reposition the frame members).

Apply silicone adhesive to the sink rim and then carefully replace the countertop section before the silicone adhesive sets up. Reattach the countertop.

Hook up the drain plumbing and install the faucet. If you are drilling through the countertop material to install a faucet, make sure your installation hole or holes align with the preformed holes in the back flange of the sink.

Option for Unremovable Countertops ▸

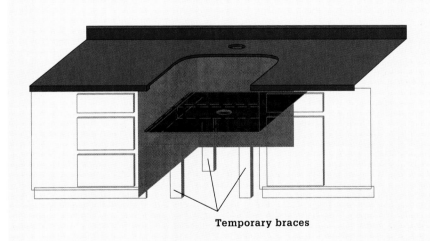

Temporary braces

If you are not able to remove the countertop, you'll need to raise the sink up against the underside of the countertop once you've caulked the rim. Create a 3-piece 2 × 4 frame and platform (as seen in step 8) but do not attach it to the cabinets. Instead, support the platform with braces. With help, set the sink on the platform and raise it from below after the silicone adhesive has been applied to the sink rim. When the sink rim is tight against the countertop, attach the frame members to the cabinet sides with screws.

RADIATORS: DRAINING

Hot water and steam systems, also known as hydronic systems, feature a boiler that heats water and circulates it through a closed network of pipes to a set of radiators or convectors. Because water expands and contracts as it heats and cools, these systems include expansion tanks to ensure a constant volume of water circulating through the pipes.

Hot water and steam systems warm the surrounding air through a process called convection. Hot water radiators (photo 1) are linked to the system by pipes connected near the bottom of the radiator. As water cools inside the radiator, it is drawn back to the boiler for reheating. The radiators in steam systems (photo 2) have pipes connected near the top of the radiator. These radiators can be very hot to the touch. Convectors (photo 3) are smaller and lighter and may be used to replace hot water radiators, or to extend an existing hot water system.

Although the delivery of hot water or steam to the rooms in your house is considered a closed system, some air will make its way into the system. Steam radiators have an automatic release valve that periodically releases hot, moist air. Hot water radiators contain a bleed valve that must periodically be opened to release trapped air. It is usually necessary to bleed convector systems using a valve near the boiler.

Today's hot water and steam systems are often fueled by natural gas. Older systems may use fuel oil. Fuel oil systems require more frequent maintenance of the filter and blower.

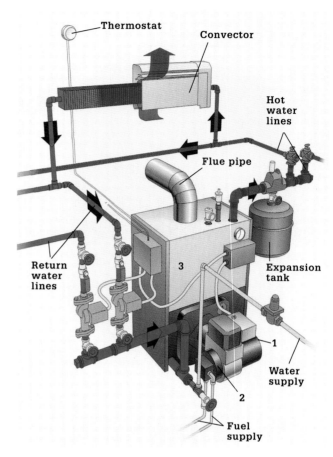

A blower draws in air through the air intake (1) while a fuel pump (2) maintains a constant supply of fuel oil. The mixture is ignited by a high-voltage spark as it enters the combustion chamber (3) and heats water.

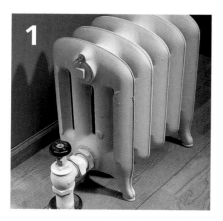

Hot water radiators circulate heated water through pipes. As it cools, water is drawn back to the boiler for reheating.

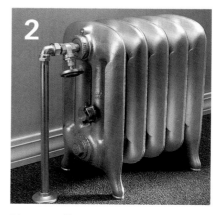

Steam radiators operate at a higher temperature. Steam cools in the radiators, returns to a liquid state, and then flows back to the boiler.

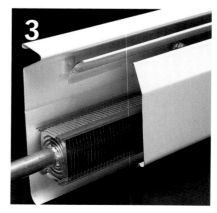

Space-saving hot water convectors work on the same principle as radiators, but use thin sheet-metal fins to transfer heat to the air.

DRAINING + FILLING A SYSTEM

Sediment gradually accumulates in any water-based system, reducing the system's efficiency and damaging internal parts. Draining the boiler every season reduces the accumulation of sediment. Be aware that draining the system can take a long time, and the water often has an unpleasant odor. This doesn't indicate a problem. Drain the system during warm weather, and open the windows and run a fan to reduce any odor.

Start by shutting off the boiler and allowing the hot system to cool. Attach a garden hose to the drain at the bottom of the boiler, and place the other end in a floor drain or utility sink. Open a bleed valve on the highest radiator in the house.

When water stops draining, open a bleed valve on a radiator closer to the boiler. When the flow stops, locate the valve or gauge on top of the boiler, and remove it with a wrench.

Make sure the system is cool before you add water. Close the drain valve on the boiler. Insert a funnel into the gauge fitting and add rust inhibitor, available from heating supply dealer. Check the container for special instructions. Reinstall the valve or gauge in the top of the boiler, close all radiator bleed valves, and slowly reopen the water supply to the boiler.

When the water pressure gauge reads 5 psi, bleed the air from the radiators on the first floor, then do the same on the upper floors. Let the boiler reach 20 psi before you turn the power on. Allow 12 hours for water to circulate fully, then bleed the radiators again.

Tools + Materials ▸

Open-end wrench set	Drop cloth
Pipe wrenches	Boiler rust inhibitor
Garden hose	Eye protection
Funnel	Heavy-duty, heat-
Plastic bucket	resistant work gloves

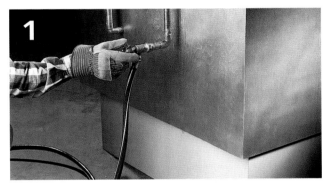

Use a garden hose to drain water from the boiler. Keep the drain end of the hose lower than the drain cock on the boiler.

If the valve or gauge on top of the boiler is attached to a separate fitting, hold the fitting still with one wrench while removing the valve or gauge with another.

Using a funnel, add a recommended rust inhibitor to the boiler through the valve or gauge fitting.

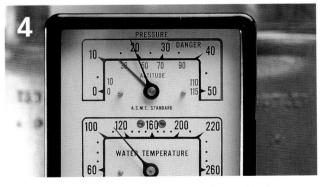

The boiler should reach a pressure of 20 psi before you turn the power back on.

RADIATORS: HOT WATER HEATING SYSTEMS

Hot water systems operate more quietly and efficiently if you bleed them of trapped air once a year. To bleed a hot water system, the boiler must be on. Start with the radiator that's highest in the house and farthest from the boiler. Place a cloth under the bleed valve, and open the valve slowly.

Close it as soon as water squirts out. Some bleed valves have knobs that open with a half turn; others must be opened with a screwdriver or valve key, available at hardware stores.

Steam radiators have automatic bleed valves. To clear a clogged valve, close the shutoff at the radiator and let the unit cool. Unscrew the bleed valve and clear the orifice with a fine wire or needle .

Older hot water convector systems may have bleed valves on or near the convectors. Bleed these convectors as you would radiators.

Most convector systems today don't have bleed valves. For these, locate the hose bib where the return water line reaches the boiler. Close the gate valve between the bib and the boiler. Attach a short section of hose to the bib and immerse the other end in a bucket of water. Open the bib while adding water to the boiler by opening the supply valve. The supply valve is located on the supply pipe, usually the smallest pipe in the system. Flush the system until no air bubbles come out of the hose in the bucket. Open the gate valve to bleed any remaining air. Close the hose bib before restarting the boiler.

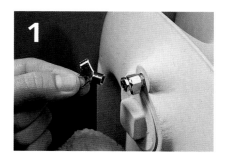

If you can't find a key for your radiators, a local hardware store or home center may have a replacement.

If the radiator isn't heating, clear the orifice with a fine wire or needle.

A convector-based heating system is usually bled at the boiler by holding a hose underwater and flushing the system until there are no more air bubbles coming from the hose.

Replace Radiator Control Valves ▸

A radiator control valve that won't operate should be replaced. You'll first need to drain the system. Then use a pipe wrench to disconnect the nut on the outlet side of the valve, then disconnect the valve body from the supply pipe. Thread the tailpiece of the new valve into the radiator. Thread the valve body onto the supply pipe. Make sure the arrow on the valve body points in the direction of the water flow. Thread the connecting nut on the tailpiece onto the outlet side of the valve. When you recharge the system, open the bleed valve on the radiator until a trickle of water runs out.

Use a pipe wrench to remove the control valve (left). Thread the tailpiece of the new valve into the radiator (right).

Fasten the valve to the supply tube, then secure the connecting nut on the tailpiece to the valve.

MAINTAINING THE BLOWER MOTOR

Inspect the blower motor before the start of the heating season. Inspect it again before the start of the cooling season if your central air conditioning uses the same blower.

Turn off the power to the furnace. Remove the access panel to the blower housing and inspect the motor. Some motors have oil ports and an adjustable, replaceable drive belt. Others are self-lubricating and have a direct-drive mechanism. Wipe the motor clean with a damp cloth and check for oil fill ports. The access panel may include a diagram indicating their location. Remove the covers to the ports (if equipped) and add a few drops of light machine oil. Place the covers on the ports.

With the power still off, inspect the drive belt. If it is cracked, worn, glazed, or brittle, replace it. Check the belt tension by pushing down gently midway between the pulleys. The belt should flex about 1". To tighten or loosen the belt, locate the pulley tension adjustment nut on the blower motor. Loosen the locknut, and turn the adjustment nut slightly. Check the belt tension, and readjust as required until the tension is correct.

If the belt is out of alignment or the bearings are worn, adjusting the tension will not solve the problem. With the power off, hold a straightedge so it's flush with the edge of both pulleys. To align the belt, locate the mounting bolts on the motor's sliding bracket. Loosen the bolts, and move the motor carefully until the pulleys are aligned. Tighten the bolts and check the tension and alignment again. Repeat until the pulley is aligned and the tension adjusted. Replace the furnace access panels. Restore power and switch on the furnace.

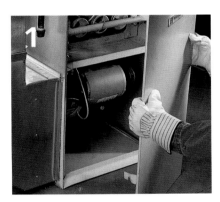

Remove the access panel to the blower housing and inspect the motor.

Remove the covers to the oil ports and add a few drops to each port.

Check the tension by pushing down on the middle of the belt.

Loosen the pulley tension adjustment nut slightly to tighten the belt.

Check the pulley alignment, using a straightedge.

Loosen the bolts that hold the motor on its sliding bracket, and move the motor carefully until the pulleys are aligned.

INSPECTING THE PILOT + THERMOCOUPLE

The pilot light (it's actually a flame used to ignite gas flowing through the burners) plays a large role in the efficiency of the entire system, and a clean-burning pilot saves money, improves indoor air quality, and extends furnace life.

If your furnace has a standing pilot light, always check the flame before the start of the heating season to ensure that it's burning cleanly and with the proper mix of air and fuel. Start by removing the main furnace access panel. If you can't see the pilot flame clearly, turn off the gas supply and the pilot gas shutoff switch (if equipped). Wait 10 minutes for the pilot to cool, and remove the pilot cover. Relight the pilot, following the instructions on the control housing or access cover. If the pilot won't stay lit, shut off the gas supply once again and inspect the thermocouple.

Inspect the flame. If the flame is too weak (left photo), it will be blue and may barely touch the thermocouple. If the flame is too strong (center photo), it will also be blue, but may be noisy and lift off the pilot. A well-adjusted flame (right photo) will be blue with a yellow tip, and cover ½" at the end of the thermocouple. Turn the pilot adjustment screw on the control housing or gas valve to reduce the pressure. If it's weak, turn the screw in the other direction to increase the pressure. If the flame appears weak and yellow even after adjustment, remove the pilot jet and clean the orifice.

If the pilot in your furnace or boiler goes out quickly, and you have made sure the gas supply is sufficient, you may need to replace the thermocouple. Turn off the gas supply. Using an open-end wrench, loosen the thermocouple tube fitting from the control housing or gas valve. Unscrew the thermocouple from the pilot housing and install a new one. Tighten it with a wrench just until it's snug.

Turn off the main gas supply and the pilot gas supply (if your furnace has a separate one).

Adjust the flame so it is steady, has a yellow tip, and covers the thermocouple's tip (right).

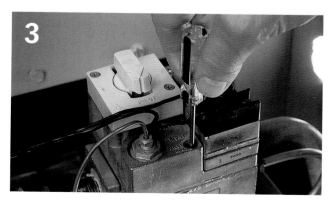

Turn the screw to adjust the height of the flame so it covers the top of the thermocouple.

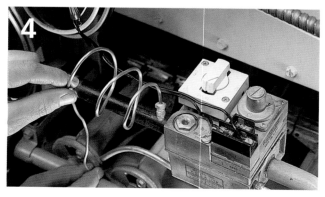

Remove the thermocouple from the control housing and install a new one.

HVAC + APPLIANCES

CLEANING THE BURNERS

Burners work by mixing together gas and air that is then ignited by a pilot flame or a heated element. Gas is delivered by a manifold and enters each burner tube through a small orifice, known as a spud. Burners and spuds gradually become encrusted with soot and other products of the combustion process and must be cleaned occasionally to keep them working efficiently.

To clean the burners, turn off the furnace's main shutoff, and switch off the power to the furnace at the main service panel. Shut off the gas supply, including the pilot gas supply if your unit has a separate one. Wait at least 30 minutes for the parts to cool. Remove the burner tubes by unscrewing them from their retaining brackets, by pulling out the metal pan that holds them, or by loosening the screws that attach the gas manifold to the furnace. On some furnaces, you need to remove the pilot housing to reach the burners.

Twist each burner carefully to remove it from its spud. Fill a laundry tub with water and soak the burners. Carefully clean the outside of the burner tubes and the burner ports with a soft-bristled brush. Replace any tubes that are cracked, bent, or severely corroded.

Inspect the spuds: clean burners won't work effectively if the spuds are dirty or damaged. Use a ratchet wrench to loosen and remove each spud. Clean the outside of each spud with a soft-bristled brush. Then, use a pilot jet tool to clean the inside of each spud. The tool is designed for cleaning small orifices, but take special care to avoid scratching or enlarging a spud's opening. Reinstall the spuds in the manifold. Tighten them just until they're snug. Once the burner tubes are dry, install them on the spuds, and attach them to the burner tube brackets or burner pan. Connect the pilot housing, if equipped. Turn the power and gas supply back on. On furnaces with a standing pilot, relight the pilot flame.

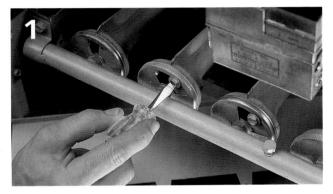

Remove the screws holding the burners to their brackets or to a slide-out pan.

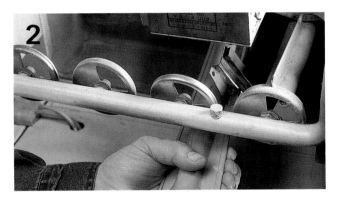

If a burner is difficult to remove, twist it carefully from side to side while lifting and pulling.

To avoid bending or damaging the spud threads, hold the manifold steady with one hand as you remove each spud.

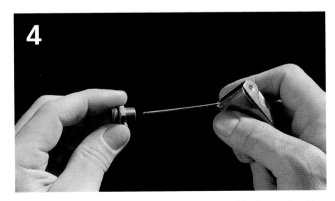

Clean each spud orifice carefully with a pilot jet tool, taking care not to scratch or enlarge the orifice.

SERVICING ELECTRONIC IGNITION FURNACES

Newer furnaces include an intermittent pilot light or hot-surface igniter as well as an electronic control center, with warning lights to help you recognize problems.

On some newer models, the temperature difference between the supply and return ducts needs to be within a narrow range to avoid damaging the heat exchanger. To find out whether this applies to your furnace, check the information plate on the burner compartment—it may include an indication of the acceptable range.

Each season, check the differential by slipping the probe of a pocket thermometer into a slit in an expansion joint in the supply duct. Record the reading and compare it with the temperature in the return air duct. Call a professional technician if the difference between the two numbers falls outside the recommended range.

Your furnace may contain an intermittent pilot, which is lit with a spark when signaled by the thermostat. An intermittent pilot consumes gas only when necessary, reducing home fuel costs. If the electronic ignition fails to spark, call a technician for service.

Some furnace models ignite the gas with a glowing element, known as a hot-surface igniter. If the igniter fails, replace it. Remove the main furnace panel and locate the igniter just beyond the ignition end of the burner tubes. Disconnect the igniter plug and remove the nut on the mounting bracket with a nut driver or ratchet wrench. Replace the igniter.

If the igniter still doesn't function properly, check with the manufacturer: you may need to replace the control center. Detach the wires from the old control center one at a time and attach them to the replacement. Then, disconnect the old control center, using a screwdriver, and connect the new one.

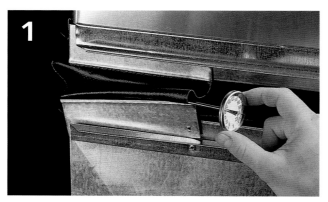

Check the temperature inside the supply duct and compare it with the temperature in the return duct.

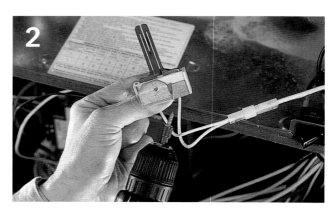

Disconnect the faulty hot-surface igniter from the mounting bracket.

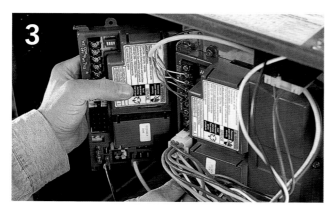

Remove the control center wires one at a time and switch them over to the new control center.

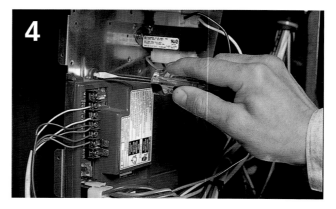

Unscrew the control center's mounting screws and install the replacement unit.

MAINTAINING A HIGH-EFFICIENCY GAS FURNACE

A high-efficiency gas furnace is defined as a furnace that's at least 90% "efficient," as determined by an annual fuel utilization efficiency (AFUE) rating.

Furnaces made as late as 1992 can have ratings as low as 60%. A standard, mid-efficient unit sold today is about 80%, while high-efficiency units can be as high as 96% efficient.

Like other furnaces, high-efficiency gas furnaces require maintenance. The air filters must be cleaned regularly—electronic filters need to be cleaned on a monthly basis, and disposable filters should be changed every three months.

If the drain line cannot drain properly, moisture can build up inside the heat exchanger and restrict gas flow. Inspect the drain line to make sure it's free of kinks. Some furnaces have several drain connections that should be inspected.

Clean the drain line once a year by disconnecting it from the furnace and forcing water from a garden hose through the line. If the drain line is black plastic, remove it at a connection point, then reattach once it's clean. If the line is white, then it's PVC, and you'll need to reconnect it to the unit with a coupling after cleaning.

Some furnaces have a removable condensate trap. If your unit has one, remove it at the beginning of the winter season and clean it out with water. Check the trap periodically throughout the season and dump the water as necessary.

Check the vent pipes and furnace unit for signs of corrosion. The water produced by the furnace is acidic and will corrode metal quickly. If pipes are leaking, they must be replaced.

Make sure the areas around the air intake and exhaust are unobstructed. Plants and other materials that block the intake and exhaust can cause the furnace to shut down.

Clean electronic filters every month, then reinsert them in your furnace.

Clean the drain line once a year by running water through it from a garden hose.

Inspect the areas around vent pipes for signs of corrosion. Corroded pipes will need to be replaced.

Remove any debris and materials that could block the air intake and exhaust.

DISHWASHER: INSTALLING

Shut off the electrical power to the dishwasher circuit at the electrical panel. Also, turn off the water supply at the shutoff valve, usually located directly under the floor.

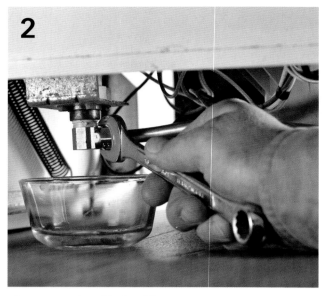

Disconnect the old plumbing connections. First unscrew the front access panel. Once the access panel is removed, disconnect the water supply line from the L-fitting on the bottom of the unit. This is usually a brass compression fitting, so just turning the compression nut counterclockwise with an adjustable wrench should do the trick. Use a bowl to catch any water that might leak out when the nut is removed.

Disconnect the old wiring connections. The dishwasher has an integral electrical box at the front of the unit where the power cable is attached to the dishwasher's fixture wires. Take off the box cover and remove the wire connectors that join the wires together.

Disconnect the discharge hose, which is usually connected to the dishwasher port on the side of the garbage disposer. To remove it, loosen the screw on the hose clamp and pull it off. You may need to push this hose back through a hole in the cabinet wall and into the dishwasher compartment so it won't get caught when you pull the dishwasher out.

5

Detach the unit from the surrounding cabinets. Remove the screws that hold the brackets to the underside of the countertop. Then put a piece of cardboard or old carpet under the front legs to protect the floor from getting scratched, and pull the dishwasher out.

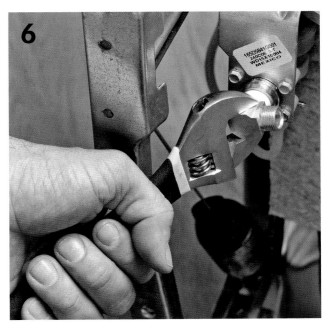

6

Prepare the new dishwasher. Tip it on its back and attach the new L-fitting into the threaded port on the solenoid. Apply some Teflon tape or pipe sealant to the fitting threads before tightening it in place to prevent possible leaks.

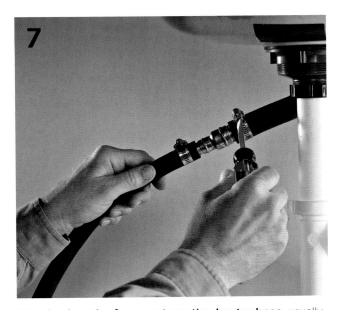

7

Attach a length of new automotive heater hose, usually ⅝" diameter, to the end of the dishwasher's discharge hose nipple with a hose clamp. The new hose you are adding should be long enough to reach from the discharge nipple to the port on the side of the kitchen sink garbage disposer.

8

Prepare for the wiring connections. Like the old dishwasher, the new one will have an integral electrical box for making the wiring connections. To gain access to the box, remove the box cover. Then install a cable connector on the back of the box and bring the power cable from the service panel through this connector. Power should be shut off at the main electrical panel at all times.

(continued)

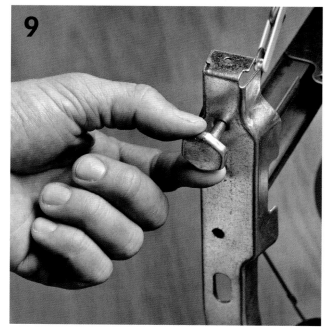

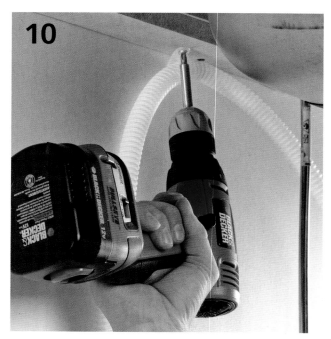

Install a leveling leg at each of the four corners while the new dishwasher is still on its back. Just turn the legs into the threaded holes designed for them. Leave about ½" of each leg projecting from the bottom of the unit. These will have to be adjusted later to level the appliance. Tip the appliance up onto the feet and slide it into the opening. Check for level in both directions and adjust the feet as required.

Once the dishwasher is level, attach the brackets to the underside of the countertop to keep the appliance from moving. Then pull the discharge hose into the sink cabinet and install it so there's a loop that is attached with a bracket to the underside of the countertop. This loop prevents waste water from flowing from the disposer back into the dishwasher.

Lengthening a Discharge Hose ▶

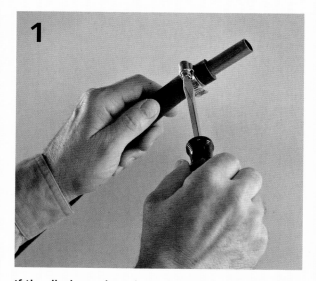

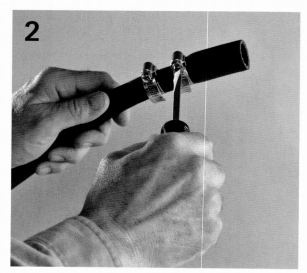

If the discharge hose has to be modified to fit onto the disposer port, first insert a 4"-long piece of ½" copper tubing into the hose and hold it in place with a hose clamp. This provides a nipple for the rubber adapter that fits onto the disposer.

Clamp the rubber disposer adapter to the end of the copper tubing nipple. Then tighten the hose clamp securely.

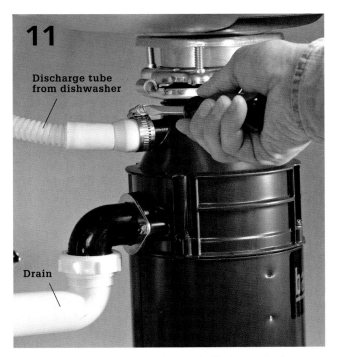

11

Discharge tube
from dishwasher

Drain

Push the adapter over the disposer's discharge nipple and tighten it in place with a hose clamp. If you don't have a disposer, this discharge hose can be clamped directly to a modified sink tailpiece that's installed below a standard sink strainer.

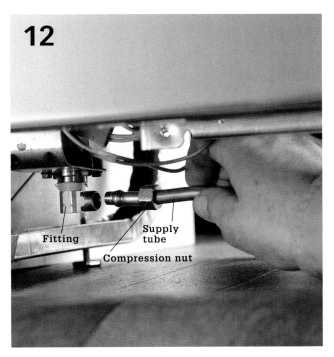

12

Fitting

Supply
tube

Compression nut

Adjust the L-fitting on the dishwasher's water inlet valve until it points directly toward the water supply tubing. Lubricate the threads slightly with a drop of dishwashing liquid and tighten the tubing's compression nut onto the fitting. Use an adjustable wrench and turn the nut clockwise.

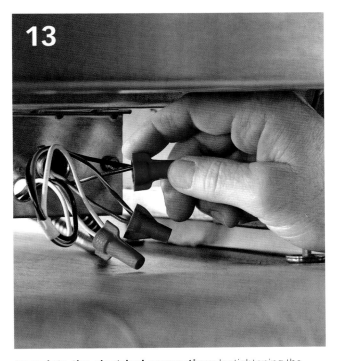

13

Complete the electrical connections by tightening the connector's clamp on the cable and then joining the power wires to the fixture wires with wire connectors. Attach the ground wire (or wires) to the grounding screw on the box, and replace the cover.

14

Install the access panel, usually by hooking it on a couple of prongs just below the dishwasher's door. Install the screws (if any) that hold it in place, and turn on the water and power supplies. Replace the toe-kick panel at the bottom of the dishwasher.

GARBAGE DISPOSERS

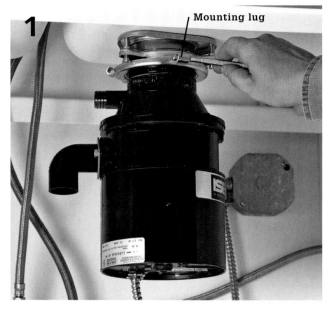

1

Mounting lug

Remove the old disposer if you have one. You'll need to disconnect the drain pipes and traps first. If your old disposer has a special wrench for the mounting lugs, use it to loosen the lugs. Otherwise, use a screwdriver. If you do not have a helper, place a solid object directly beneath the disposer to support it before you begin removal. *Important: Shut off electrical power at the main service panel before you begin removal. Disconnect the wire leads, cap them, and stuff them into the electrical box.*

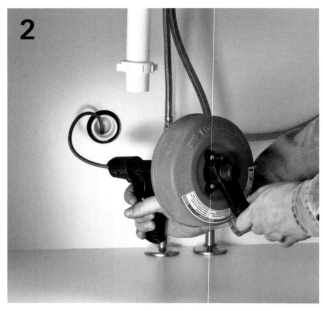

2

Clear the drain lines all the way to the branch drain before you begin the new installation. Remove the trap and trap arm first.

3

Upper mounting ring

Lower mounting ring

Snap ring

Disassemble the mounting assembly and then separate the upper and lower mounting rings and the backup ring. Also remove the snap ring from the sink sleeve.

4

Sink sleeve

Press the flange of the sink sleeve for your new disposer into a thin coil of plumber's putty that you have laid around the perimeter of the drain opening. The sleeve should be well-seated in the putty.

HVAC + APPLIANCES

5

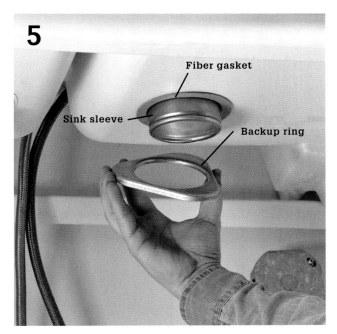

Fiber gasket

Sink sleeve

Backup ring

Slip the fiber gasket and then the backup ring onto the sink sleeve, working from inside the sink base cabinet. Make sure the backup ring is oriented the same way it was before you disassembled the mounting assembly.

6

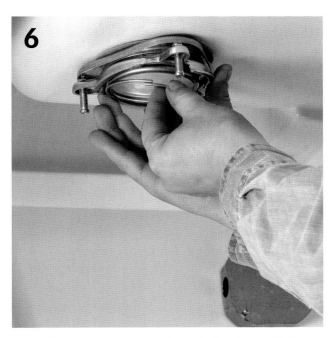

Insert the upper mounting ring onto the sleeve with the slotted ends of the screws facing away from the backup ring so you can access them. Then, holding all three parts at the top of the sleeve, slide the snap ring onto the sleeve until it snaps into the groove.

7

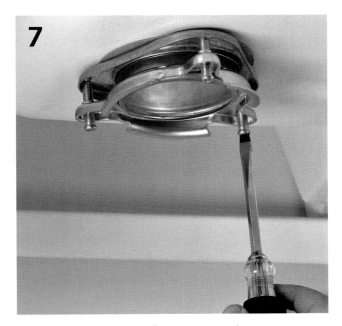

Tighten the three mounting screws on the upper mounting ring until the tips press firmly against the backup ring. It is the tension created by these screws that keeps the disposer steady and minimizes vibrating.

8

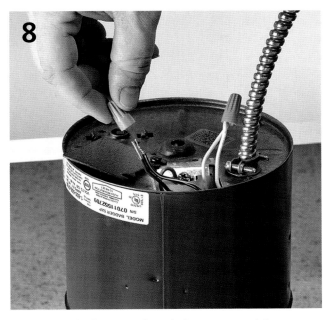

Make electrical connections before you mount the disposer unit on the mounting assembly. Shut off the power at the electrical panel if you have turned it back on. Remove the access plate from the disposer. Attach the white and black feeder wires from the electrical box to the white and black wires (respectively) inside the disposer. Twist a small wire nut onto each connection and wrap it with electrical tape for good measure. Also attach the green ground wire from the box to the grounding terminal on your disposer.

(continued)

9

Knock out the plug in the disposer port if you will be connecting your dishwasher to the disposer. If you have no dishwasher, leave the plug in. Insert a large flathead screwdriver into the port opening and rap it with a mallet. Retrieve the knock-out plug from inside the disposer canister.

10

Hang the disposer from the mounting ring attached to the sink sleeve. To hang it, simply lift it up and position the unit so the three mounting ears are underneath the three mounting screws and then spin the unit so all three ears fit into the mounting assembly. Wait until after the plumbing hookups have been made to lock the unit in place.

11

Attach the discharge tube to the disposer according to the manufacturer's instructions. It is important to get a very good seal here, or the disposer will leak. Go ahead and spin the disposer if it helps you access the discharge port.

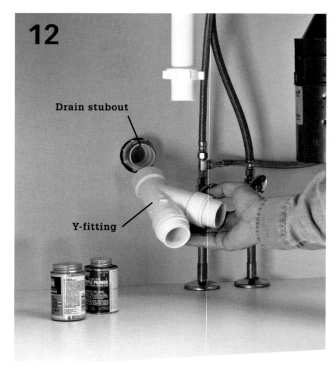

12

Drain stubout

Y-fitting

Attach a Y-fitting at the drain stubout. The Y-fitting should be sized to accept a drain line from the disposer and another from the sink. Adjust the sink drain plumbing as needed to get from the sink P-trap to one opening of the Y.

HVAC + APPLIANCES

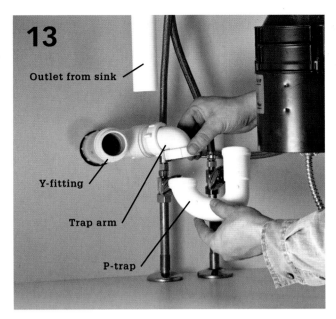

13

Outlet from sink

Y-fitting

Trap arm

P-trap

Install a trap arm for the disposer in the open port of the Y-fitting at the wall stubout. Then, attach a P-trap or a combination of a tube extension and a P-trap so the trap will align with the bottom of the disposer discharge tube.

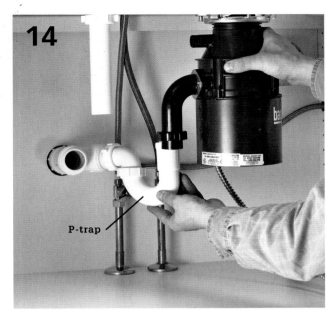

14

P-trap

Spin the disposer so the end of the discharge tube is lined up over the open end of the P-trap and confirm that they will fit together correctly. If the discharge tube extends down too far, mark a line on it at the top of the P-trap and cut at the line with a hacksaw. If the tube is too short, attach an extension with a slip joint. You may need to further shorten the discharge tube first to create enough room for the slip joint on the extension. Slide a slip nut and beveled compression washer onto the discharge tube and attach the tube to the P-trap.

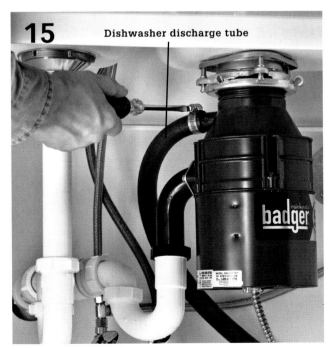

15

Dishwasher discharge tube

Connect the dishwasher discharge tube to the inlet port located at the top of the disposer unit. This may require a dishwasher hookup kit. Typically, a hose clamp is used to secure the connection.

16

Lock the disposer into position on the mounting ring assembly once you have tested to make sure it is functioning correctly and without leaks. Lock it by turning one of the mounting lugs until it makes contact with the locking notch.

HOW TO HOOK UP A REFRIGERATOR ICEMAKER

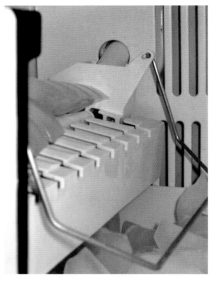

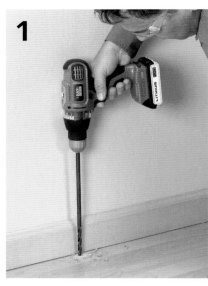

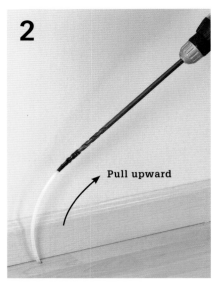

Pull upward

Aftermarket automatic icemakers are simple to install as long as your refrigerator is icemaker ready. Make sure to buy the correct model for your appliance and do careful installation work—icemaker water supply lines are very common sources for leaks.

Locate a nearby cold-water pipe, usually in the basement or crawl space below the kitchen. Behind the refrigerator and near the wall, use a long ½" bit to drill a hole through the floor. Do not pull the bit out.

From below, fasten plastic icemaker tubing to the end of the drill bit by wrapping firmly with electrician's tape. From above, carefully pull the bit up, to bring the tubing up into the kitchen.

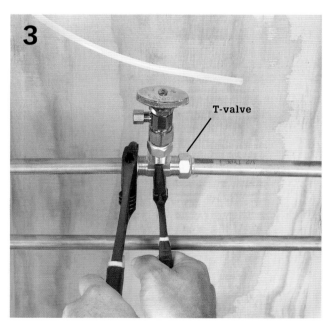

T-valve

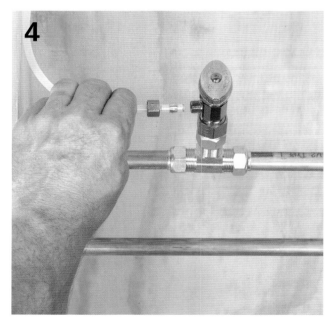

Shut off the water and open nearby faucets to drain the line. Cut into a cold-water pipe and install a compression T-valve. Tighten all the nuts, close the valve and nearby faucets, and restore water to test for leaks.

Connect the tubing. Arrange the tubing behind the fridge so you have about 6 ft. of slack, making it easy to pull the fridge out for cleaning. Cut the tubing with a knife. Slide on a nut and a ferrule. Insert the tubing into the valve, slide the ferrule tight against the valve, and tighten the nut. To finish the installation, connect the tubing to the refrigerator, using a nut and ferrule. Keep the tubing neatly coiled and kink-free for future maintenance.

HOW TO INSTALL A NEW ICEMAKER

Remove all the contents from the refrigerator and freezer. Unplug the unit and pull it out from the wall. Open the freezer door and remove the icemaker cover plate (inset). On the back of the refrigerator, remove the backing or unscrew the icemaker access panel.

Install the tube assembly. Remove two insulation plugs to expose two openings, one for the water line and the other for a wiring harness. Install the water tube assembly (part of the icemaker kit) in its access hole; it has a plastic elbow attached to the plastic tube that reaches into the freezer compartment.

Hook up the harness. Icemaker kits usually come with a wiring harness that joins the icemaker motor inside the freezer box to the power supply wires. Push this harness through its access hole and into the freezer compartment. Then seal the hole with the plastic grommet that comes with the harness.

Join the end of the icemaker wiring harness to the power connector that was preinstalled on the back of the refrigerator. This connection should lay flat against the back. If it doesn't, just tape it down with some duct tape.

(continued)

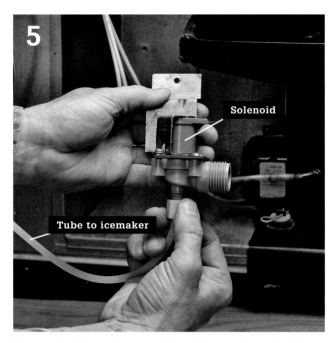

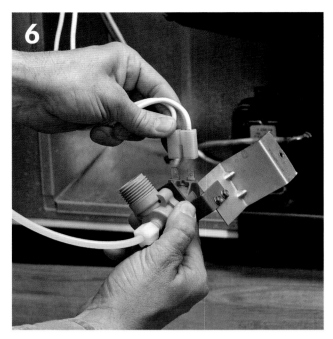

The water tube at the top of the refrigerator is attached to the solenoid that is mounted at the bottom with a plastic water line. To install the line, first attach it to the water tube, then run it down the back of the refrigerator and attach it to the solenoid valve with a compression fitting. This job is easier to do before you attach the solenoid assembly to the refrigerator cabinet.

The icemaker wiring harness comes with two snap connectors. One goes to the preinstalled wires on the refrigerator and the other is attached to the solenoid. Just push this second connector onto the brass tabs, usually at the top of the solenoid.

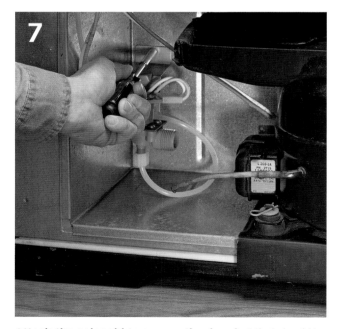

Attach the solenoid to a mounting bracket that should be installed on the cabinet wall at the bottom of the refrigerator. Mounting holes may be predrilled in the cabinet for this purpose. But if not, drill holes to match the bracket and the size of the screws. Then attach the bracket and make sure to attach the solenoid ground wire to one of these screws.

Install the water-inlet copper tube once the solenoid is mounted. Attach it by tightening the nut on one end with channel-type pliers. The other end of the tube is held to the refrigerator cabinet with a simple clamp. Make sure the end of this tubing is pointing straight up.

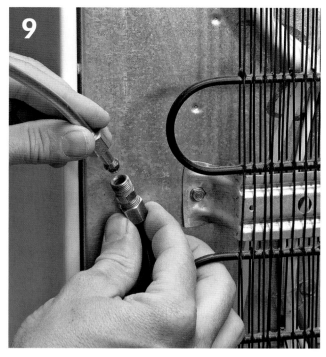

9

The end of the water-inlet tube is joined to the water supply tubing (from the house plumbing system) with a brass compression coupling. Tighten the compression nuts with an open-end or adjustable wrench.

10

From inside the freezer compartment, make sure the water tube and the wiring harness (from the back of the refrigerator) are free. If they are caught on the cabinet, loosen them until they are easily accessible.

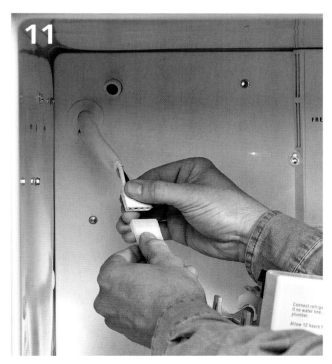

11

Connect the wire harness to the plug on the icemaker unit. Also connect the water supply tube to the back of the icemaker with a spring clip or hose clamp.

12

Install the icemaker. Remove any small rubber caps that may be installed in the mounting screw holes with a narrow putty knife. Lift the unit and screw it to the freezer wall. The mounting bracket holes are usually slotted to permit leveling the unit. Plug in the refrigerator and test the icemaker.

"SMART" THERMOSTATS

Advancing digital technology has impacted just about every aspect of our home systems, including the thermostat. What used to be a fairly simple device (often containing small amounts of mercury) has been replaced in most homes by "smart" thermostats.

These offer many advantages over traditional analog thermostats. The biggest benefit is cost savings, thanks to the ability to program heating and cooling for only when they're need and ensure you don't accidentally leave the furnace or AC running when you're not home, or you're asleep. These are also convenient. They are essentially "set-it-and-forget-it" technology.

The good news, for those who may be slower to embrace new technology, is that how you install a "smart" thermostat is really not that different from the old way of doing it. Each unit has four to eight 20-gauge copper wires that are color coded. You simply mount the thermostat body in the old location and make like-to-like connections to the thermostat cable coming through the wall and leading to your furnace and air conditioner. It is a relatively simple remove-and-replace procedure as long as your existing cable matches the colored wire combination in your new unit. If the cable does not match the device you will need to upgrade it, starting from the appliances and fishing the cable through to the thermostat location.

Once you have made the connections and mounted the thermostat to the wall, you simply need to download the correct app to your smartphone and follow the setup and usage directions. Bluetooth enabled thermostats are not cheap. But once they are set up they typically do not require any monthly usage fees.

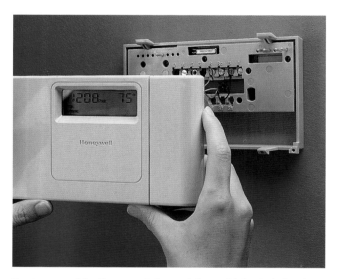

Programmable thermostats contain sophisticated circuitry that allows you to set the heating and cooling systems in your house to adjust automatically at set times of the day. Replacing a manual thermostat with a programmable model is a relatively simple job that can have big payback on heating and cooling energy savings.

Internet-connected thermostats can be controlled by using an app installed on your smartphone. They are relatively expensive. Installation is similar to older programmable thermostats—the real trick is making sure you have the right number of colored wires and that you connect them properly.

HOW TO UPGRADE TO A PROGRAMMABLE THERMOSTAT

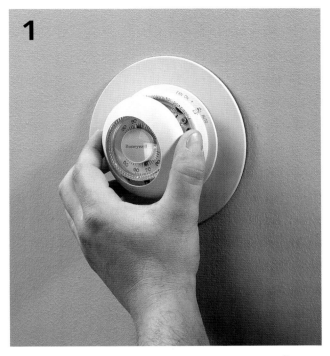

1

Start by removing the existing thermostat. Turn off the power to the furnace at the main service panel and test for power. Then remove the thermostat cover.

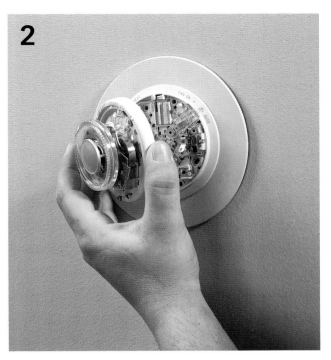

2

The body of the thermostat is held to a wall plate with screws. Remove these screws and pull the body away from the wall plate. Set the body aside.

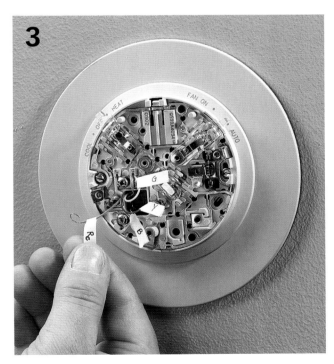

3

The low-voltage wires that power the thermostat are held by screw terminals to the mounting plate. Do not remove the wires until you label them with tape according to the letter printed on the terminal to which each wire is attached.

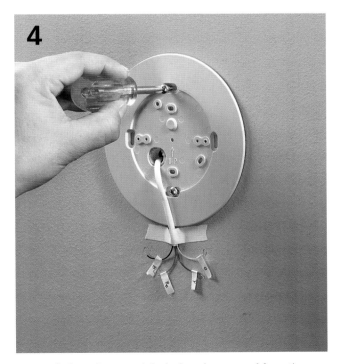

4

Once all the wires are labeled and removed from the mounting plate, tape the cable that holds these wires to the wall to keep it from falling back into the wall. Then unscrew the mounting plate and set it aside.

(continued)

5

Position the new thermostat base on the wall and guide the wires through the central opening. Screw the base to the wall using wall anchors if necessary.

6

Check the manufacturer's instructions to establish the correct terminal for each low-voltage wire. Then connect the wires to these terminals, making sure each screw is secure.

7

Programmable thermostats require batteries to store the programs so they won't disappear if the power goes out in a storm. Make sure to install batteries before you snap the thermostat cover in place. Program the new unit to fit your needs, and then turn on the power to the furnace.

Mercury Thermostats ▸

Older model thermostats (and even a few still being made today) often contained one or more small vials of mercury totaling 3 to 4 grams in weight. Because mercury is a highly toxic metal that can cause nerve damage in humans, along with other environmental problems, DO NOT dispose of an old mercury thermostat with your household waste. Instead, bring it to a hazardous waste disposal site or a mercury recycling site if your area has one (check with your local solid waste disposal agency). The best way to determine if your old thermostat contains mercury is simply to remove the cover and look for the small glass vials containing the silverish mercury substance. If you are unsure, it is always better to be safe and keep the device in question out of the normal waste stream.

HOW TO INSTALL AN INTERNET-BASED THERMOSTAT

1

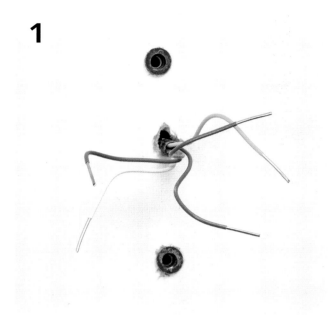

Remove the old thermostat and compare the color and quantity of wires from the wall to the instructions that came with the new thermostat. If they are not compatible you will have to purchase new thermostat wire that is compatible with the new unit and run it from the furnace/air conditioner to the thermostat location.

2

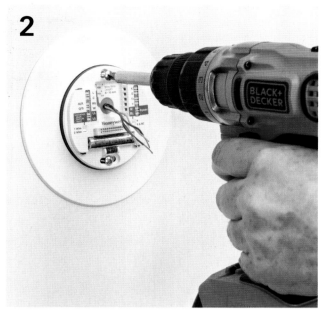

Thread the thermostat wires through the access hole in the thermostat base plate and attach the plate and mounting ring (optional) to the wall.

3

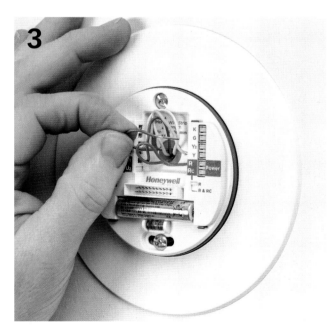

Attach the color coded wires to the correct terminal on the base plate unit according to the manufacturer's directions.

4

Make sure a new battery of the correct size is installed in the thermostat and then snap the cover/sensor onto the base plate. To engage the new thermostat for internet usage you will need to download an app for your smartphone from the thermostat manufacturer's website.

ELECTRICITY: BASICS

The service mast (metal pole) and the weatherhead create the entry point for electricity into your home. The mast is supplied with three wires two of which (the insulated wires) each carry 120 volts and originate at the nearest transformer. In some areas electricity enters from below ground as a lateral, instead of the overhead drop shown above.

The meter measures the amount of electricity consumed. It is usually attached to the side of the house, and connects to the service mast. A thin metal disc inside the meter rotates when power is used. The electric meter belongs to your local power utility company. If you suspect the meter is not functioning properly, contact the power company.

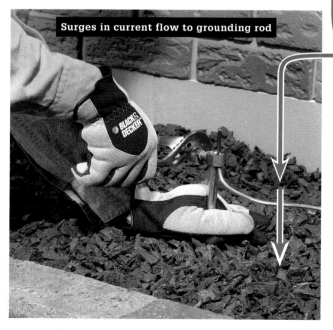

Surges in current flow to grounding rod

A grounding wire connects the electrical system to the earth through a metal grounding rod driven next to the house or through another type of grounding electrode.

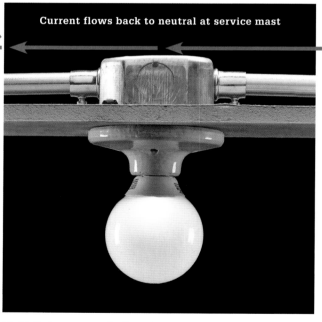

Current flows back to neutral at service mast

Light fixtures attach directly to a household electrical system. They are usually controlled with wall switches.

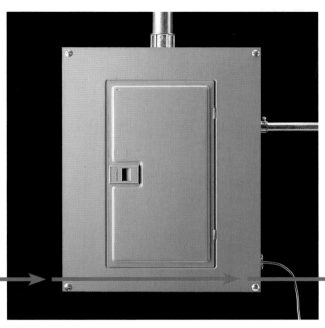

The main service panel, or "breaker box," distributes power to individual circuits. Individual circuit breakers protect each circuit from short circuits and overloads. Circuit breakers also are used to shut off power to individual circuits while repairs are made. Older homes may have fuses instead of circuit breakers.

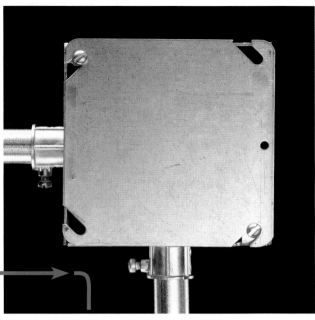

Electrical boxes enclose wire connections. According to the National Electrical Code, all wire splices and connections must be contained entirely in a covered plastic or metal electrical box. This box must be accessible for inspection and for service.

Switches control electricity passing through hot circuit wires. Switches can be wired to control light fixtures, ceiling fans, appliances, and receptacles.

Receptacles, sometimes called outlets, provide plug-in access to electricity. A 120-volt, 15-amp receptacle with a grounding hole is the most typical receptacle in wiring systems installed after 1965. Most receptacles have two plug-in locations and are called duplex receptacles.

Glossary of Electrical Terms ▸

Ampere (or amp): Refers to the rate at which electrical power flows to a light, tool, or appliance.

Armored cable: Two or more wires that are grouped together and protected by a flexible metal covering.

Box: A device used to contain wiring connections.

BX: See armored cable (Bx is the older term).

Cable: Two or more wires that are grouped together and protected by a covering or sheath.

Circuit: A continuous loop of electrical current flowing along wires or cables.

Circuit breaker: A safety device that interrupts an electrical circuit in the event of an overload or short circuit.

Conductor: Any material that allows electrical current to flow through it. Copper wire is an especially good conductor.

Conduit: A metal or plastic pipe used to protect wires.

Continuity: An uninterrupted electrical pathway through a circuit or electrical fixture.

Current: The movement of electrons along a conductor.

Duplex receptacle: A receptacle that provides connections for two plugs.

Feed wire: A conductor that carries 120-volt current uninterrupted from the service panel.

Fuse: A safety device, usually found in older homes, that interrupts electrical circuits during an overload or short circuit.

Greenfield: Materials used in flexible metal conduit. See armored cable.

Grounded wire: See neutral wire.

Grounding wire: A wire used in an electrical circuit to conduct current to the earth in the event of a short circuit. The grounding wire often is a bare copper wire.

Hot wire: Any wire that carries voltage. In an electrical circuit, the hot wire usually is covered with black or red insulation.

Insulator: Any material, such as plastic or rubber, that resists the flow of electrical current. Insulating materials protect wires and cables. Also called the ungrounded wire.

Junction box: See box.

Meter: A device used to measure the amount of electrical power being used.

Neutral wire: A wire that returns current at zero voltage to the source of electrical power. Usually covered with white or light gray insulation. Also called the grounded wire.

Nonmetallic sheathed cable: NM cable consists of two or more insulated conductors and, in most cases, a bare ground wire housed in a durable PVC casing.

Outlet: See receptacle.

Overload: A demand for more current than the circuit wires or electrical device was designed to carry. Usually causes a fuse to blow or a circuit breaker to trip.

Pigtail: A short wire used to connect two or more circuit wires to a single screw terminal.

Polarized receptacle: A receptacle designed to keep hot current flowing along black or red wires, and neutral current flowing along white or gray wires. The wider slot is neutral.

Power: The result of hot current flowing for a period of time. Use of power makes heat, motion, or light.

Receptacle: A device that provides plug-in access to electrical power.

Romex: A brand name of plastic-sheathed electrical cable that is commonly used for indoor wiring. Commonly known as NM cable.

Screw terminal: A place where a wire connects to a receptacle, switch, or fixture.

Service panel: A metal box usually near the site where electrical power enters the house. In the service panel, electrical current is split into individual circuits. The service panel has circuit breakers or fuses to protect each circuit.

Short circuit: An accidental and improper contact between two current-carrying wires, or between a current-carrying wire and a grounding conductor.

Switch: A device that controls electrical current passing through hot circuit wires. Used to turn lights and appliances on and off.

UL: An abbreviation for Underwriters Laboratories, an organization that tests electrical devices and manufactured products for safety.

Voltage (or volts): A measurement of electricity in terms of pressure.

Wattage (or watt): A measurement of electrical power in terms of total energy consumed. Watts can be calculated by multiplying the voltage times the amps.

Wire connector: A device used to connect two or more wires together. Also called a wire nut.

Best Practices for Home Wiring ▸

BY MATERIAL
Service Panel
- Maintain a minimum 30" wide by 36" deep of clearance in front of all electrical panels.
- Ground all 120-volt and 240-volt circuits.
- Match the amperage rating of the circuit when replacing fuses.
- Use handle-tie breakers for 240-volt loads (line to line) and on 120 breakers on multiwire branch circuits.
- Close all unused service panel openings.
- Label each fuse and breaker clearly on the panel.

Electrical Boxes
- Use boxes that are large enough to accommodate the number of wires entering the box.
- Locate all receptacle boxes 12" above the finished floor (standard).
- Locate all switch boxes 48" above the finished floor (standard). For special circumstances, inspectors will allow switch and location measurements to be altered, such as receptacles at 24" above the floor to make them more accessible for someone using a wheelchair.
- Install all boxes so they remain accessible.
- Mount electrical boxes flush with the finished wall board surface. Leave a minimum of 3" of usable cable or wire extending past the front of the electrical box.
- Place receptacle boxes flush with combustible surfaces.

Wires + Cables
- Use wires that are large enough for the amperage rating of the circuit (see Wire Size Chart, page 240).
- Drill holes at least 2" from exposed edge of joists to run cables. Don't attach cables to the joists' bottom edge.
- Do not run cables diagonally between framing members.
- Run cable between receptacles 20" above the floor.
- Use nail plates to protect cable run through holes in studs less than 1¼" from front edge of stud.
- Do not crimp cables sharply.
- Contain spliced wires or connections entirely in a plastic or metal electrical box.
- Use approved wire connectors to join wires.
- Secure cables within 8" of an electrical box and every 54" along its run.
- Leave a minimum ¼" (maximum 1") of sheathing where cables enter an electrical box.

- Clamp cables and wires to electrical boxes with approved NM clamp. No clamp is necessary for one-gang plastic boxes if cables are secured within 8".
- Label all cables and wires at each box to show circuits served for rough-in inspection.
- Connect only a single wire to a single screw terminal. Use pigtails to join more than one wire to a screw terminal.

Switches
- Use a switch-controlled receptacle in rooms without a built-in light fixture operated by a wall switch.
- Use three-way switches at the top and bottom on stairways with six steps or more.
- Use switches with grounding screw with plastic electrical boxes.
- Locate all wall switches within easy reach of the room entrance.

Receptacles
- Match amp rating of a receptacle to circuit size.
- Install receptacles on all walls 24" long.
- Install receptacles so a 6-ft. cord can be plugged in from any point along a wall or every 12 ft. along a wall.
- Include receptacles in any living areas and hallway that is 10 ft. long or more.
- Use three-slot, grounded receptacles for all 15- or 20-amp, 120-volt branch circuits.
- Use a switch-controlled receptacle in rooms with no built-in light fixture operated by a wall switch.
- Install GFCI-protected receptacles in bathrooms, kitchens, garages, crawl spaces, unfinished basements, and outdoor receptacle locations.
- Install one 15-amp or 20-amp, 120-volt, GFCI-protected receptacle for each parking space in a garage. Use the garage receptacle circuit only for garage and receptacles on garage exterior walls.

Light Fixtures
- Use mounting straps that are anchored to the electrical boxes to mount ceiling fixtures.
- Keep non-IC-rated recessed light fixtures 3" from insulation and ½" from combustibles.
- Include at least one switch-operated lighting outlet in every habitable room, kitchen, bathroom, basement, hallway, stairway, attached garage, and attic and crawlspace used for storage or containing equipment requiring service. Outlet may be a switched receptacle in areas other than kitchens and bathrooms.

(continued)

Grounding

- Ground all receptacles by connecting receptacle grounding screws to the circuit grounding wires.
- Use switches with grounding screws whenever possible. Always ground switches installed in plastic electrical boxes and all switches in kitchens, bathrooms, and basements.

BY ROOM
Kitchens/Dining Rooms

- Install a dedicated 40- or 50-amp, 120/240-volt circuit for a range (or two circuits for separate oven and countertop units).
- Install two 20-amp small appliance circuits.
- Install dedicated 15-amp, 120-volt circuits for dishwashers and food disposals (required by many local codes). The dishwasher circuit should be GFCI protected.
- Use GFCI receptacles for all accessible countertop receptacles; within 6 ft. from the sink, including all receptacles, such as a refrigerator receptacle, range receptacle, unused undersink receptacles, and receptacles along walls.
- Position receptacles for appliances that will be installed within cabinets, such as microwaves or food disposals, according to the manufacturer's instructions.
- Include receptacles on counters wider than 12".
- Space receptacles a maximum of 48" apart above countertops and closer together in areas where many appliances will be used.
- Locate receptacles 4" above the top of the backsplash. If backsplash is more than the standard 4" or the bottom of cabinet is less than 18" from countertop, center the box in space between countertop and bottom of wall cabinet but not more than 20" above the counter.
- Do not connect lights to small appliance circuits.
- Install additional lighting in work areas at a sink or range for convenience and safety.

Bathrooms

- Install a 20-amp circuit only for bathroom receptacles, or install a 20-amp circuit that serves receptacles and lighting in only one bathroom and no other rooms.
- Install at least one ceiling-mounted light fixture.
- Provide GFCI protection for all bathroom receptacles.
- Install a dedicated circuit for an exhaust fan with heater or other type of heating appliance, if required.
- Install at least one receptacle not more than 36" from each sink.
- Ensure light fixtures in tub/shower areas are rated for damp or wet locations, as required.

Utility/Laundry Rooms

- Install at least one 20-amp, GFCI-protected receptacle on its own circuit, located within 6 ft. of a washing machine.
- Install a separate receptacle for an electric dryer, as applicable. This must be 30-amp (minimum), 240-volt, GFCI protected, and on a dedicated four-conductor circuit.
- Install approved conduit for cable runs in unfinished rooms.
- Use GFCI-protected receptacles.

Living, Entertainment, Bedrooms

- Install a minimum of two 15-amp circuits in living rooms.
- Install a minimum of one 15- or 20-amp basic lighting/receptacle circuit for each 600 sq. ft. of living space.
- Install a dedicated circuit for each permanent appliance, like an air conditioner or group of electric baseboard heaters.
- Use electrical boxes listed and labeled for ceiling fans wherever a ceiling fan is installed.
- Space receptacles on basic lighting/receptacle circuits a maximum of 12 ft. apart. For convenience you can space them as close as 6 ft.
- Install permanently wired smoke alarms in room additions that include sleeping areas and hallways.

Outdoors

- Check for underground utilities before digging.
- Use UF cable for outdoor wiring needs.
- Run cable and wires in approved conduit, as required by local code.
- Install in-use rated weatherproof box covers.
- Bury cables housed in conduit at least 18" deep; cable not in conduit must be buried at least 24" deep.
- Use weatherproof electrical boxes with watertight covers.
- Use GFCI-protected receptacles.
- Install receptacles a minimum of 12" above ground level.
- Anchor freestanding receptacles not attached to a structure by embedding the conduit in a concrete footing, so that it is at least 12" but no more than 18" above ground level.
- Plan on installing a 20-amp, 120-volt circuit if the circuit contains more than one light fixture rated for 300 watts, or more than four receptacles.

Stairs/Hallways

- Use three-way switches at the top and bottom on stairways with six risers or more.
- Include receptacles in hallways 10 ft. long or more.
- Position stairway lights so each step and landing is illuminated.

ELECTRICITY: SAFETY BASICS

Safety should be the primary concern of anyone working with electricity. Although most household electrical repairs are simple and straightforward, always use caution and good judgment when working with electrical wiring or devices. Common sense can prevent accidents.

The basic rule of electrical safety is: Always turn off power to the area or device you are working on. At the main service panel, remove the fuse or shut off the circuit breaker that controls the circuit you are servicing. Then check to make sure the power is off by testing for power with a voltage tester. *TIP: Test a live circuit with the voltage tester to verify that it is working before you rely on it.* Restore power only when the repair or replacement project is complete.

Follow the safety tips shown on these pages. Never attempt an electrical project beyond your skill or confidence level. Never attempt to repair or replace your main service panel or service entrance head. These are jobs for a qualified electrician and require that the power company shut off power to your house.

Shut power OFF at the main service panel or the main fuse box before beginning any work.

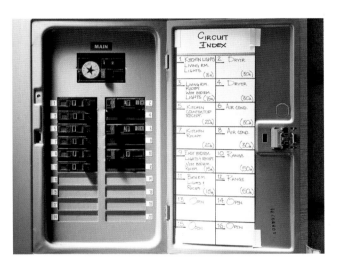

Create a circuit index and affix it to the inside of the door to your main service panel. Update it as needed.

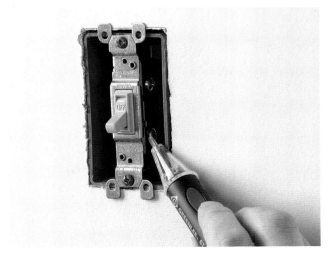

Confirm power is OFF by testing at the outlet, switch, or fixture with a voltage tester.

Use only UL-approved electrical parts or devices. These devices have been tested for safety by Underwriters Laboratories.

ELECTRICAL CIRCUITS

An electrical circuit is a continuous loop. Household circuits carry eletricity from the main service panel, throughout the house, and back to the main service panel. Several switches, receptacles, light fixtures, or appliances may be connected to a single circuit.

Current enters a circuit loop on hot wires and returns along neutral wires. These wires are color coded for easy identification. Hot wires are black or red, and neutral wires are white or light gray. For safety, all modern circuits include a bare copper or green insulated grounding wire. The grounding wire conducts current in the event of a ground fault, and helps reduce the chance of severe electrical shock. The service panel also has a bonding wire connected to a metal water pipe and a grounding wire connected to a metal grounding rod buried underground or to another type of grounding electrode.

If a circuit carries too much current, it can overload. A fuse or a circuit breaker protects each circuit in case of overloads.

Current returns to the service panel along a neutral circuit wire. Current then leaves the house on a large neutral service wire that returns it to the utility transformer.

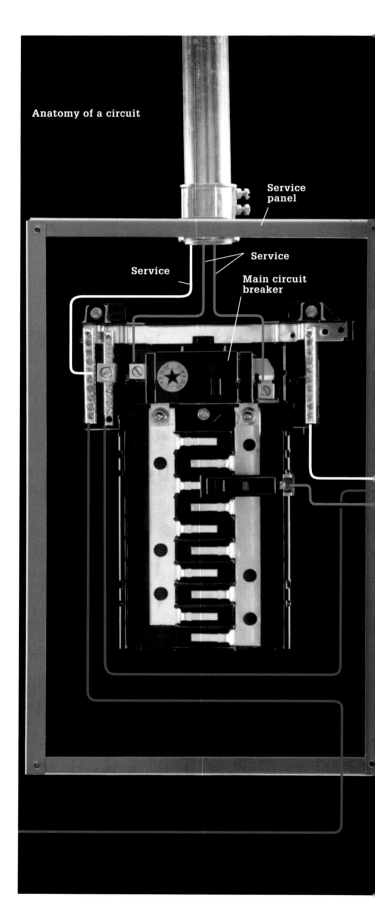

Anatomy of a circuit

Service panel

Service

Service

Main circuit breaker

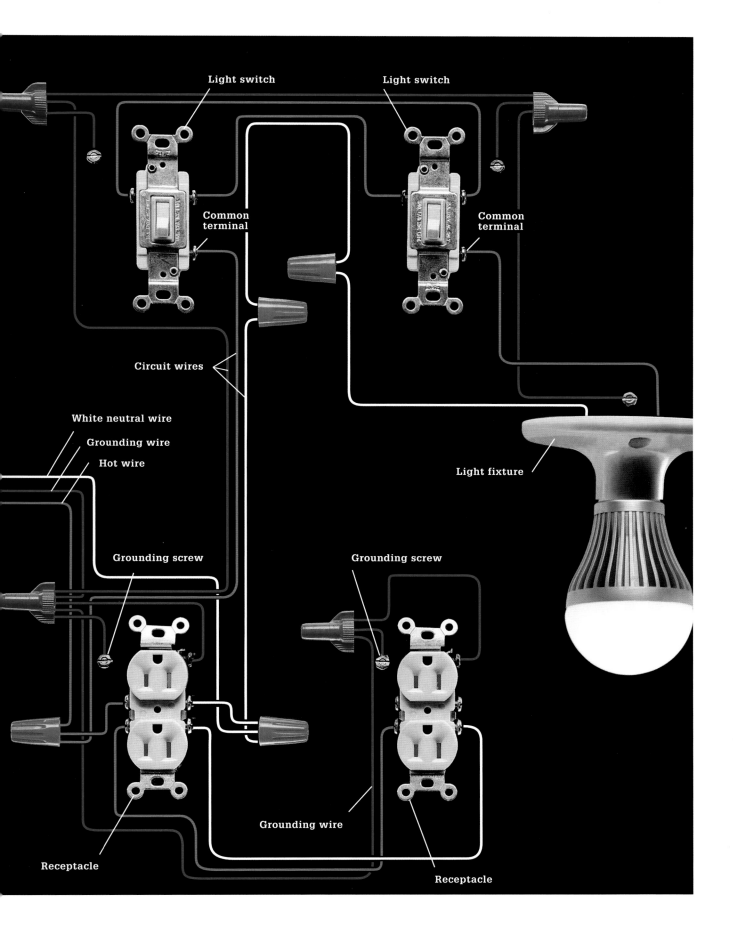

Light switch

Light switch

Common terminal

Common terminal

Circuit wires

White neutral wire

Grounding wire

Hot wire

Light fixture

Grounding screw

Grounding screw

Receptacle

Grounding wire

Receptacle

WIRES + CABLE

Wires are made of copper or aluminum in most houses. Copper is a better conductor of electricity and is used in most houses. Copper-coated aluminum wires may be found in a few houses built in the early 1970s, but this wire is uncommon. "Tin"-coated copper wires may be found in houses built in the 1940s and 1950s.

A group of two or more wires enclosed in a metal, rubber, or plastic sheath is called a cable. The sheath protects the wires from damage and people from shock. Metal conduit also protects wires, but it is not considered a cable.

Individual wires are covered with rubber or plastic vinyl insulation. An exception is a bare copper grounding wire, which does not need an insulation cover. The insulation is color coded (chart, below) to identify the wire as a hot wire, a neutral wire, or a grounding wire. New cable sheathing is also color coded to indicate the size of the wires inside. White means #14 wire, yellow means #12 wire, and orange means #10 wire.

In most wiring systems installed after 1965, the wires and cables are insulated with PVC. This type of insulation is very durable and can last as long as the house itself.

Before 1965, wires and cables were insulated with rubber. Rubber insulation has a life expectancy of about 25 years. Old insulation that is cracked or damaged can be reinforced temporarily by wrapping the wire with plastic electrical tape. However, old wiring with cracked or damaged insulation should be inspected by a qualified electrician to make sure it is safe. Homeowner insurance companies may refuse to provide coverage for houses with cloth-covered and knob-and-tube wiring.

Wires must be large enough for the amperage rating of the circuit. A wire that is too small can become dangerously hot. Wire sizes are categorized according to the American Wire Gauge (AWG) system. To check the size of a wire, use the wire stripper openings of a combination tool as a guide.

Wire Color Chart ▶

Wire color		Function
	White	Neutral wire carrying current at zero voltage.
	Black	Hot wire carrying current at full voltage.
	Red	Hot wire carrying current at full voltage.
	White, black markings	Hot wire carrying current at full voltage.
	Green	Serves as a bonding pathway.
	Bare copper	Serves as a bonding pathway.

Individual wires are color-coded to identify their function. In some circuit installations, the white wire serves as a hot wire that carries voltage. If so, this white wire may be labeled with black tape or paint to identify it as a hot wire.

Wire Size Chart ▶

Wire gauge		Wire capacity & use
	#6	55 amps, 240 volts; central air conditioner, electric furnace.
	#8	40 amps, 240 volts; electric range, central air conditioner.
	#10	30 amps, 240 volts; window air conditioner, water heater, clothes dryer.
	#12	20 amps, 120 volts; light fixtures, receptacles, microwave oven.
	#14	15 amps, 120 volts; light fixtures, receptacles.
	#16	Light-duty extension cords.
	#18 to 22	Thermostats, doorbells, security systems.

Wire sizes (shown actual size) are categorized by the American Wire Gauge system. The larger the wire size, the smaller the AWG number. The ampacities in this table are for copper wires in NM cable. The ampacity for the same wire in conduit is usually more. The ampacity for aluminum wire is less.

CONNECTING WIRES + CABLE

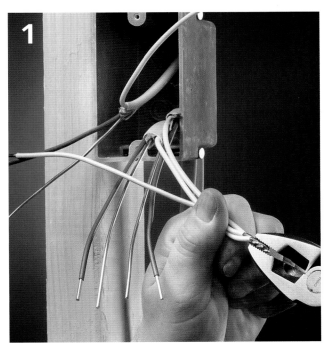

Ensure power is off and test for power. Grasp the wires to be joined in the jaws of a pair of linesman's pliers. The ends of the wires should be flush and they should be parallel and touching. Rotate the pliers clockwise two or three turns to twist the wire ends together.

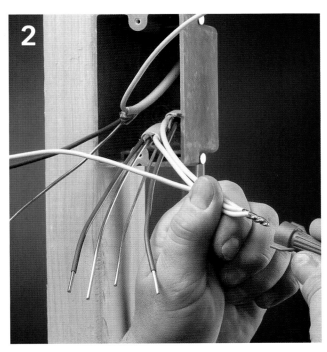

Twist a wire connector over the ends of the wires. Make sure the connector is the right size. Hand-twist the connector as far onto the wires as you can. There should be no bare wire exposed beneath the collar of the connector.

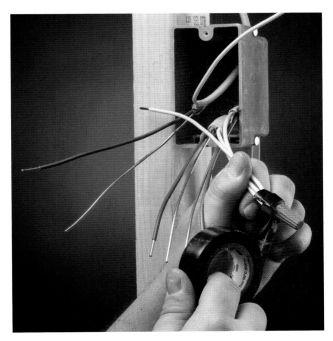

OPTION: Reinforce the joint by wrapping it with electrician's tape. By code, you cannot bind the wire joint with tape only, but it can be used as insurance. Few professional electricians use tape for purposes other than tagging wires for identification.

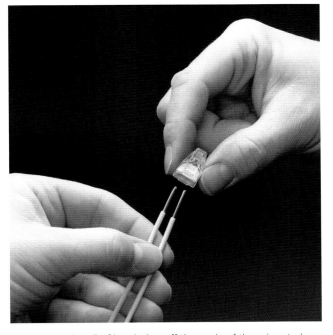

OPTION: Strip ¾" of insulation off the ends of the wires to be joined, and insert each wire into a push-in connector. Gently tug on each wire to make sure it is secure. Always read and follow the connector manufacturer's instructions.

HOW TO PIGTAIL WIRES

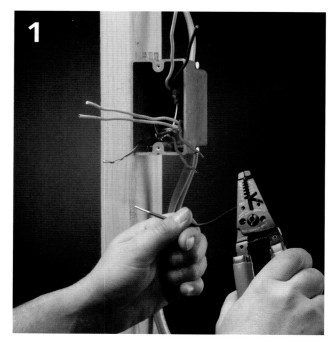

Cut a 6" length from a piece of insulated wire the same gauge and color as the wires it will be joining. Strip ¾" of insulation from each end of the insulated wire. *NOTE: Pigtailing is done mainly to avoid connecting multiple wires to one terminal, which is a code violation.*

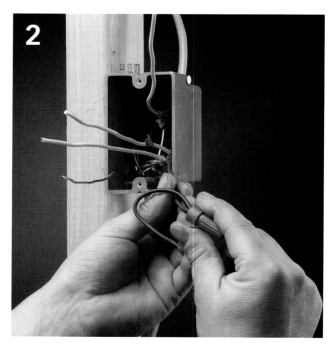

Join one end of the pigtail to the wires that will share the connection using a wire nut (see previous page).

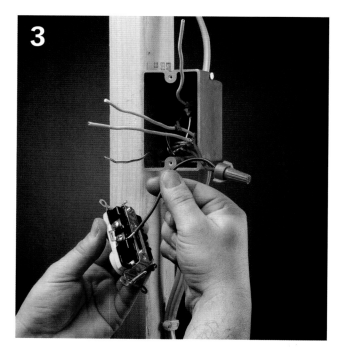

Connect the pigtail to the appropriate terminal on the receptacle or switch. Fold the wires neatly and press the fitting into the box.

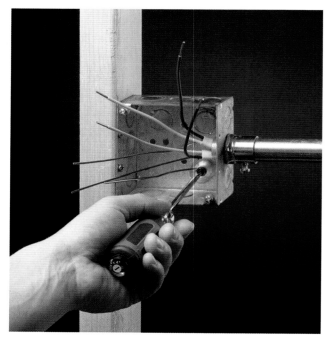

ALTERNATIVE: If you are pigtailing to a grounding screw or grounding clip in a metal box, you may find it easier to attach one end of the wire to the grounding screw before you attach the other end to the other wires.

INSTALLING WIRES + CABLES IN WALLS

From the unfinished space below the finished wall, look for a reference point, like a soil stack, plumbing pipe s, or electrical cables, that indicates the location of the wall above. Choose a location for the new cable that does not interfere with existing utilities. Drill a 1" hole up into the stud cavity.

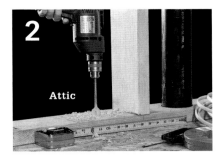

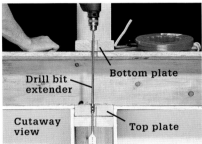

From the unfinished space above the finished wall, find the top of the stud cavity by measuring from the same fixed reference point used in step 1. Drill a 1" hole down through the top plate and into the stud cavity using a drill bit extender.

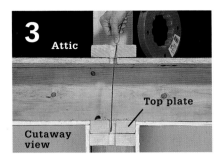

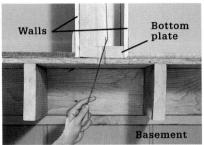

Extend a fish tape down through the top plate, twisting the tape until it reaches the bottom of the stud cavity. From the unfinished space below the wall, use a piece of stiff wire with a hook on one end to retrieve the fish tape through the drilled hole in the bottom plate.

Trim back 2" of sheathing from the end of the NM cable, then insert the wires through the loop at the tip of the fish tape.

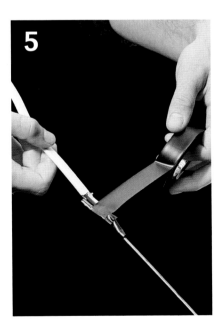

Bend the wires against the cable, then use electrical tape to bind them tightly. Apply cable-pulling lubricant to the taped end of the fish tape.

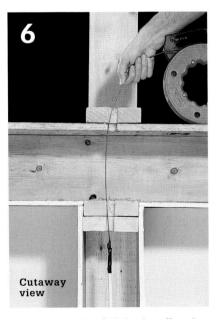

From above the finished wall, pull steadily on the fish tape to draw the cable up through the stud cavity. This job will be easier if you have a helper feed the cable from below as you pull.

ELECTRICAL BOXES

The National Electrical Code requires that wire connections and cable splices be contained inside an approved metal or plastic box. This shields framing members and other flammable materials from electrical sparks.

Electrical boxes come in several shapes. Rectangular and square boxes are used for switches and receptacles. Rectangular (2 × 3-inch) boxes are used for single switches or duplex receptacles. Square (4 × 4-inch) boxes are used any time it is convenient for two switches or receptacles to be wired, or "ganged," in one box, an arrangement common in kitchens or entry hallways. Octagonal electrical boxes contain wire connections for ceiling fixtures.

All electrical boxes are available in different depths. A box must be deep enough so a switch or receptacle can be removed or installed easily without crimping and damaging the circuit wires. Replace an undersized box with a larger box using the Electrical Box Fill Chart (right) as a guide. The NEC also says that all electrical boxes must remain accessible. Never cover an electrical box with drywall, paneling, or wallcoverings.

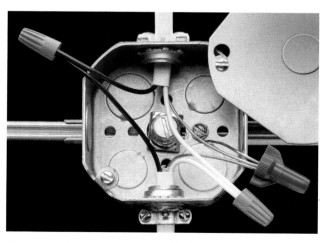

Octagonal boxes usually contain wire connections for ceiling fixtures. Because the ceiling fixture attaches directly to the box, the box should be anchored firmly to a framing member. A properly installed octagonal box should support a ceiling fixture weighing up to 50 pounds. Any box must be covered with a tightly fitting cover plate, and the box must not have open knockouts. Do not overfill the box.

Electrical Box Fill Chart ▶

Box size and shape	Maximum number of conductors permitted (see Notes below)			
	8 AWG	10 AWG	12 AWG	14 AWG
Junction Boxes				
4 × 1¼" R or O	5	5	5	6
4 × 1½" R or O	5	6	6	7
4 × 2⅛" R or O	7	8	9	10
4 × 1¼" S	6	7	8	9
4 × 1½" S	7	8	9	10
4 × 2⅛" S	10	12	13	15
4¹¹⁄₁₆ × 1¼" S	8	10	11	12
4¹¹⁄₁₆ × 1½" S	9	11	13	14
4¹¹⁄₁₆ × 2⅛" S	14	16	18	21
Device Boxes				
3 × 2 × 1½"	2	3	3	3
3 × 2 × 2"	3	4	4	5
3 × 2 × 2¼"	3	4	4	5
3 × 2 × 2½"	4	5	5	6
3 × 2 × 2¾"	4	5	6	7
3 × 2 × 3½"	6	7	8	9
4 × 2⅛ × 1½"	3	4	4	5
4 × 2⅛ × 1⅞"	4	5	5	6
4 × 2⅛ × 2⅛"	4	5	6	7

Notes:
- R = Round; O = Octagonal; S = Square or rectangular
- Each hot or neutral wire entering the box is counted as one conductor.
- Grounding wires are counted as one conductor in total—do not count each one individually.
- Raceway fittings and external cable clamps do not count. Internal cable connectors and straps count as either half or one conductor, depending on type.
- Devices (switches and receptacles mainly) each count as two conductors.
- When calculating total conductors, any nonwire components should be assigned the gauge of the largest wire in the box.
- For wire gauges not shown here, contact your local electrical inspections office.

COMMON ELECTRICAL BOXES

Rectangular boxes are used with wall switches and duplex receptacles. Single-size rectangular boxes (shown above) may have detachable sides that allow them to be ganged together to form double-size boxes.

Detachable side

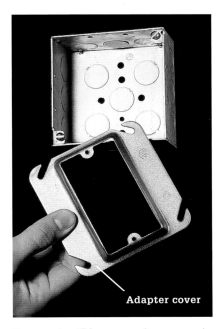

Adapter cover

Square 4 x 4" boxes are large enough for most wiring applications. They are used for cable splices and ganged receptacles or switches. To install one switch or receptacle in a square box, use an adapter cover.

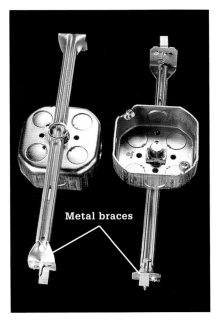

Metal braces

Braced octagonal boxes fit between ceiling joists. The metal braces extend to fit any joist spacing and are nailed or screwed to framing members.

Foam gasket

Outdoor boxes have sealed seams and foam gaskets to guard a switch or receptacle against moisture. Corrosion-resistant coatings protect all metal parts. Code compliant models include a watertight hood.

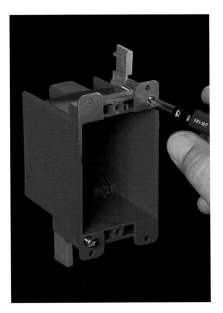

Retrofit boxes can be installed to upgrade older boxes or to allow you to add new additional receptacles and switches. One type (above) has built-in clamps that tighten against the inside of a wall and hold the box in place.

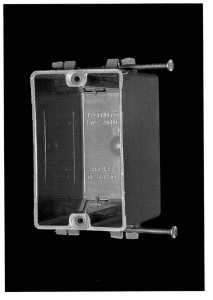

Plastic boxes are common in new construction. They can be used only with NM (nonmetallic) cable. The box may include preattached nails for anchoring it to framing members. Wall switches must have grounding screws if installed in plastic boxes.

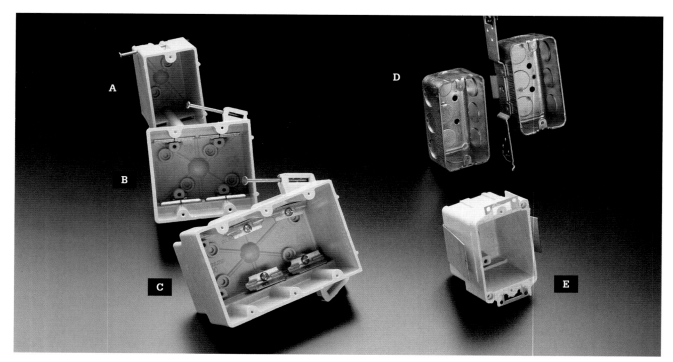

3½"-deep plastic boxes with preattached mounting nails are used for any wiring project protected by finished walls. Common styles include single-gang (A), double-gang (B), and triple-gang (C). Double-gang and triple-gang boxes require internal cable clamps. Metal boxes (D) should be used for exposed indoor wiring, such as conduit installations in an unfinished basement. Metal boxes also can be used for wiring that will be covered by finished walls. Plastic retrofit boxes (E) are used when a new switch or receptacle must fit inside a finished wall. Use internal cable clamps.

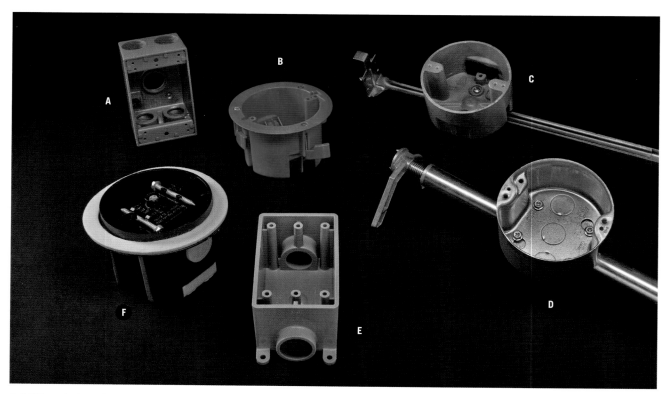

Additional electrical boxes include cast aluminum box (A) for use with outdoor fixtures, including receptacles that are wired through metal conduit (these must have in-use covers if they house receptacles); old work ceiling box (B) used for light fixtures; light-duty ceiling fan box (C) with brace that spans ceiling joists; heavy-duty retrofit ceiling fan box (D) designed for retrofit; PVC box (E) for use with PVC conduit in indoor or outdoor setting; vapor-proof ceiling box with foam gasket (F).

Box Specifications ▸

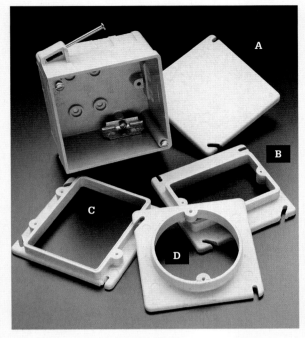

High-quality nonmetallic boxes are rigid and don't contort easily. A variety of adapter plates are available, including junction box cover plate (A), single-gang (B), double-gang (C), and light fixture (D). Adapter plates come in several thicknesses to match different wall constructions.

Boxes larger than 2" × 4" and all retrofit boxes must have internal cable clamps. After installing cables in the box, tighten the cable clamps over the cables so they are gripped firmly, but not so tightly that the cable sheathing is crushed.

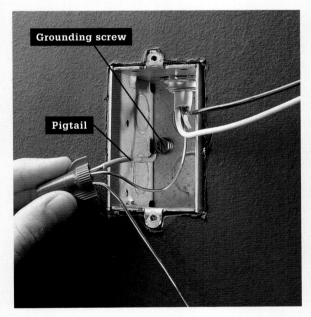

Grounding screw

Pigtail

Metal boxes must be bonded to the circuit grounding system. Connect the circuit grounding wires to the box with a green insulated pigtail wire and wire connector (as shown) or with a grounding clip.

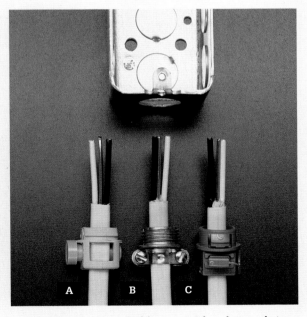

Cables entering a metal box must be clamped. A variety of clamps are available, including plastic clamps (A, C) and threaded metal clamps (B).

RECEPTACLES

Several different types of receptacles are found in the typical home. Each has a unique arrangement of slots that accepts only a certain kind of plug, and each is designed for a specific job.

Household receptacles provide two types of voltage: normal and high voltage. Although voltage ratings have changed slightly over the years, normal receptacles should be rated for 110, 115, 120, or 125 volts. For purposes of replacement, these ratings are considered identical. High-voltage receptacles are rated at 220, 240, or 250 volts. These ratings are considered identical.

When replacing a receptacle, check the amperage rating of the circuit at the main service panel, and buy a receptacle with the correct amperage rating.

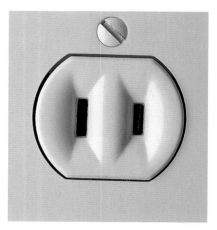

15 amps, 120 volts. Polarized two-slot receptacle is common in homes built before 1960. Slots are different sizes to accept polarized plugs.

15 amps, 120 volts. Three-slot grounded receptacle has two different sized slots and a U-shaped hole for grounding. It is required in all new wiring installations.

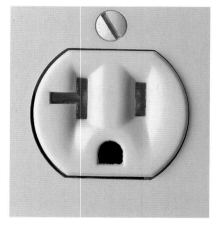

20 amps, 120 volts. This three-slot grounded receptacle features a special T-shaped slot. It is installed for use with large appliances or portable tools that require 20 amps of current.

15 amps, 250 volts. This receptacle is used primarily for window air conditioners. It is available as a single unit or as half of a duplex receptacle with the other half wired for 120 volts.

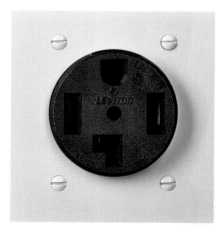

30 amps, 120/240 volts. This grounded receptacle is used for clothes dryers. It provides high-voltage current for heating coils and 120 volts to run lights and timers.

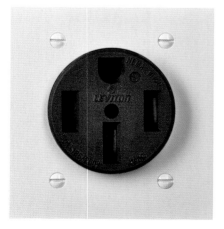

50 amps, 120/240 volts. This grounded receptacle is used for ranges. The high voltage powers heating coils, and the 120-volts run clocks and lights.

RECEPTACLES: HIGH-VOLTAGE

High-voltage receptacles provide current to large appliances like clothes dryers, ranges, water heaters, and air conditioners. The slot configuration of a high-voltage receptacle will not accept a plug rated for 120 volts.

A high-voltage receptacle can be wired in one of two ways. In a standard high-voltage receptacle, voltage is brought to the receptacle with two hot wires, each carrying a maximum of 120 volts. No white neutral wire is necessary, but a grounding wire should be attached to the receptacle and to the metal receptacle box.

A clothes dryer or range also may require normal current (a maximum of 120 volts) to run lights, timers, and clocks. If so, a white neutral wire will be attached to the receptacle. The appliance itself will split the incoming current into a 120-volt circuit and a 240-volt circuit.

It is important to identify and tag all wires on the existing receptacle so that the new receptacle will be properly wired.

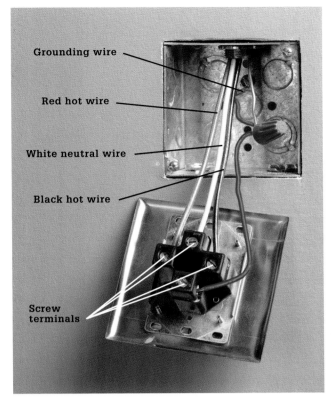

A receptacle rated for 120/240 volts has two incoming hot wires, each carrying 120 volts, a white neutral wire, and a copper grounding wire. Connections are made with setscrew terminals at the back of the receptacle.

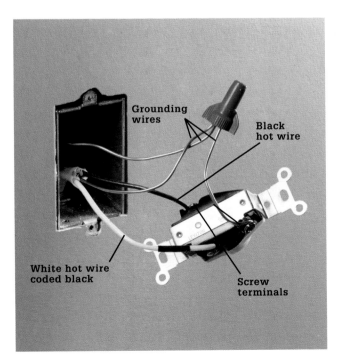

Standard receptacle rated for 240 volts has two incoming hot wires and no neutral wire. A grounding wire is pigtailed to the receptacle and to the metal receptacle box.

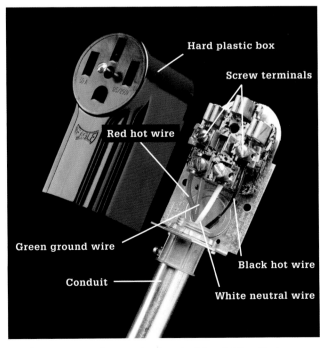

Surface-mounted receptacle rated for 240 volts has a hard plastic box that can be installed on concrete or block walls. Surface-mounted receptacles are often found in basements and utility rooms.

RECEPTACLES: REPLACING

A 120-volt duplex receptacle can be wired to the electrical system in a number of ways. The most common are shown on these pages.

Extending a branch circuit or adding a new branch to install new receptacles, lights, or switches requires a permit. The electrical inspector may require that you install arc-fault protection on the entire circuit. Check with the electrical inspector before starting such projects.

Wiring configurations may vary slightly from these photographs, depending on the kind of receptacles used, the type of cable, or the technique of the electrician who installed the wiring. To make dependable repairs or replacements, use masking tape and label each wire according to its location on the terminals of the existing receptacle.

Receptacles are wired as either end-of-run or middle-of-run. These two basic configurations are easily identified by counting the number of cables entering the receptacle box. End-of-run wiring has only one cable, indicating that the circuit ends. Middle-of-run wiring has two cables, indicating that the circuit continues on to other receptacles, switches, or fixtures.

A split-circuit receptacle is shown on the next page. Each half of a split-circuit receptacle is wired to a separate circuit. This allows two appliances of high wattage to be plugged into the same receptacle without blowing a fuse or tripping a breaker. This wiring configuration is similar to a receptacle that is controlled by a wall switch. Code requires a switch-controlled receptacle in most rooms that do not have a built-in light fixture operated by a wall switch.

Split-circuit and switch-controlled receptacles are connected to two hot wires, so use caution during repairs or replacements. Make sure the connecting tab between the hot screw terminals is removed.

Two-slot receptacles are common in older homes. There is no grounding wire attached to the receptacle, but the box may be grounded with armored cable or conduit. Tamper-resistant receptacles are now required in all new residential installations.

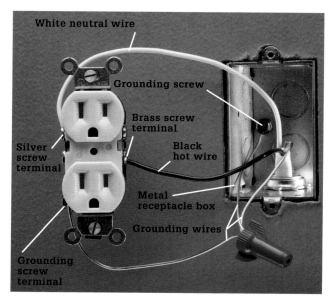

Single cable entering the box indicates end-of-run wiring. The black hot wire is attached to a brass screw terminal, and the white neutral wire is connected to a silver screw terminal. If the box is metal, the grounding wire is pigtailed to the grounding screws of the receptacle and the box. In a plastic box, the grounding wire is attached directly to the grounding screw terminal of the receptacle.

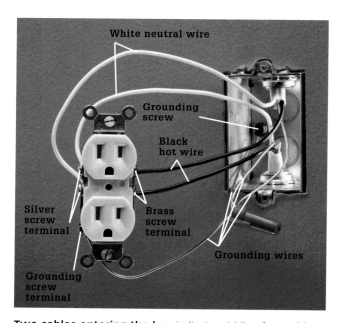

Two cables entering the box indicate middle-of-run wiring. Black hot wires are connected to brass screw terminals, and white neutral wires to silver screw terminals. The grounding wire is pigtailed to the grounding screws of the receptacle and the box.

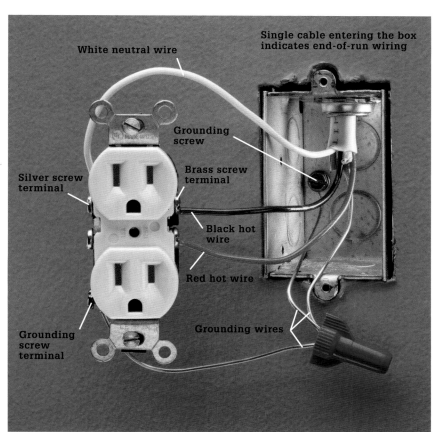

White neutral wire

Single cable entering the box indicates end-of-run wiring

Grounding screw

Brass screw terminal

Silver screw terminal

Black hot wire

Red hot wire

Grounding screw terminal

Grounding wires

A split-circuit receptacle (technically a multiwire branch circuit) is attached to a black hot wire, a red hot wire, a white neutral wire, and a bare grounding wire. The wiring is similar to a switch-controlled receptacle. The hot wires are attached to the brass screw terminals, and the connecting tab or fin between the brass terminals is removed. The white wire is attached to a silver screw terminal, and the connecting tab on the neutral side remains intact. The grounding wire is pigtailed to the grounding screw terminal of the receptacle and to the grounding screw attached to the box. *NOTE: A receptacle wired like this must be fed by a double-pole circuit breaker (with each hot wire connecting to a terminal on the breaker) or by two single-pole breakers connected with a handle tie. This ensures that both halves of the receptacle are always shut off at the same time, to prevent accidents.*

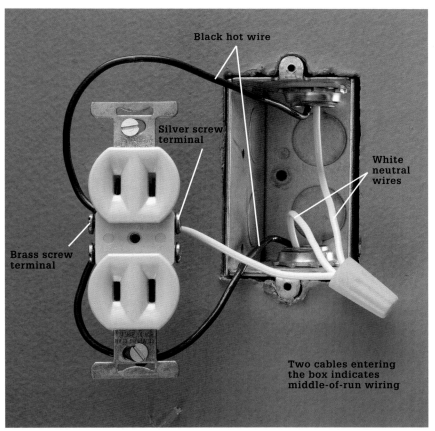

Black hot wire

Silver screw terminal

White neutral wires

Brass screw terminal

Two cables entering the box indicates middle-of-run wiring

A two-slot receptacle is often found in older homes. The black hot wires are connected to the brass screw terminals, and the white neutral wires are pigtailed to a silver screw terminal. Two-slot receptacles may be replaced with three-slot types, but only if a means of grounding exists at the receptacle box. In some municipalities, you may replace a two-slot receptacle with a GFCI receptacle as long as the receptacle has a sticker that reads "No equipment ground."

HOW TO INSTALL A NEW RECEPTACLE

Position the new old work box on the wall and trace around it. Consider the location of hidden utilities within the wall before you cut.

Remove baseboard between the new and existing receptacle. Cut away the drywall about 1" below the baseboard with a jigsaw, wallboard saw, or utility knife.

Drill a ⅝" hole in the center of each stud along the opening between the two receptacles. A drill bit extender or a flexible drill bit will allow you a better angle and make drilling the holes easier.

Run the branch cable through the holes from the new location to the existing receptacle. Secure the cable to the stud below the box. Install a metal nail plate on the front edge of each stud that the cable routes through.

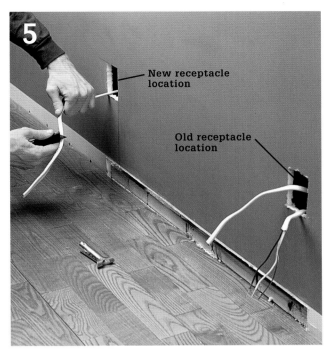

5

New receptacle location

Old receptacle location

Turn off the power at the panel and test for power.
Remove the old receptacle and its box, and pull the new branch cable up through the hole. Remove sheathing and insulation from both ends of the new cable.

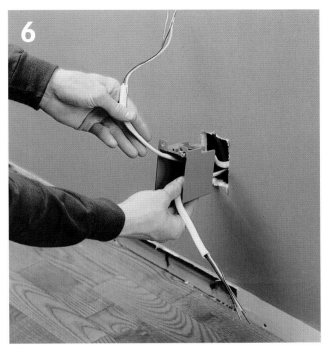

6

Thread the new and old cables into an old work box large enough to contain the added wires and clamp the cables. Fit the box into the old hole and attach it.

7

Reconnect the old receptacle by connecting its neutral, hot, and grounding screws to the new branch cable and the old cable from the panel with pigtails.

8

Pull the cable through another old work box for the new receptacle. Secure the cable and install the box. Connect the new receptacle to the new branch cable. Insert the receptacle into the box and attach the receptacle and cover plate with screws. Patch the opening with drywall. Reattach the baseboard to the studs.

GFCI RECEPTACLES

The ground-fault circuit-interrupter (GFCI) receptacle protects against electrical shock caused by a faulty appliance, or a worn cord or plug. It senses small changes in current flow and can shut off power in as little as 1/40 of a second.

GFCIs are now required in bathrooms, kitchens, garages, crawl spaces, unfinished basements, and outdoor receptacle locations, and within 6 feet of all sinks. Consult your local codes for any requirements regarding the installation of GFCI receptacles. Most GFCIs use standard screw terminal connections, but some have wire leads and are attached with wire connectors. Because the body of a GFCI receptacle is larger than a standard receptacle, small crowded electrical boxes may need to be replaced with more spacious boxes.

The GFCI receptacle may be wired to protect only itself (single location), or it can be wired to protect all receptacles, switches, and light fixtures from the GFCI "forward" to the end of the circuit (multiple locations).

Because the GFCI is so sensitive, it is most effective when wired to protect a single location. The more receptacles any one GFCI protects, the more susceptible it is to "phantom tripping," shutting off power because of tiny, normal fluctuations in current flow. GFCI receptacles installed in outdoor locations must be rated for outdoor use and weather resistance (WR) along with ground fault protection.

Tools + Materials ▸

Screwdriver
Wire connectors
Non-contact
  voltage tester

Eye protection
Rubberized work gloves
Masking tape

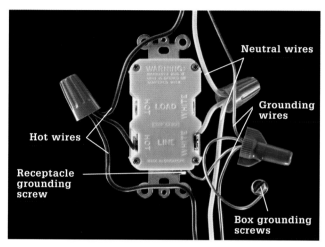

A GFCI wired for single-location protection (shown from the back) has hot and neutral pigtail wires connected only to the screw terminals marked LINE. A GFCI connected for single-location protection may be wired as either an end-of-run or middle-of-run configuration.

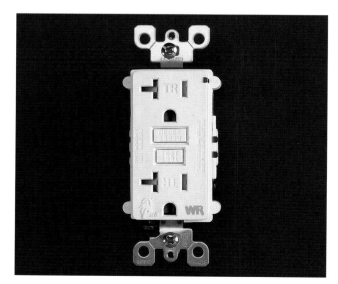

Modern GFCI receptacles have tamper-resistant slots. Look for a model that's rated "WR" (for weather resistance) if you'll be installing it outdoors or in a wet location.

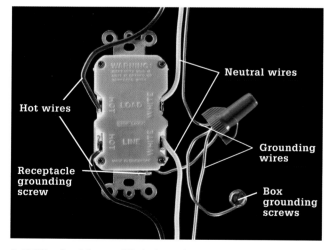

A GFCI wired for multiple-location protection (shown from the back) has one set of hot and neutral pigtail wires connected to the LINE pair of screw terminals, and the other set connected to the LOAD pair of screw terminals. A GFCI receptacle connected for multiple-location protection may be wired only as a middle-of-run configuration.

HOW TO INSTALL A GFCI FOR SINGLE-LOCATION PROTECTION

1

Shut off power to the receptacle at the main service panel. Test for power with a noncontact tester. Be sure to check both halves of the receptacle.

2

Remove cover plate. Loosen the mounting screws, and gently pull the receptacle from the box. Do not touch the wires. Confirm power is off with the tester.

3

Disconnect all wires from the silver screw terminals of the old receptacle. Remove the old receptacle.

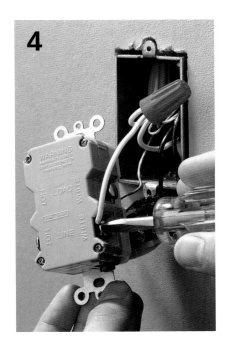

4

Pigtail all the white neutral wires together, and connect the pigtail to the terminal marked WHITE LINE on the GFCI (see photo, opposite page).

5

Disconnect all black hot wires from the brass screw terminals of the old receptacle. Pigtail these wires together, and connect them to the terminal marked HOT LINE on the GFCI.

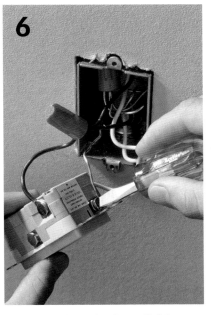

6

If a grounding wire is available, connect it to the green grounding screw terminal of the GFCI. Mount the GFCI in the receptacle box, and reattach the cover plate. Restore power, and test the GFCI according to the manufacturer's instructions. If a grounding wire is not available, label the receptacle cover plate: NO EQUIPMENT GROUND.

HOW TO INSTALL A GFCI FOR MULTIPLE-LOCATION PROTECTION

Use a map of your house circuits to determine a location for your GFCI. Indicate all receptacles that will be protected by the GFCI installation.

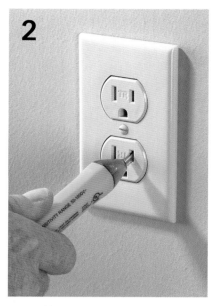

Turn off power to the correct circuit at the panel. Test all the receptacles in the circuit with a non-contact voltage tester to make sure the power is off. Always check both halves of each duplex receptacle.

Remove the cover plate from the receptacle that will be replaced with the GFCI. Loosen the mounting screws and gently pull the receptacle from its box. Take care not to touch any bare wires. Confirm the power is off with the tester.

Disconnect all black hot wires. Carefully separate the hot wires and position them so that the bare ends do not touch anything. Restore power to the circuit at the panel. Determine which black wire is the feed wire by testing for hot wires. The feed wire brings power to the receptacle from the service panel. Use caution: This is a live wire test, during which the power is turned on temporarily.

When you have found the hot feed wire, turn off power at the panel. Identify the feed wire by marking it with masking tape.

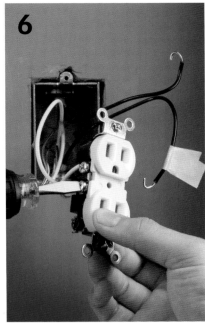

6

Disconnect the white neutral wires from the old receptacle. Identify the white feed wire and label it with masking tape. The white feed wire will be the one that shares the same cable as the black feed wire.

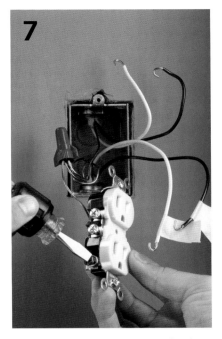

7

Disconnect the grounding wire from the grounding screw terminal of the old receptacle. Remove the old receptacle.

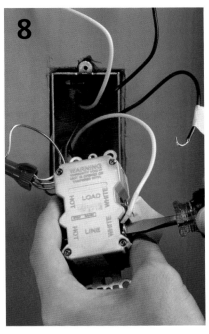

8

Connect the white feed wire to the terminal marked WHITE LINE on the GFCI. Connect the black feed wire to the terminal marked HOT LINE on the GFCI.

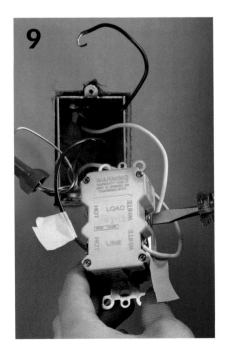

9

Connect the other white neutral wire to the terminal marked WHITE LOAD on the GFCI.

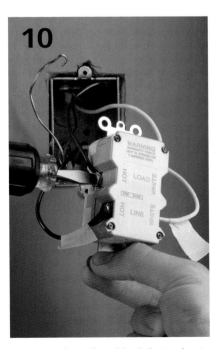

10

Connect the other black hot wire to the terminal marked HOT LOAD on the GFCI. Connect the grounding wire to the grounding screw terminal of the GFCI.

11

Carefully tuck all wires into the receptacle box. Mount the GFCI in the box and attach the cover plate. Turn on power to the circuit at the panel. Test the GFCI according to the manufacturer's instructions.

SWITCHES: ELECTRICAL

Wall switches are available in three general types. To repair or replace a switch, it is important to identify its type.

Single-pole switches are used to control a set of lights from one location. Three-way switches are used to control a set of lights from two different locations and are always installed in pairs. Four-way switches are used in combination with a pair of three-way switches to control a set of lights from three or more locations.

Identify switch types by counting the screw terminals. Single-pole switches have two screw terminals, three-way switches have three screw terminals, and four-way switches have four. Most switches include a grounding screw terminal, which is identified by its green color.

When replacing a switch, choose a new switch that has the same number of screw terminals as the old one. The location of the screws on the switch body varies depending on the manufacturer, but these differences will not affect the switch operation.

Whenever possible, connect switches using the screw terminals rather than push-in fittings. Some specialty switches have wire leads instead of screw terminals. They are connected to circuit wires with wire connectors.

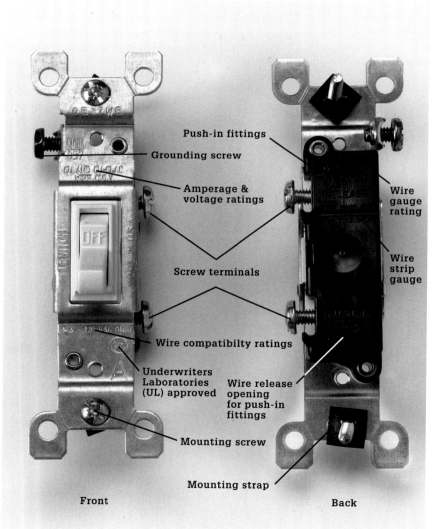

Push-in fittings

Grounding screw

Amperage & voltage ratings

Screw terminals

Wire compatibilty ratings

Underwriters Laboratories (UL) approved

Wire release opening for push-in fittings

Mounting screw

Mounting strap

Wire gauge rating

Wire strip gauge

Front

Back

The recommended way to connect a wall switch to circuit wires is to the screw terminals. The push-in fittings on the back may be used, with restrictions. A switch may have a stamped strip gauge that indicates how much insulation must be stripped from the circuit wires to make the connections.

The switch body is attached to a metal mounting strap that allows it to be mounted in an electrical box. Several rating stamps are found on the strap and on the back of the switch. The abbreviation UL or UND. LAB. INC. LIST means that the switch meets the safety standards of the Underwriters Laboratories. Switches also are stamped with maximum voltage and amperage ratings. Standard wall switches are rated 15A or 125V. Voltage ratings of 110, 120, and 125 are considered to be identical for purposes of identification.

For standard wall switch installations, choose a switch that has a wire gauge rating of #12 or #14. For wire systems with solid-core copper wiring, use only switches marked COPPER, CU, or CO/ALR. For aluminum wiring, use only switches marked CO/ALR. Note that while CO/ALR switches and receptacles are approved by the National Electrical Code for use with aluminum wiring, the Consumer Products Safety Commission does not recommend using these. Switches and receptacles marked AL/CU can no longer be used with aluminum wiring, according to the National Electrical Code.

SINGLE-POLE WALL SWITCHES

A single-pole switch is the most common type of wall switch. It has ON-OFF markings on the switch lever and is used to control a set of lights, an appliance, or a receptacle from a single location. A single-pole switch has two screw terminals and a grounding screw. When installing a single-pole switch, check to make sure the ON marking shows when the switch lever is in the up position.

In a correctly wired single-pole switch, a hot circuit wire is attached to each screw terminal. However, the color and number of wires inside the switch box will vary, depending on the location of the switch along the electrical circuit.

If two cables enter the box, then the switch lies in the middle of the circuit. In this installation, both of the hot wires attached to the switch are black.

If only one cable enters the box, then the switch lies at the end of the circuit. In this installation (sometimes called a switch loop), one of the hot wires is black, but the other hot wire usually is white. A white hot wire should be coded with black tape or paint.

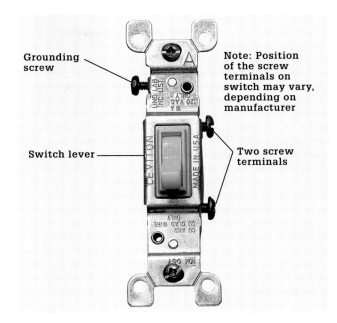

Grounding screw

Switch lever

Note: Position of the screw terminals on switch may vary, depending on manufacturer

Two screw terminals

A single-pole switch is essentially an interruption in the black power supply wire that is opened or closed with the toggle. Single-pole switches are the simplest of all home wiring switches.

TYPICAL SINGLE-POLE SWITCH INSTALLATIONS

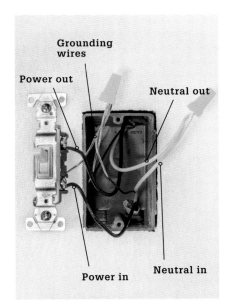

Grounding wires

Power out

Neutral out

Power in

Neutral in

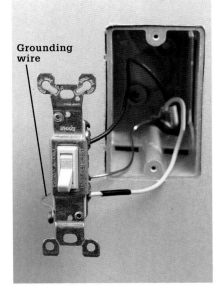

Grounding wire

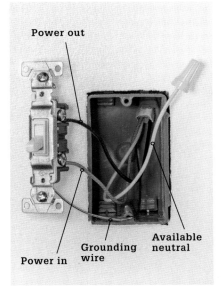

Power out

Available neutral

Grounding wire

Power in

Two cables enter the box when a switch is located in the middle of a circuit. Each cable has a white and a black insulated wire, plus a bare copper grounding wire. The black wires are hot and are connected to the screw terminals on the switch. The white wires are neutral and are joined together with a wire connector. Grounding wires are pigtailed to the switch.

Old method: One cable enters the box when a switch is located at the end of a circuit. In this installation, both of the insulated wires are hot. The white wire should be labeled with black tape or paint to identify it as a hot wire. The grounding wire is connected to the switch grounding screw.

New method: In new switch wiring, the white wire should not supply current to the switched device and a separate neutral wire should be available in the switch box.

THREE-WAY WALL SWITCHES

Three-way switches have three screw terminals and do not have ON-OFF markings. Three-way switches are always installed in pairs and are used to control lights from two locations.

One of the screw terminals on a three-way switch is darker than the others. This screw is the common screw terminal. The position of the common screw terminal on the switch body may vary, depending on the manufacturer. Before disconnecting a three-way switch, always label the wire that is connected to the common screw terminal. It must be reconnected to the common screw terminal on the new switch.

The two lighter-colored screw terminals on a three-way switch are called the traveler screw terminals. The traveler terminals are interchangeable, so there is no need to label the wires attached to them.

Because three-way switches are installed in pairs, it sometimes is difficult to determine which of the switches is causing a problem. The switch that receives greater use is more likely to fail, but you may need to inspect both switches to find the source of the problem.

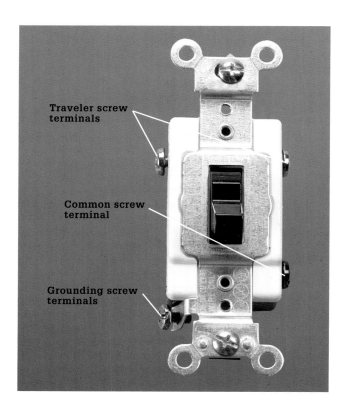

Traveler screw terminals

Common screw terminal

Grounding screw terminals

TYPICAL THREE-WAY SWITCH INSTALLATIONS

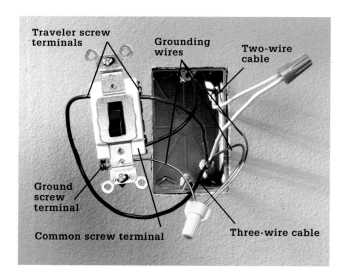

Traveler screw terminals

Grounding wires

Two-wire cable

Ground screw terminal

Common screw terminal

Three-wire cable

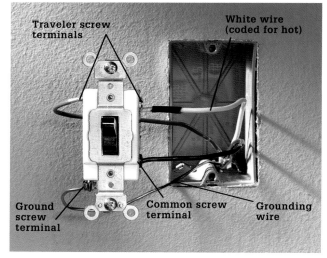

Traveler screw terminals

White wire (coded for hot)

Ground screw terminal

Common screw terminal

Grounding wire

Two cables enter the box if the switch lies in the middle of a circuit. One cable has two wires, plus a bare copper grounding wire; the other cable has three wires, plus a ground. The black wire from the two-wire cable is connected to the dark common screw terminal. The red and black wires from the three-wire cable are connected to the traveler screw terminals. The white neutral wires are joined together with a wire connector, and the grounding wires are pigtailed to the switch grounding terminal.

One cable enters the box if the switch lies at the end of the circuit. The cable has a black wire, red wire, and white wire, plus a bare copper grounding wire. The black wire must be connected to the common screw terminal, which is darker than the other two screw terminals. The white and red wires are connected to the two traveler screw terminals. The white wire is taped to indicate that it is hot. The bare copper grounding wire is connected to the switch grounding terminal.

DIMMER SWITCHES

A dimmer switch makes it possible to vary the brightness of a light fixture. Dimmers are often installed in dining rooms, recreation areas, or bedrooms. Do not install a dimmer at stairway light switches unless you install a dimmer at all switches.

Any standard single-pole switch can be replaced with a dimmer, as long as the switch box is of adequate size. Dimmer switches have larger bodies than standard switches. They also generate a small amount of heat that must dissipate. For these reasons, dimmers should not be installed in undersized electrical boxes or in boxes that are crowded with circuit wires. Always follow the manufacturer's specifications for installation.

In lighting configurations that use three-way switches (opposite page), replace the standard switches with special three-way dimmers. Buy a packaged pair of three-way dimmers designed to work together.

Dimmer switches are available in several styles (photo, right). All types have wire leads instead of screw terminals, and they are connected to circuit wires using wire connectors. Some types have a green grounding lead that should be connected to the grounded metal box or to the bare copper grounding wires. Until recently, dimmers were designed to work only with incandescent lamps. They may not work well, or may not work at all, with CFL and LED lamps. When replacing incandescent lamps with CFL and LED lamps, make sure the new lamps are designed to work with older dimmers. When replacing dimmers, make sure the new dimmers are designed to work with CFL and LED lamps.

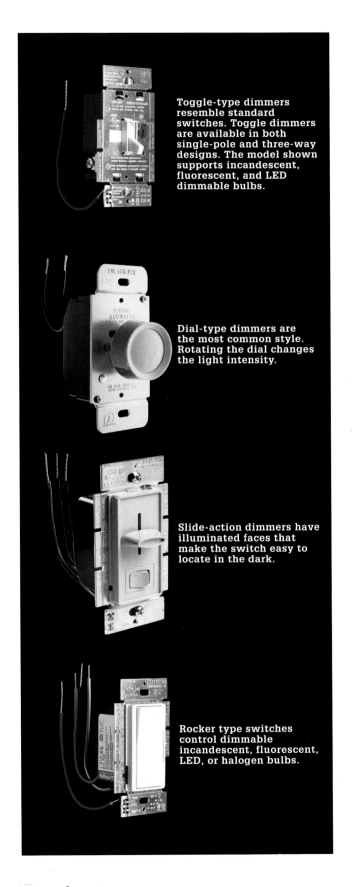

Toggle-type dimmers resemble standard switches. Toggle dimmers are available in both single-pole and three-way designs. The model shown supports incandescent, fluorescent, and LED dimmable bulbs.

Dial-type dimmers are the most common style. Rotating the dial changes the light intensity.

Slide-action dimmers have illuminated faces that make the switch easy to locate in the dark.

Rocker type switches control dimmable incandescent, fluorescent, LED, or halogen bulbs.

▶ Tools + Materials ▸

Screwdriver
Circuit tester
Needlenose pliers
Wire connectors
Masking tape

CIRCUIT BREAKERS + FUSES

The circuit breaker panel is the electrical distribution center for your home. It divides the current into branch circuits that are carried throughout the house. Each branch circuit is protected by a circuit breaker that protects the wires from dangerous current overloads. When installing new circuits, the last step is to connect the wires to new circuit breakers at the panel. Working inside a circuit breaker panel is not dangerous if you follow basic safety procedures. Always shut off the main circuit breaker and test for power before touching any parts inside the panel, and never touch the service wire lugs. If unsure of your own skills, hire an electrician to make the final circuit connections. (If you have an older electrical service with fuses instead of circuit breakers, always have an electrician make these final hookups.)

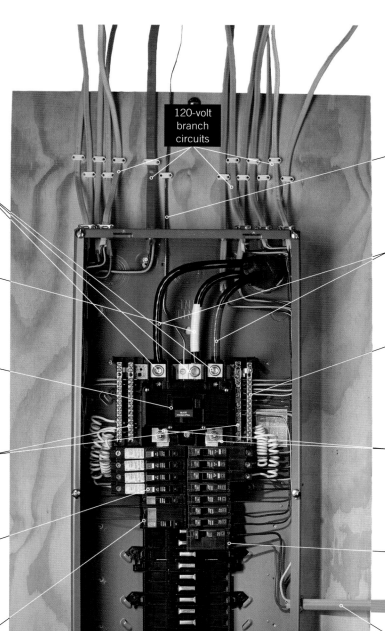

Main circuit breaker panel distributes the power entering the home into branch circuits.

Service lugs: Never touch these. They are always live unless the utility shuts off the service to the panel. The NEC requires protective covers (service barriers) on the two hot service lugs.

Neutral service wire carries current back to the power source after it has passed through the home.

Main circuit breaker protects the panelboard from overloads and disconnects power to all circuits in the panel.

Neutral bus bar has setscrew terminals for linking all neutral circuit wires to the neutral service wire.

Single-pole breaker connects to one hot bus bar to provide 120 volts to circuit.

Double-pole breaker connects to both hot legs of the bus bar to provide 240 volts.

120-volt branch circuits

Grounding conductor leads to metal grounding rods driven into the earth or to other grounding electrodes.

Two hot service wires provide 120/240 volts of power to the main circuit breaker. These wires are always HOT.

Grounding bus bar has terminals for linking grounding wires to the main grounding conductor. It is bonded to the neutral bus bar.

Two hot bus bars run through the center of the panel, supplying power to the circuit breakers. Each carries 120 volts.

Subpanel feeder breaker is a double-pole breaker. It is wired in the same way as a 120/240-volt circuit.

120/240-volt branch circuit

If a circuit breaker panel does not have enough open slots for new full-size circuit breakers, you may be able to install ½-height (slimline) circuit breakers. Otherwise, you will need to install a subpanel.

Before installing any new wiring, evaluate your electrical service to make sure it provides enough current to support both the existing wiring and any new circuits. If your service does not provide enough power, have an electrician upgrade it to a higher amp rating. During the upgrade, the electrician will install a new circuit breaker panel with enough extra breaker slots for the new circuits you want to install.

Safety Warning ›

Never touch any parts inside a circuit breaker panel until you have checked for power. Circuit breaker panels differ in appearance, depending on the manufacturer. Never begin work in a circuit breaker panel until you understand its layout and can identify the parts.

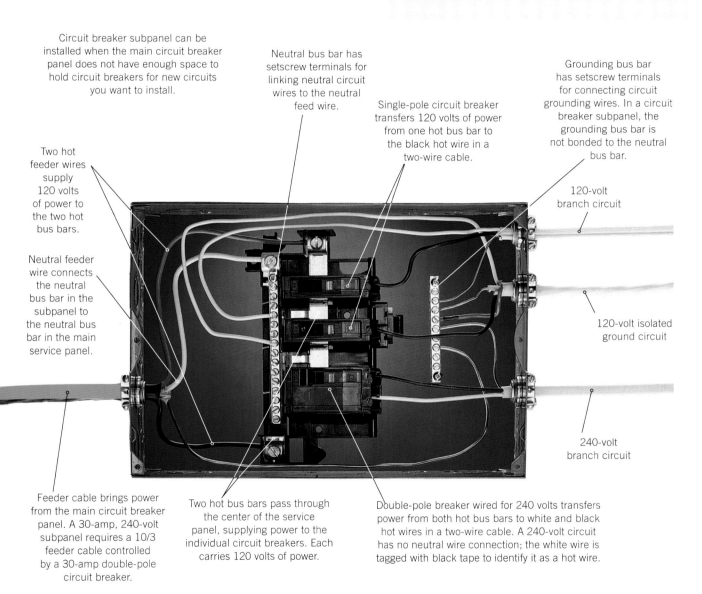

Circuit breaker subpanel can be installed when the main circuit breaker panel does not have enough space to hold circuit breakers for new circuits you want to install.

Neutral bus bar has setscrew terminals for linking neutral circuit wires to the neutral feed wire.

Single-pole circuit breaker transfers 120 volts of power from one hot bus bar to the black hot wire in a two-wire cable.

Grounding bus bar has setscrew terminals for connecting circuit grounding wires. In a circuit breaker subpanel, the grounding bus bar is not bonded to the neutral bus bar.

Two hot feeder wires supply 120 volts of power to the two hot bus bars.

Neutral feeder wire connects the neutral bus bar in the subpanel to the neutral bus bar in the main service panel.

120-volt branch circuit

120-volt isolated ground circuit

240-volt branch circuit

Feeder cable brings power from the main circuit breaker panel. A 30-amp, 240-volt subpanel requires a 10/3 feeder cable controlled by a 30-amp double-pole circuit breaker.

Two hot bus bars pass through the center of the service panel, supplying power to the individual circuit breakers. Each carries 120 volts of power.

Double-pole breaker wired for 240 volts transfers power from both hot bus bars to white and black hot wires in a two-wire cable. A 240-volt circuit has no neutral wire connection; the white wire is tagged with black tape to identify it as a hot wire.

Exercise Your Breakers ›

Your breakers (including the main) should be "exercised" once a year to ensure proper mechanical function. Simply turn them off and then back on. A convenient time to perform the exercise is at daylight saving time, when you'll need to reset all of your clocks anyway.

FUSES + CIRCUIT BREAKERS

Fuses and circuit breakers are safety devices designed to protect the electrical system from short circuits and overloads. Fuses and circuit breakers are located in the main service panel and in subpanels.

Most service panels installed before 1965 rely on fuses to protect individual circuits. Screw-in plug fuses protect 120-volt circuits that power lights and receptacles. Cartridge fuses protect 240-volt appliance circuits and the main shutoff of the service panel.

Inside each fuse is a current-carrying metal alloy ribbon. If a circuit is overloaded, the metal ribbon melts and stops the flow of power. A fuse must match the amperage rating of the circuit. Never replace a fuse with one that has a larger amperage rating.

In most service panels installed after 1965, circuit breakers protect and control individual circuits. Single-pole circuit breakers protect 120-volt circuits, and double-pole circuit breakers protect 240-volt circuits. Amperage ratings for circuit breakers range from 0 to more than 200.

Each circuit breaker has a permanent metal strip that heats up and bends when voltage passes through it. If a circuit is overloaded, the metal strip inside the breaker bends enough to "trip" the switch and stop the flow of power. Circuit breakers are listed to trip twice. After the second trip they weaken and tend to nuisance trip at lower currents. Replace breakers that have tripped more than twice—they may fail. Worn circuit breakers should be replaced by an electrician.

When a fuse blows or a circuit breaker trips, it is usually because there are too many light fixtures and plug-in appliances drawing power through the circuit. Move some of the plug-in appliances to another circuit, then replace the fuse or reset the breaker. If the fuse blows or the breaker trips again immediately, there may be a short circuit in the system. Call a licensed electrician if you suspect a short circuit.

Tools + Materials ▸

Fuse puller and continuity tester
   (for cartridge fuses only)
Replacement fuse

Circuit breakers are found in the majority of panels installed since the 1960s. Single-pole breakers control 120-volt circuits. Double-pole breakers rated for 20 to 60 amps control 240-volt circuits. Ground-fault circuit interrupter (GFCI) and arc-fault circuit interrupter (AFCI) breakers provide protection from shocks and fire-causing arcs for the entire circuit.

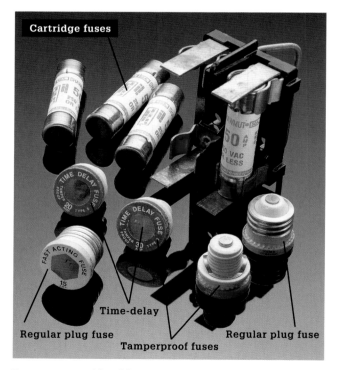

Fuses are used in older service panels. Plug fuses usually control 120-volt circuits rated for 15, 20, or 30 amps. Tamper-proof plug fuses have threads that fit only matching sockets, making it impossible to install a wrong-sized fuse. Time-delay fuses absorb temporary heavy power loads without blowing. Cartridge fuses control 240-volt circuits and range from 30 to 100 amps.

HOW TO IDENTIFY + REPLACE A BLOWN PLUG FUSE

Locate the blown fuse at the panel. If the metal ribbon inside is cleanly melted (right), the circuit was overloaded. If window is discolored (right), there was a short circuit.

Unscrew the fuse, being careful to touch only the insulated rim of the fuse. Replace it with a fuse that has the same amperage rating.

HOW TO REMOVE, TEST + REPLACE A CARTRIDGE FUSE

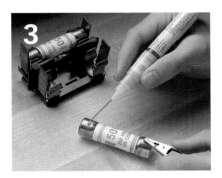

Remove cartridge fuses by gripping the handle of the fuse block and pulling sharply.

Remove the individual cartridge fuses from the block using a fuse puller.

Test each fuse using a continuity tester. If the tester glows, the fuse is good. If not, install a new fuse with the same amperage rating.

HOW TO RESET A CIRCUIT BREAKER

Open the panel and locate the tripped breaker. The lever on the tripped breaker will be either in the OFF position, or in a position between ON and OFF.

Reset the tripped circuit breaker by pressing the circuit breaker lever all the way to the OFF position, then pressing it to the ON position.

Test AFCI and GFCI circuit breakers by pushing the TEST button. The breaker should trip to the OFF position. If not, the breaker is faulty and must be replaced by an electrician.

CONNECTING CIRCUIT BREAKERS

The last step in a wiring project is connecting circuits at the breaker panel. After this is done, the work is ready for the final inspection.

Circuits are connected at the main panel, if it has enough open slots, or at a circuit breaker subpanel. When working at a subpanel, make sure the feeder breaker at the main panel has been turned off, and test for power (see photo, right) before touching any parts in the subpanel.

Make sure the circuit breaker amperage does not exceed the ampacity of the circuit wires you are connecting to it. Also be aware that circuit breaker styles and installation techniques vary according to manufacturer. Use breakers approved by the panel manufacturer. You should install AFCI circuit breakers for most 15- and 20-amp, 120-volt circuits inside the home.

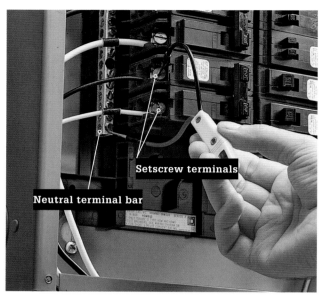

Test for current before touching any parts inside a circuit breaker panel. With the main breaker turned off but all other breakers turned on, touch one probe of a neon tester to the neutral terminal bar, and touch the other probe to each setscrew on one of the double-pole breakers (not the main breaker). If the tester does not light for either setscrew, it is safe to work in the panel.

NOTE: Noncontact circuit testers are preferred in most situations where you are testing for current because they're safer. But in some instances, you'll need a tester with individual probes to properly check for current.

Tools + Materials ▸

Screwdriver
Hammer
Pencil
Combination tool
Cable ripper

Circuit tester
Pliers
Cable clamps
Single- and double-pole AFCI circuit breakers

HOW TO CONNECT CIRCUIT BREAKERS

Shut off the main circuit breaker (if you are working in a subpanel, shut off the feeder breaker in the main panel). Remove the panel cover plate, taking care not to touch the parts inside the panel. Test for power.

Open a knockout in the side of the circuit breaker panel using a screwdriver and hammer. Attach a cable clamp to the knockout.

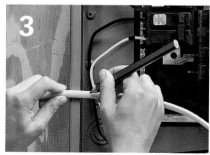

Hold the cable across the front of the panel near the knockout, and mark the sheathing about ½" inside the edge of the panel. Strip the cable from the marked line to the end using a cable ripper. (There should be 18" to 24" of excess cable.) Insert the cable through the clamp and into the service panel, and then tighten the clamp.

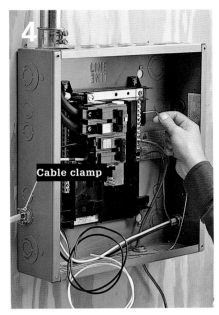

Bend the bare copper grounding wire around the inside edge of the panel to an open setscrew terminal on the grounding terminal bar. Insert the wire into the opening on the terminal bar, and tighten the setscrew. Fold excess wire around the inside edge of the panel.

For 120-volt circuits, bend the white circuit wire around the outside of the panel to an open setscrew terminal on the neutral terminal bar. Clip away excess wire, and then strip ½" of insulation from the wire using a combination tool. Insert the wire into the terminal opening, and tighten the setscrew.

Strip ½" of insulation from the end of the black circuit wire. Insert the wire into the setscrew terminal on a new single-pole circuit breaker, and tighten the setscrew.

Slide one end of the circuit breaker onto the guide hook, and then press it firmly against the terminal bar until it snaps into place. (Breaker installation may vary, depending on the manufacturer.) Fold excess black wire around the inside edge of the panel.

For 120–240-volt circuit (top): Connect red and black wires to the double-pole breaker. Connect white wire to the neutral terminal bar, and the grounding wire to grounding terminal bar. For 240-volt circuits without a neutral (bottom), attach white and black wires to the double-pole breaker, tagging white wire with black tape. There is no neutral terminal bar connection on this circuit.

Remove the appropriate breaker tab on the panel cover plate to make room for the new circuit breaker. A single-pole breaker requires one tab, while a double-pole breaker requires two tabs. Reattach the cover plate, and label the new circuit on the panel index.

CONDUIT: INSTALLING

All individual wires (such as THHN/THWN) must be installed in conduit or in thinner material called tubing. Cables and wires that are subject to physical damage must be installed in conduit or some types of tubing to protect them. Whether a location is subject to physical damage depends on the judgment of the electrical inspector. Cables that are exposed and are within the reach of an adult and most cables installed outside are often considered subject to physical damage. Other exposed locations may also qualify.

The interior of conduit and tubing installed outside is considered a wet area. Don't install NM cable inside conduit being run outdoors. Use UF cable instead or pull individual wires rated for wet area use. Conduit and tubing installed outdoors must be rated for exterior use.

At one time, conduit could only be fitted by using elaborate bending techniques and special tools. Now, however, a variety of shaped fittings are available to let a homeowner join conduit easily.

ELECTRICAL BONDING IN METAL CONDUIT

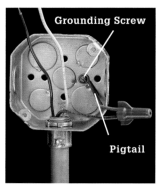

Grounding Screw

Pigtail

Pigtail

Grounding Clip

Install a green insulated grounding wire for any circuit that runs through metal conduit. Although code allows the metal conduit to serve as the grounding conductor, most electricians install a green insulated wire as a more dependable means of grounding the system. The grounding wires must be connected to metal boxes with a pigtail and grounding screw (left) or grounding clip (right).

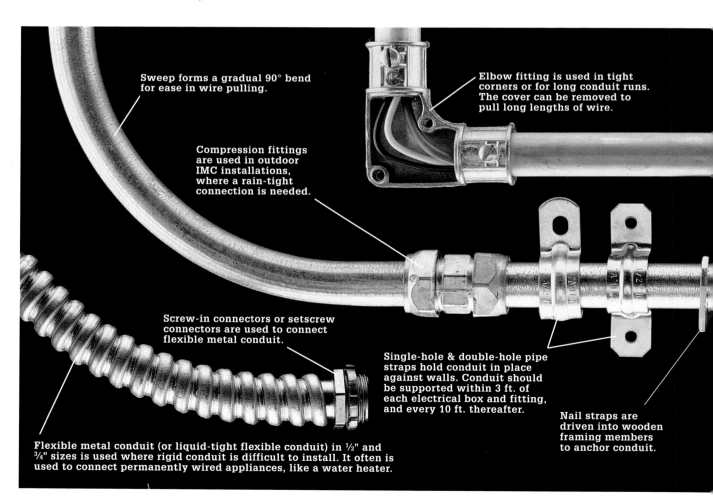

Sweep forms a gradual 90° bend for ease in wire pulling.

Elbow fitting is used in tight corners or for long conduit runs. The cover can be removed to pull long lengths of wire.

Compression fittings are used in outdoor IMC installations, where a rain-tight connection is needed.

Screw-in connectors or setscrew connectors are used to connect flexible metal conduit.

Single-hole & double-hole pipe straps hold conduit in place against walls. Conduit should be supported within 3 ft. of each electrical box and fitting, and every 10 ft. thereafter.

Nail straps are driven into wooden framing members to anchor conduit.

Flexible metal conduit (or liquid-tight flexible conduit) in ½" and ¾" sizes is used where rigid conduit is difficult to install. It often is used to connect permanently wired appliances, like a water heater.

FILL CAPACITY

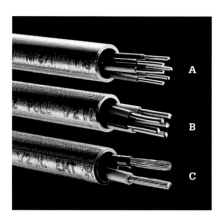

EMT ½" in diameter can hold up to twelve 14-gauge or nine 12-gauge THHN/THWN wires (A), five 10-gauge wires (B), or two 8-gauge wires (C). Use ¾" conduit for greater capacity.

METAL CONDUIT

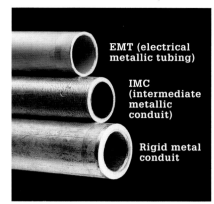

EMT (electrical metallic tubing)

IMC (intermediate metallic conduit)

Rigid metal conduit

EMT (electrical metallic conduit) is lightweight and easy to install. IMC (intermediate metallic conduit) has thicker galvanized walls and is a good choice for exposed outdoor use. Rigid metal conduit provides the greatest protection for wires, but it is more expensive and requires threaded fittings. EMT is the preferred metal material for home use.

PLASTIC CONDUIT

PVC conduit (Schedule 80) and tubing are allowed by many local codes. It is assembled with solvent glue and PVC fittings that resemble those for metal conduit. When wiring with PVC conduit and tubing, always run a green grounding wire. Use material approved for use in electrical applications. Do not use PVC plumbing pipes.

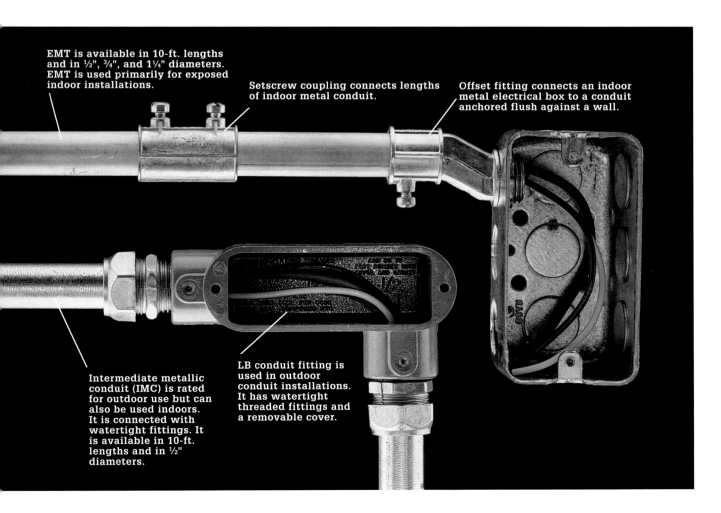

EMT is available in 10-ft. lengths and in ½", ¾", and 1¼" diameters. EMT is used primarily for exposed indoor installations.

Setscrew coupling connects lengths of indoor metal conduit.

Offset fitting connects an indoor metal electrical box to a conduit anchored flush against a wall.

Intermediate metallic conduit (IMC) is rated for outdoor use but can also be used indoors. It is connected with watertight fittings. It is available in 10-ft. lengths and in ½" diameters.

LB conduit fitting is used in outdoor conduit installations. It has watertight threaded fittings and a removable cover.

WORKING WITH CONDUIT

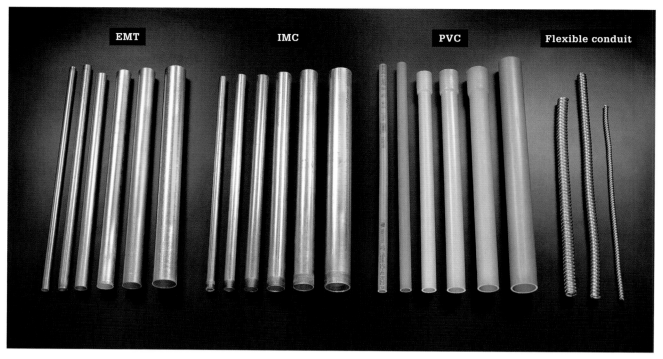

Conduit types used most in homes are EMT (electrical metallic tubing), IMC (intermediate metallic conduit), RNC (rigid nonmetallic conduit), and flexible metal conduit. The most common diameters by far are ½" and ¾", but larger sizes, which carry more wires, are stocked at most building centers.

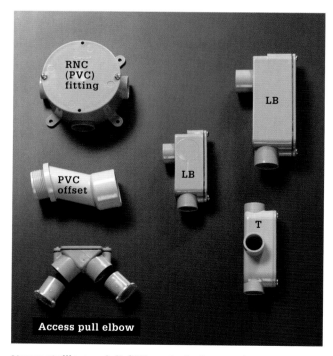

Nonmetallic conduit fittings typically are solvent welded to nonmetallic conduit, as opposed to metal conduit, which can be threaded and screwed into threaded fittings or attached with setscrews or compression fittings.

A thin-wall conduit bender is used to bend sweeps into EMT or IMC conduit.

HOW TO MAKE NONMETALLIC CONDUIT CONNECTIONS

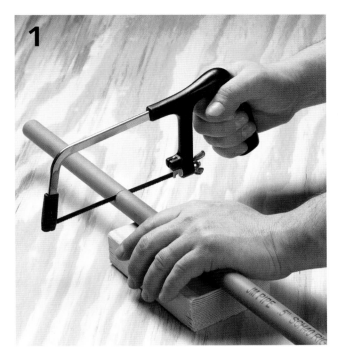

Cut the rigid nonmetallic conduit (PVC) to length with a fine-tooth saw, such as a hacksaw. For larger diameter (1½" and above), use a power miter box with a fine-tooth or plastic cutting blade.

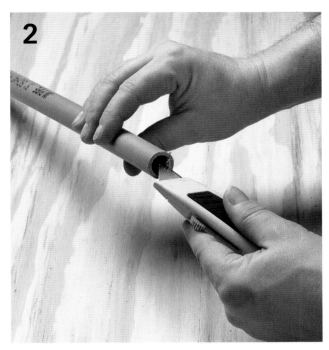

Deburr the cut edges with a utility knife or fine sandpaper such as emery paper. Wipe the cut ends with a dry rag. Also wipe the coupling or fitting to clean it.

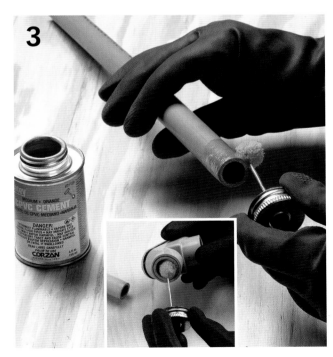

Apply a coat of PVC cement to the end of the conduit and to the inside walls of the coupling (inset). Wear latex gloves to protect your hands. The cement should be applied past the point on the conduit where it enters the fitting or coupling.

Insert the conduit into the fitting or coupling and rotate it a quarter turn to help spread the cement. Allow the joint to set undisturbed for 10 minutes.

SURFACE-MOUNTED WIRING

Surface-mounted wiring is a network of electrical circuits that run through small, decorative conduit. The systems include matching elbows, T-connectors, and various other fittings and boxes that are also surface mounted. The main advantage to a surface mounted wiring system is that you can add a new fixture onto a circuit without cutting into your walls.

Although they are extremely convenient and can even contribute to a room's decor when used thoughtfully, surface-mounted wiring systems do have some limitations. They are not allowed for some specific applications (damp areas such as bathrooms, for example) in many areas, so check with the local electrical inspector before beginning a project. And the boxes that house the switches and receptacles tend to be very shallow and more difficult to work with than ordinary boxes.

In some cases, you may choose to run an entirely new circuit with surface-mounted wiring components (at least starting at the point where the branch circuit wire reaches the room from the service panel). But more often, a surface-mounted wiring circuit ties into an existing receptacle or switch. If you are tying into a standard switch box for power, make sure the load wire for the new surface-mounted wiring circuit is connected to the hot wire in the switch box before it is connected to the switch (otherwise, the surface-mounted wiring circuit will be off whenever the switch is off).

Surface-mounted wiring circuits are networks of cable channels and electrical boxes that allow you to run new wiring without cutting into walls. If you have a room with too much demand on a single receptacle (inset), installing a surface-mounted circuit with one or more new outlets is a good solution.

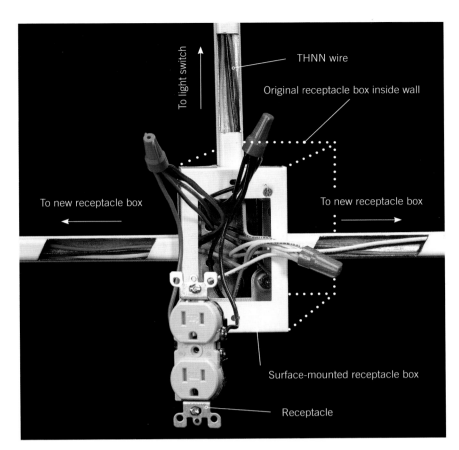

A surface-mounted receptacle box is mounted directly to the original electrical box (usually for a receptacle) and raceway tracks are attached to it. The tracks house THNN wires that run from the new box to new receptacles and light switches.

Labels on image:
- To light switch
- THNN wire
- Original receptacle box inside wall
- To new receptacle box
- To new receptacle box
- Surface-mounted receptacle box
- Receptacle

PARTS OF A SURFACE-MOUNTED SYSTEM

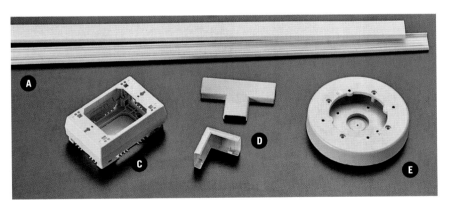

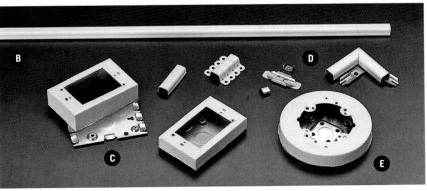

Surface-mounted wiring systems employ two-part tracks that are mounted directly to the wall surface to house cable. Lighter-duty plastic raceways (A), used frequently in office buildings, are made of snap-together plastic components. For home wiring, look for a heavier metal-component system (B). Both systems include box extenders for tying in to a receptacle (C), elbows, T-connectors, and couplings (D), and boxes for fixtures (E).

HOW TO INSTALL SURFACE-MOUNTED RACEWAY

1

Confirm that the receptacle you'll be tying into can support additional load and shut off power to that circuit at the main service panel. Remove the cover plate from the receptacle and test with a voltage tester to make sure the circuit is not getting current.

2

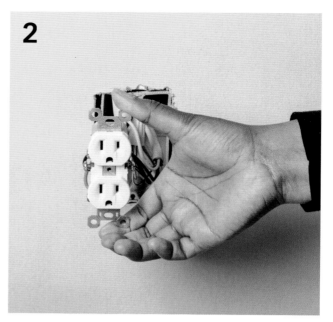

Pull the receptacle from the electrical box to access the wire connections. Test that the wires are not hot and that no power is coming into the receptacle, and then disconnect the receptacle. Cap the free wires in the box.

3

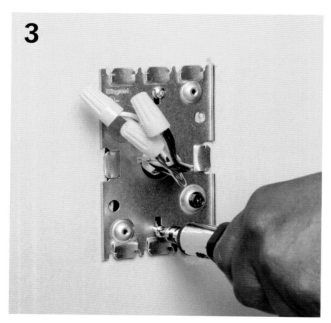

Feed the wires in the box through the access hole in the back of the mounting plate for a surface-mounted receptacle box. Attach the mounting plate to the mounting holes for the cover plate in the existing electrical box.

4

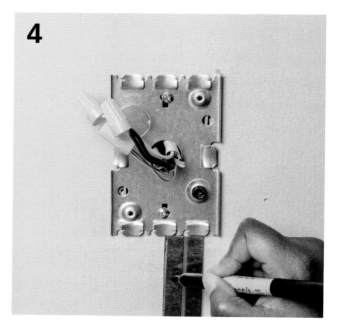

Select an entry point into the new box from the knockout options on the box. Find the corresponding tab on the mounting plate for the box, and draw a straight line from the center of the tab to the next box or fitting in the layout plan. The basic theory of installing the raceway track is to install each segment and then mark and move on to the next one in line.

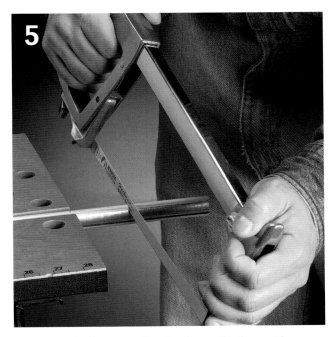

Hold or tack the mounting hardware for the next box or fitting against the wall in position, based on your layout line. You'll need to cut a section of track that is roughly ½" longer than the distance between the mounting tabs on the two pieces of mounting hardware (this ensures that the track will fully seat on the mounting tabs with the ends concealed by the box or fitting covers). Cut the track to length with a hacksaw after securing it in a vise or clamping work support. Deburr the cut edges of the track with a metal file.

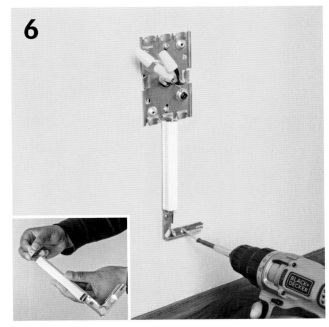

Insert a metal bushing (included in the raceway accessory kit) into each end of the track to protect the wires that will pass through the track. Insert the cut track over the mounting hardware tab on the second box or fitting and then insert the free end of the track onto the tab on the receptacle box (inset). If the piece of track you have cut is longer than a foot or so, you should also have installed a mounting clip for the track (see step 8). Attach the second mounting hardware piece to the wall by screwing it into wall stud locations or drywall anchors.

Plot out the path for the next section of track and hold or tack the mounting hardware in position so you can get an accurate cutting length (see step 5). Cut the track to that length, deburr, and add bushings. Insert the new mounting hardware in one end of the track and slip the other end over the tab on the previous hardware. Test with a level and mark the fastener locations for the new fitting and then install the new fitting.

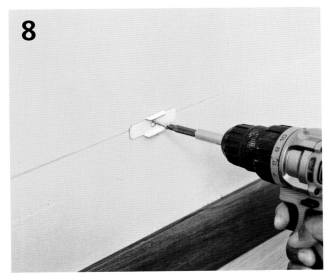

Install a mounting clip every 24" or so along the path, selecting stud locations where possible. The clips shown here are intended for use on flat-surface walls. If your wall has irregularities, look for strap clips that fit over the track.

(continued)

9

With the new fitting plate attached to the end of the track section, fit the other end over the previous plate and then snap the track onto the clips so the edges grip the track sides.

10

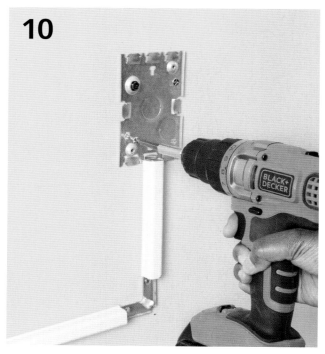

Attach the new fitting plate and continue working in this manner until you have reached the end of the run.

11

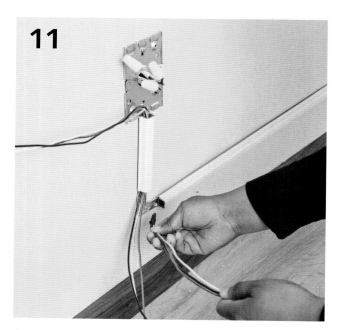

Cut strands of THNN wire (one white, one black, one ground) slightly longer than the total run of the circuit from the original receptacle box. Tape the ends of the wires together and begin feeding them through the track. Start at the beginning and pull the wire through to each subsequent fitting or box until you reach the end of the run. Make sure that the wires follow the curved guides on the elbow plates so they are not damaged when you install the covers.

12

Snap the covers onto the elbow fitting plates, taking care to get a neat fit over the wires. You may need to use a rubber mallet to get the cover to snap so it is gripped by the plate.

13

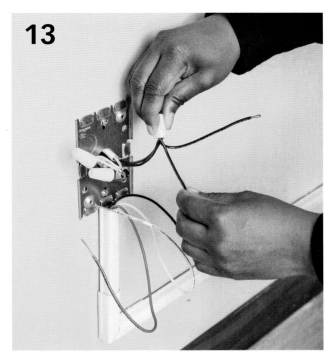

Strip and connect the ends of the new THNN wires and then join them with incoming wires and pigtails in the original box, using wire caps. Be sure the caps are the correct size for the connections.

14

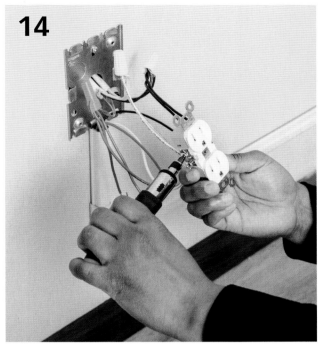

Connect the new receptacle to the THNN wires in the original box using standard wiring practices. Connect all other devices, including the terminal one, in the same manner.

15

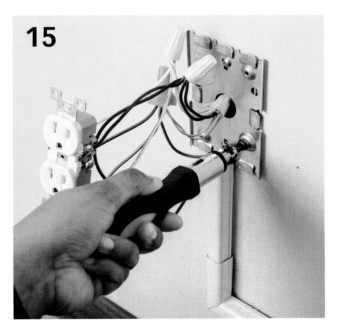

Connect a pigtail grounding wire to a green grounding screw mounted on the base plate for the starting receptacle.

16

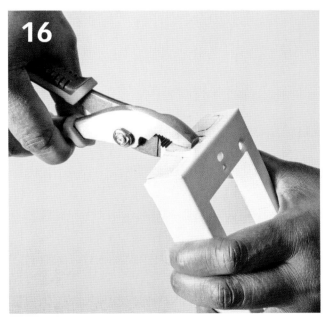

Remove knockout from the box cover, using pliers. Note that there are two height options on each knockout. Select the height that matches your track profile.

(continued)

17

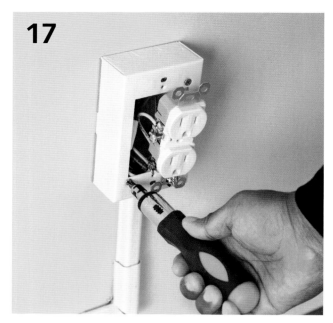

Connect the new receptacle to the THNN wires in the original box using standard wiring practices.

18

Cover the installed receptacles with the cover plate(s), check that the raceway is complete and secure to the wall, and then turn the power on and check that the receptacles are live.

TIPS FOR WORKING WITH SURFACE-MOUNTED RACEWAY

MAKING CORNERS WITH RACEWAY

Use corner pieces to guide around corners. Fittings are available for inside or outside corners and consist of a mounting plate and a cap piece. Inside corners may be used at wall/ceiling junctures.

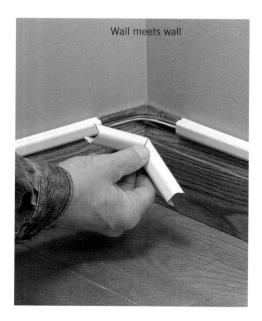

Wall meets wall

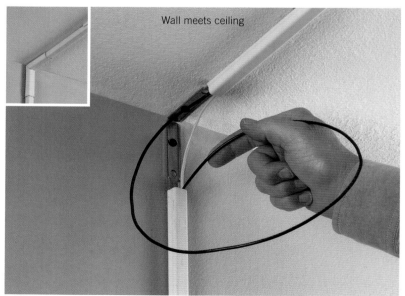

Wall meets ceiling

SPLICING RACEWAY

What if I need a piece of track that's longer than the longest piece available at the hardware store (usually 5 ft.)? You can use straight connector pieces to join two lengths of track. Much like an elbow piece, they have a mounting plate and a cover that snaps over the wiring.

Tool Tip ▸

Metal raceway can be cut like metal conduit. Secure the track or conduit in a vise or clamping work support, and cut with a hacksaw. For best results, use long, slow strokes and don't bear down too hard on the saw. Once the cut is made, file the metal burrs smooth with a metal file.

Wall Anchors ▸

Here's how to install wall anchors: Mark screw locations on the wall, and then drill a narrow guide hole for the screw anchor. Drive the anchor into the guide holes until the flange is flush with the wall surface.

Ideally anything you attach to a drywall wall should be anchored at a wall stud location. Of course, in the real world this often is not possible. You'll find many kinds of wall anchors for sale at the local hardware store. Some work better than others. The common tapered plastic sleeves that are driven into guide holes will work for lighter duty, but they don't grip the wall well enough to secure surface-mounted wiring components. For this, use coarse-threaded, screw-in anchors.

LIGHTS: CEILING

Ceiling fixtures don't have any moving parts and their wiring is very simple, so, other than changing bulbs, you're likely to get decades of trouble-free service from a fixture. This sounds like a good thing, but it also means that the fixture probably won't fail and give you an excuse to update a room's look with a new one. Fortunately, you don't need an excuse. Upgrading a fixture is easy and can make a dramatic impact on a room. You can substantially increase the light in a room by replacing a globe-style fixture by one with separate spot lights, or you can simply install a new fixture that matches the room's décor.

Tools + Materials ▸

Replacement light
  fixture
Wire stripper
Voltage sensor
Insulated
  screwdrivers
Wire connectors
Eye protection

Hacksaw
Pliers
Hammer

Installing a new ceiling fixture can provide more light to a space, not to mention an aesthetic lift. It's one of the easiest upgrades you can do. Check the weight rating of the box to which you will attach your fixture. Older boxes may not handle a heavy fixture.

HOW TO REPLACE A CEILING LIGHT

1

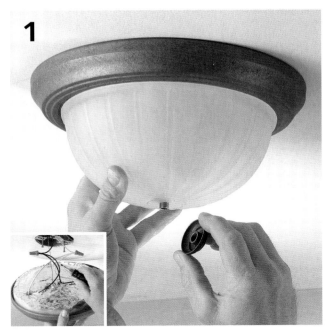

Shut off power to the ceiling light and remove the shade or diffuser. Loosen the mounting screws and carefully lower the fixture, supporting it as you work (do not let light fixtures hang by their electrical wires alone). Test with a voltage sensor to make sure no power is reaching the connections.

2

Remove the twist connectors from the fixture wires or unscrew the screw terminals and remove the white neutral wire and the black lead wire (inset).

3

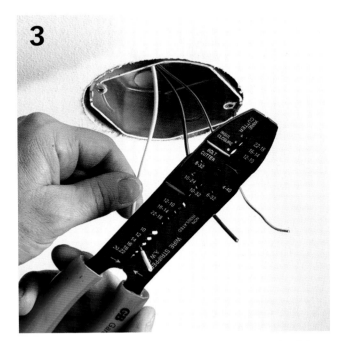

Before you install the new fixture, check the ends of the wires coming from the ceiling electrical box. They should be clean and free of nicks or scorch marks. If they're dirty or worn, clip off the stripped portion with your combination tool. Then strip away about ¾" of insulation from the end of each wire.

4

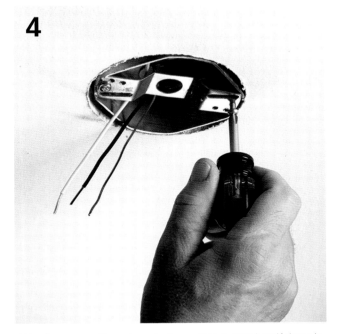

Attach a mounting strap to the ceiling fixture box if there is not one already present. Your new light may come equipped with a strap, otherwise you can find one for purchase at any hardware store.

(continued)

5

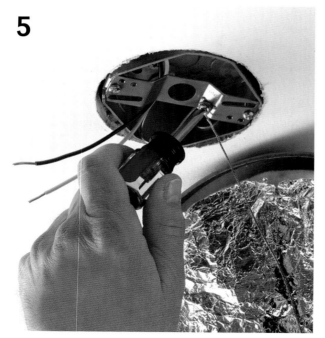

Lift the new fixture up to the ceiling (you may want a helper for this) and attach the bare copper ground wire from the power supply cable to the grounding screw or clip on the mounting strap. Also attach the ground wire from the fixture to the screw or clip.

6

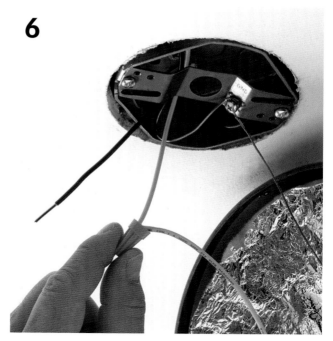

With the fixture supported by a ladder or a helper, join the white wire lead and the white fixture wire with a wire connector (often supplied with the fixture).

7

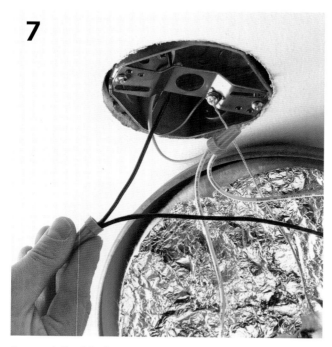

Connect the black power supply wire to the black fixture wire with a wire connector.

8

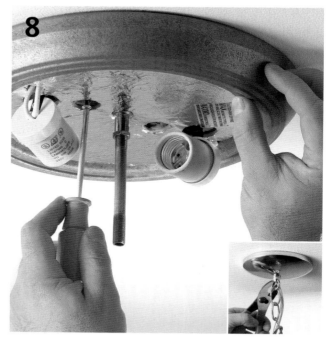

Position the new fixture mounting plate over the box so the mounting screw holes align. Drive the screws until the fixture is secure against the ceiling. *NOTE: Some fixtures are supported by a threaded rod or nipple in the center that screws into a female threaded opening in the mounting strap (inset).*

RECESSED CEILING LIGHTS

Mark the location for the light canister. If you are installing multiple lights, measure out from the wall at the start and end of the run, and connect them with a chalkline snapped parallel to the wall.

Install the housing for the recessed fixture. Housings for new construction (or remodeling installations where the installation area is fully accessible from either above or below) have integral hanger bars that you attach to the each joist in the joist bay.

Run electric cable from the switch to each canister location. Multiple lights are generally installed in series. Make sure to leave enough extra cable at each location to feed the wire into the housing and make the connection.

Run the feeder cables into the electrical boxes attached to the canister housings. You'll need to remove knockouts first and make sure to secure the cable with a wire staple within 8" of the entry point to the box.

(continued)

5

Connect the circuit wires to the fixture wires inside the junction box. Twist the hot lead together with the black fixture wire, as well as the black lead to other fixtures further downline. Also connect the neutral white wires. Join the ground wires and pigtail them to the grounding screw or clip in the box. Finish the ceiling, as desired.

6

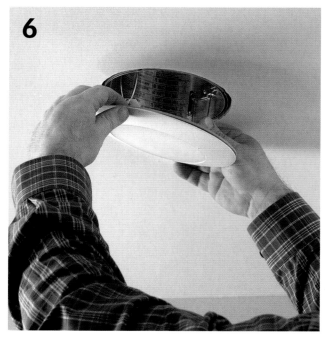

Attach your trim kit of choice. Normally, these are hung with torsion spring clips from notches or hooks inside the canister. This should be done after the ceiling is installed and finished for new construction projects. With certain types of trim kits, such as eyeball trim, you'll need to install the light bulb before the trim kit.

Canless Lights for Retrofitting ▸

Installing recessed lighting in existing ceilings is much easier now than it was a decade ago. New "canless" wafer LED lights are now widely available for installations in existing ceilings. The simplest (and most expensive) versions are battery powered and are simply clipped into holes you cut in the ceiling based on the manufacturer's supplied template. In most cases, however, homeowners will choose to install wired canless fixtures. These include a self-contained junction box for each fixture, which is wired to the room's light switch. The junction box is connected to the fixture by a snap-in cable. The fixture is held in the ceiling hole with spring clips, making installation incredibly easy.

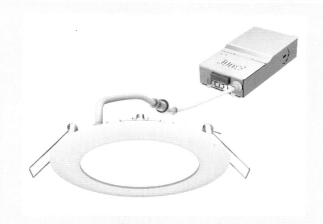

TRACK LIGHTING

Disconnect the old ceiling light fixture (for remodeling projects) after shutting off power to the circuit at the electrical panel. The globe or diffuser and the lamps should be removed before the fixture mounting mechanism is detached. Carefully pull the fixture away from the ceiling without touching any wires.

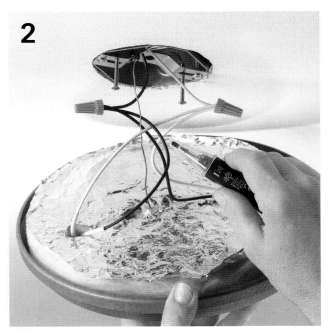

Test the fixture wires with a voltage tester to make sure the circuit is dead. Support the fixture from below while you work—never allow a light fixture to hang by its electrical wires alone. Remove the wire connectors and pull the wires apart. Remove the old light fixture.

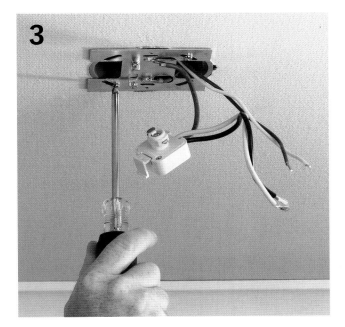

Attach the mounting strap for the new track light to the old ceiling box. If the mounting strap has a hole in the center, thread the circuit wires through the hole before screwing the strap to the box. The green or bare copper ground from the circuit should be attached to the grounding screw or clip on the strap or box.

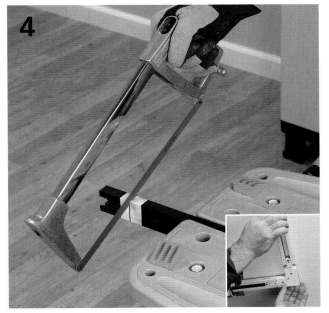

Cut the track section to length, if necessary, using a hack saw. Deburr the cut end with a metal file. If you are installing multiple sections of track, assemble the sections with the correct connector fittings (sold separately from your kit). You can also purchase T-fittings or L-fittings (inset) if you wish to install tracks in either of these configurations.

(continued)

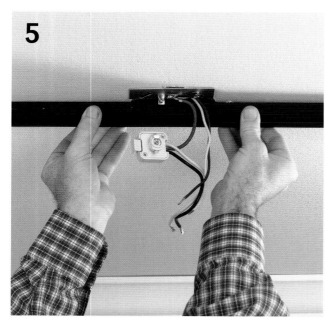

5

Position the track section in the mounting saddle on the mounting strap and hold it temporarily in place in the location where it will be installed. The track section will have predrilled mounting holes in the back. Draw a marking point on the ceiling at each of these locations. If your track does not have predrilled mounting holes, remove it and drill a ³⁄₁₆" hole in the back every 16".

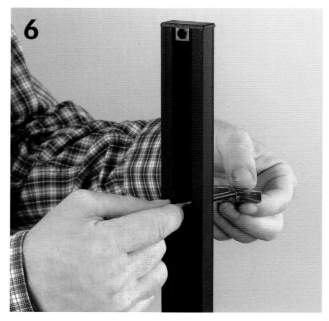

6

Insert the bolt from a toggle bolt or molly bolt into each predrilled screw location and twist the toggle or molly back onto the free end. These types of hardware have greater holding power than anchor sleeves. Drill a ⅝" dia. access hole in the ceiling at each of the mounting hole locations you marked on the ceiling in step 5.

7

Insert the toggle or molly into the access hole far enough so it clears the top of the hole and the wings snap outward. Then tighten each bolt so the track is snug against the ceiling. If the mounting hole happens to fall over a ceiling joint, simply drive a drywall screw at that hole location.

8

Hook up wires from the track's power supply fitting to the circuit wires. Connect black to black and white to white. The grounding wire from the power supply fitting can either be pigtailed to the circuit ground wire and connected to the grounding screw or clip, or it can be twisted together with the circuit grounding wire at the grounding terminal. Snap the fitting into the track if you have not already done so.

9

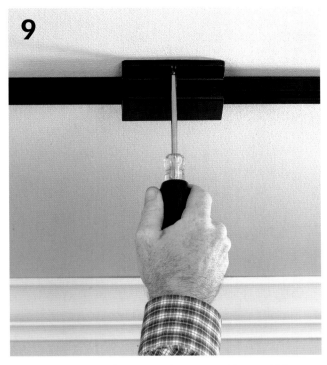

Attach the protective cover that came with your kit to conceal the ceiling box and the electrical connections. Some covers simply snap in place, others require a mounting screw.

10

Dead end

Cap the open ends of the track with a dead end cap fitting. These also may require a mounting screw. Leaving track ends open is a safety violation.

11

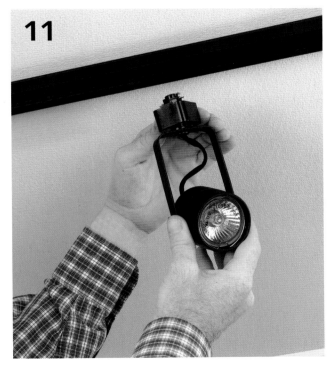

Insert the light heads into the track by slipping the stem into the track slot and then twisting it so the electrical contact points on the head press against the electrified inner rails of the track slot. Tug lightly on the head to make sure it is secure before releasing it.

12

Arrange the track light heads so their light falls in the manner you choose, and then depress the locking tab on each fixture to secure it in position. Restore power and test the lights.

UNDERCABINET LIGHTING

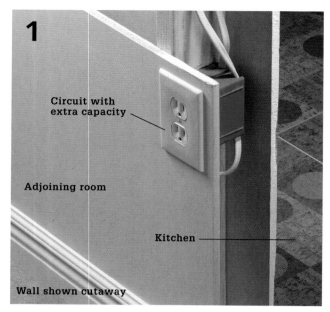

Look in the adjoining room for a usable power source in the form of a receptacle that has a box located in the wall behind your base cabinets. Unlike the small-appliance circuit with outlets in your backsplash area, these typically are not dedicated circuits (which can't be expanded). Make sure that the receptacle's circuit has enough capacity to support another load. Shut the power to the receptacle off at the main service panel and test for power. *NOTE: Expanding a branch circuit may require a permit. Check with your local electrical inspector before doing this project.*

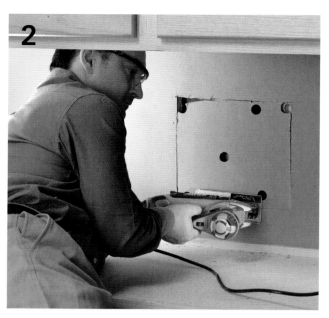

Cut a hole in the base cabinet back panel to get access to the wall behind it in roughly the area where you know the next-door receptacle to be. Use a keyhole saw or drywall saw and make very shallow cuts until you have positively identified the locations of the electrical box and cables. Then finish the cuts with a jigsaw.

Drill an access hole into the kitchen wall for the cable that will feed the undercabinet light. A ½" dia. hole should be about the right size if you are using 12-ga. or 14-ga. sheathed NM cable.

Cut a small access hole (4 × 4" or so) in the back panel of the base cabinet directly below the undercabinet light location.

5

Feed the cable into the access hole at the light location until the end reaches the access hole below. Don't cut the cable yet. Reach into the access hole and feel around for the free cable end and then pull it out through the access hole once you've found it. Cut the cable, making sure to leave plenty of extra on both ends.

6

Feed the cable into a piece of flexible conduit that's long enough to reach between the two access holes in the base cabinets. Attach a connector to each end of the conduit to protect the cable sheathing from the sharp edges of the cut metal. *TIP: To make patching the cabinet back easier, drill a new access hole for the cable near the square access hole.*

7

Hang the conduit with hanger straps attached to the base cabinet frame or back panel, drilling holes in the side walls of the cabinet where necessary to thread the conduit through. On back panels, use small screws to hang the straps instead of brads or nails. Support the conduit near both the entrance and the exit holes (the conduit should extend past the back panels by a couple of inches).

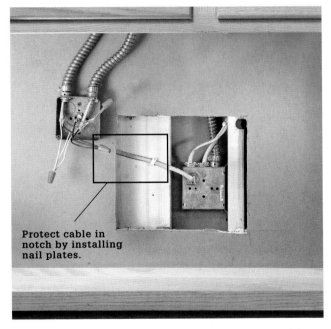

Protect cable in notch by installing nail plates.

VARIATION: If you are installing more than one undercabinet light, run the cable down from each installation point as you did for the first light. Mount an electrical junction box to the cabinet back near the receptacle providing the power. Run the power cables from each light through flexible conduit and make connections inside the junction box. Be sure to attach the junction box cover once the connections are made.

(continued)

8

Remove the receptacle from the box you are tying into and insert the new circuit cable into one of the knockouts using a cable clamp. Check the wire capacity chart on page 240 to ensure the box is acceptable for the number of new conductors. Replace it with a larger box if necessary. Reinstall the receptacle once the connections are made.

9

Install the undercabinet light. Some models have a removable diffuser that allows access to the fixture wires, and these should be screwed to the upper cabinet prior to making your wiring hookups. Other models need to be connected to the circuit wires before installation. Check your manufacturer's installations.

10

Connect wires inside the light fixture according to the light manufacturer's directions. Make sure the incoming cable is stapled just before it enters the light box and that a cable clamp is used at the knockout in the box to protect the cable. Restore the power and test the light.

11

Cut patches of hardboard and fit them over the access holes, overlapping the edges of the cutouts. Adhere them to the cabinet backs with panel adhesive.

VANITY LIGHTS

Many bathrooms have a single fixture positioned above the vanity, but a light source in this position casts shadows on the face and makes grooming more difficult. Light fixtures on either side of the mirror is a better arrangement.

For a remodel, mark the mirror location, run cable, and position boxes before drywall installation. You can also retrofit by installing new boxes and drawing power from the existing fixture.

The light sources should be at eye level; 66" is typical. The size of your mirror and its location on the wall may affect how far apart you can place the sconces, but 36" to 40" apart is a good guideline.

Extending a branch circuit or adding a new branch to install new receptacles, lights, or switches requires a permit. Check with the electrical inspector before starting such projects.

Tools + Materials ▸

Drywall saw
Drill and bits
Combination tool
Circuit tester
Screwdrivers
Hammer

Electrical boxes
  and braces
NM cable
Vanity light fixtures
Wire connectors

Vanity lights on the sides of the mirror provide good lighting. The are also a wonderful way to easily and inexpensively accessorize the room.

HOW TO REPLACE VANITY LIGHTS IN A FINISHED BATHROOM

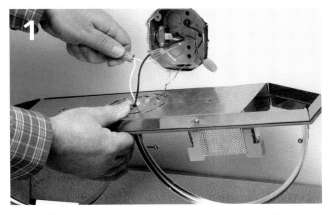

Turn off the power at the panel. Remove the old fixture from the wall, and test to make sure that the power is off. Then remove a strip of drywall from around the old fixture to the first studs beyond the approximate location of the new fixtures. Make the opening large enough that you have room to route cable from the existing fixture to the boxes.

Mark the location for the fixtures, and install new boxes. Install the boxes about 66" above the floor and 18" to 20" from the centerline of the mirror (the mounting base of some fixtures is above or below the bulb, so adjust the height of the bracing accordingly). If the correct location is on or next to a stud, you can attach the box directly to the stud; otherwise you'll need to install blocking or use boxes with adjustable braces (shown).

(continued)

3

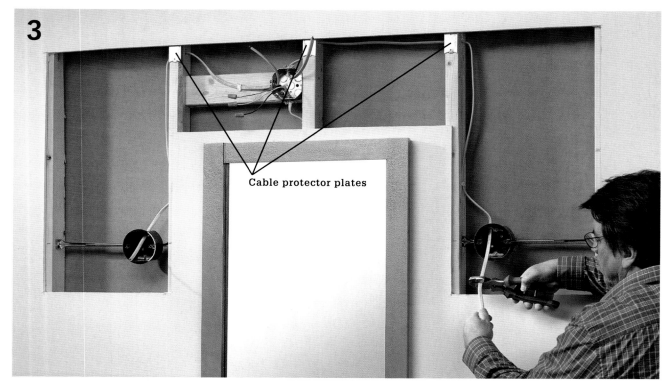

Cable protector plates

Open the side knockouts on the electrical box above the vanity. Then drill ⅝" holes in the centers of any studs between the old fixture and the new ones. Run two NM cables from the new boxes for the fixtures to the box above the vanity. Protect the cable with metal protector plates. Secure the cables with cable clamps, leaving 11" of extra cable for making the connection to the new fixtures. Remove sheathing, and strip insulation from the ends of the wires.

4

Connect the white wires from the new cables to the white wire from the old cable, and connect the black wires from the new cables to the black wire from the old cable. Connect the ground wires. Cover all open boxes, and then replace the drywall, leaving openings for the fixture and the old box. (Cover the old box with a solid junction box cover plate and leave it accessible.)

5

Install the fixture mounting braces on the boxes. Attach the fixtures by connecting the black circuit wire to the black fixture wire and connecting the white circuit wire to the white fixture wire. Connect the ground wires. Position each fixture over each box, and attach with the mounting screws. Restore power, and test the circuit.

HOW TO INSTALL A NEW EXTERIOR FIXTURE BOX

On the outside of the house, make the cutout for the motion-sensor light fixture. Outline the light fixture box on the wall, drill a pilot hole, and complete the cutout with a wallboard saw or jigsaw.

Estimate the distance between the indoor switch box and the outdoor motion-sensor box, and cut a length of NM cable about 2 ft. longer than this distance. Use a fish tape to pull the cable from the switch box to the motion-sensor box. See page 239 for tips on running cable through finished walls.

Mounting bracket

Retrofit box

Strip about 10" of outer insulation from the end of the cable using a cable ripper. Open a knockout in the retrofit light fixture box with a screwdriver. Insert the cable into the box so that at least ¼" of outer sheathing reaches into the box. Apply a heavy bead of silicone or polyurethane caulk to the flange of the electrical box before attaching it to the wall.

Mounting screws

Insert the box into the cutout opening, and tighten the mounting screws until the brackets draw the outside flange firmly against the siding. Follow the siding manufacturer's instructions about flashing this wall pentration.

PLUGS + CORDS: REPLACING

Replace an electrical plug whenever you notice bent or loose prongs, a cracked or damaged casing, or a missing insulating faceplate. A damaged plug poses a shock and fire hazard.

Replacement plugs are available in different styles to match common appliance cords. Always choose a replacement that is similar to the original plug. Flat-cord and quick-connect plugs are used with light-duty appliances, like lamps and radios. Round-cord plugs are used with larger appliances, including those that have three-prong grounding plugs.

Some tools and appliances use polarized plugs. A polarized plug has one wide prong (neutral) and one narrow (hot) prong, corresponding to the hot and neutral slots found in a standard receptacle.

If there is room in the plug body, tie the individual wires in an underwriter's knot to secure the plug to the cord.

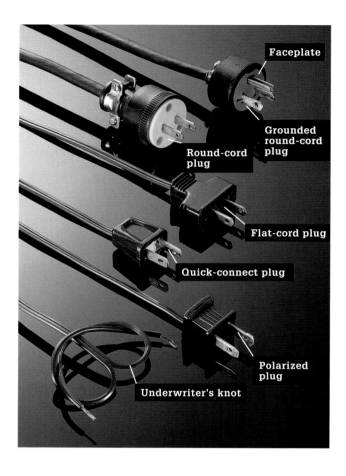

Faceplate

Grounded round-cord plug

Round-cord plug

Flat-cord plug

Quick-connect plug

Polarized plug

Underwriter's knot

Tools + Materials ▸

Combination tool
Needlenose pliers

Screwdriver
Replacement plug

HOW TO INSTALL A QUICK-CONNECT PLUG

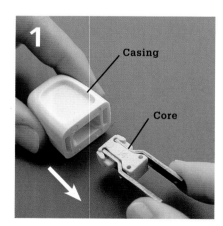

Casing

Core

Squeeze the prongs of the new quick-connect plug together slightly and pull the plug core from the casing. Cut the old plug from the flat-cord wire with a combination tool, leaving a clean cut end.

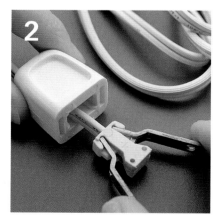

Feed unstripped wire through rear of plug casing. Spread prongs, then insert wire into opening in rear of core. Squeeze prongs together; spikes inside core penetrate cord. Slide the casing over the core until it snaps into place.

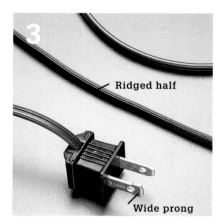

Ridged half

Wide prong

When replacing a polarized plug, make sure that the ridged half of the cord lines up with the wider (neutral) prong of the plug.

HOW TO REPLACE A ROUND-CORD PLUG

Cut off round cord near the old plug using a combination tool. Remove the insulating faceplate on the new plug and feed cord through rear of plug. Strip about 3" of outer insulation from the round cord. Strip ¾" insulation from the individual wires.

Underwriter's knot

Tie an underwriter's knot with the black and the white wires. Make sure the knot is located close to the edge of the stripped outer insulation. Pull the cord so that the knot slides into the plug body.

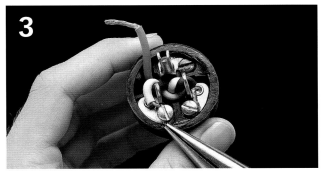

Hook end of black wire clockwise around brass screw and white wire around silver screw. On a three-prong plug, attach the third wire to the grounding screw. If necessary, excess grounding wire can be cut away.

Tighten the screws securely, making sure the copper wires do not touch each other. Replace the insulating faceplate.

HOW TO REPLACE A FLAT-CORD PLUG

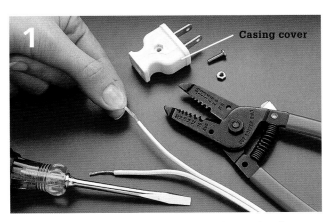

Casing cover

Cut old plug from cord using a combination tool. Pull apart the two halves of the flat cord so that about 2" of wire are separated. Strip ¾" insulation from each half. Remove casing cover on new plug.

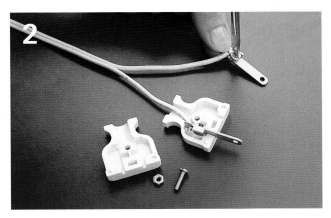

Hook ends of wires clockwise around the screw terminals, and tighten the screw terminals securely. Reassemble the plug casing. Some plugs may have an insulating faceplate that must be installed.

CEILING FANS: INSTALLING

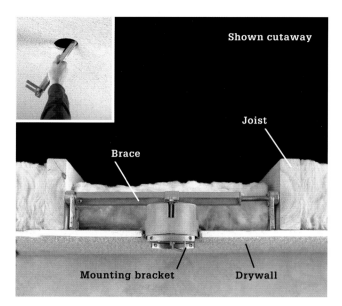

Add a wood brace above the ceiling box if you have access from above (as in an attic). Cut a 2 × 4 brace to fit and nail it between the ceiling joists. Drive a couple of deck screws through the ceiling box and into the brace. If the box is not fan-rated, replace it with one that is.

Install an adjustable fan brace if the ceiling is closed and you don't want to remove the drywall. Remove the old light and the electrical box and then insert the fan brace into the box opening (inset photo). Twist the brace housing to cause it to telescope outward. The brace should be centered over the opening and at the right height so the ceiling box is flush with the ceiling surface once it is hung from the brace.

BRACKET-MOUNTED FANS

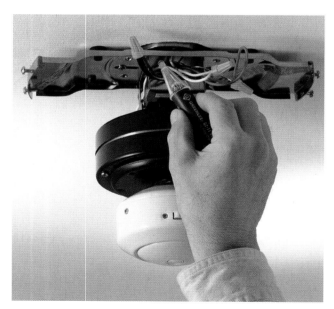

Direct-mount fan units have a motor housing with a mounting tab that fits directly into a slot on the mounting bracket. Fans with this mounting approach are secure and easy to install but difficult to adjust.

Ball-and-socket fan units have a downrod, but instead of threading into the mounting bracket, the downrod has an attached ball that fits into a hanger "socket" in the mounting bracket. This installation allows the fan to move in the socket and find its own level for quiet operation.

HOW TO INSTALL DOWNROD CEILING FANS

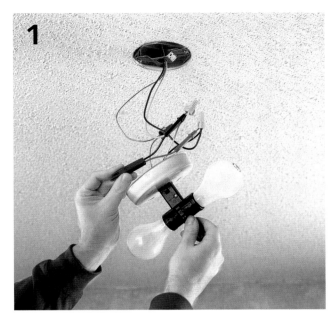

1

Shut off the power to the circuit at the panel. Unscrew the existing fixture and carefully pull it away from the ceiling. Test for power with a voltage tester to confirm the power is off. Disconnect and remove the old fixture.

2

Canopy

Rod hanger pipe

Run the wires from the top of the fan motor through the canopy and then through the rod hanger pipe. Slide the rod hanger pipe through the canopy and attach the pipe to the motor collar using the included hanging pin. Tighten the mounting screws firmly.

3

Hanging pin

Hang the motor assembly by the hook on the mounting bracket. Connect the wires according to manufacturer's directions using wire connectors to join the fixture wires to the circuit wires in the box. Gather the wires together and tuck them inside the fan canopy. Lift the canopy and attach it to the mounting bracket.

4

Fan housing

Attach the fan blades with the included hardware. Connect the wiring for the fan's light fixture according to the manufacturer's directions. Tuck all wires into the switch housing and attach the fixture. Install light bulbs. Restore power and test the fan.

REPAIRING CEILING FANS

Ceiling fans contain rapidly moving parts, making them more susceptible to trouble than many other electrical fixtures. Installation is a relatively simple matter, but repairing a ceiling fan can be very frustrating. The most common problems you'll encounter are balance and noise issues and switch failure, usually precipitated by the pull chain breaking. In most cases, both problems can be corrected without removing the fan from the ceiling. But if you have difficulty on ladders or simply don't care to work overhead, consider removing the fan when replacing the switch.

Ceiling fans are subject to a great deal of vibration and stress, so it's not uncommon for switches and motors to fail. Minimize wear and tear by making sure blades are in balance so the fan doesn't wobble.

Tools + Materials ▸

Screwdriver
Combination tool

Replacement switch
Voltage tester

HOW TO TROUBLESHOOT BLADE WOBBLE

Start by checking and tightening all hardware used to attach the blades to the mounting arms and the mounting arms to the motor. Hardware tends to loosen over time, and this is frequently the cause of wobble.

If wobble persists, try switching around two of the blades. Often this is all it takes to get the fan back into balance. If a blade is damaged or warped, replace it.

OPTION: Fan-blade wobble also may be corrected using small weights that are affixed to the tops of the blades. For an easy DIY fix, you can use electrical tape and washers and some trial-and-error. You can also purchase fan-blade weight kits for a couple of dollars. These kits include clips for marking the position of the weights as you relocate them as well as self-adhesive weights that can be stuck to the blade once you have found the sweet spot.

HOW TO FIX A LOOSE WIRE CONNECTION

A leading cause of fan failure is loose wire connections. To inspect these connections, first shut off the power to the fan. Remove the fan blades to gain access, and then remove the canopy that covers the ceiling box and fan mounting bracket. Most canopies are secured with screws on the outside shell. Have a helper hold the fan body while you remove the screws so it won't fall.

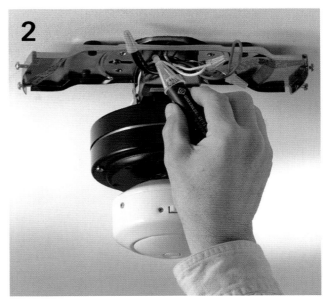

Once the canopy is lowered, you'll see black, white, green, copper, and possibly blue wires. Hold a voltage tester within ½" of these wires with the wall switch that controls the fan in the ON position. The black and blue wires should cause the sensor to beep if power is present.

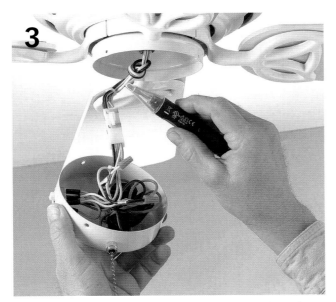

Shut off power and test the wires by touching the voltage tester to each one. If the sensor beeps or lights up, then the circuit is still live and is not safe to work on. When the sensor does not beep or light up, the circuit is dead and may be worked upon.

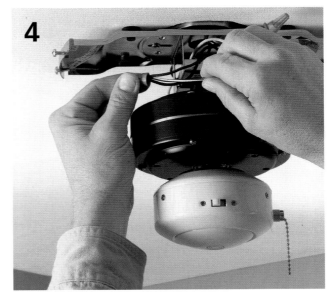

When you have confirmed that there is no power, check all the wire connections to make certain each is tight and making good contact. You may be able to see that a connection has come apart and needs to be remade. But even if you see one bad connection, check them all by gently tugging on the wire connectors. If the wires pull out of the wire connector or the connection feels loose, unscrew the wire connector from the wires. Turn the power back on and see if the problem has been solved.

HOW TO REPLACE A CEILING FAN PULL-CHAIN SWITCH

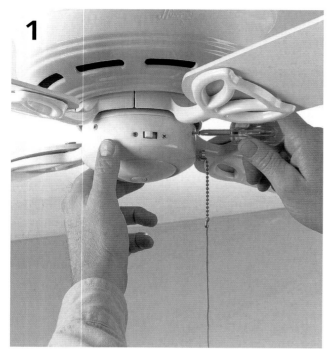

Turn off the power at the panel. Use a screwdriver to remove the three to four screws that secure the bottom cap on the fan switch housing. Lower the cap to expose the wires that supply power to the pull-chain switch.

Test the wires with a voltage tester. If the tester beeps or lights up, then the circuit is still live and is not safe to work on. When the sensor does not beep or light up, the circuit is dead and may be worked upon.

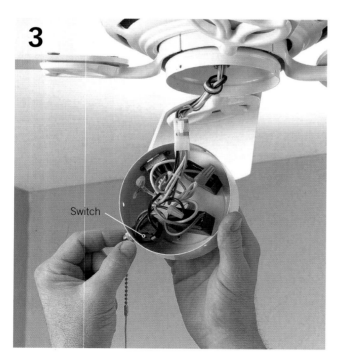

Switch

Locate the switch unit (the part that the pull chain used to be attached to if it broke off); it's probably made of plastic. You'll need to replace the whole switch. Fan switches are connected with three to eight wires, depending on the number of speed settings.

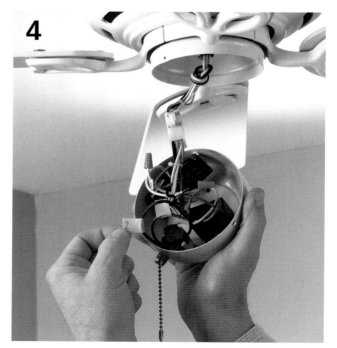

Attach a small piece of tape to each wire that enters the switch, and write an identifying number on the tape. Start at one side of the switch, and label the wires in the order they're attached.

5

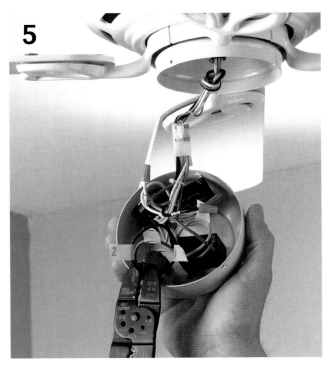

Disconnect the old switch wires, in most cases by cutting the wires off as close to the old switch as possible. Unscrew the retaining nut that secures the switch to the switch housing.

6

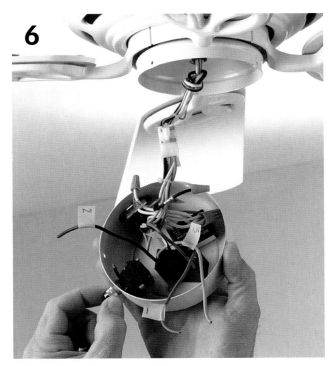

Remove the switch. There may be one or two screws that hold it in place or it may be secured to the outside of the fan with a small knurled nut, which you can loosen with needle-nose pliers. Purchase an identical new switch.

7

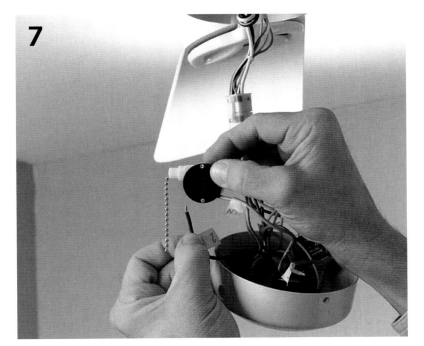

Connect the new switch using the same wiring configuration as on the old model. To make connections, first use a wire stripper to strip ¾" of insulation from the ends of each of the wires coming from the fan motor (the ones you cut in step 5). Attach the wires to the new switch in the same order and configuration as they were attached to the old switch. Secure the new switch in the housing, and make sure all wires are tucked neatly inside. Reattach the bottom cap. Restore power to the fan. Test all the fan's speeds to make sure all the connections are good.

> **Buyer's Tip ▶**
>
> **Here's how to buy a new switch.** Bring the old switch to the hardware store or home center, and find an identical new switch—one with the same number and color of wires. It should also attach to the fan motor wires in the same way (slots or screw terminals or with integral wires and wire connectors) and attach to the fan in the same way. If you are unable to locate an identical switch, find the owners manual for your ceiling fan and contact the manufacturer. Or, find the brand and model number of the fan and order a switch from a ceiling fan dealer or electronics supply store.

BASEBOARD HEATERS

Baseboard heaters are a popular way to provide additional heating for an existing room or primary heat to a converted attic or basement. Extending a branch circuit or adding a new branch to install new receptacles, lights, switches, or equipment requires a permit. The electrical inspector may require that you install arc-fault protection on the entire circuit. Check with the electrical inspector before starting such projects.

Heaters are generally wired on a dedicated 240-volt circuit controlled by a thermostat. Several heaters can be wired in parallel and controlled by a single thermostat.

Baseboard heaters are generally surface-mounted without boxes, so in a remodeling situation, you only need to run cables before installing wallboard. Be sure to mark cable locations on the floor before installing drywall. Retrofit installations are also not difficult. You can remove existing baseboard and run new cable in the space behind. Baseboard heaters (and other heating equipment) get very hot and can ignite nearby combustible materials. Maintain the manufacturer's recommended distance between the heater and materials such as curtains, blinds, and wood.

Tools + Materials ▸

Drill/driver	12/2 NM cable
Wire stripper	Electrical tape
Cable ripper	Basic wiring supplies
Wallboard saw	Kneepads
Baseboard heater or heaters	Work gloves
240-thermostat (in-heater or in-wall)	

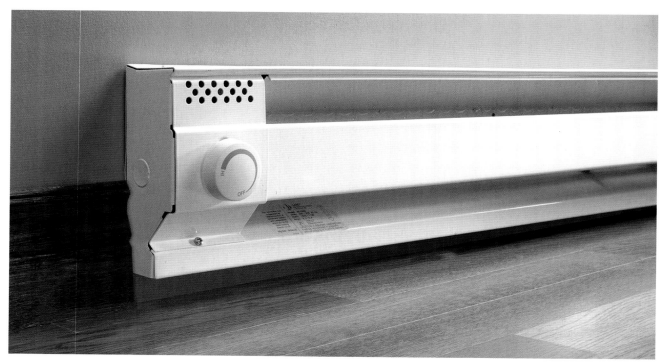

Baseboard heaters can provide primary or supplemental heat for existing rooms or additions. Install heaters with clear space between the heater and the floor.

BASEBOARD THERMOSTATS

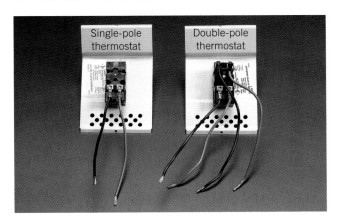

Single-pole thermostat Double-pole thermostat

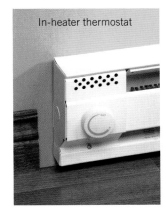

In-heater thermostat

Wall-mount thermostat

Single-pole and double-pole thermostats work in a similar manner, but double-pole models are safer. The single-pole model will open the circuit (causing shutoff) in only one leg of the power service. Double-pole models have two sets of wires to open both legs, lessening the chance that a person servicing the heater will contact a live wire.

In-heater and wall-mount are the two types of baseboard thermostats you can choose from. If you are installing multiple heaters, a single wall-mount thermostat is more convenient. Individual in-heater thermostats give you more zone control, which can result in energy savings.

HOW MUCH HEATER DO YOU NEED?

If you don't mind doing a little math, determining how many lineal feet of baseboard heater a room requires is not hard. For the most precise estimate, contact a professional.

1. Measure the area of the room in square feet (length × width): _____

2. Multiply the area by 10 to get the baseline minimum wattage: _____

3. Add 5% for each newer window or 10% for each older window: _____

4. Add 10% for each exterior wall in the room: _____

5. Add 10% for each exterior door: _____

6. Add 10% if the space below is not insulated: _____

7. Add 20% if the space above is not well insulated: _____

8. Add 10% if ceiling is more than 8 ft. high: _____

9. Total of the baseline wattage plus all additions: _____

10. Divide this number by 250 (the wattage produced per foot of standard baseboard heater): _____

11. Round up to a whole number. This is the minimum number of feet of heater you need. _____

NOTE: It is much better to have more feet of heater than is required than fewer. Having more footage of heater does not consume more energy; it does allow the heaters to work more efficiently.

PLANNING TIPS FOR BASEBOARD HEATERS

- Baseboard heaters require a dedicated circuit. A 20-amp, 240-volt circuit of 12-gauge copper wire may power up to 16 ft. of heater. Refer to the manufacturer's instructions for specific circuit load information.

- Do not install a heater beneath a wall receptacle. Cords hanging down from the receptacle are a fire hazard.

- Do not mount heaters directly on the floor. You should maintain at least 1" of clear space between the baseboard heater and the floor covering.

- Installing heaters directly beneath windows is a good practice.

- Locate wall thermostats on interior walls only, and do not install directly above a heat source.

HOW TO INSTALL A 240-VOLT BASEBOARD HEATER

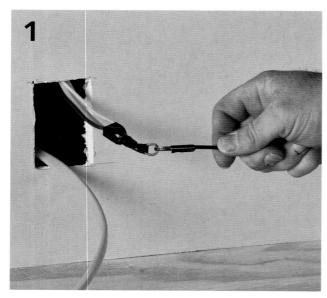

At the heater locations, cut a small hole in the drywall 3" to 4" above the floor. Pull 12/2 NM (or the wire gauge specified by the heater manufacturer) cables through the first hole: one from the thermostat, the other to the next heater. Pull all the cables for subsequent heaters. Middle-of-run heaters will have two cables, while end-of-run heaters have only one cable.

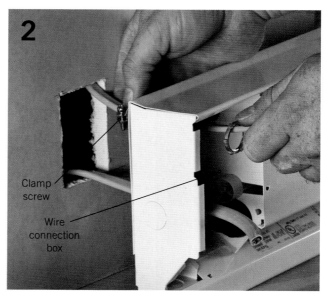

Clamp screw

Wire connection box

Remove the cover on the wire connection box. Open a knockout for each cable that will enter the box, and then feed the cables through the cable clamps and into the wire connection box. Attach the clamps to the wire connection box, and tighten the clamp screws until the cables are gripped firmly.

Anchor the heater against wall about 1" off floor by driving flathead screws through the back of the housing and into studs. Strip away cable sheathing so at least ½" of sheathing extends into the heater. Strip ¾" of insulation from each wire using a combination tool.

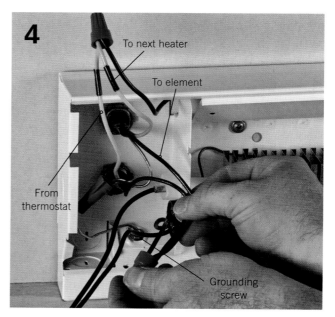

To next heater

To element

From thermostat

Grounding screw

Make connections to the heating element if the power wires are coming from a thermostat or another heater controlled by a thermostat. See the next page for other wiring schemes. Connect the white circuit wires to one of the wire leads on the heater. Tag white wires with black tape to indicate they are hot. Connect the black circuit wires to the other wire lead. Connect a grounding pigtail to the green grounding screw in the box, and then join all grounding wires with a wire connector. Reattach the cover.

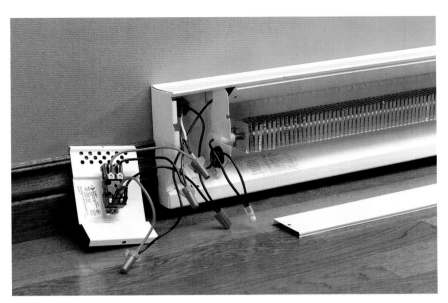

One heater with end-cap thermostat. Run both power leads (black plus tagged neutral) into the connection box at either end of the heater. If installing a single-pole thermostat, connect one power lead to one thermostat wire and connect the other thermostat wire, to one of the heater leads. Connect the other hot LINE wire to the other heater lead. If you are installing a double-pole thermostat, make connections with both legs of the power supply.

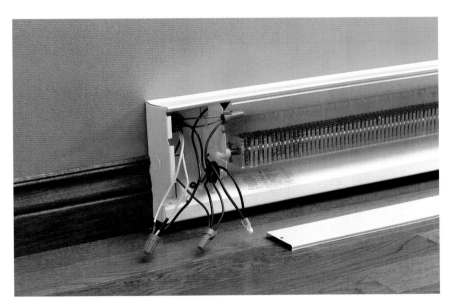

Multiple heaters. At the first heater, join both hot wires from the thermostat to the wires leading to the second heater in line. Be sure to tag all white neutrals hot. Twist copper ground wires together and pigtail them to the grounding screw in the baseboard heater junction box. This parallel wiring configuration ensures that power flow will not be interrupted to the downstream heaters if an upstream heater fails.

Wall-mounted thermostat. If installing a wall-mounted thermostat, the power leads should enter the thermostat first and then be wired to the individual heaters singly or in series. Hookups at the heater are made as shown in step 4. Be sure to tag the white neutral as hot in the thermostat box as well as in the heater box.

SMOKE + CARBON MONOXIDE DETECTORS

Smoke and carbon monoxide (CO) alarms are essential safety components of any living facility. All national fire protection codes require that new homes have a hard-wired smoke alarm in every sleeping room and on every level of a residence, including basements, attics, and attached garages. A smoke alarm needs to be protected with an AFCI circuit if it is installed in a bedroom. Most authorities also recommend CO detectors on every level of the house and in every sleeping area.

Heat alarms, which detect heat instead of smoke, are often specified for locations like utility rooms, basements, or unfinished attics, where conditions may cause nuisance tripping of smoke alarms.

Hard-wired alarms operate on your household electrical current but have battery backups in case of a power outage. On new homes, all smoke alarms must be wired in a series so that every alarm sounds regardless of the fire's location. When wiring a series of alarms, be sure to use alarms of the same brand to ensure compatibility. Always check local codes before starting the job. Ceiling-installed alarms should be 4"

away from the nearest wall. Smoke alarms and CO alarms are considered such important safety devices that national codes require updating these alarms to current code requirements during some types of remodeling projects. Enforcement of this requirement varies by jurisdiction, so check with your building department before remodeling.

Tools + Materials ▸

Screwdriver	Two- and three-wire
Combination tool	14-gauge
Fish tape	NM cable
Drywall saw	Alarms
Wall or ceiling	Wire connectors
outlet boxes	15-amp single-pole
Cable clamps	breaker
(if boxes are not	Eye protection
self-clamping)	Work gloves

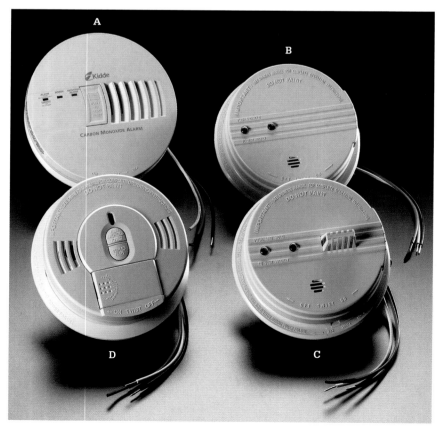

Smoke detectors and carbon monoxide (CO) detectors are required in new construction. Hard-wired carbon monoxide detectors (A) are triggered by the presence of carbon monoxide gas. Smoke detectors are available in photoelectric and ionizing models. In ionizing detectors (B), a small current flows in an ionization chamber. When smoke enters the chamber, it interrupts the current, triggering the alarm. Photoelectric detectors (C) rely on a beam of light, interrupted by smoke triggers an alarm. Heat alarms (D) sound when they detect areas of high. In existing homes where it is impractical to install hardwired smoke alarms, battery-powered alarms are allowed. Use battery-powered smoke alarms that are wirelessly interconnected. CO alarms are required in homes with fuel-burning appliances, including fireplaces. If more than one CO alarm is required, they should be hardwired and interconnected. Combination alarms are available, and may be installed instead of separate alarms. Typical service life of a CO alarm is 7 years, so combination alarms will need more frequent replacement.

HOW TO CONNECT A SERIES OF HARD-WIRED SMOKE ALARMS

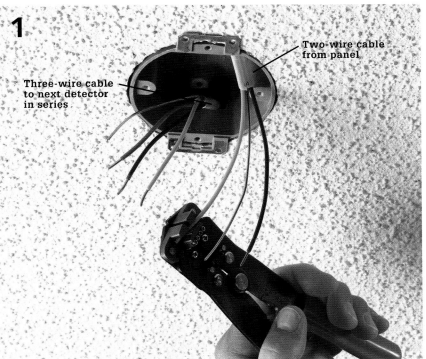

1

Three-wire cable to next detector in series

Two-wire cable from panel

Pull 14/2 NM cable from the panel into the first ceiling electrical box in the smoke alarm series. Pull 14/3 NM cable between the remaining alarm outlet boxes. Use cable clamps to secure the cable in each outlet box. Remove sheathing and strip insulation from wires.

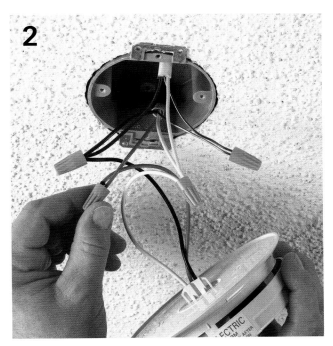

2

Ensure power is off and test for power. Wire the first alarm in the series. Use a wire connector to connect the ground wires. Splice the black circuit wire with the alarm's black lead and the black wire going to the next alarm in the series. Splice the white circuit wire with the alarm's white wire and the white (neutral) wire going to the next alarm in the series. Splice the red traveler wire with the odd-colored alarm wire (in this case, also a red wire).

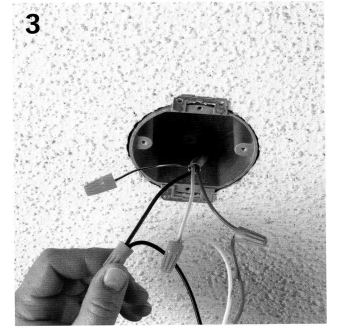

3

Wire the remaining alarms in the series by connecting the like-colored wires in each outlet box. Always connect the red traveler wire to the odd-colored (in this case, red) alarm wire. This red traveler wire connects all the alarms together so that when one alarm sounds, all the alarms sound. If the alarm doesn't have a grounding wire, cap the ground with a wire connector. When all alarms are wired, install and connect the new 15-amp AFCI breaker.

LED-BACKLIT MIRROR

Traditionally, the standard light source for smaller bathrooms and powder rooms is a light fixture above the mirror. This was often the only solution for vanity mirror lighting where there is little or no space on the sides of the mirror. Now, however, there is an interesting option: lighting that is emitted by the mirror itself.

LED-illuminated mirrors use a base that contains LED strips that provide backlight from around the edges of the mirror or an LED frame that actually shines through the mirror when turned on. This type of mirror is not particularly expensive, is fairly easy to install, and can add brilliantly useful lighting in cramped quarters.

The wiring for our mirror features an ordinary circuit plug that fits into a standard 115- or 120-volt outlet. Installation is quite easy if you happen to have a wall outlet located on the wall directly behind where your mirror will be installed. If not, then you will need to install (or have an electrician install) a standard wall outlet behind the mirror location. Our project assumes that this wall outlet already exists or has been preinstalled. You will need competent wiring skills if you expect to do this work yourself; if you are not skilled at such work, hire an electrician to run new cable and install the wall outlet.

An LED-backlit mirror adds a special element to a small—or even a large—bathroom, but the real benefit is a true-to-life representation in the mirror so you'll see exactly what other people will see.

Tools + Materials ▸

Tape measure
Carpenter's pencil
Stud finder
Drill and bits

Torpedo level
Eye protection
Work gloves

HOW TO INSTALL AN LED-ILLUMINATED MIRROR

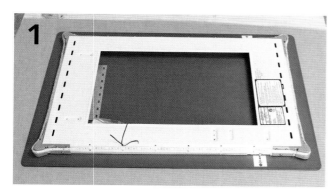

Unpack the LED mirror and place it face down on a soft, flat surface. Examine the kit to make sure all parts are included. Make sure the necessary circuit wiring is done, based on the instructions with the LED kit. The following steps assume that the circuit wiring is complete. In our example, the assumption is that a simple circuit extension from the wall vanity light has been installed, so that the same switch that controls the light fixture will control the LED mirror.

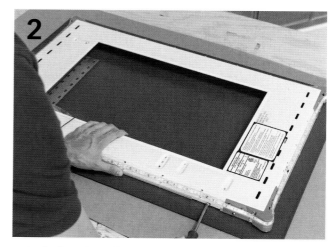

Detach the mirror from the base by loosening the mounting screws. If your mirror has illuminated LED strips, there may also be wire connections running from the base to the mirror panel that need to be detached.

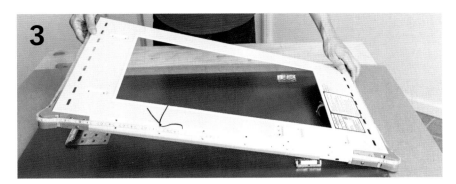

3

Remove the mirror base from the mirror panel. Establish a level line on the wall to mark where the bottom of the mirror will go. Installing a temporary ledger board along this line can help make installation easier.

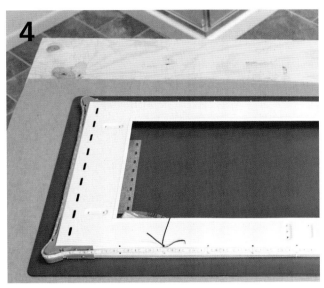

4

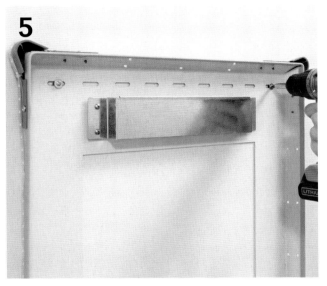

5

Position the mirror base against the wall, and mark the location for the mounting holes on the wall. Ideally, you should be able to find locations over studs where you can mount the mirror base securely. Should this not be possible, you will need to attach plastic wall anchors to secure the mirror base or use toggle bolts to secure the mirror to the wall.

Secure the mirror base to the wall by driving mounting screws into wall studs, both at the top and bottom of the mirror on both sides. If you have access to wall studs on both sides, four screws driven near each corner should be sufficient to mount the mirror base securely. Plug in the electrical cord on the mirror base into the wall outlet.

6

7

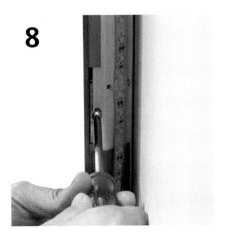

8

Holding the mirror panel in place, use the quick-fit connector to establish the electrical connection between the mirror panel and the base. This work is easiest if you have a helper hold the mirror panel as you plug in the wiring.

Carefully hang the mirror panel onto the mounting bracket on the base. Align the mirror panel so the mounting screws are properly positioned.

Secure the mirror panel to the base using the mounting screws included with the kit. Test the LED mirror to make sure it works properly.

WIRELESS SWITCHES

Sometimes a light switch is just in the wrong place, or it would be more convenient to have two switches controlling a single fixture. Adding a second switch the conventional way generally requires hours of work and big holes in walls. (Electricians call this a three-way switch installation.) Fortunately wireless switch kits are available to perform basically the same function for a fraction of the cost and effort. There is a bit of real wiring involved here, but it's not nearly as complicated as the traditional method of adding a three-way switch installation.

The kits work by replacing a conventional switch with a unit that has a built-in radio frequency receiver that will read a remote device mounted within a 50-foot radius. The kits come with a remote, battery-powered switch (it looks like a standard light switch) that you can attach to a wall with double-sided tape.

Two other similar types of wireless switch kits are also available. One allows you to control a plugged-in lamp or appliance with a remote light switch. The second type allows you to control a conventional light fixture remotely, but instead of replacing the switch, the receiver screws in below the light bulb. This is particularly useful if you want to control a pull-chain light from a wall switch.

Tools + Materials ▸

Voltage tester
Screwdrivers
Wire connectors

Wireless switch
  transmitter and
  receiver/switch

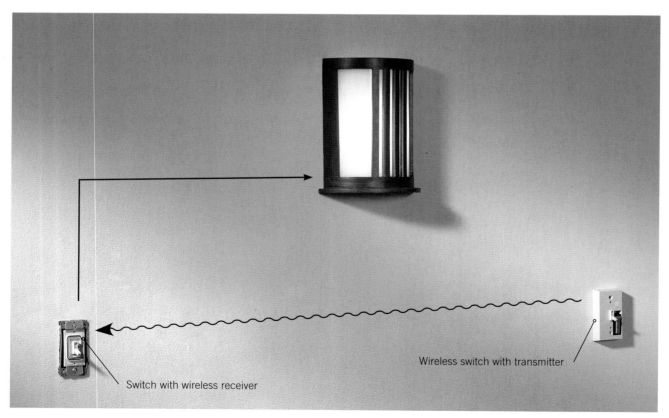

Switch with wireless receiver

Wireless switch with transmitter

A wireless switch is a two-part switching system: a wireless switch with a battery-powered transmitter can be attached to any wall surface; an existing switch is then replaced with a new switch containing a receiver that is triggered by signals from the wireless transmitter, effectively creating a three-way switch condition.

WIRELESS SWITCH PRODUCTS

Wireless lamp switch

Wireless wall switch kit

Wireless plug-in switch

Wireless kits are available to let you switch lights on and off remotely in a variety of ways: at the switch, at the plug, or at the bulb socket.

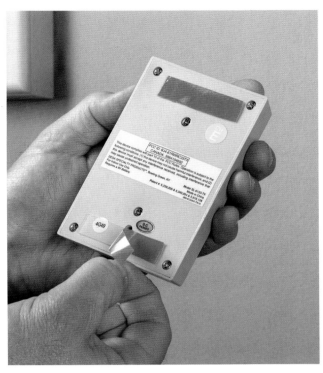

The remote switch is a wireless transmitter that requires a battery. The transmitter switch attaches to the wall with adhesive tape or velcro strips.

A receiver with a receptacle can be plugged into any receptacle to give it wireless functionality. The switch is operated with a remote control transmitter.

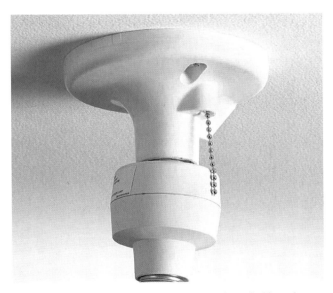

A radio-controlled light fixture can be threaded into the socket of any existing light fixture so it can be turned on and off with a remote control device.

HOW TO INSTALL A WIRELESS WALL SWITCH

1

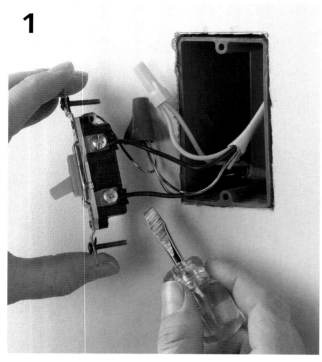

Remove the old switch. Shut off power to the switch circuit, and then disconnect and remove the old switch.

2

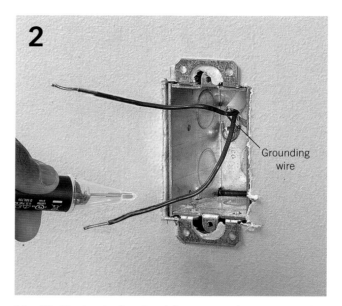

Grounding wire

Identify the lead wire. Carefully separate the power supply wires (any color but white or green) in the switch box so they are not contacting each other or any other surface. Restore power and test each lead wire with a noncontact voltage tester to identify which wire carries the power (the LINE) and which is headed for the fixture the switch controls (the LOAD). Shut power off, and then label the wires.

3

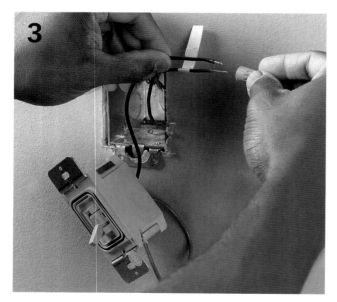

Connect the LINE wire to the LINE terminal or wire on the switch. Connect the LOAD wire (or wires) to the LOAD terminal or wire. The neutral whites (if present) and green grounding wires should be twisted together with a connector. The green wires should be grounded to the grounding clip or terminal in the box. *Some switch boxes, such as the one above, are wired with NM2 cable that has two blacks and a green wire and no white.*

4

Once the wires are firmly connected, you can attach the switch to the box. Tuck the new switch and wires neatly back into the box. Then drive the two long screws that are attached to the new switch into the two holes in the electrical box.

5

Attach the cover plate to the new wireless switch.
Turn the power back on, and test to make sure the switch
operates normally.

6

Remove the backing from the adhesive pads on the
back of the wireless switch transmitter box. Install a new 9-volt
battery (or other type as required) in the box, and connect it to
the switch transmitter terminals.

7

Stick the transmitter box to the wall at the desired location.
The box should be no more than 50 ft. from the receiver switch
(see manufacturer's suggestions). The box should be at the
same height (usually 48") as the other switch boxes.

8

Test the operation of both switches. Each switch
should successfully turn the light fixture on and off. You've
just successfully created a three-way switch installation
without running any new wires.

PLUMBING MATERIALS

Common Pipe + Tube Types ▶

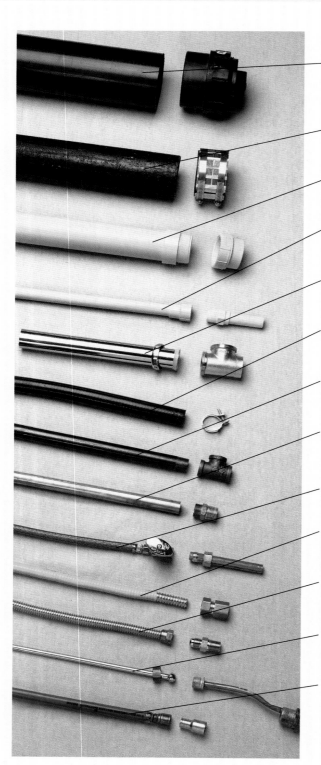

BENEFITS & CHARACTERISTICS

Acrylonitrile butadiene styrene (ABS) is an approved DWV pipe (although it has its detractors) and is commonly used in many markets, especially in the western U.S.

Cast iron is strong but hard to work with. Repairs should be made with plastic pipe.

Polyvinyl chloride (PVC) is rigid plastic that resists heat and chemicals. Schedule 40 is the minimum thickness, although Schedule 80 pipe minimizes water noise.

Chlorinated polyvinyl chloride (CPVC) rigid plastic is inexpensive and withstands high temperature and pressure.

Chromed brass has an attractive shiny surface and is used for drain traps where appearance is important.

Polyethylene (PE) plastic is a black or bluish flexible pipe sometimes used for main water service lines as well as irrigation systems.

Black pipe (iron pipe) generally is threaded at the ends to accept female-threaded fittings. Usually used for gas lines; it is not for potable water.

Rigid copper is used for water supply pipes. It resists corrosion and has smooth surfaces for good water flow.

Braided metal is used for water supply tubes that connect shutoff valves to fixtures.

Flexible stainless-steel (protective coated) connectors are used to attach gas appliances to supply stopcocks.

Flexible stainless-steel (uncoated) connectors are used to attach gas appliances to supply stopcocks.

Chromed copper supply tube is used in areas where appearance is important. It is easy to bend and fit.

Cross-linked polyethylene (PEX) is flexible and is approved by major building codes for water supply.

Flexible copper tubing (not shown) bends easily and requires fewer couplings than rigid copper.

COMMON USES	LENGTHS	DIAMETERS	FITTING METHODS	TOOLS USED FOR CUTTING
DWV pipes, sewer pipes, drain traps	10'	1¼, 1½, 2, 3, 4"	ABS solvent cement or threaded fittings	Tubing cutter, miter box, or hacksaw
DWV pipes, sewer pipes	5', 10'	1½, 2, 3, 4"	Oakum & lead, banded neoprene couplings	Snap cutter or hacksaw
DWV pipes, sewer pipes, drain traps	10', 20'; or sold by linear feet	1¼, 1½, 2, 3, 4"	Solvent cement, threaded fittings	Tubing cutter, miter box, or hacksaw
Hot & cold water supply pipes	10'	⅜, ½, ¾, 1"	Solvent cement & plastic fittings, or with compression fittings	Tubing cutter, miter box, or hacksaw
Valves & shutoffs; drain traps, supply risers	Lengths vary	1¼, ½, ¾, 1¼, 1½"	Compression fittings, or with metal solder	Tubing cutter, hacksaw, or reciprocating saw
Outdoor cold water supply pipes	Sold in coils of 25 to hundreds of feet	¼ to 1"	Rigid PVC fittings & stainless steel hose clamps	Ratchet-style plastic pipe cutter or miter saw
Gas supply pipe	Sold in lengths up to 10'	⅜, 1, 1¼, 1½"	Threaded connectors	Hacksaw, power cutoff saw, or reciprocating saw with bi-metal blade
Hot & cold water supply pipes	10', 20'; or sold by linear feet	⅜, ½, ¾, 1"	Metal solder, compression fittings, threaded fittings, press connect fittings, push connect fittings, flared fittings	Tubing cutter, hacksaw, or jigsaw
Supply tubes	12" or 20"	⅜, ½, ¾"	Attached threaded fittings	Do not cut
Gas ranges, dryers, water heaters	12" to 60"	⅝, ½" (OD)	Attached threaded fittings	Do not cut
Gas ranges, dryers, water heaters	12" to 60"	⅝, ½" (OD)	Attached threaded fittings	Do not cut
Supply tubing	12", 20", 30"	⅜"	Brass compression fittings	Tubing cutter or hacksaw
Hot & cold water supply; PEX-AL-PEX (usually orange) is used in radiant floors	Sold in coils of 25 feet to hundreds of feet	¼ to 1"	Crimp fittings, push connect fittings, expansion fittings	Tubing cutter
Gas supply; hot & cold water supply	30', 60' coils; or by feet	¼, ⅜, ½, ¾, 1"	Brass flare fittings, solder, compression fittings	Tubing cutter or hacksaw

COPPER

Copper is nearly ideal for water supply pipes. A purely natural (and consequently environmentally friendly) material, it resists corrosion and has a smooth surface that allows efficient water flow. The pipes are available in several diameters, but most home plumbing is done with ½- or ¾-inch pipe. The pipe comes in both rigid and flexible forms, although any copper pipe is going to be somewhat rigid.

The drawbacks to copper pipe are its susceptibility to leaks if it comes in contact with highly acidic well water, as well as its expense—also, traditional soldering or "sweating" of copper fittings is a skill that takes some practice to get right. PEX is an increasingly popular option because it is cheaper and the semiflexible tubes can be quickly and easily routed through framing without concern for kinks or the need for meticulous bending.

Rigid copper, sometimes called hard copper, is approved for home water supply systems by all local codes. It comes in three wall-thickness grades: Types M, L, and K. Type M is the thinnest, the least expensive, and a good choice for do-it-yourself home plumbing.

Rigid Type L usually is required by code for commercial plumbing systems. Because it is strong and solders easily, Type L may be preferred by some professional plumbers and do-it-yourselfers for home use. Type K has the heaviest wall thickness and is used most often for underground water service lines.

Flexible copper, also called soft copper, comes in two wall-thickness grades: Types L and K. Both are approved for most home water supply systems, although flexible Type L copper is used primarily

Soldering is a traditional way to join copper pipe and fittings, but it takes some practice to master (lead-free solders, now a requirement, can be a little more finicky). But push-fit fittings and other connection and material options are largely replacing soldered fittings and pipe.

for gas service lines. Because it is bendable and will resist a mild frost, Type L may be installed as part of a water supply system in unheated indoor areas, such as crawl spaces. Type K is used for underground water service lines.

A third form of copper, called DWV, is used for drain systems. Because most codes now allow low-cost plastic pipes for drain systems, DWV copper is seldom used.

Copper pipes are connected with soldered, compression, flare, or push-fit fittings (see chart below). Always follow your local code for the correct types of pipes and fittings allowed in your area.

Copper Pipe + Fitting Chart ▸

FITTING METHOD	RIGID COPPER			FLEXIBLE COPPER		GENERAL COMMENTS
	TYPE M	TYPE L	TYPE K	TYPE L	TYPE K	
Soldered	yes	yes	yes	yes	yes	Inexpensive, strong, and trouble-free fitting method. Requires some skill.
Compression	yes	not applicable		no	no	Makes repairs and replacement easy. More expensive than solder. Best used on flexible copper.
Flare	no	no	no	yes	yes	Use only with flexible copper pipes. Usually used as a gas-line fitting. Requires some skill.
Push-fit fittings	no	yes	yes	no	no	Easy to use. Flexible and inexpensive.

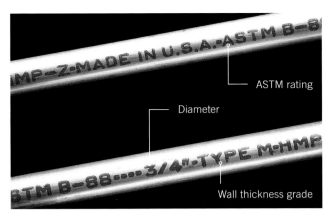

ASTM rating

Diameter

Wall thickness grade

Grade stamp information includes the pipe diameter, the wall-thickness grade, and a stamp of approval from the ASTM (American Society for Testing and Materials). Type M pipe is identified by red lettering, Type L by blue lettering.

Bend flexible copper pipe with a coil-spring tubing bender to avoid kinks. Select a bender that matches the outside diameter of the pipe. Slip the bender over the pipe using a twisting motion. Bend pipe slowly until it reaches the correct angle, but not more than 90°.

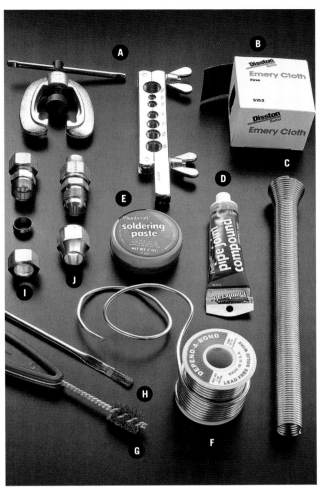

Specialty tools and materials for working with copper include: flaring tools (A), emery cloth (B), coil-spring tubing bender (C), pipe joint compound (D), soldering paste (flux) (E), lead-free solder (F), wire brush (G), flux brush (H), compression fitting (I), flare fitting (J).

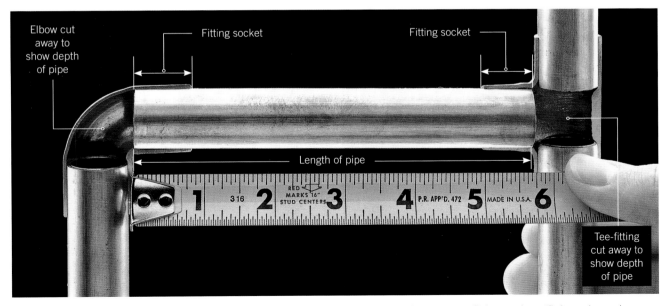

Elbow cut away to show depth of pipe

Fitting socket

Fitting socket

Length of pipe

Tee-fitting cut away to show depth of pipe

Find the length of copper pipe needed by measuring between the bottom of the copper fitting sockets (fittings shown in cutaway). Mark the length on the pipe with a felt-tipped pen.

CUTTING + SOLDERING COPPER

The best way to cut rigid and flexible copper pipe is with a tubing cutter. A tubing cutter makes a smooth, straight cut, an important first step toward making a watertight joint. Remove any metal burrs on the cut edges with a reaming tool or round file.

Copper can also be cut with a hacksaw. A hacksaw is useful in tight areas where a tubing cutter will not fit. Take care to make a smooth, straight cut when cutting with a hacksaw.

A soldered pipe joint, also called a sweated joint, is made by heating a copper or brass fitting with a propane torch until the fitting is just hot enough to melt metal solder. The heat draws the solder into the gap between the fitting and pipe to form a watertight seal. A fitting that is overheated or unevenly heated will not draw in solder. Copper pipes and fittings must be clean and dry to form a watertight seal.

Tools + Materials ▶

Tubing cutter with
   reaming tip
   (or hacksaw
   and round file)
Wire brush
Flux brush
Propane torch
Spark lighter (or
   matches)
Round file
Cloth

Adjustable wrench
Channel-type pliers
Copper pipe
Copper fittings
Emery cloth
Soldering paste
   (flux)
Sheet metal
Lead-free solder
Rag
Eye protection
Work gloves

Soldering Tips ▶

Use caution when soldering copper. Pipes and fittings become very hot and must be allowed to cool before handling.

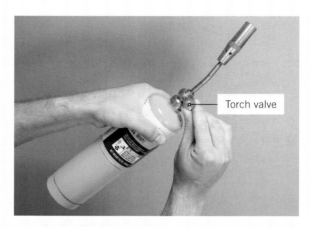

Torch valve

Prevent accidents by shutting off the torch immediately after use. Make sure the valve is closed completely.

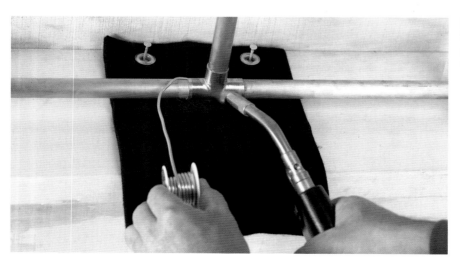

Protect wood from the heat of the torch flame while soldering. Use an old cookie sheet, two sheets of 26-gauge metal, or a fiber shield, as shown.

HOW TO CUT RIGID + FLEXIBLE COPPER PIPE

Place the tubing cutter over the pipe and tighten the handle so that the pipe rests on both rollers and the cutting wheel is on the marked line.

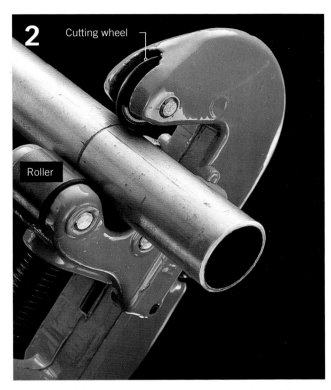

Cutting wheel

Roller

Turn the tubing cutter one rotation so that the cutting wheel scores a continuous straight line around the pipe.

Rotate the cutter in the opposite direction, tightening the handle slightly after every two rotations, until the cut is complete.

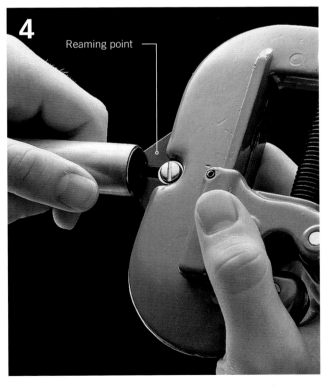

Reaming point

Remove sharp metal burrs from the inside edge of the cut pipe using a round file or the reaming point on the tubing cutter.

HOW TO SOLDER COPPER PIPES + FITTINGS

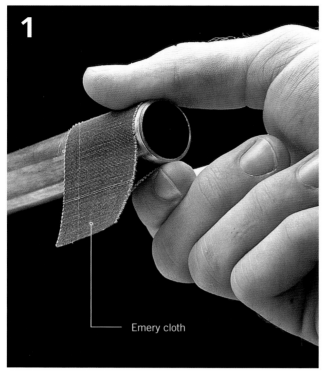

Emery cloth

Clean the end of each pipe by sanding with an emery cloth. Ends must be free of dirt and grease to ensure that the solder forms a good seal.

Clean the inside of each fitting by scouring with a wire brush or emery cloth.

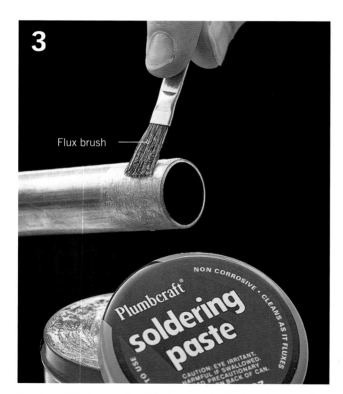

Flux brush

Apply a thin layer of soldering paste (flux) to the end of each pipe using a flux brush. Soldering paste should cover about 1" of pipe end. Don't use too much flux.

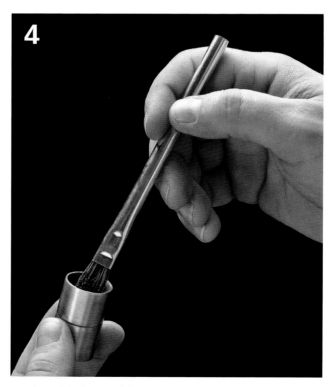

Apply a thin layer of flux to the inside of the fitting.

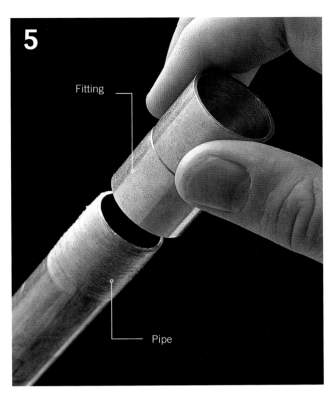

5

Fitting

Pipe

Assemble each joint by inserting the pipe into the fitting so it is tight against the bottom of the fitting sockets. Twist each fitting slightly to spread soldering paste.

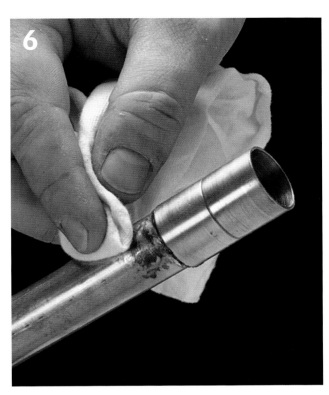

6

Use a clean dry cloth to remove excess flux before soldering the assembled fitting.

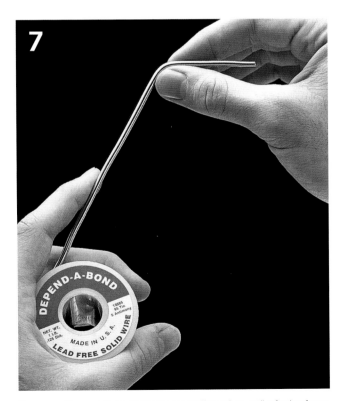

7

Prepare the wire solder by unwinding 8" to 10" of wire from the spool. Bend the first 2" of the wire to a 90° angle.

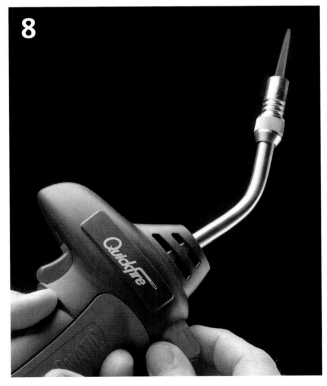

8

Open the gas valve and trigger the spark lighter to ignite the torch. Adjust the torch valve until the inner portion of the flame is 1" to 2" long.

(continued)

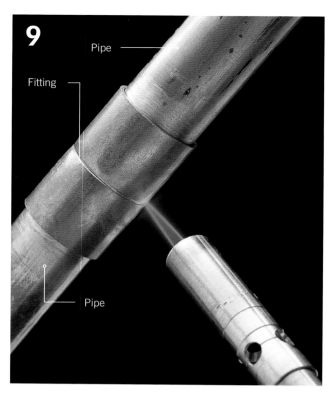

9

Pipe

Fitting

Pipe

Move the torch flame back and forth and around the pipe and the fitting to heat the area evenly.

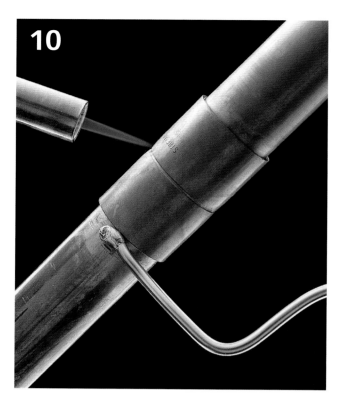

10

Heat the other side of the copper fitting to ensure that heat is distributed evenly. Touch the solder to the pipe. The solder will melt when the pipe is at the right temperature.

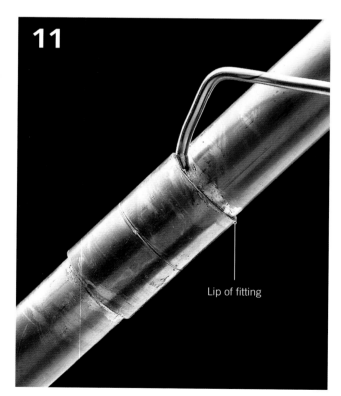

11

Lip of fitting

When the solder melts, remove the torch and quickly push ½" to ¾" of solder into each joint. Capillary action fills the joint with liquid solder. A correctly soldered joint should show a thin bead of solder around the lips of the fitting.

12

Allow the joint to cool briefly, then wipe away excess solder with a dry rag. *CAUTION: Pipes will be hot. If joints leak after water is turned on, disassemble and resolder.*

HOW TO SOLDER BRASS VALVES

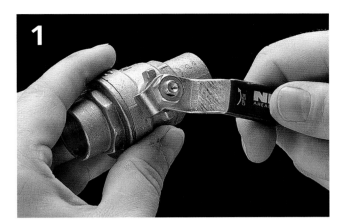

Valves should be fully open during all stages of the soldering process. If a valve has any plastic or rubber parts, remove them prior to soldering.

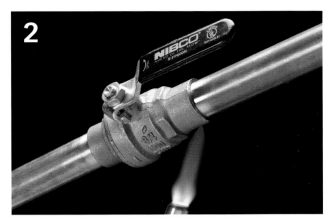

To prevent valve damage, quickly heat the pipe and the flanges of the valve, not the valve body. After soldering, cool the valve by spraying it with water.

HOW TO TAKE APART SOLDERED JOINTS

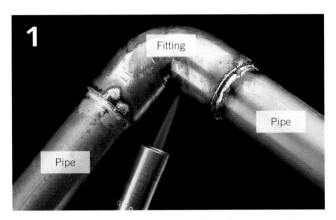

Fitting

Pipe

Pipe

Turn off the water and drain the pipes by opening the highest and lowest faucets in the house. Light your torch. Hold the flame tip to the fitting until the solder becomes shiny and begins to melt.

Use channel-type pliers to separate the pipes from the fitting.

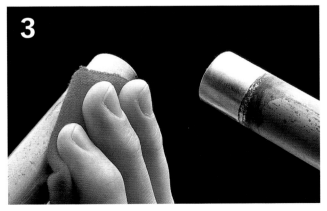

Remove old solder by heating the ends of the pipe with your torch. Use a dry rag to wipe away melted solder quickly. *CAUTION: Pipes will be hot.*

Use emery cloth to polish the ends of the pipe down to bare metal. Never reuse fittings.

PUSH-FIT FITTINGS

Also known as "push-to-connect," push-fit fittings have been around roughly since the turn of the latest century. They were originally developed for naval use, which is an indicator of how reliable they are—when installed correctly and under the right circumstances. These are the height of ease-of-use in plumbing connections, requiring no soldering, chemicals such as glue or solvent, or even tools.

The fittings are manufactured with a ring of stainless-steel teeth pointed to allow the fitting to slide over the end of a pipe and secure it in place. An EPDM rubber O-ring makes a watertight connection around the outside of the pipe, and the O-ring is pre-lubricated to ensure it seals on the surface of the pipe and remains supple.

Push-fit fittings can be used on copper, CPVC, and PEX-A and -B pipes. When used with PEX pipe, a plastic sleeve is fitted inside the pipe and stiffens the PEX to allow the fitting to hold tight. This plastic sleeve must be removed from the push-fit fittings when they are used with copper and CPVC. In every case, the fittings themselves are generally rated at about 200 psi and 200°F.

Still, cost may ultimately affect whether you choose push-fit fittings; the fittings are far more expensive than their more traditional counterparts. That's why most homeowners and professionals tend to use the fittings only for small projects and repairs.

Push-fit fittings may be used on several types of supply pipes and can even join dissimilar pipes in the same run. The fittings freely spin on a pipe end, making their application more versatile. Given that you don't need any tools to install them, these are great options for tight spaces that would not allow for a soldering iron, torch, or other tools.

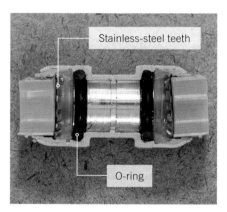

Push-fit fittings make a watertight seal with a EPDM rubber O-ring. A row of stainless-steel teeth grab and hold the pipe in place. Plastic insert sleeves (right) are employed only when the fitting is used with PEX and should be removed for copper or CPVC joints.

Dos for Pushing Push-Fit Fittings

- **Start with a clean cut.** The fitting's seal relies on solidly sitting on the end of the pipe. Use a copper pipe cutter—not a saw—when cutting copper pipe for push-fit fittings, and cut PEX with a PEX tubing cutter.

- **Limit reuse.** Although manufacturers regularly specify that these fittings can be reused four or five times in some cases, most professionals tend to limit reuse to two or three times. There is concern that the lubricant that helps the O-ring maintain a seal could wear away and create leaks after too many reuses.

- **Ream carefully.** Clean up the end of any pipe that will be used with these fittings. Even a small burr can damage push-fit rubber O-rings.

Don'ts for Pushing Push-Fit Fittings

- **Never** use a push-fit fitting in a system weatherized with glycol, such as in a plumbed recreational vehicle. The glycol may react with the O-ring lubricant and damage the seal.

- **Do not** use push-fit fittings with any lubricants, glues, solvents, Teflon tape, or other compounds.

- **Don't** sand the end of copper pipe prior to installing a push-fit fitting.

- **Never** use push-fit fittings with PEX-AL-PEX (PEX-A and PEX-B are fine).

- **Don't** use the fittings for exterior applications where they'll be consistently exposed to sunlight.

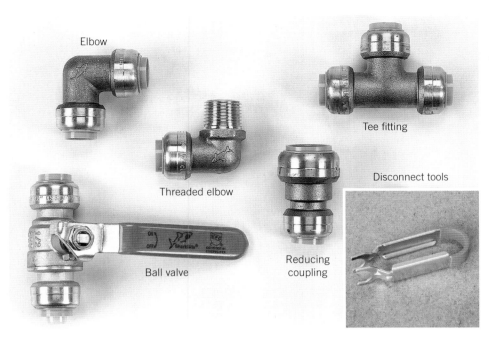

Elbow

Threaded elbow

Tee fitting

Ball valve

Reducing coupling

Disconnect tools

Push-fit fittings for copper pipe are available as couplings, elbows, tees, and even shutoff valves. A special tool (inset; some have handles and some don't) can be purchased to make it easier to disassemble push-fit joints.

HOW TO INSTALL PUSH-FIT FITTINGS

Tools + Materials ▸

Pipe cutter
Push-fit fitting
Deburr tool or utility knife
Depth gauge or ruler
Marker
Disconnect tool (optional)
Work gloves
Eye protection

1

Cleanly cut the end of the pipe with a cutter meant for use on the pipe's material. Clean up the cut end and deburr with the manufacturer's tool. Use the manufacturer's depth gauge or a ruler to mark the pipe with the proper fitting depth.

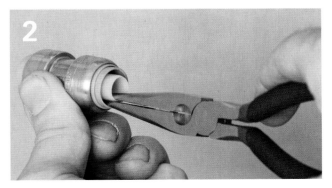

2

Remove the fittings' plastic sleeve if you're working with any pipe other than PEX. Slide the fitting onto the end of the pipe all the way until you reach the depth gauge mark. Pull on the fitting to ensure it is securely fixed to the pipe.

OPTION: If you need to remove the fitting for any reason, slip the removal tool over the pipe, snug it to the bottom of the fitting, and slowly pull the tool and the fitting off the pipe, twisting both as you pull.

PEX MATERIALS

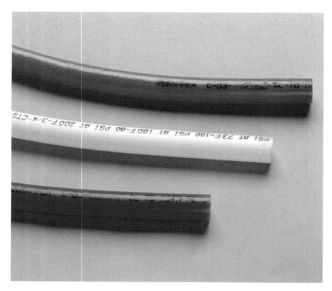

PEX pipe is manufactured in red, white, and blue. The intention is to use red for hot water lines and blue for cold water. However, the color does not affect price, and you may decide to use one color for the entire project.

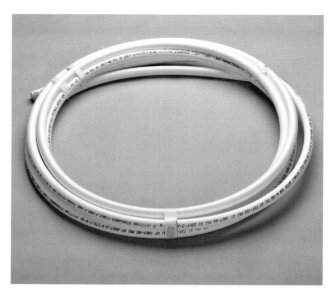

PEX combines the flexibility of plastic tubing with the durability of rigid supply pipe. It is sold in coils of common supply-pipe diameters.

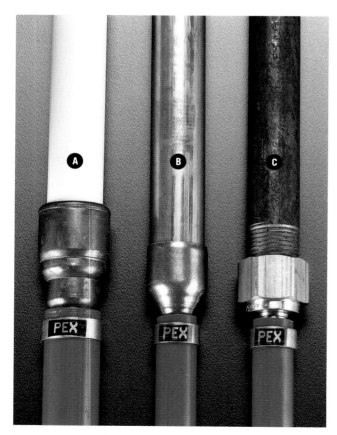

PEX is connected to other water supply materials with transition fittings, including CPVC-to-PEX (A), copper-to-PEX (B), and iron-to-PEX (C).

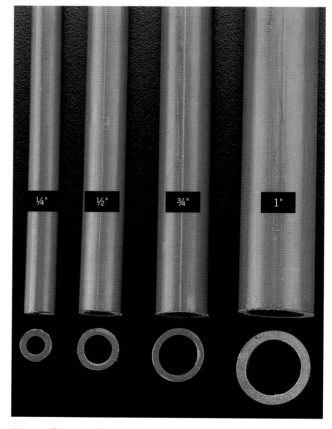

Generally, you should use the same diameter PEX as is specified for rigid supply tubing, but in some "home run" installations you can use ⅜" PEX where ½" rigid copper would normally be used.

PEX INSTALLATION

Check with your local plumbing inspector to verify that PEX is allowed in your municipality. PEX has been endorsed by all major plumbing codes in North America, but your municipality may still be using an older set of codes. Follow the guidelines below when installing PEX:

- Do not install PEX in aboveground exterior applications, because it degrades quickly from UV exposure.

- Do not use PEX for gas lines.

- Do not use plastic solvents or petroleum-based products with PEX (they can dissolve the plastic).

- Keep PEX at least 12" away from recessed light fixtures and other potential sources of high heat.

- Do not attach PEX directly to a water heater. Make connections at the heater with metallic tubing (either flexible water-heater connector tubing or rigid copper) at least 18" long; then join it to PEX with a transition fitting.

- Do not install PEX in areas where there is a possibility of mechanical damage or puncture. Always fasten protective plates to wall studs through which PEX runs.

- Always leave some slack in installed PEX lines to allow for contraction and in case you need to cut off a bad crimp.

- Use the same minimum branch and distribution supply-pipe dimensions for PEX that you'd use for copper or CPVC, according to your local plumbing codes.

- You can use push fittings to join PEX to itself or to CPVC or copper.

Do not connect PEX directly to a water heater. Use metal connector tubes. Solder the connector tubes to the water heater before attaching PEX. Never solder metal tubing that is already connected to PEX lines.

General Codes for PEX

PEX has been endorsed for residential use by all major building codes, although some municipal codes may be more restrictive. The specific design standards may also vary, but here are some general rules:

- For PEX, maximum horizontal support spacing is 32" and maximum vertical support spacing is 10'.

- Maximum length of individual distribution lines is 60'.

- PEX is designed to withstand 210°F water for up to 48 hours. For ongoing use, most PEX is rated for 180°F water up to 100 pounds per square inch of pressure.

- Directional changes of more than 90°F require a guide fitting.

- A mid-story guide is required for most PEX installations in walls. The guide should prevent movement perpendicular to the pipe direction.

Connectors for PEX systems are not interchangeable and all require specific crimping or connecting tools. The most common types you'll find in building centers today are: (A) pinching tool with jaws that snag a tab on a stainless-steel ring, drawing the ring tight when the tool is squeezed; (B) stainless-steel sleeve crimping tool that is similar to the full-circle crimping tool (right) but uses stainless-steel sleeves with flared ends; (C) expansion connectors with conical tips that fit into the PEX and a nylon union ring, then temporarily expand it as a barbed fitting is inserted, then squeezed tight as the memory in the PEX causes it to shrink back to a nonexpanded state.

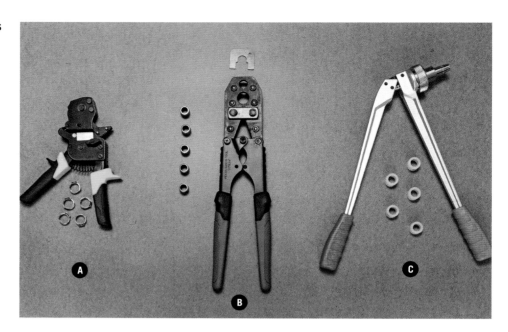

A full-circle crimping tool (A) compresses a crimping ring (usually copper) onto the PEX union to seal the joint. It was the original system used by most professionals before the PEX options expanded into more DIY-friendly systems. Crimping tools and rings are still used widely and are very reliable. With any PEX system you'll need a tubing cutter (B) for clean, square cuts, and a go/no-go gauge (C) to test connectors to make sure they are fitted properly after installation.

CHOOSING PEX PIPE + CONNECTORS

Deciding on a connection method for your PEX pipes can seem confusing as first, given that some connectors can only work with certain types of PEX. There are four possible connection types: push-to-connect fittings will work with any PEX pipe, compression fittings work only with PEX-AL-PEX, expansion connectors work only with PEX-A, and crimp fittings will work with any PEX pipe. The types most commonly used in home plumbing are crimp fittings and expansion fittings. Both are extremely reliable, but expansion fittings take a bit more practice and expertise. They are also marginally more expensive, but the fittings themselves feature a larger internal diameter, which translates to improved water flow.

HOW TO MAKE PEX FULL-CIRCLE CRIMP CONNECTIONS

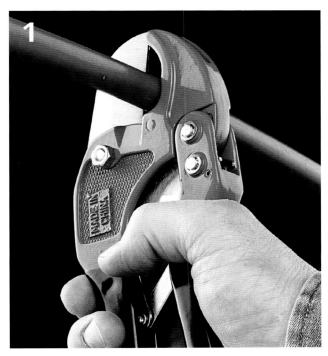

Cut the pipe to length, making sure to leave enough extra material so the line will have a small amount of slack once the connections are made. A straight, clean cut is very important. For best results, use a tubing cutter.

Inspect the cut end to make sure it is clean and smooth. If necessary, deburr the end of the pipe with a sharp utility knife. Slip a crimp ring over the end.

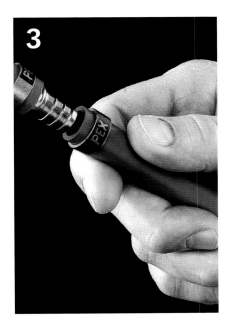

Insert the barbed end of the fitting into the pipe until it is snug against the cut edges. Position the crimp ring so it is ⅛" to ¼" from the end of the pipe, covering the barbed end of the fitting. Pinch the fitting to hold it in place.

Fit the crimping tool with the appropriate head for the size pipe and fitting you're crimping. Align the jaws of the tool over the crimp ring (the ring should be exactly perpendicular to the pipe) and squeeze the handles to apply strong, even pressure to the ring until you hear a click.

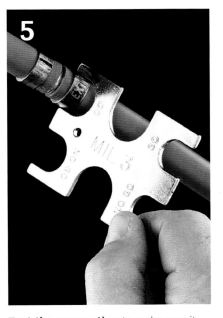

Test the connection to make sure it is mechanically acceptable using a go/no-go gauge. If the ring does not fit into the gauge properly, cut the pipe near the connection and try again.

HOW TO MAKE STAINLESS-STEEL SLEEVE PEX CONNECTIONS

Mark and cut the PEX tubing (either type A or type B), then cut it to length using a tubing cutter. Hold the PEX firmly against the registration ridges in the tool jaws to ensure a square cut, and then squeeze firmly until the blade slices through cleanly.

Slip a stainless-steel sleeve onto the cut end of the PEX so it is firmly seated with the flared grommet-style end flush against the end of the PEX.

Insert the fitting or union into the open end of the PEX to the required depth. Check to make sure the part is properly seated and square to the tubing.

Wrap the jaws of the connector tool around the sleeve, making sure you are using the jaw opening of the correct diameter (either ½" or ¾"). Squeeze the tool handles together with even pressure, keeping the sleeve centered in the hole of the tool jaws. Squeeze until the tool handles are as close together as the tool will allow.

Test the sleeve with the go/no-go gauge provided with the connector tool to make sure it is fastened securely.

HOW TO MAKE PEX PINCH CONNECTIONS

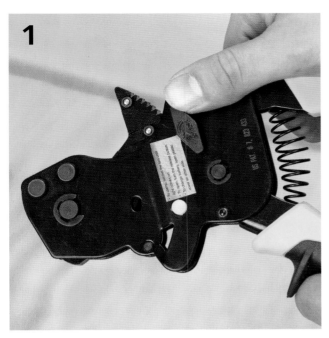

Press the release button on the pinch connector tool handle to unlock the tool, and test to make sure the ratcheting action occurs when you squeeze the handles together.

Slip a pinch ring over the cut end of the PEX. Grasp the tab "knuckle" on the pinch ring in the ends of the tool jaws. Partially tighten the ring to keep it from sliding, but do not fully tighten.

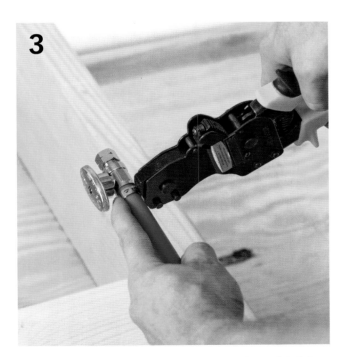

Insert the fitting or union into the PEX opening so it is fully seated. Adjust the pinch ring so it is parallel to the cut end of the PEX and 1/8" back from the tube end. With the pinch ring knuckle in the tool jaws, squeeze several times to further tighten the ring—four to six squeezes total is typical. On some tool models, an on-board alert light will glow when you have achieved the right amount of torque. Release the pinch ring from the tool.

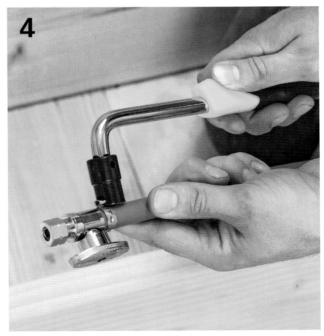

OPTION: If you are not satisfied with the connection or need to undo it for any reason, slip the pinch ring knuckle into the slot in the end of the pinch ring removal tool. Hold the PEX joint securely and twist the removal tool back and forth until the ring snaps and can be removed easily.

HOW TO MAKE PEX EXPANSION CONNECTIONS

Fit the expansion connector tool with the head that corresponds to the diameter of the fitting and PEX pipe. Lightly grease the head.

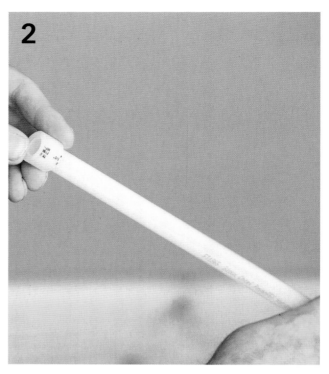

Slide the expansion ring onto the end of the PEX pipe (PEX-A only) until you reach the stop at the end of the ring. The ring should be flush against the cut end of the tubing.

Insert the expansion tool head into the end of the PEX pipe and begin opening and closing the expansions jaws. Push the PEX pipe onto the head as it widens until the edge of the PEX pipe is flush against the base of the expansion head.

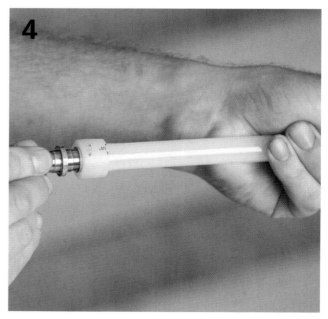

When the pipe and expansion sleeve are fully expanded, quickly remove the expansion tool head and slip the fitting into the end of the pipe. Allow the pipe to return to its original shape, firmly grabbing the fitting's barbed end, before using.

TIPS FOR WORKING WITH PEX

PEX tubing hangers can be attached to framing members to guide and support the semi-flexible tubing.

Install a 2 × 4 brace between wall framing or floor or ceiling joists to support in-line fittings, such as this two-port manifold.

Attach plastic corner guides if you are making a 90° turn with the tubing. The guides smooth out the curve, help prevent the PEX from kinking, and keep it contained too.

Use a hole-saw slightly larger in diameter than the PEX to drill access holes in framing for making tubing runs. Holes or pairs of holes should be at least 1" from the edges of framing members and at least 1" apart. Smooth the inside of the each hole to avoid snags.

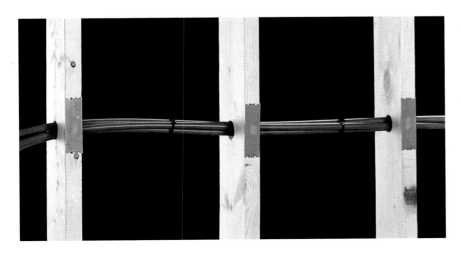

Attach nail protector plates to the edges of any framing members the PEX passes through. To keep them manageable, use plastic ties to secure parallel tubes together. *TIP: Leave some slack in the PEX lines so they can expand or contract slightly without stressing the connections.*

RIGID PLASTIC PIPE

Cut rigid ABS, PVC, or CPVC plastic pipes with a tubing cutter or with any saw. Cuts must be straight to ensure watertight joints.

Rigid plastics are joined with plastic fittings and solvent cement. Use a solvent cement that is made for the type of plastic pipe you are installing. For example, do not use ABS solvent on PVC pipe. Some solvent cements, called "all-purpose" or "universal" solvents, may not comply with local plumbing codes.

Solvent cement hardens in about 30 seconds, so test-fit all plastic pipes and fittings before cementing the first joint. For best results, the surfaces of plastic pipes and fittings should be dulled with emery cloth and liquid primer before they are joined. However, there are several new self-priming cements on the market that eliminate the need for a separate primer. These save time, effort, and expense.

Liquid solvent cements and primers are toxic and flammable. Provide adequate ventilation when fitting plastics, and store the products away from any source of heat.

Tools + Materials ▶

Tape measure	Fittings
Felt-tipped pen	Emery cloth
Tubing cutter	Plastic pipe primer
(or miter box	Solvent cement
or hacksaw)	Rag
Utility knife	Petroleum jelly
Channel-type pliers	Eye protection
Latex gloves	Work gloves
Plastic pipe	

Solvent welding is a chemical bonding process used to permanently join PVC pipes and fittings. The primer is always purple but may not be needed if you use a self-priming cement.

Primer and solvent cement are specific to the plumbing material being used. Avoid using all-purpose or multipurpose products. Light- to medium-body cements are appropriate for DIYers as they allow the longest working time and are easiest to use. When working with large pipe, 3 or 4" in diameter, buy a large-size can of cement, which has a larger dauber. If you use the small dauber (which comes with the small can), you may need to apply twice, which will slow you down and make connections difficult. (The smaller can of primer is fine for any other size pipe, since there's no rush in applying primer.) Cement (though not primer) goes bad in the can within a month or two after opening, so you may need to buy a new can for a new project.

HOW TO CUT RIGID PLASTIC PIPE

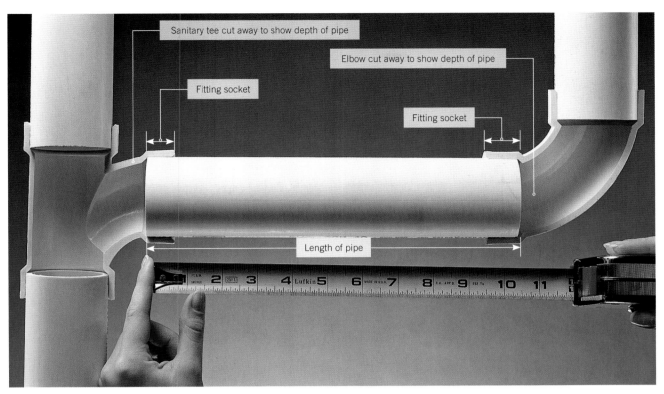

Find the length of plastic pipe needed by measuring between the bottoms of the fitting sockets (fittings shown in cutaway). Mark the length on the pipe with a felt-tipped pen.

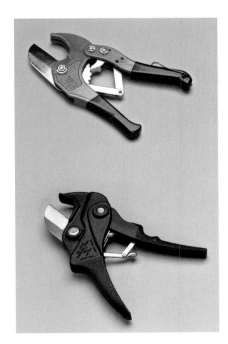

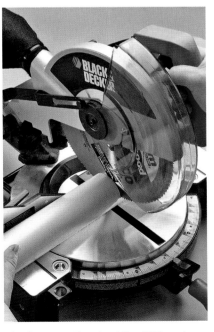

Plastic tubing cutters do a fast, neat job of cutting. They are not interchangeable with metal tubing cutters and don't work on larger-diameter pipe.

The best cutting tool for PVC and some other plastic pipe is a power miter saw with a fine tooth woodworking blade.

A ratcheting plastic-pipe cutter can cut smaller diameter PVC and CPVC pipe in a hurry.

HOW TO CEMENT PVC PIPE

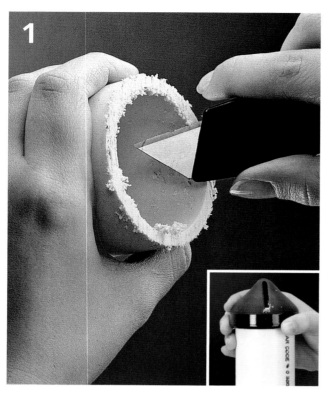

1

Remove rough burrs on cut ends of plastic pipe using a utility knife or deburring tool (inset).

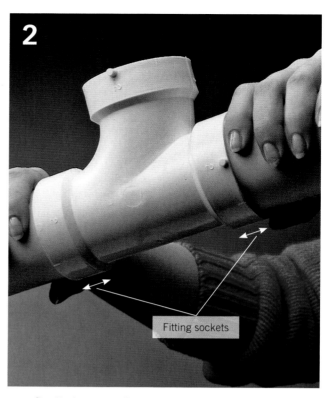

2

Fitting sockets

Test-fit all pipes and fittings. Pipes should fit tightly against the bottom of the fitting sockets.

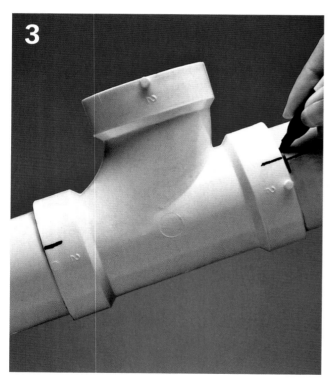

3

Mark the depth of the fitting sockets on the pipes. Take pipes as well as key marks where needed to maintain positioning of pipe and fittings apart. Clean the ends of the pipes and fitting sockets with emery cloth.

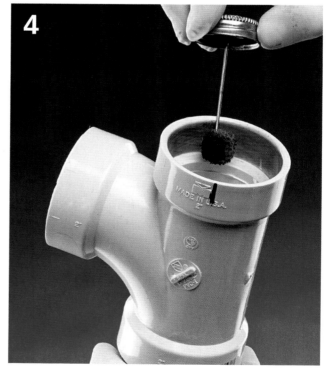

4

Apply a light coat of plastic pipe primer to the ends of the pipes and to the insides of the fitting sockets. Primer dulls glossy surfaces and ensures a good seal. (Skip this step if using a self-priming cement.)

PLUMBING

5

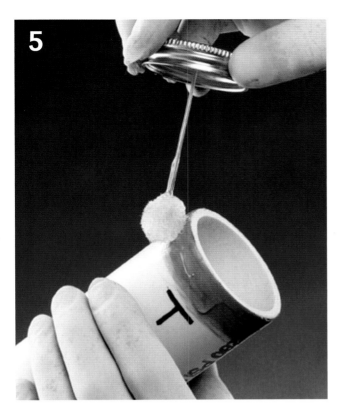

Solvent-cement each joint by applying a thick coat of solvent cement to the end of the pipe. Apply a thin coat of solvent cement to the inside surface of the fitting socket. Work quickly: solvent cement hardens in about 30 seconds.

6

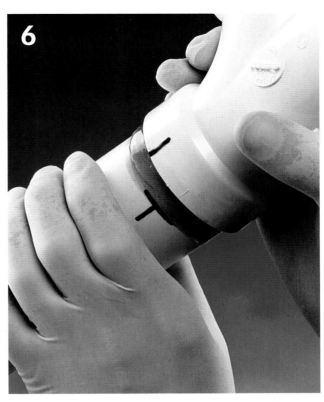

Quickly position the pipe and fitting so that the alignment marks are offset by about 2". Force the pipe into the fitting until the end fits flush against the bottom of the socket.

7

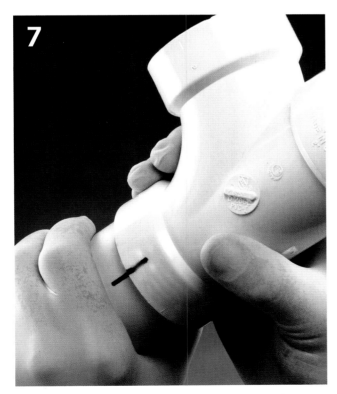

Spread solvent by twisting the pipe until the marks are aligned. Hold the pipe in place for about 20 seconds to prevent the joint from slipping.

8

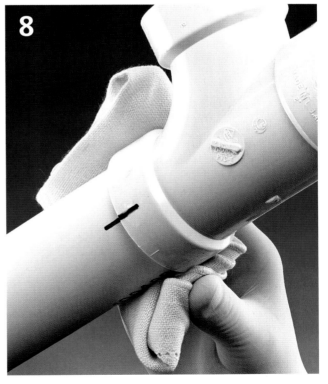

Wipe away excess solvent cement with a rag. Do not disturb the joint for 30 minutes after gluing.

SHUTOFF VALVES

Worn-out shutoff valves or supply tubes can cause water to leak underneath a sink or other fixture. First, try tightening the fittings with an adjustable wrench. If this does not fix the leak, replace the shutoff valves and supply tubes.

Shutoff valves are available in several fitting types. For copper pipes, valves with compression-type fittings are easiest to install. For plastic pipes, use grip-type valves. For galvanized steel pipes, use valves with female threads.

Older plumbing systems often were installed without fixture shutoff valves. When repairing or replacing plumbing fixtures, you may want to install shutoff valves if they are not already present.

Tools + Materials ▸

Hacksaw
Tubing cutter
Adjustable wrench
Tubing bender
Work gloves

Eye protection
Felt-tipped pen
Shutoff valves
Supply tubes
Pipe joint compound

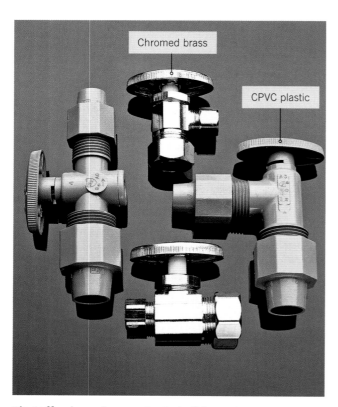

Shutoff valves allow you to shut off the water to an individual fixture so it can be repaired. They can be made from durable chromed brass or lightweight plastic. Shutoff valves come in ½" and ¾" diameters to match common water pipe sizes.

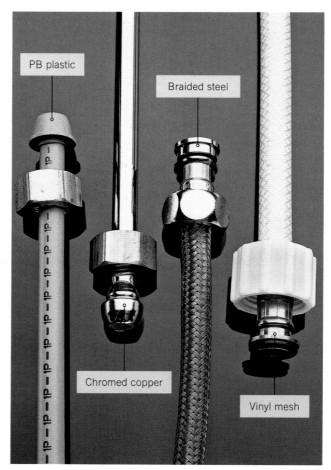

Supply tubes are used to connect water pipes to faucets, toilets, and other fixtures. They come in 12", 20", and 30" lengths. PB plastic and chromed copper tubes are inexpensive. Braided steel and vinyl mesh supply tubes are easy to install.

HOW TO INSTALL SHUTOFF VALVES + SUPPLY TUBES

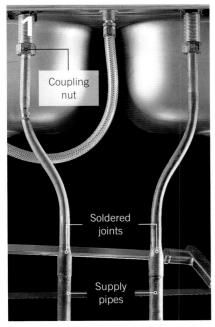

Turn off water at the main shutoff valve. Remove old supply pipes. If pipes are soldered copper, cut them off just below the soldered joint using a hacksaw or tubing cutter. Make sure the cuts are straight. Unscrew the coupling nuts and discard the old pipes.

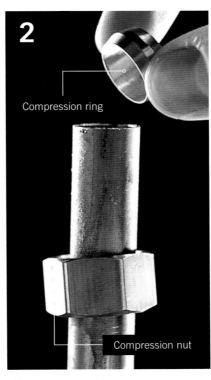

Slide a compression nut and a compression ring over the copper water pipe. Threads of the nut should face the end of the pipe.

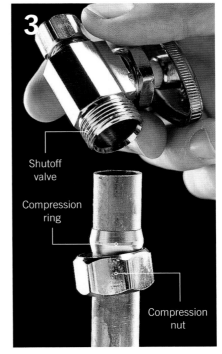

Apply pipe joint compound to the threads of the shutoff valve or compression nut. Screw the compression nut onto the shutoff valve and tighten with an adjustable wrench.

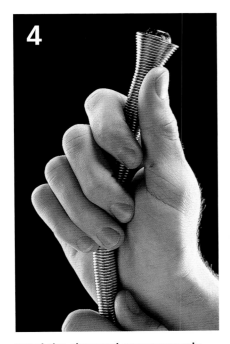

Bend the chromed copper supply tube to reach from the tailpiece of the fixture to the shutoff valve using a tubing bender. Bend the tube slowly to avoid kinking the metal.

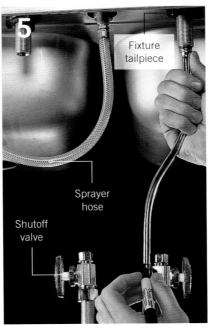

Position the supply tube between the fixture tailpiece and the shutoff valve, and mark the tube to length. Cut the supply tube with a tubing cutter.

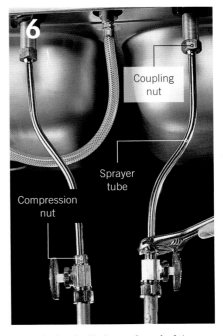

Attach the bell-shaped end of the supply tube to the fixture tailpiece with a coupling nut, then attach the other end to the shutoff valve with a compression ring and nut. Tighten all fittings with an adjustable wrench.

COMPRESSION FITTINGS

Compression fittings are used to make connections that may need to be taken apart. Compression fittings are easy to disconnect and are often used to install supply tubes and fixture shutoff valves. Use compression fittings in places where it is unsafe or difficult to solder, such as in crawl spaces.

Compression fittings are used most often with flexible copper pipe. Flexible copper is soft enough to allow the compression ring to seat snugly, creating a watertight seal. Compression fittings also may be used to make connections with Type M rigid copper pipe.

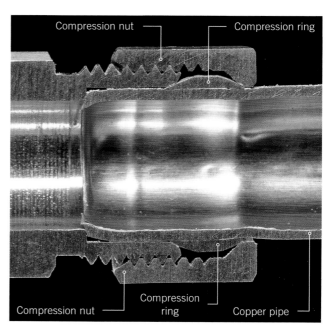

This compression fitting (shown in cutaway) shows how a threaded compression nut forms a seal by forcing the compression ring against the copper pipe. The compression ring is covered with pipe joint compound before assembly to ensure a perfect seal.

Tools + Materials ▸

Felt-tipped pen
Tubing cutter
  or hacksaw
Adjustable wrenches
Work gloves

Eye protection
Brass compression
  fittings
Pipe joint compound
  or Teflon tape

HOW TO ATTACH SUPPLY TUBES TO FIXTURE SHUTOFF VALVES WITH COMPRESSION FITTINGS

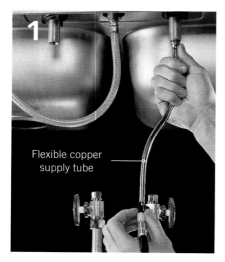

Bend flexible copper supply tube and mark to length. Include ½" for the portion that will fit inside valve. Cut the tube.

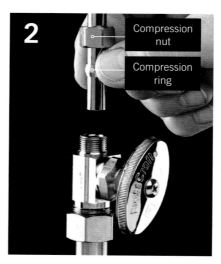

Slide the compression nut and then the compression ring over the end of the pipe. The threads of the nut should face the valve.

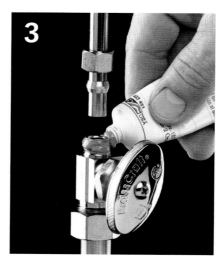

Apply a small amount of pipe joint compound to the threads to lubricate them.

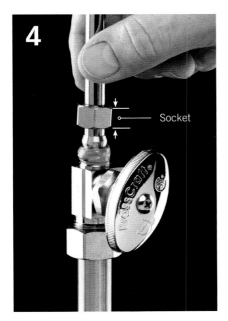

Insert the end of the pipe into the fitting so it fits flush against the bottom of the fitting socket.

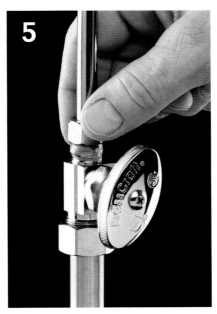

Slide the compression ring and nut against the threads of the valve. Hand tighten the nut onto the valve.

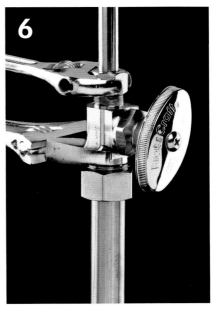

Tighten the compression nut with adjustable wrenches. Do not overtighten. Turn on the water and watch for leaks. If the fitting leaks, tighten the nut gently.

HOW TO JOIN TWO COPPER PIPES WITH A COMPRESSION UNION FITTING

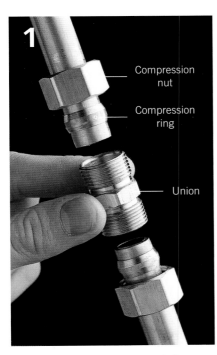

Slide compression nuts and rings over the ends of pipes. Place a threaded union between the pipes.

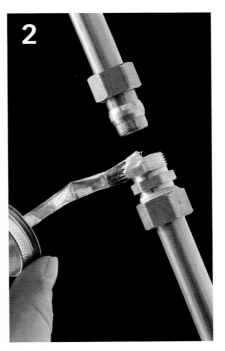

Apply a layer of pipe joint compound or Teflon tape to the union's threads, then screw compression nuts onto the union.

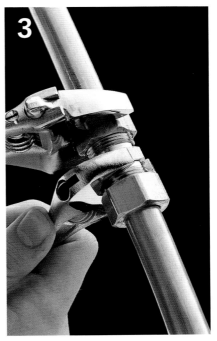

Hold the center of the union fitting with an adjustable wrench and use another wrench to tighten each compression nut one complete turn. Turn on the water. If the fitting leaks, tighten the nuts gently.

HOW TO REMOVE A TOILET

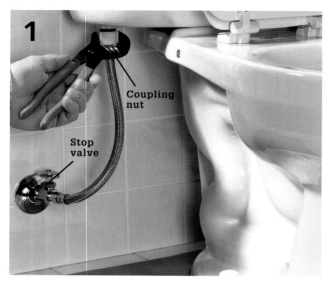

1

Coupling
nut

Stop
valve

Remove the old supply tube. First, turn off the water at the stop valve. Flush the toilet, holding the handle down for a long flush, and sponge out the tank. Use a wet/dry vac to clear any remaining water out of the tank and bowl. Unfasten the coupling nut for the water supply below the tank using channel-type pliers.

2

Grip each tank bolt nut with a box wrench or pliers and loosen it as you stabilize each tank bolt from inside the tank with a large slotted screwdriver. If the nuts are stuck, apply penetrating oil to the nut and let it sit before trying to remove them again. You may also cut the tank bolts between the tank and the bowl with an open-ended hacksaw. Remove and discard the tank.

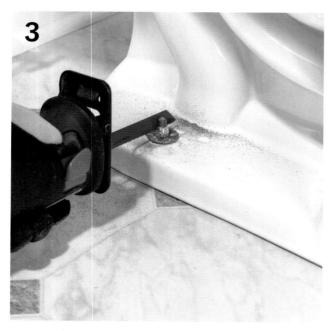

3

Remove the nuts that hold the bowl to the floor.
First, pry off the bolt covers with a screwdriver. Use a socket wrench, locking pliers, or your channel-type pliers to loosen the nuts on the tank bolts. Apply penetrating oil and let it sit if the nuts are stuck, then take them off. As a last resort, cut the bolts off with a hacksaw by first cutting down through one side of the nut. Tilt the toilet bowl over and remove it.

Prying Up Wax Rings ▸

Removing an old wax ring is one of the more disgusting jobs you'll encounter in the plumbing universe (the one you see here is actually in relatively good condition). Work a stiff putty knife underneath the plastic flange of the ring (if you can) and start scraping. In many cases the wax ring will come off in chunks. Discard each chunk right away—they stick to everything. If you're left with a lot of residue, scrub with mineral spirits. Once clean, stuff a rag-in-a-bag in the drain opening to block sewer gas.

HOW TO INSTALL A TOILET

Clean and inspect the old closet flange. Look for breaks or wear. Also inspect the flooring around the flange. If either the flange or floor is worn or damaged, repair the damage. Use a rag and mineral spirits to completely remove residue from the old wax ring. Place a rag-in-a-bag into the opening to block odors.

Installation Tip ▸

If you will be replacing your toilet flange or if your existing flange can be unscrewed and moved, orient the new flange so the slots are parallel to the wall. This allows you to insert bolts under the slotted areas, which are much stronger than the areas at the ends of the curved grooves.

Insert new tank bolts (don't reuse old ones) into the openings in the closet flange. Make sure the heads of the bolts are oriented to catch the maximum amount of flange material. To firmly hold the bolts upright, slide on the plastic washers and press them down.

Remove the wax ring and apply it to the underside of the bowl, around the horn. Remove the protective covering. Do not touch the wax ring. It is very sticky. Remove the rag-in-a-bag. If you have an older 4" flange, place the ring on the flange rather than the toilet to make sure it is centered.

(continued)

4

Lower the bowl onto the flange, taking care not to disturb the wax ring. The holes in the bowl base should align perfectly with the tank bolts. Add a washer and tighten a nut on each bolt. Hand tighten each nut and then use channel-type pliers to further tighten the nuts. Alternate back and forth between nuts until the bowl is secure. Do not overtighten.

5

Spud nut

Spud washer

Install the flush valve. Some tanks come with a flush valve and a fill valve preinstalled. For models that do not have this, insert the flush valve through the tank opening and tighten a spud nut over the threaded end of the valve. Place a foam spud washer on top of the spud nut.

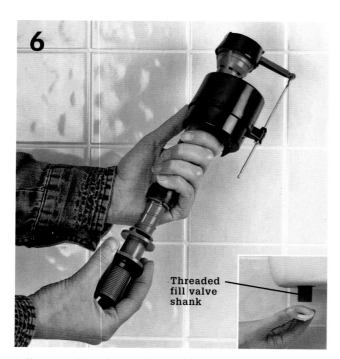

6

Threaded fill valve shank

Adjust the fill valve as directed by the manufacturer to set the correct tank water level height and install the valve inside the tank. Hand tighten the nylon lock nut that secures the valve to the tank (inset photo) and then tighten it further with channel-type pliers.

7

Intermediate nut goes between tank and bowl

With the tank lying on its back, thread a rubber washer onto each tank bolt and insert it into the bolt holes from inside the tank. Then, thread a brass washer and hex nut onto the tank bolts from below and tighten them to a quarter turn past hand tight. Do not overtighten.

8

Intermediate nut

Position the tank on the bowl, spud washer on the opening, and bolts through the bolt holes. Put a rubber washer, followed by a brass washer and a wing nut, on each bolt and tighten these up evenly.

9

You may stabilize the bolts with a large slotted screwdriver from inside the tank, but tighten the nuts, not the bolts. You may press down a little on a side, the front, or the rear of the tank to level it as you tighten the nuts by hand. Do not overtighten and crack the tank. The tank should be level and stable when you're done. Do not overtighten.

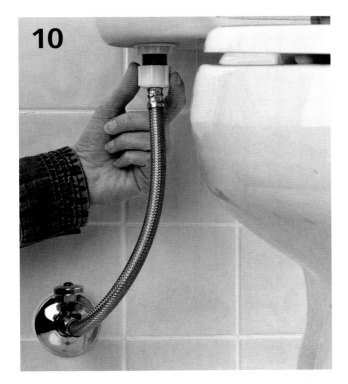

10

Hook up the water supply by connecting the supply tube to the threaded fill valve with the coupling nut provided. Turn on the water and test for leaks. Do not overtighten.

11

Attach the toilet seat by threading the plastic or brass bolts provided with the seat through the openings on the back of the rim and attaching nuts.

TOILET: CLEARING CLOGS

The toilet is clogged and has overflowed. Have patience. Now is the time for considered action. A second flush is a tempting but unnecessary gamble. First, do damage control. Mop up the water if there's been a spill. Next, consider the nature of the clog. Is it entirely "natural" or might a foreign object be contributing to the congestion? Push a natural blockage down the drain with a plunger. A foreign object should be removed, if possible, with a closet auger. Pushing anything more durable than toilet paper into the sewer may create a more serious blockage in your drain and waste system.

If the tub, sink, and toilet all back up at once, the branch drainline that serves all the bathroom fixtures is probably blocked and your best recourse is to call a drain clearing service.

Tools + Materials ▶

Towels
Closet auger
Eye protection

Rubberized work
   gloves
Plunger with foldout
   skirt (force cup)

A blockage in the toilet bowl leaves flush water from the tank nowhere to go but on the floor. Depending on the nature of the clog, this may be a sanitary issue, so always start with the least disruptive solution that has the lowest chance of spilling waste water onto the bathroom floor.

The trap is the most common catching spot for toilet clogs. Once the clog forms, flushing the toilet cannot generate enough water power to clear the trap, so flush water backs up. Traps on modern 1.6-gallon toilets have been redesigned to larger diameters and are less prone to clogs than the first generation of 1.6-gallon toilets.

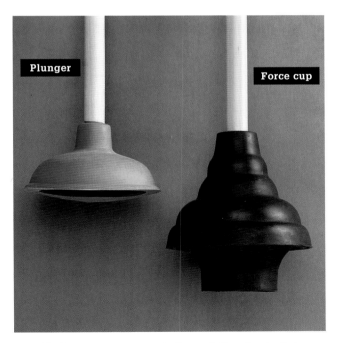

Plunger

Force cup

Not all plungers were created equal. The standard plunger (left) is simply an inverted rubber cup and is used to plunge sinks, tubs, and showers. The flanged plunger, also called a force cup, is designed to get down into the trap of a toilet drain. You can fold the flange up into the flanged plunger cup and use it as a standard plunger.

Drain Clearers ▸

The home repair marketplace is filled with gadgets and gimmicks, as well as well-established products, that are intended to clear drains of all types. Some are caustic chemicals, some are natural enzymes, others are more mechanical in nature. Some help, some are worthless, some can even make the problem worse. Nevertheless, if you are the type of homeowner who is enamored with new products and the latest solutions, you may enjoy testing out new drain cleaners as they become available. In this photo, for example, you'll see a relatively new product that injects blasts of compressed CO_2 directly into your toilet, sink, or tub drain to dislodge clogs. It does not cause any chemicals to enter the waste stream, and the manufacturers claim the CO_2 blast is very gentle and won't damage pipes. As with any new product, use it with caution. But if a plunger or a snake isn't working, it could save you the cost of a plumber's house call.

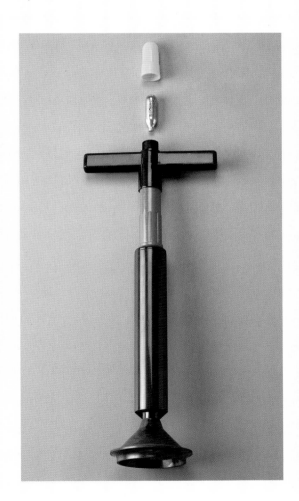

HOW TO PLUNGE A CLOGGED TOILET

1

Plunging is the easiest way to remove "natural" blockages. Take time to lay towels around the base of the toilet and remove other objects to a safe, dry location, since plunging may result in splashing. Often, allowing a very full toilet to sit for 20 or 30 minutes will permit some of the water to drain to a less precarious level.

Force Cups ▶

A flanged plunger (force cup) fits into the mouth of the toilet trap and creates a tight seal so you can build up enough pressure in front of the plunger to dislodge the blockage and send it on its way.

2

There should be enough water in the bowl to completely cover the plunger. Fold out the skirt from inside the plunger to form a better seal with the opening at the base of the bowl. Pump the plunger vigorously half-a-dozen times, take a rest, and then repeat. Try this for four to five cycles.

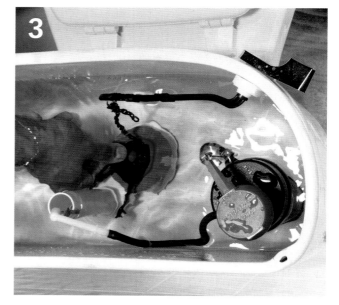

3

If you force enough water out of the bowl that you are unable to create suction with the plunger, put a controlled amount of water in the bowl by lifting up on the flush valve in the tank. Resume plunging. When you think the drain is clear, you can try a controlled flush, with your hand ready to close the flush valve should the water threaten to spill out of the bowl. Once the blockage has cleared, dump a five-gallon pail of water into the toilet to blast away any residual debris.

HOW TO CLEAR CLOGS WITH A CLOSET AUGER

1

Protective rubber boot

Place the business end of the auger firmly in the bottom of the toilet bowl with the auger tip fully withdrawn. A rubber sleeve will protect the porcelain at the bottom bend of the auger. The tip will be facing back and up, which is the direction the toilet trap takes.

Closet Augers ▶

A closet auger is a semirigid cable housed in a tube. The tube has a bend at the end so it can be snaked through a toilet trap (without scratching it) to snag blockages.

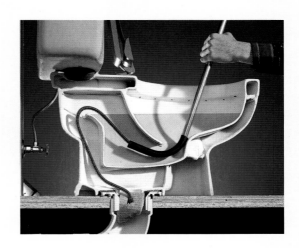

2

Rotate the handle on the auger housing clockwise as you push down on the rod, advancing the rotating auger tip up into the back part of the trap. You may work the cable backward and forward as needed, but keep the rubber boot of the auger firmly in place in the bowl. When you feel resistance, indicating you've snagged the object, continue rotating the auger counterclockwise as you withdraw the cable and the object.

3

Fully retract the auger until you have recovered the object. This can be frustrating at times, but it is still a much easier task than the alternative—to remove the toilet and go fishing.

INSTALLING BATHTUBS

Prepare for the new tub. Inspect and remove old or deteriorated wall surfaces or framing members in the tub area. With today's mold-resistant wallboard products, it makes extra sense to strip off the old alcove wallcoverings and ceiling down to the studs so you can replace them. This also allows you to inspect for hidden damage in the wall and ceiling cavities.

Check the subfloor for level—if it is not level, use pour-on floor leveler compound to correct it (ask at your local flooring store). Make sure the supply and drain pipes and the shutoff valves are in good repair and correct any problems you encounter. If you have no bath fan in the alcove, now is the perfect time to add one.

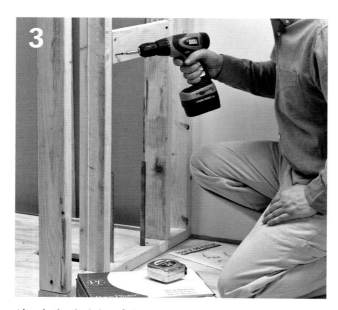

Check the height of the crossbraces for the faucet body and the showerhead. If your family members needed to stoop to use the old shower, consider raising the brace for the showerhead. Read the instructions for your new faucet/diverter and check to see that the brace for the faucet body will conform to the requirements (this includes distance from the surround wall as well as height). Adjust the brace locations as needed.

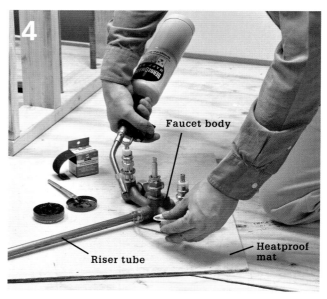

Faucet body

Riser tube

Heatproof mat

Begin by installing the new water supply plumbing. Measure to determine the required height of your shower riser tube and cut it to length. Attach the bottom of the riser to the faucet body and the top to the shower elbow.

5

Attach the faucet body to the cross brace with pipe hanger straps. Then, attach supply tubing from the stop valves to the faucet body, making sure to attach the hot water to the left port and cold to the right port. Also secure the shower elbow to its cross brace with a pipe strap. Do not attach the shower arm yet.

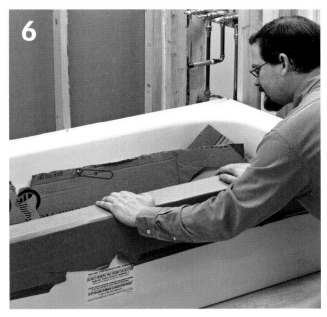

6

Slide the bathtub into the alcove. Make sure tub is flat on the floor and pressed flush against the back wall. If your tub did not come with a tub protector, cut a piece of cardboard to line the tub bottom, and tape pieces of cardboard around the rim to protect the finish from shoes and dropped tools.

7

Mark locations for ledger boards. To do this, trace the height of the top of the tub's nailing flange onto the wall studs in the alcove. Then remove the tub and measure the height of the nailing flange. Measure down this same amount from your flange lines and mark the new ledger board location.

8

Install 1 × 4 ledger boards. Drive two or three 3"-galvanized deck screws through the ledger board at each stud. All three walls should receive a ledger. Leave an open space in the wet wall to allow clearance for the DWO (drain-waste-overflow) kit. Measure to see whether the drain will line up with the tub's DWO. If not, you may need to cut and reassemble the drain.

(continued)

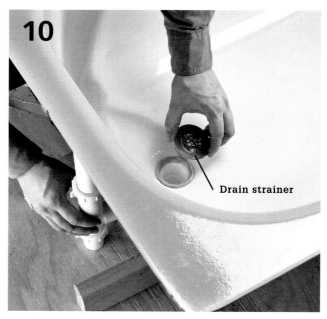

Install the drain-waste-overflow pipes before you install the tub. Make sure to get a good seal on the slip nuts at the pipe joints. Follow the manufacturer's instructions to make sure the pop-up drain linkage is connected properly. Make sure rubber gaskets are positioned correctly at the openings on the outside of the tub.

Thread the male-threaded drain strainer into the female-threaded drain waste elbow. Wrap a coil of plumber's putty around the drain outlet underneath the plug rim first. Hand tighten only.

Attach the overflow coverplate, making sure the pop-up drain controls are in the correct position. Tighten the mounting screws that connect to the mounting plate to sandwich the rubber gasket snugly between the overflow pipe flange and the tub wall. Then, finish tightening the drain strainer against the waste elbow by inserting the handle of a pair of pliers into the strainer body and turning.

Working with a helper, place the tub in position, taking care not to bump the DWO assembly. If the DWO assembly does not line up with the drainpipe, remove the tub and adjust the drain location. Many acrylic, fiberglass, and steel tubs will have a much firmer feeling if they are set in a bed of sand-mix concrete. Check manufacturer's instructions, and pour concrete or mortar as needed. Set the tub carefully back in the alcove.

13

Attach the drain outlet from the DWO assembly to the drain P-trap. This is the part of the job where you will appreciate that you spent the time to create a roomy access panel for the tub plumbing. Test the drain and overflow to make sure they don't leak. Also test the water supply plumbing, temporarily attaching the handles, spout, and shower arm so you can operate the faucet and the diverter.

14

Drive a 1½" galvanized roofing nail at each stud location, just over the top of the tub's nailing flange. The nail head should pin the flange to the stud. Be careful here—an errant blow or overdriving can cause the enameled finish to crack or craze. *OPTION: You may choose to drill guide holes and nail through the flange instead.*

15

Install the wallcoverings and tub surround. You can also make a custom surround from tileboard or cementboard and tile.

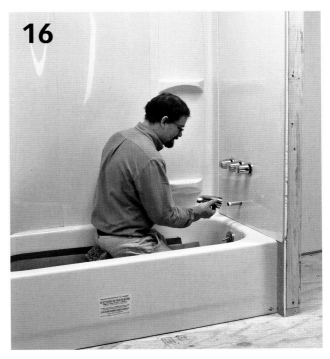

16

Install fittings. First, thread the shower arm into the shower elbow and attach the spout nipple to the valve assembly. Also attach the shower head and escutcheon, the faucet handle/diverter with escutcheon, and the tub spout. Use thread lubricant on all parts.

INSTALLING SLIDING TUB DOORS

Curtains on your bathtub shower are a hassle. If you forget to tuck them inside the tub, water flows freely onto your bathroom floor. If you forget to slide them closed, mildew sets up shop in the folds. And every time you brush against them, they stick to your skin. Shower curtains certainly don't add much elegance or charm to a dream bath. Neither does a deteriorated door. Clean up the look of your bathroom, and even give it an extra touch of elegance, with a new sliding tub door.

When shopping for a sliding tub door, you have a choice of framed or frameless. A framed door is edged in metal. The metal framing is typically aluminum but is available in many finishes, including those that resemble gold, brass, or chrome. Glass options are also plentiful. You can choose between frosted or pebbled glass, clear, mirrored, tinted, or patterned glass. Doors can be installed on ceramic tile walls or onto a fiberglass tub surround.

Tools + Materials ▸

Measuring tape	Marker
Pencil	Masonry bit for tile wall
Hacksaw	Phillips screwdriver
Miter box	Caulk gun
Level	Masking tape
Drill	Silicone sealant and remover
Center punch	Tub door kit
Razor blade	Work gloves

A sliding tub door framed in aluminum gives the room a sleek, clean look and is just one of the available options. A model like this fits into a 60" alcove, so it can replace a standard tub, as long as you can provide access to the plumbing and an electrical connection.

HOW TO INSTALL SLIDING TUB DOORS

Remove the existing door and inspect the walls. Use a razor blade to cut sealant from tile and metal surfaces. Do not use a razor blade on fiberglass surfaces. Remove remaining sealant by scraping or pulling. Use a silicone sealant remover to remove all residue. Remove shower curtain rods, if present. Check the walls and tub ledge for plumb and level.

Measure the distance between the finished walls along the top of the tub ledge. Refer to the manufacturer's instructions for figuring the track dimensions. For the product seen here, $\frac{3}{16}$" is subtracted from the measurement to calculate the track dimensions.

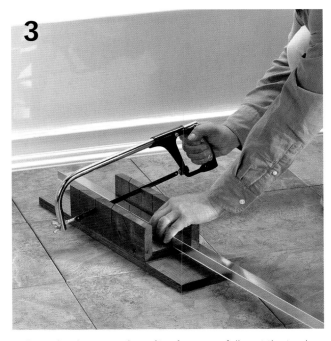

Using a hacksaw and a miter box, carefully cut the track to the proper dimension. Center the track on the bathtub ledge with the taller side out and so the gaps are even at each end. Tape into position with masking tape.

Place a wall channel against the wall with the longer side out and slide into place over the track so they overlap. Use a level to check the channel for plumb, and then mark the locations of the mounting holes on the wall with a marker. Repeat for the other wall channel. Remove the track.

(continued)

Drill mounting holes for the wall channel at the marked locations. In ceramic tile, nick the surface of the tile with a center punch, use a ¼" masonry bit to drill the hole, and then insert the included wall anchors. For fiberglass surrounds, use a ⅛" drill bit; wall anchors are not necessary.

Apply a bead of silicone sealant along the joint between the tub and the wall at the ends of the track. Apply a minimum ¼" bead of sealant along the outside leg of the track underside.

Position the track on the tub ledge and against the wall. Attach the wall channels using the provided screws. Do not use caulk on the wall channels at this time.

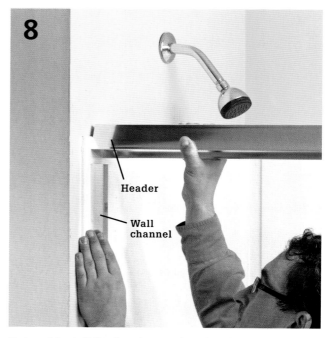

Header

Wall channel

Cut and install the header. At a location above the tops of the wall channels, measure the distance between the walls. Refer to the manufacturer's instructions for calculating the header length. For the door seen here, the length is the distance between the walls minus ¹⁄₁₆". Measure the header and carefully cut it to length using a hacksaw and a miter box. Slide the header down on top of the wall channels until seated.

9

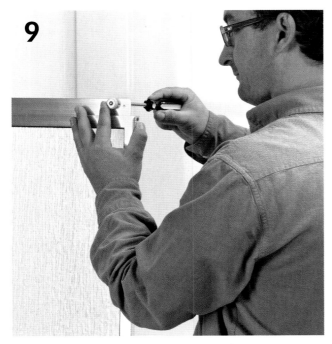

Mount the rollers in the roller mounting holes. To begin, use the second-from-the-top roller mounting holes. Follow the manufacturer's instructions for spacer or washer placement and orientation.

10

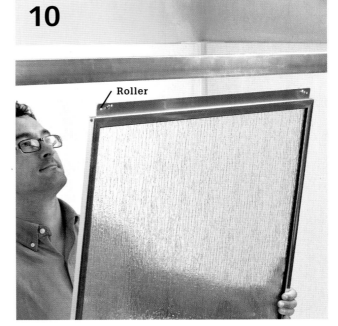

Roller

Carefully lift the inner panel by the sides and place the rollers on the inner roller track. Roll the door toward the shower end of the tub. The edge of the panel should touch both rubber bumpers. If it doesn't, remove the door and move the rollers to different holes. Drive the screws by hand to prevent overtightening.

11

Lift the outer panel by the sides with the towel bar facing out from the tub. Place the outer rollers over the outer roller track. Slide the door to the end opposite the shower end of the tub. If the door does not contact both bumpers, remove the door and move the rollers to different mounting holes.

12

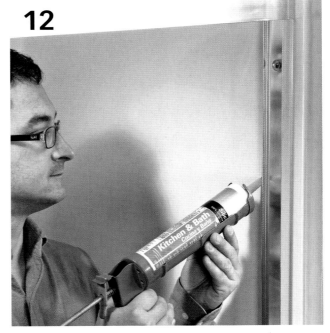

Apply a bead of clear silicone sealant to the inside seam of the wall and wall channel at both ends and to the U-shaped joint of the track and wall channels. Smooth the sealant with a fingertip dipped in water.

CORNER SHOWER

One method for creating a quick shower stall is with a glass-wall kit, ideal for small bathrooms. It tucks neatly into the corner of your bathroom and can make use of either a custom-built shower pan or a prefabricated shower pan like that commonly used in framed-in alcoves. Many such showers come with the base pan as part of the kit, while with others you will need to buy or build a separate shower pan.

The kit we've used to demonstrate a corner shower installation includes the shower pan, three wall pieces (two flat panels and a corner shelf/connector unit), and the glass panels and frames for the sliding door. All connectors and hardware are included, but this isn't the case with all such kits. When buying a shower kit, always examine the components and read the instructions carefully to see if additional parts and materials are needed.

The key to smooth installation with a kit shower is making sure the wall panels, frames, and shower pan fit squarely in the corners and against the existing walls. Walls that are out of square or not perfectly flat can complicate this job, so correcting faulty walls is time well spent if you're installing a corner shower.

Any shower kit will require very diligent and careful sealing of the joints using siliconized latex caulk and silicone sealant. Do not rush this step, because it is crucial to achieving a workable, leak-free shower.

Tools + Materials ▶

Corner shower kit
  with shower pan
Tape measure
Pencil or marker
4' level

Drill bits and
  hole saw
Straightedge
Utility knife
Silicone sealant
Wall (panel)
  adhesive

Siliconized latex
  caulk
Caulk gun
Carpenter's square
Hammer
Center punch
Phillips screwdriver

Masking tape
Mineral spirits
Clean cloths
Plastic wall anchors
Eye protection
Work gloves

HOW TO INSTALL A CORNER SHOWER

1

Prepare the floor drain and install a prefabricated shower pan in the corner of the room. Make sure the outside diameter of the drain pipe matches the requirements of the shower pan (ours required a 2⅜" outside diameter for the drain pipe). The shower pan must sit perfectly level on the floor and tight against the wall studs on the two adjoining walls for the installation to proceed smoothly.

2

Draw centerlines along the top of the outer thresholds of the shower pan. Position one of the metal wall channels vertically against the wall, so the bottom edge is centered on the centerline. Use a level to adjust the wall channel for plumb, then mark the mounting-hole locations on the wall through the holes in the wall channel.

3

Drill holes and drive plastic wall anchors for the metal shower channels. The plastic wall anchors are included in most shower kits.

4

Position the wall channels in place and secure them to the wall with mounting screws driven through the mounting holes and into the wall anchors.

5

Fill the gaps between the shower base and the wall with siliconized latex caulk. Install the other wall channel in the same way, and seal the remaining gap between the shower pan and the wall. Lightly sand the top face of the shower pan curbs with the sandpaper included in the kit. This will create a better bonding surface when you seal the pan at the end of the project.

(continued)

6

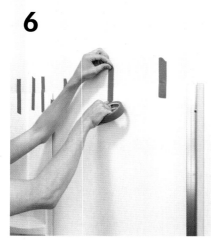

Prepare the walls in whatever manner recommended by the kit instructions. Test-fit the side panels and the corner panel by taping them in place temporarily with masking tape, with the shiny side of the panels facing out. The wall panels should butt against the wall channels and rest flat against the shower-pan curbs. If the wall panels don't line up correctly, it indicates that the wall channels are out of plumb or the shower pan is not level. The corner panel should slightly overlap the side wall panels, by about ½". Some trimming may be necessary if the overlap is greater.

7

To prepare the side wall that will contain the plumbing fixtures, cut a cardboard template to the same size as the wall panel and place the template against the wall. Mark the location of the shower and faucet on the template. Make an X against this side of the cardboard for reference. Remove the cardboard template, then use a utility knife to cut away openings for the plumbing stub-outs on the template. Test-fit the cardboard template against the wall, making sure the plumbing pipes fit correctly.

8

Use the template to mark the opening on the wall panel that will hold the shower plumbing fixtures, then use an appropriately sized hole saw to cut openings in the wall panel. Make sure to align the wall panel correctly when marking: the shiny side will face into the shower.

9a

9b

9c

Beginning with the panel without plumbing cutouts, spread a continuous ¼" bead of panel adhesive along the four edges of the back of the wall panel, no closer than 2" to the edges. Leave gaps at the ends so air can escape when you press the panels against the wall. Also apply an S-shaped continuous bead to the center of the panel. Position the panel against the wall so the bottom rests firmly against the shower-pan curb and side edges are against the wall channel and the corner of the room. Press the panel against the wall firmly, and smooth it with even hand pressure until the panel is perfectly flat. Repeat with the wall that has plumbing cutouts, making sure to apply a bead of panel adhesive around the cutouts. Finally, apply panel adhesive to the back of the corner panel and press it into place. (Some shower models may have a connecting rod that joins the corner panel to the shower-pan unit.) If any excess adhesive has squeezed out around the edges of the panel, clean it away with a rag moistened with mineral spirits.

10

Following the kit instructions, begin assembling the doorframes. With our kit, the first step is to attach the center guide to the bottom rail using the screws included with the kit.

11

Stand the sliding door panels upright so the hanging brackets are at the top. Install the rollers on the same side of the door panels as the door stops.

12

Most shower kits have both stationary glass panels and sliding panels. Begin by installing the first stationary panel by inserting it into the wall channel so the roller channel at the side of the top rail is facing inside the shower stall. Now insert the sliding door panel on this side, so that the rollers engage the roller channel inside the top rail. Repeat this step with the opposite-side stationary panel and sliding door panel. Secure the top and bottom rails of the glass panels to the side channels and to one another using the corner connectors included with the kit.

(continued)

Install the seal strips on the back of both sliding door panels, as per the kit instructions. These pliable strips will allow the door to form a watertight seal against the stationary panels.

13

Make small adjustments to the entire assembly to center it on the top face of the shower pan curbs. Once you've positioned it correctly, so that the entire unit is plumb and the bottoms of the stationary panels are flat and level on the shower pan, drill holes in the frame through the adjustment holes in the glass frames and secure the unit to the wall channels with the provided screws. Test the doors and, if necessary, make small adjustments by loosening and then reattaching the roller screws at the top of the doors. Allow the shower unit to sit in place for 12 hours before beginning the waterproofing step.

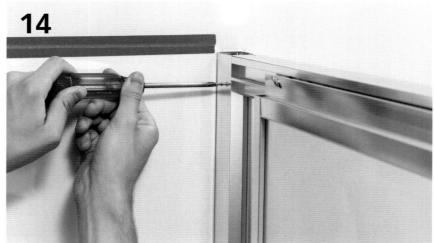

14

15

Waterproofing the shower requires the use of two different but similar-sounding products: siliconized latex caulk and silicone sealant. First, apply siliconized caulk to the seams between the wall panels and corner panel, between the wall panels and the metal wall channels, the seam where the wall panels and corner panel meet the shower pan, and along the tops of the wall panels. Apply silicone sealant to the heads of all screws in the upright panel frames. From inside of the shower, apply silicone sealant along the seams where the bottom rails lie on the shower pan curb and along the bottoms of the wall channels and glass panel upright frames. Also apply silicone sealant around the center guide. Apply silicone sealant around the joint where the bottom rails butt up against the bottom connector. Finally, apply sealant to the heads of any exposed screws.

16

Let the caulked and sealed seams dry completely. To complete your shower, make the plumbing hookups of the shower faucet spray head and the shower valve. Test the shower to check for leaks.

CURBLESS SHOWER

Whether it's part of a complete "wet room," or installed as a standalone feature, a curbless shower combines easy access for those with limited mobility, convenience for other users, and a look that is trendy, sophisticated, and attractive. The trick to installing one of these water features is to ensure the moisture stays inside the shower.

Once upon a time, creating a reliably waterproof enclosure for a curbless shower was no small chore. It meant putting a lot of work into creating a custom shower pan. This kind of project was usually above the skill level or desire of the weekend DIYer, and it generally meant hiring a contractor.

Now you can buy curbless shower pan kits that make installation a breeze. The manufacturers have thought through all the issues that can arise and have developed the kits and shower pans to be as foolproof as possible, while also meeting prevailing codes and best standards and practices. Installing a curbless shower using one of these kits is a realistic project for any home handyperson with even moderate DIY skills and a weekend to spare.

These pans come with preconfigured slopes to ensure optimal drainage away from the shower's edges. The product we used for this project, the Tuff Form kit from Access Reliability Center, includes an offset drain hole that offers the option of rotating the pan in the event of a joist or mechanicals that are in the way. This product is offered in nine different sizes and can be cut with a circular saw to just about any shape—including more unusual, curvy shapes for a truly custom look.

Curbless shower pan manufacturers also sell pans with trench drains for an even sleeker look. The pan we used for this project is typical of the prefab curbless pan construction; it can support 1,100 pounds even though the pan itself weighs less than 70 pounds. It sits right on floor joists, with the addition of blocking to support the area around the drain, and to provide nailing surfaces around the edges.

Kits like these offer advantages beyond the ease of installation and a thoughtful configuration of parts. Usually, the plumbing can be completely adjusted and connected from above, so you won't need to work in the basement or a crawl space, or open up a first-floor ceiling to install a second-floor shower. The kits themselves generally include almost everything you'll need for the installation.

Tools + Materials ›

Circular saw	Synthetic paintbrush
Jigsaw	Waterproof latex sealant
Caulking gun	Caulk gun
Torpedo level	Waterproofing tape
Drill and bits	Liquid waterproofing
PVC cement and brush	membrane
Screwdriver	Roller and roller handle
Speed square	Tiles
Screws	Thinset tile adhesive
Putty knife	Notched trowel
Palm sander and	Tile saw
120-grit pad	Adhesive mat
Scissors	Eye and ear protection
Rubber gloves	

A curbless shower kit includes almost everything you need. All you have to supply are some basic tools, the tile, and a little elbow grease.

Wet Rooms + Universal Design ▸

Because a wet room allows the bathroom to be designed with fewer barriers and a single-level floor surface, these rooms are natural partners to a Universal Design approach. If you're thinking about converting a bathroom to a wet room, it's worthwhile to consider a little extra effort to make the space as accessible as possible for the maximum number of users.

Walls. Where codes allow it, consider using thick plywood rather than cementboard for the wall sub-surfaces. Plywood allows for direct installation of grab bars without the need for blocking or locating studs. If you're set on using cementboard, plan out locations for grab bars near toilets, behind and alongside bathtubs, and

in showers. Most codes specify that grab bars must be able to support up to 200 pounds—which usually means adding blocking in the walls behind the grab bars.

Shower stall. One of the benefits to adding a curbless shower is easy wheelchair (or walker) access. For maximum accessibility, the shower area should be at least 60" wide by at least 36" deep (60" by 60" is preferable). This allows a wheelchair-bound user to occupy the stall with a helper. And, although the idea is a wide-open shower space, it's always a good idea to add a fold down seat. This allows for transfer from a wheelchair, or a place for someone with limited leg strength and endurance to sit.

HOW TO INSTALL A WATERPROOF SUBBASE FOR A CURBLESS SHOWER

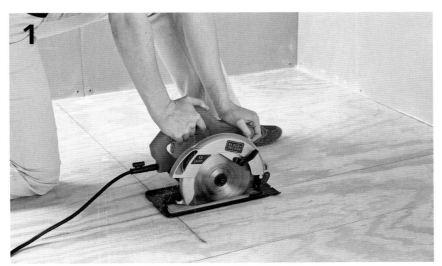

Remove the existing flooring material in the area of the shower pan (if you're remodeling an existing bathroom). Use a circular saw to cut out and remove the subfloor in the exact dimensions of the shower pan. Finish the cuts with a jigsaw or handsaw.

Reinforce the floor with blocking between joists as necessary. Toenail bridge blocking in on either side of the drain waste pipe location, and between joists anywhere you'll need a nailing surface along the edges of the shower pan. If trusses or joists are spaced more than 16" on center, add bridge blocking to adequately support the pan.

(continued)

3

Set the pan in the opening to make sure it fits and is level. If it is not level, screw shims to the tops of any low joists and check again: repeat if necessary until the pan is perfectly level in all directions.

4

Install or relocate drain pipes as needed. Check with your local building department: if the drain and trap are not accessible from below you may need to have an on-site inspection before you cover up the plumbing.

5

Check the height of the drainpipe—its top should be exactly 2⅜" from the bottom of the pan—measure down from the top of the joist. If the drainpipe is too high, remove it and trim with a tubing cutter. If it is too low, replace the assembly with a new assembly that has a longer tailpiece.

6

Lay a thick bead of construction adhesive along the contact areas on all joists, nailing surfaces, and blocking.

7

Set the pan in place and screw it down, using at least 2 screws along each side. Do not overtighten the screws. If you've cut off the screwing flange on one or more sides to accommodate an unusual shape, drill ⅛" pilot holes in the cut edges at joist or blocking locations, and drive the screws through the holes.

8

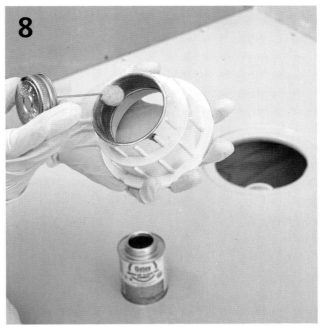

Disassemble the supplied drain assembly. Be careful not to lose any of the screws. Place the drain tailpiece on the waste pipe under where the pan's drainhole will be located, and measure to check that it sits at the correct level. Solvent-glue the tailpiece to the end of the waste pipe.

9

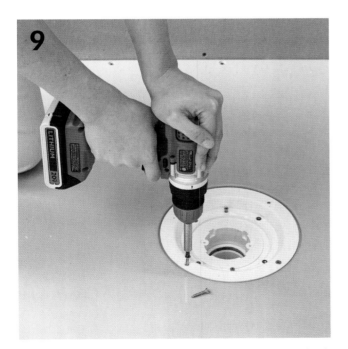

Position the supplied gaskets on top of the tailpiece (check the manufacturer's instructions; the gaskets usually need to be layered in the correct order). Set the drain flange piece on top of the tail, and into the drain hole in the pan. Drill ⅛" pilot holes through the flange and into the pan. Screw the flange to the pan.

10

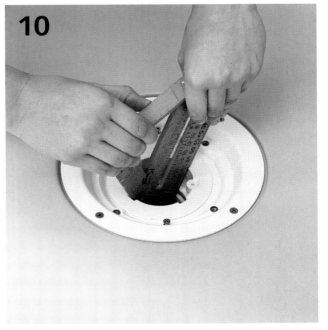

Thread the tail top piece into the tail through the drain flange. Use a speed square or other lever, such as spread channel lock pliers, to snugly tighten the tail top piece in place.

(continued)

11

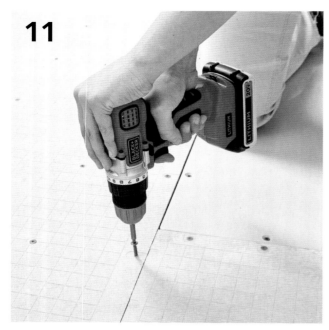

Install tile underlayment for the rest of the project area. If the underlayment is higher than the top of the pan once it is installed, you'll have to sand it to level, gradually tapering away from the pan.

12

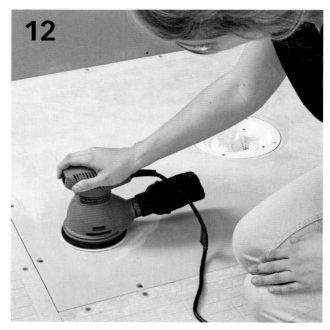

Scrape any stickers or other blemishes off the pan with a putty knife. Lightly sand the entire surface of the pan using 120-grit sandpaper to help the sealant adhere. After you're done sanding, wipe down the sanded pan with a damp sponge. Make sure the entire area is clean.

13

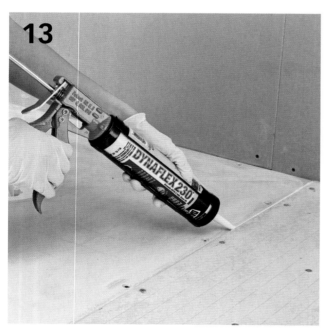

Seal the edge seams at the wall and between the pan and subfloor with waterproof latex sealant. Caulk any pan screw holes that were not used.

14

Cut strips of waterproofing tape to cover all seams in the tile underlayment (both walls and floor). Also cut strips for the joints where walls and floor meet. Open the pail of liquid waterproofing membrane and mix the liquid thoroughly. Beginning at the top and working down, brush a bed of waterproofing liquid over the seams. Before it dries, set the tape firmly into the waterproofing. Press and smooth the tape. Then brush a layer of waterproofing compound over the tape.

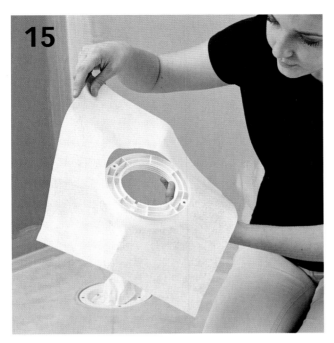

15

Trace a hole in the center of the waterproof drain gasket, using the bottom of the drain clamping donut. Cut the hole out using scissors. Be careful cutting the gasket because it is a crucial part of the drain waterproofing. Check the fit with the gasket against the underside of the clamping donut top flange.

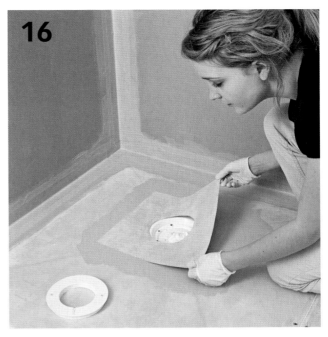

16

Apply a thin coat of the waterproofing compound around the drain hole and to the back of the drain gasket. Don't apply too much; if the waterproofing is too thick under the gasket, it may not dry correctly.

17

Put the gasket in place and brush a coat of the waterproofing over the gasket. Screw the clamping donut in place on the top of the drain and over the membrane. Hand-tighten the bolts and then cover the clamping donut with the waterproofing compound (avoid covering the slide lock for the drain grate).

18

Use a roller to roll waterproofing compound across the walls and over the entire pan surface. The ideal is 4mm thick (about the thickness of a credit card). Allow this first coat to dry for 2 hours, then cover with a second coat. This should conclude the waterproofing phase of the project and you're ready to begin laying tile once the waterproofing compound has dried thoroughly.

HOW TO INSTALL TILE FOR A CURBLESS SHOWER

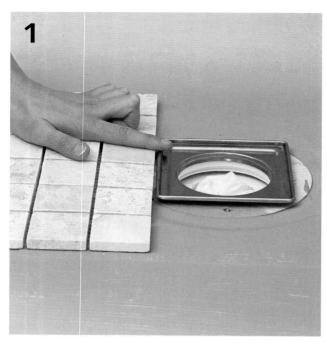

1

Set the floor tile first. Begin by placing a sample of the floor tile directly next to the drain so you can set the drain grate height to match. The adjustable mounting plate for the grate should be flush with the tops of the tile.

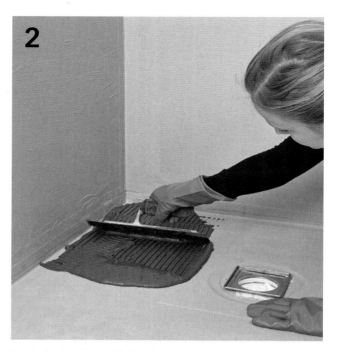

2

Begin laying floor tile in the corner of the shower. Lay a bed of thinset tile adhesive, using a notched trowel. The thinset container should specify the notch size (⅜" square notch is common).

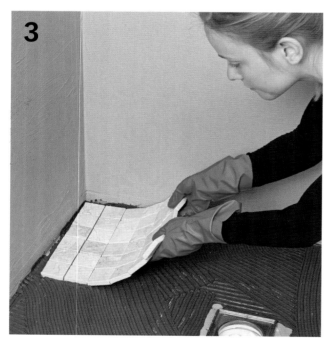

3

Place the corner tile into the bed of thinset and press it to set it. Don't press down too hard or you will displace too much of the material. Continue laying tile, fanning out from the corner toward the drain opening. Leave space around the drain opening as it is likely you'll need to cut tiles to fit.

4

Install tile so a small square of untiled area is left around the drain opening (which, in the system seen here, is square, making for an easier cutting job).

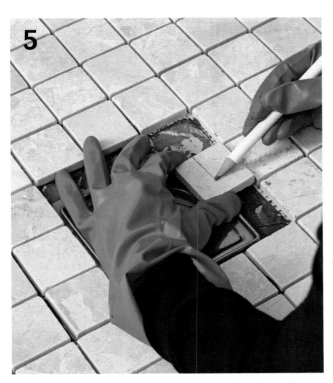

5

Mark the tiles that surround the drain opening for cutting. Leave a small gap between the tiles next to the drain grate mounting plate.

6

Cut the tiles along the trim lines using a tile saw. If you are not comfortable using a tile saw, score the tiles and cut them with tile nippers.

7

Apply thinset onto the shower pan, taking care not to get any on the drain grate mounting plate. You may need to use a small trowel or a putty knife to get into small gaps.

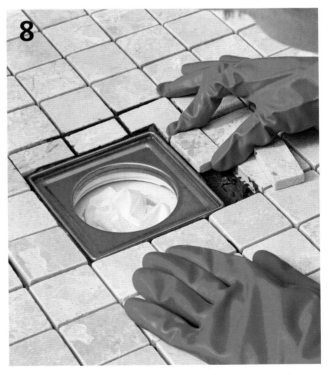

8

Set the cut tiles around the drain opening, doing your best to maintain even gaps that match the gaps in the rest of the floor. Once you've finished tiling around the drain, complete setting floor tile in the rest of the project area.

(continued)

9

Let the floor tile set overnight and then apply grout. Using a grout float held at about a 30° angle, wipe the grout over the gaps so all gaps are filled evenly. After the grout dries, buff the floor with a towel to wipe up excess residue.

10

Snap the grate cover into the cover mounting plate (if you've stuffed a rag into the drain opening to keep debris out, be sure to remove it first). The grate cover seen here locks in with a small key that should be saved in case you need to remove the grate cover.

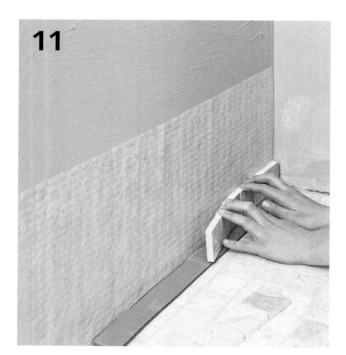

11

Begin setting the wall tile. Generally, it's easiest if you start at the bottom and work upward. Instead of thinset adhesive, an adhesive mat is being used here. This relatively new product is designed for walls and is rated for waterproof applications. It is a good idea to use a spacer (¼" thick or so) to get an even border at the bottoms of the first tiles.

12

In the design used here, a border of the same mosaic tile used in the floor is installed all around the shower area to make the first course. Dark brown accent tiles are installed in a single vertical column running upward, centered on the line formed by the shower faucet and showerhead. This vertical column is installed after the bottom border.

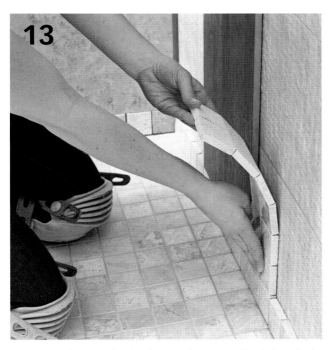

13

Next, another vertical column of accent tiles is installed on each side of the large, dark tiles. These columns are also laid using the floor tile, which connects the walls and floor visually in an effective way.

14

Finally, larger field tiles that match the floor tile used outside the shower area are installed up to the corner and outward from the shower area. Starting at the bottom, set a thin spacer on top of the border tiles to ensure even gaps.

15

Grout the gaps in the wall tiles. It's usually a good idea to protect any fittings, such as the shower faucet handle escutcheon, with painters tape prior to grouting. If you wish, a clear surround may be installed to visually define the shower area, as in the photo to the right, but because the shower pan is pitched toward the drain it really is not necessary.

HOW TO INSTALL A CLAWFOOT TUB

PLUMBING

1

Position the tub exactly where you'd like it to rest, ideally over existing supply and drain lines. Install the feet first if they were not preattached (inset photo).

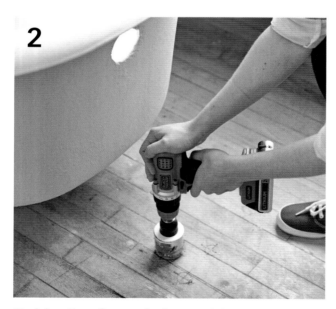

2

Mark locations for supply risers and drain tailpipe on the floor. Drill starter holes and double check below the floor to make sure floor joists will not be directly under the access holes. Use a hole saw slightly wider than each pipe to drill access holes. Install supply lines and drainline.

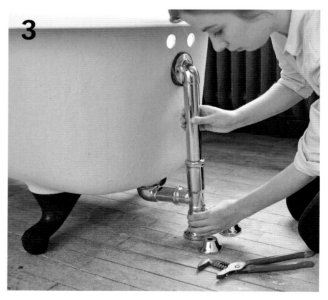

3

Install the drain-waste-overflow assembly according to the manufacturer's instructions. With a freestanding tub, it is often easiest to join the assembly parts working upward from the drainpipe connection in the floor. Install the drain flange in the tub, fastening it from the top into the drain shoe. Make the connection to the drain pipe in the floor—if the kit comes with a floor escutcheon that covers the drain connection, make sure it is in place before you attach the tailpipe to the T.

4

Fasten the overflow cover to the overflow receiver with the bolt or bolts that are provided. Be sure to position the rubber gasket that came with the drain kit so it fits neatly against the tub wall. Do not overtighten the fasteners.

5

Assemble the faucet according to the manufacturer's instructions. Most older clawfoot tubs have a two-valve faucet with a gooseneck spigot that mounts directly to the wall of the tub at the foot end. Many newer freestanding tubs utilize a wall-mounted faucet.

6

Mount the faucet body to the tub wall with the retainer nuts that thread onto the faucet valve stems.

7

Attach the supply risers to the valve inlets for the faucet. Put the supply pipe base escutcheons in place on the floor over the supply line connections. Secure the risers into the supply connections below the floor. Turn on the water supply and test to make sure there are no leaks in any of the pipes or fitting connections, including the drain and overflow.

Feet First ▸

Despite their great weight, it is always a good idea to anchor cast-iron tubs—even a small shift in position can cause the drain or supply connections to fail. Older tubs often have screwholes in the bottoms of the feet so they may be fastened to the floor once the hookups are made. Newer lighter-weight tubs generally use floor pins to stabilize the tub. Some manufacturers recommend using rubber pads and epoxy under each foot, in conjunction with dowels or mounting studs. Some tubs have self-leveling feet, with integral adjustment posts—check and follow the manufacturer's installation instructions.

ADDING A SHOWER TO A FREESTANDING TUB

Complete kits for converting a freestanding tub to a shower are widely available through plumbing-supply retailers. A quick online search will give you an idea of what's out there (use key phrases such as "clawfoot tub to shower," "clawfoot tub shower set," or "shower enclosure"). Kits include a special faucet with a built-in diverter, a riser pipe (extending from the faucet to the showerhead), and a rectangular shower-curtain frame that mounts to the ceiling and wall. Prices range from less than $100 to more than $500, depending on the style of the faucet and showerhead and the quality of the materials.

Examine your faucet and its water hookups carefully before ordering a kit. Measure the distance between the faucet tailpieces and the length and offset of the water-supply risers. The new faucet must fit into the existing holes in your tub. You may need to buy new supply risers to connect to the faucet.

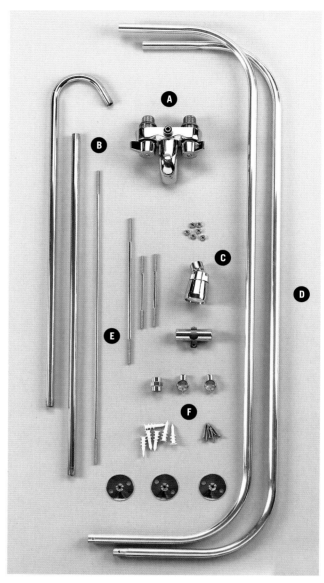

A packaged kit for adding a shower to your tub features a faucet with diverter (A), shower-riser plumbing (B), showerhead (C), a frame for the shower curtain (D) that mounts on the wall and ceiling with threaded rods (E), and fasteners and fittings (F).

A spout with a diverter, some metal supply tubing, and a shower-curtain frame can add showering capacity to a standalone tub.

Tools + Materials ▸

Adjustable wrench	Drill and bits
Plumber's putty or	Shower-conversion kit
silicone plumber's	Tubing cutter
grease	Ear and eye protection
Teflon tape	Work gloves

PLUMBING

HOW TO INSTALL A SHOWER-CONVERSION KIT

Remove the old tub faucet and replace it with the new diverter-type faucet from the kit. Fit the assembled shower riser into the top of the faucet and hand-tighten. Apply Teflon tape to the threads before making the connection. This assembly includes one straight and one curved section, joined by a coupling. The top, curved pipe includes a connector to a wall brace. Shorten the straight section using a tubing cutter, to lower the showerhead height, if desired. Slip the compression nut and washer onto the bottom end of the shower riser, and attach the riser to the top of the faucet, hand-tightening for the time being.

Assemble the curtain frame with a helper, securing it with setscrews. Hold the frame level and measure to the ceiling to determine the ceiling-brace pipe length. Cut the pipe and complete the ceiling-brace assembly. Set the shower riser to the desired height and connect the brace to the wall (ensure strong connections by driving the mounting screws into a wall stud and ceiling joist, if possible).

After the curtain frame is completely assembled and secured, tighten the faucet connection with a wrench. Full-size shower kits require one shower curtain on each side of the curtain frame. The hooks seen here feature roller bearings on the tops so they can be operated very smoothly with minimal resistance.

HOW TO INSTALL A VESSEL SINK

Secure the vanity cabinet or other countertop that you'll be using to mount the vessel sink.

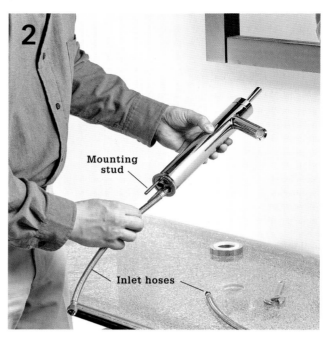

Begin hooking up the faucet. Insert the brass mounting stud into the threaded hole in the faucet base with the slotted end facing out. Hand tighten and then use a slotted screwdriver to tighten another half turn. Insert the inlet hoses into the faucet body and hand tighten. Use an adjustable wrench to tighten another half turn. Do not overtighten.

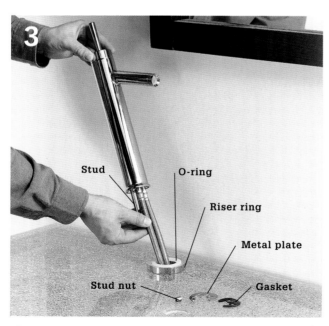

Place the O-ring on top of the riser ring over the faucet cutout in the countertop. From underneath, slide the rubber gasket and the metal plate over the mounting stud. Thread the mounting stud nut onto the mounting stud and hand tighten. Use an adjustable wrench to tighten another half turn.

To install the sink and pop-up drain, first place the small metal ring between two O-rings and place over the drain cutout.

5

Place the vessel bowl on top of the O-rings. In this installation, the vessel is not bonded to the countertop.

6

Put the small rubber gasket over the drain hole in the vessel. From the top, push the pop-up assembly through the drain hole.

7

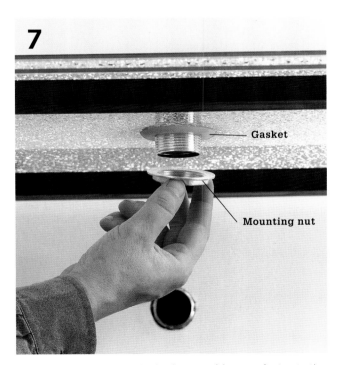

Gasket

Mounting nut

From underneath, push the large rubber gasket onto the threaded portion of the pop-up assembly. Thread the nut onto the pop-up assembly and tighten. Use an adjustable wrench or basin wrench to tighten an additional half turn. Thread the tailpiece onto the pop-up assembly.

8

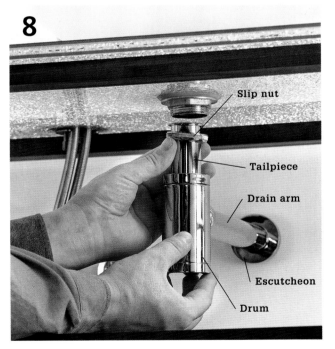

Slip nut

Tailpiece

Drain arm

Escutcheon

Drum

Install the drum trap. Loosen the rings on the top and outlet of the drum trap. Slide the drum trap top hole over the tailpiece. Slide the drain arm into the side outlet, with the flat side of the rubber gasket facing away from the trap. Insert the drain arm into the wall outlet. Hand tighten the rings.

WALL-MOUNTED SINKS

There are many benefits to a wall-mounted sink that, depending on your situation and needs, will offset the inherent lack of storage space. In contrast to the footprint of a traditional vanity-mounted sink, wall-mounted units can save space on the sides and in front of the fixture. More importantly, they are an essential addition to a Universal Design bathroom where wheelchair accessibility is a key consideration. It's why these particular fixtures are sometimes called "roll-under" sinks.

All that practicality aside, early models at the lower end of the price spectrum were somewhat unattractive because their designs simply left the drain tailpiece, trap, and supply shut-off valves in plain sight. But there's no need for you to settle for a less-than-handsome wall-mounted sink. Manufacturers have developed two solutions to the problem of exposed plumbing. Some are designed with a bowl that conceals supply line shut-offs, replacing the trap with sleekly designed tailpieces and squared off trap bends. The other solution, and one more widely available, is a wall-mounted pedestal that covers the plumbing. Sinks with this feature are sometimes called "semi-pedestal."

We've opted to illustrate the installation of just such a sink in the instructions that follow. Keep in mind that different manufacturers sometimes use very different mounting procedures. In any case, the idea remains the same: strongly secure the sink to studs or blocking, so that it is completely stable and will not fall.

The most involved part of the installation process is usually rerouting water supply and drain lines as necessary. You should hire a licensed plumber for this if you're not comfortable with the work. Once the plumbing is in place, the installation is quick and easy.

Tools + Materials ▸

Carpenter's level	Phillips screwdriver
Adjustable wrenches	Standard screwdriver
Pipe wrench	Jigsaw
Channel-type pliers	Basin wrench
Drill and bits	Tape measure
Tubing cutter	Hacksaw
Work gloves	2 × 8 lumber
Eye protection	

Although a wall-mounted sink offers many benefits—accessibility to wheelchair users among them—there's no need to sacrifice chic style for that functionality.

HOW TO INSTALL A WALL-MOUNTED SINK

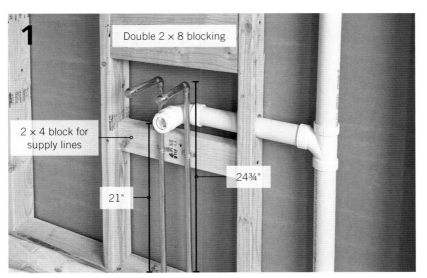

1

Double 2 × 8 blocking

2 × 4 block for supply lines

21"

24¾"

Remove the existing sink, if any. Remove wall coverings as necessary to install blocking for mounting the sink. Reroute water supply and drain lines as necessary, according to the sink manufacturer's directions. The sink in this project required the centerpoints of the waste pipe be 21" and the supply lines 24¾" up from the finished floor. If unsure of your plumbing skills or code requirements, hire a professional plumber for this part of the project. Install blocking between the studs for attaching the mounting bracket for the sink. A doubled 2 × 8 is installed here. Have your plumbing inspected, if required by your municipality, before you install the drywall and finished wall surface.

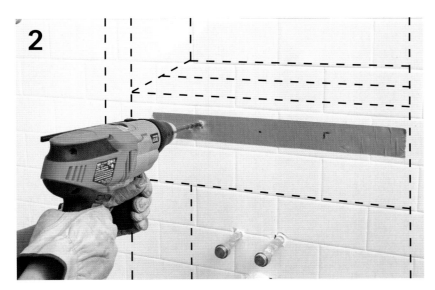

2

Drill guide holes for the mounting bolts if your sink is a direct-mount model, as this one is. Some wall-hung sinks are hung from a mounting bracket. The bolts used to hang this sink are threaded like lag screws on one end, with a bolt end that projects from the wall. The guide holes should be spaced exactly as the manufacturer specifies so they align with the mounting holes in the back mounting flange on the sink.

TIP: Protect tile surfaces with masking tape in the drilling areas to avoid chip-out.

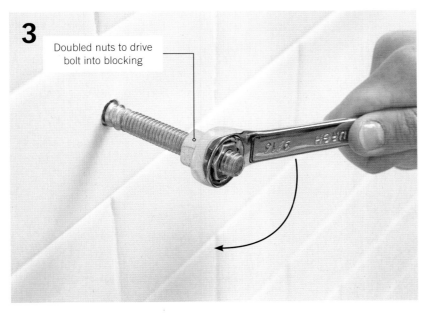

3

Doubled nuts to drive bolt into blocking

Drive the threaded mounting bolts (screw end first) into the guide holes. There should be pilot holes (smaller than the guide holes) driven into the blocking. To drive this hardware, spin a pair of nuts onto the bolt end and turn the bolt closest to you with a wrench. Drive the mounting bolt until the end is projecting out from the wall by a little more than 1½". Remove the nuts. Install the pop-up drain in the sink, and then slide the sink over the ends of the mounting bolts so the mounting flange is flush against the wall. You'll want help for this. Thread the washers and nuts onto the ends of the mounting bolts, and hand-tighten. Check to make sure the sink is level, and then tighten the nuts with a socket wrench, reaching up into the void between the basin and the flange. Don't overtighten—you could crack the sink flange.

(continued)

4

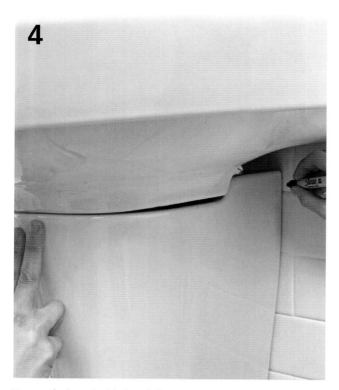

Have a helper hold the sink pedestal (in this model, a half-pedestal) in position against the underside of the sink. Mark the edges of the pedestal on the wall covering as reference for installing the pedestal-mounting hardware.

5

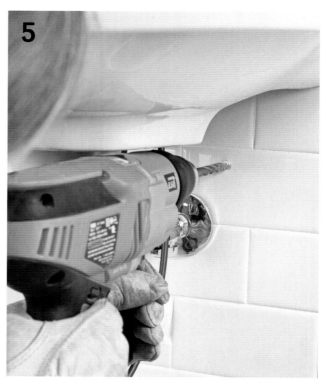

Remove the pedestal, and drill the pilot holes for the pedestal-mounting bolts, which work much in the same way as the sink-mounting bolts. Drill guide and pilot holes, then drive the mounting bolts, leaving about 1¼" of the bolt end exposed.

6

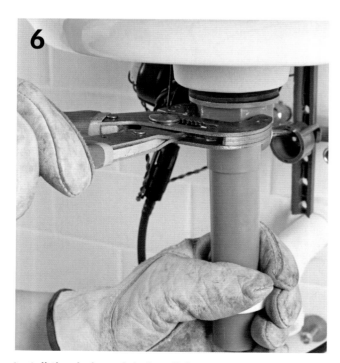

Install the drain and drain tailpiece on the sink. Also mount the faucet body to the sink deck if you have not done so already. Attach the drain trap arm to the drain stub out in the wall, and attach shutoff valves to the drain supply lines.

7

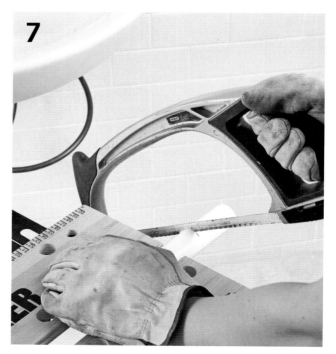

Complete the drain connection by installing a P-trap assembly that connects the tailpiece and the trap arm. Also connect the drain pop-up rod that projects out of the tailpiece to the pop-up plunger mechanism you've already installed.

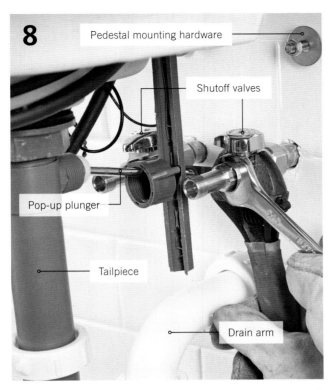

8

Pedestal mounting hardware

Shutoff valves

Pop-up plunger

Tailpiece

Drain arm

Make sure the shutoff valve fittings are tight and oriented correctly, and then hook up the faucet supply risers to the shutoff valves. Turn on the water supply and test.

Installation Tip ▸

To quickly and easily find an undersink leak, lay bright white paper or paper towels under the pipes and drain connections. Open the water supply valves and run water in the sinks. It should be clear exactly where the water dripped from by the location of the drip on the paper.

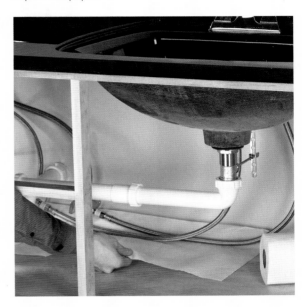

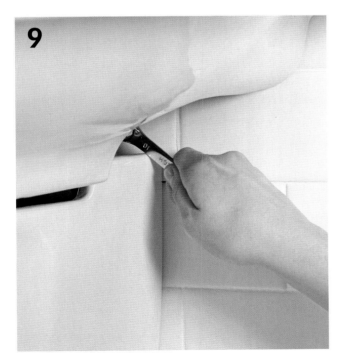

9

Slide the pedestal into place on the mounting studs. Working through the access space under the sink, use a wrench to tighten the mounting nut over the washer on the stud. Carefully tighten the nut until the pedestal is held securely in place. Be careful not to overtighten the nut.

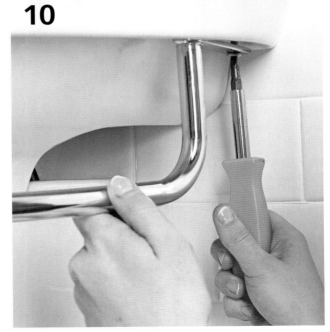

10

Attach the towel bar to the sink by first pushing the well nuts into the holes on the underside of the sink rim. Set the bar in place, and screw in the attachment screws on both sides, just until snug.

PEDESTAL + CONSOLE SINKS

Pedestal sinks remain a popular option for homeowners outfitting space-challenged bathrooms, or just looking for a more streamlined sink option. The tiny footprint of these sinks allows for easy cleaning and movement around the sinks. This bathroom fixture is available in an amazing array of design styles, and you can be confident that if you opt for a pedestal sink, you can find one to suit exactly your taste or the look of any bathroom.

The primary drawback to pedestal sinks is that they don't offer any storage. Their chief practical benefit is that they conceal plumbing some homeowners would prefer to keep out of sight. Console sinks, with their two front legs, offer some space underneath for rolling shelf units or a towel basket.

Pedestal sinks are mounted in one of two ways. Most inexpensive models are hung in much the same way as wall-mounted sinks are. The pedestal is actually installed after the sink is hung, and its purpose is purely decorative. But other, higher-end pedestal sinks have structural pedestals that bear the weight of the sink. All console sinks are mounted to the wall, although the front legs offer additional support and resistance to users leaning on the front of the sink.

Tools + Materials ▶

Pedestal sink	2 × 4 lumber
Caulk gun and	Water-resistant drywall
silicone caulk	Pencil
Stud finder	Drill
Ratchet wrench	Eye and ear protection
Basin wrench	Work gloves
Lag screws	

A console bathroom sink is a wall-mounted lavatory with two front legs that provide backup support. Many have a narrow apron to conceal the drain trap.

A pedestal sink typically is hung on the wall. The primary function of the pedestal is to conceal plumbing and provide visual appeal.

HOW TO INSTALL A PEDESTAL SINK

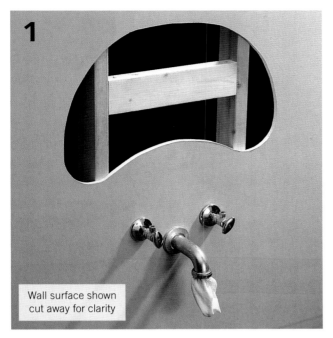

1

Wall surface shown cut away for clarity

Install 2 × 4 blocking between the wall studs behind the planned sink location. Cover the wall with water-resistant drywall.

2

Set the basin and pedestal in position and brace them with 2 × 4s. Outline the top of the basin on the wall, and mark the base of the pedestal on the floor. Mark reference points on the wall and floor through the mounting holes found on the back of the sink and the bottom of the pedestal.

3

Set aside the basin and pedestal. Drill pilot holes in the wall and floor at the reference points, then reposition the pedestal. Anchor the pedestal to the floor with lag screws.

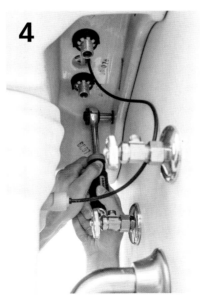

4

Attach the faucet set to the sink, then set the sink onto the pedestal. Align the holes on the back flange of the sink with the pilot holes drilled in the wall, then drive lag screws with washers into the wall brace using a ratchet wrench. Attach the sink-stopper mechanism to the sink drain.

5

Hook up the drain and supply fittings. Caulk between the back of the sink and the wall when installation is finished.

Basic Lavatory Faucet Types ▸

Widespread faucets allow you to customize the locations and orientation of the faucets and spout in your sink deck.

Single-body faucets are faster and easier to install and are extremely reliable.

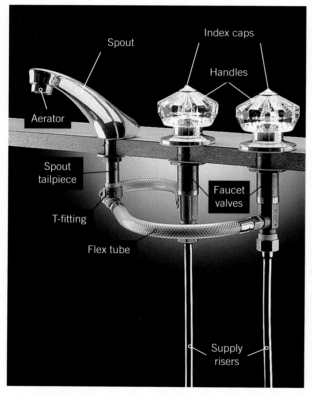

Widespread faucets come in three pieces: a spout and two valves. Supply risers carry hot and cold water to the valves, which are turned to regulate the amount of water going to the spout, where the water is mixed. Water travels from the valves to the spout through flex tubes, which in turn attach to the spout tailpiece via a T-fitting. Three-piece faucets designed to work with a pop-up stopper have a clevis and a lift rod. The handles attach with handle screws that are covered with index caps. An aerator is screwed on the faucet spout after debris is flushed from the faucet.

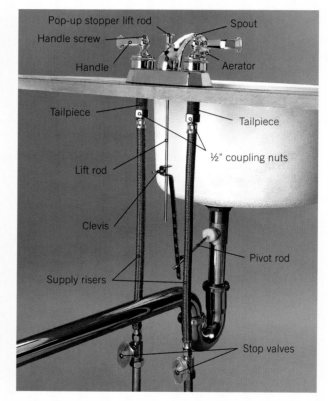

The tailpieces of a standard deck-mounted, one-piece bathroom sink faucet are 4" apart on center. As long as the 2 outside holes in the back of your sink measure 4" from center to center, and you have a middle hole for a pop-up stopper, you can put in any standard one-piece bathroom faucet with a pop-up stopper. The faucet is secured to the sink with mounting nuts that screw onto the tailpieces from below. Also get two flexible stainless-steel supply risers for sinks long enough to replace the old tubes. These typically attach to the stop valves with ⅜" compression-sized coupling nuts and to the faucet with standard faucet coupling nuts. But take your old tubes and the old compression nuts from the stop valves to the store to ensure a match. The clevis, lift rod, and pivot rod are parts of the pop-up stopper assembly. The handles attach with handle screws that are covered with index caps.

HOW TO INSTALL A WIDESPREAD FAUCET

1

Shut off the water to the existing faucet and open the valves to drain the water. Disconnect the water supply tubes from the faucet, and remove the old faucet by unscrewing the mounting nuts. *NOTE: Removing the old faucet and installing the new one may be easiest if you remove the sink from the vanity.*

2

NOTE: Shown from behind with backsplash cut away for clarity.

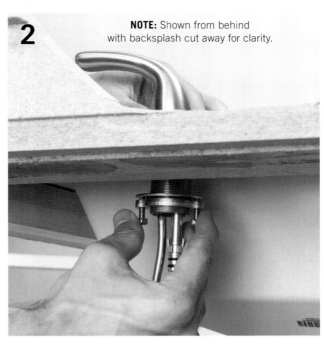

Clean away any existing plumber's putty or sealant from the surface of the sink, then lay a new bead of plumbers putty around each of the three openings. Install the two valves into the sink cutout openings by inserting the spout and valves and then threading the mounting screws onto the tailpieces from below the sink.

3

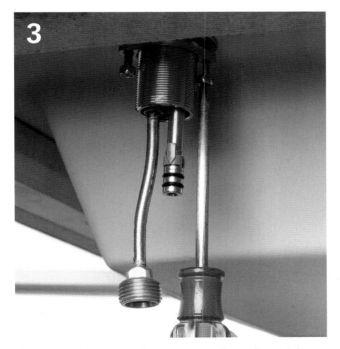

Exact mounting procedures vary; our faucet has retainer screws that are tightened after the mounting nut is threaded over the tailpieces. This secures the valves and spout tightly to the sink.

4

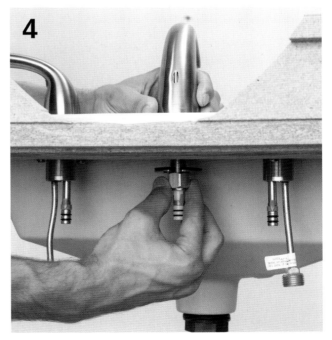

Repeat this procedure to install the center spout. Make sure the spout is aligned correctly to be perpendicular to the back of the sink.

(continued)

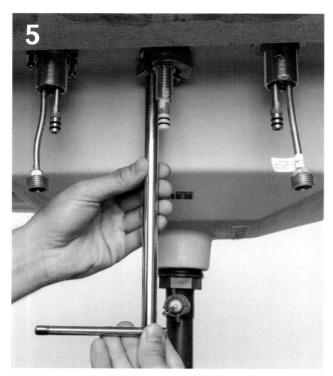

Tighten the spout mounting nut securely. A basin wrench will make this easier, since access to the mounting nut may be difficult.

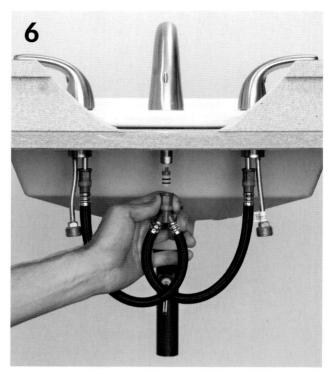

Attach the water connection tubes from the valve tailpieces to the spout tailpiece. Thread the mounting nuts by hand, then tighten slightly with channel-type pliers or an adjustable wrench (in tight quarters, this can also be done with a basin wrench).

Connect water-supply tubes from the water shutoff valves to the water-supply tubes on the faucet-valve tailpieces using an adjustable wrench (or basin wrench, where access is limited). In standard practice, the hot water normally connects to the left faucet valve and the cold water to the right. Turn on the water and test the faucet. If any fittings leak, tighten them slightly until they are watertight.

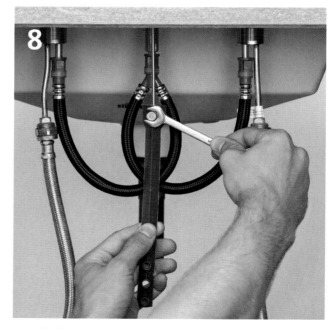

Attach the drain-stopper linkage to the push rod and to the stopper pivot lever.

VARIATION: How to Install a Single-Body Faucet ▸

1

High-quality faucets come with flexible plastic gaskets that create a durable watertight seal at the bottom of the faucet where it meets the sink deck. However, an inexpensive faucet may have a flimsy-looking foam seal that doesn't do a good job of sealing and disintegrates after a few years. If that is the case with your faucet, discard the seal and press a ring of plumber's putty into the sealant groove on the underside of the faucet body.

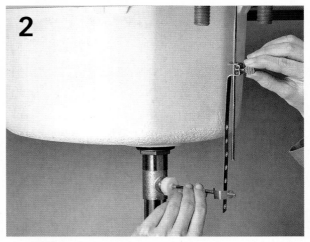

2

Insert the faucet tailpieces through the holes in the sink. From below, thread washers and mounting nuts over the tailpieces, then tighten the mounting nuts with a basin wrench until snug. Put a dab of pipe joint compound on the threads of the stop valves and thread the metal nuts of the flexible supply risers to these. Wrench tighten about a half-turn past hand tight. Overtightening these nuts will strip the threads. Now tighten the coupling nuts to the faucet tailpieces with a basin wrench.

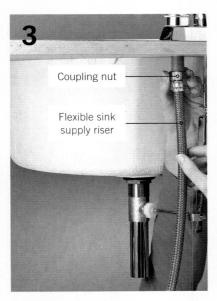

3

Coupling nut

Flexible sink supply riser

Slide the lift rod of the new faucet into its hole behind the spout. Thread it into the clevis past the clevis screw. Push the pivot rod all the way down so the stopper is open. With the lift rod also all the way down, tighten the clevis to the lift rod.

4

Grease the fluted valve stems with faucet grease, then put the handles in place. Tighten the handle screws firmly, so they won't come loose during operation. Cover each handle screw with the appropriate index cap—Hot or Cold.

5

Unscrew the aerator from the end of the spout. Turn the hot and cold water taps on full. Turn the water back on at the stop valves and flush out the faucet for a couple of minutes before turning off the water at the faucet. Check the riser connections for drips. Tighten a compression nut only until the drip stops. Replace the aerator.

POP-UP DRAINS

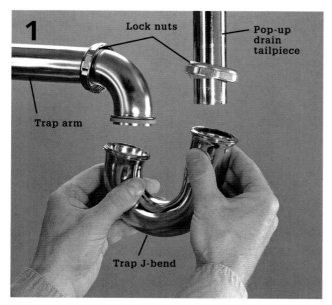

1

Lock nuts

Pop-up drain tailpiece

Trap arm

Trap J-bend

Put a basin under the trap to catch water. Loosen the nuts at the outlet and inlet to the trap J-bend by hand or with channel-type pliers and remove the bend. The trap will slide off the pop-up body tailpiece when the nuts are loose. Keep track of washers and nuts and their up/down orientation by leaving them on the tubes.

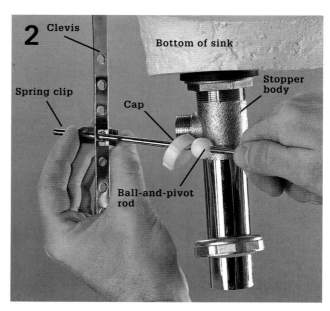

2 Clevis

Bottom of sink

Spring clip

Cap

Stopper body

Ball-and-pivot rod

Unscrew the cap holding the ball-and-pivot rod in the pop-up body and withdraw the ball. Compress the spring clip on the clevis and withdraw the pivot rod from the clevis.

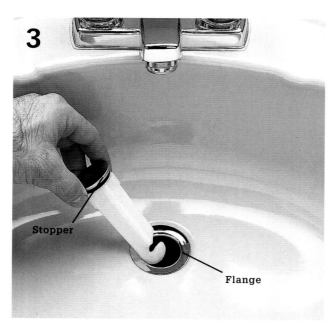

3

Stopper

Flange

Remove the pop-up stopper. Then, from below, remove the lock nut on the stopper body. If needed, keep the flange from turning by inserting a large screwdriver in the drain from the top. Thrust the stopper body up through the hole to free the flange from the basin, and then remove the flange and the stopper body.

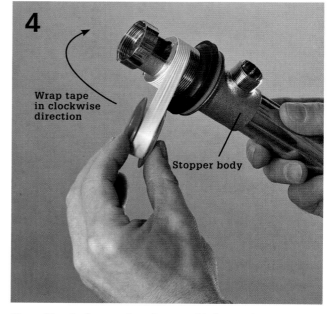

4

Wrap tape in clockwise direction

Stopper body

Clean the drain opening above and below, and then thread the locknut all the way down the new pop-up body, followed by the flat washer and the rubber gasket (beveled side up). Wrap three layers of Teflon tape clockwise onto the top of the threaded body. Make a ½"-dia. snake from plumber's putty, form it into a ring, and stick the ring underneath the drain flange.

5

Plumber's putty

From below, face the pivot rod opening directly back toward the middle of the faucet and pull the body straight down to seat the flange. Thread the locknut/washer assembly up under the sink, then fully tighten the locknut with channel-type pliers. Do not twist the flange in the process, as this can break the putty seal. Clean off the squeezeout of plumber's putty from around the flange.

6

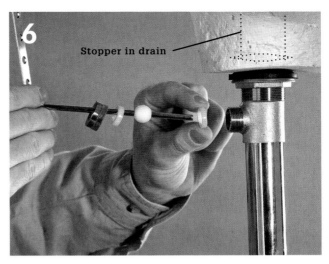

Stopper in drain

Drop the pop-up stopper into the drain hole so the hole at the bottom of its post is closest to the back of the sink. Put the beveled nylon washer into the opening in the back of the pop-up body with the bevel facing back.

7

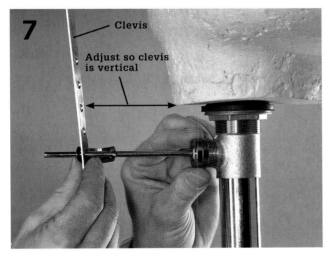

Clevis

Adjust so clevis is vertical

Put the cap behind the ball on the pivot rod as shown. Sandwich a hole in the clevis with the spring clip and thread the long end of the pivot rod through the clip and clevis. Put the ball end of the pivot rod into the pop-up body opening and into the hole in the the stopper stem. Screw the cap on to the pop-up body over the ball.

8

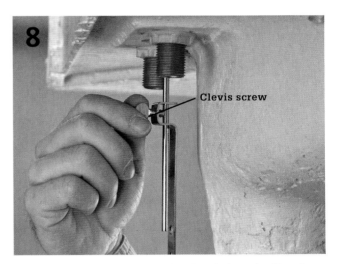

Clevis screw

Loosen the clevis screw holding the clevis to the lift rod. Push the pivot rod all the way down (which fully opens the pop-up stopper). With the lift rod also all the way down, tighten the clevis screw to the rod. If the clevis runs into the top of the trap, cut it short with your hacksaw or tin snips. Reassemble the J-bend trap.

Always Test Drain for Leaks ▸

To make sure the sink will not leak, do a thorough test. Close the stopper and turn on the faucet to fill the bowl. Once full, open the stopper and look carefully beneath the sink. Feel the trap parts; they should be dry. If there is any indication of moisture, tighten trap parts as needed.

KITCHEN SINKS: DRAINS + TRAPS

Kitchen traps, also called sink drains or trap assemblies, are made of 1½-inch pipes (also called tubes), slip washers, and nuts, so they can be easily assembled and disassembled. Most plastic types can be tightened by hand, with no wrench required. Pipes made of chromed brass will corrode in time, and rubber washers will crumble, meaning they need to be replaced. Plastic pipes and plastic washers last virtually forever. All traps are liable to get bumped out of alignment; when this happens, they should be taken apart and reassembled.

A trap's configuration depends on how many bowls the sink has, whether or not you have a food disposer and/or a dishwasher drain line, and local codes. On this page we show three of the most common assembly types. T fittings on these traps often have a baffle, which reduces the water flow somewhat. Check local codes to make sure your trap is compliant.

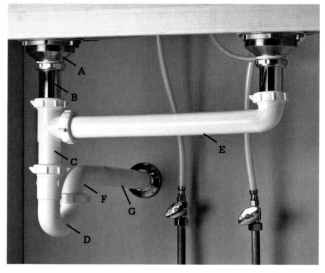

Kitchen sink drains include a strainer body (A), tailpiece (B), waste T (C), P-trap (D), outlet drain line (E), trap arm (F), and wall stubout with coupling (G).

Tools + Materials ▶

Flat screwdriver
Spud wrench
Trap arm
Mineral spirits
Cloth
Strainer kit
Plumber's putty
Utility knife

Teflon tape
Washers
Waste-T fitting
P-trap
Saw
Miter box
Work gloves
Eye protection

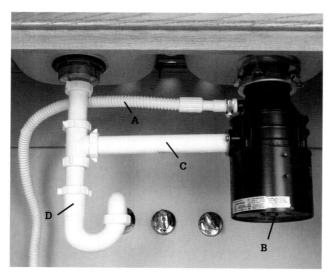

In this arrangement, the dishwasher drain hose (A) attaches to the food disposer (B), and a trap arm (C) leads from the disposer to the P-trap (D).

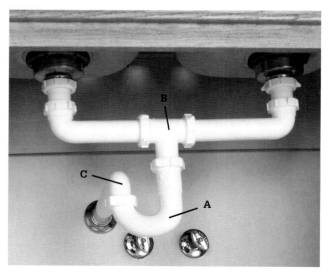

A "center tee" arrangement has a single P-trap (A) that is connected to a waste T (B) and the trap arm (C).

PLUMBING

Drain Kits ▸

Kits for installing a new sink drain include all the pipes, slip fittings, and washers you'll need to get from the sink tailpieces (most kits are equipped for a double bowl kitchen sink) to the trap arm that enters the wall or floor. For wall trap arms, you'll need a kit with a P-trap. Both drains normally are plumbed to share a trap. Chromed brass or PVC with slip fittings let you adjust the drain more easily and pull it apart and then reassemble if there is a clog. Some pipes have fittings on their ends that eliminate the need for a washer. Kitchen sink drains and traps should be 1½" o.d. pipe—the 1¼" pipe is for lavatories and doesn't have enough capacity for a kitchen sink.

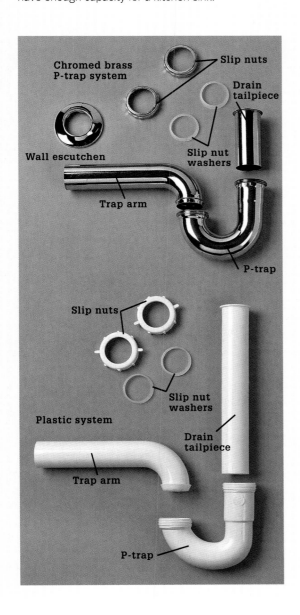

Tips for Choosing Drains ▸

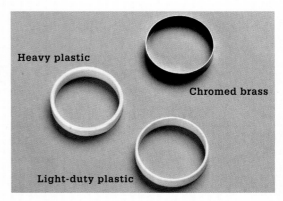

Wall thickness varies in sink drain pipes. The thinner plastic material is cheaper and more difficult to obtain a good seal with the thicker, more expensive tubing. The thin product is best reserved for lavatory drains, which are far less demanding.

Slip joints are formed by tightening a male-threaded slip nut over a female-threaded fitting, trapping and compressing a beveled nylon washer to seal the joint.

Use a spud wrench to tighten the strainer body against the underside of the sink bowl. Normally, the strainer flange has a layer of plumber's putty to seal beneath it above the sink drain and a pair of washers (one rubber, one fibrous) to seal below.

HOW TO HOOK UP A KITCHEN SINK DRAIN

If you are replacing the sink strainer body, remove the old one and clean the top and bottom of the sink deck around the drain opening with mineral spirits. Attach the drain tailpiece to the threaded outlet of the strainer body, inserting a nonbeveled washer between the parts if your strainer kits include one. Lubricate the threads or apply Teflon tape so you can get a good, snug fit.

Apply plumber's putty around the perimeter of the drain opening and seat the strainer assembly into it. Add washers below as directed and tighten the strainer locknut with a spud wrench (see photo, previous page) or by striking the mounting nubs at the top of the body with a flat screwdriver.

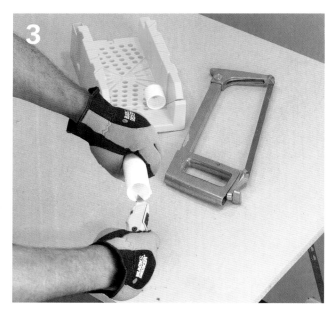

You may need to cut a trap arm or drain tailpiece to length. Cut metal tubing with a hacksaw. Cut plastic tubing with a handsaw, power miter saw, or a hand miter box and a backsaw or hacksaw. You can use a tubing cutter for any material. Deburr the cut end of plastic tubing with a utility knife.

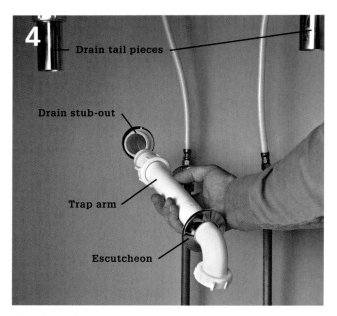

Attach the trap arm to the male-threaded drain stubout in the wall, using a slip nut and beveled compression washer. The outlet for the trap arm should point downward. *NOTE: The trap arm must be lower on the wall than any of the horizontal lines in the set-up, including lines to dishwasher, disposer, or the outlet line to the second sink bowl.*

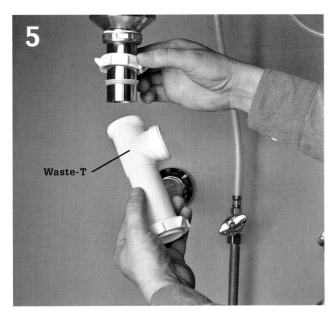

5

Attach a waste-T-fitting to the drain tailpiece, orienting the opening in the fitting side so it will accept the outlet drain line from the other sink bowl. If the waste-T is higher than the top of the trap arm, remove it and trim the drain tailpiece.

Waste-T

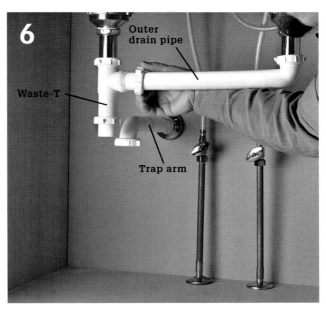

6

Outer drain pipe

Waste-T

Trap arm

Join the short end of the outlet drain pipe to the tailpiece for the other sink bowl and then attach the end of the long run to the opening in the waste-T. The outlet tube should extend into the T ½"—make sure it does not extend in far enough to block water flow from above.

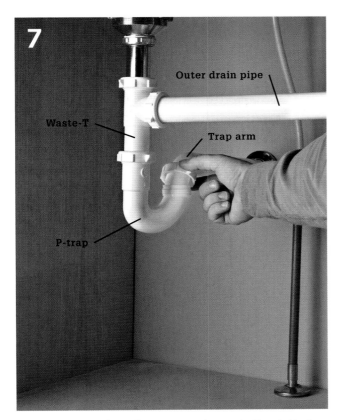

7

Outer drain pipe

Waste-T

Trap arm

P-trap

Attach the long leg of a P-trap to the waste-T and attach the shorter leg to the downward-facing opening of the trap arm. Adjust as necessary and test all joints to make sure they are still tight, and then test the system.

Variation: Drain in Floor ▸

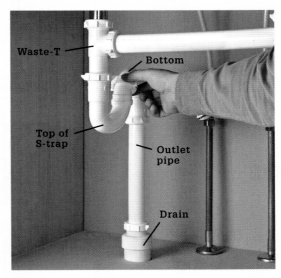

Waste-T

Bottom

Top of S-trap

Outlet pipe

Drain

If your drain stubout comes up out of the floor instead of the wall, you have an S-trap instead of a P-trap. This arrangement is illegal in many parts of the country, because a heavy surge of water can siphon the trap dry, rendering it unable to trap gases. However, if after draining the sink you run a slow to moderate stream of water for a few seconds, the trap will fill. An S-trap has two trap pipes that lead to a straight vertical pipe.

HOW TO INSTALL A PULLOUT KITCHEN SINK FAUCET

Install the base plate (if your faucet has one) onto the sink flange so it is centered. Have a helper hold it straight from above as you tighten the mounting nuts that secure the base plate from below. Make sure the plastic gasket is centered under the base plate. These nuts can be adequately tightened by hand.

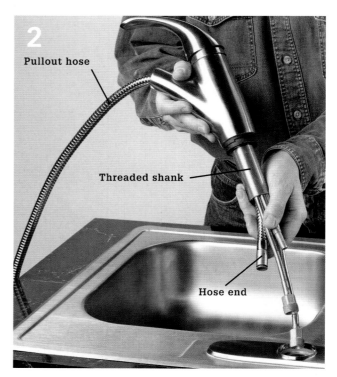

Retract the pullout hose by drawing it out through the faucet body until the fitting at the end of the hose is flush with the bottom of the threaded faucet shank. Insert the shank and the supply tubes down through the top of the deck plate.

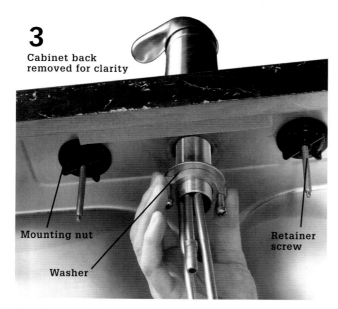

Slip the mounting nut and washer over the free ends of the supply tubes and pullout hose, then thread the nut onto the threaded faucet shank. Hand tighten. Tighten the retainer screws with a screwdriver to secure the faucet.

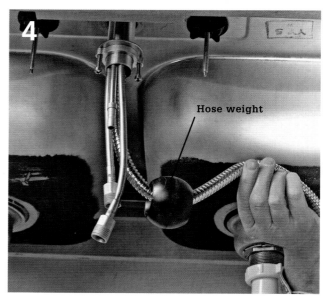

Slide the hose weight onto the pullout hose (the weight helps keep the hose from tangling and it makes it easier to retract).

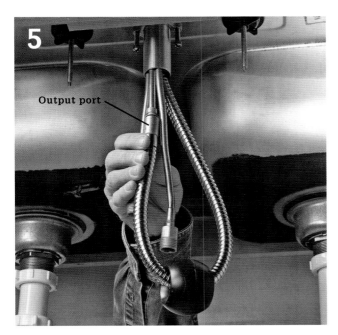

Connect the end of the pullout hose to the outlet port on the faucet body using a quick connector fitting.

Hook up the water supply tubes to the faucet inlets. Make sure the tubes are long enough to reach the supply risers without stretching or kinking.

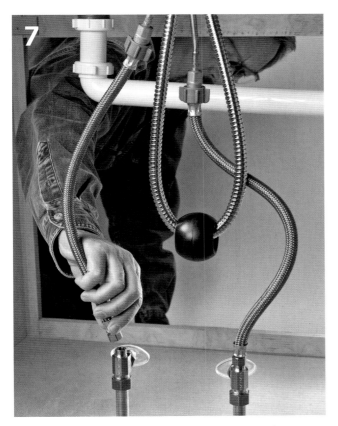

Connect the supply tubes to the supply risers at the stop valves. Make sure to get the hot lines and cold lines attached correctly.

Attach the spray head to the end of the pullout hose and turn the fitting to secure the connection. Turn on water supply and test. *TIP: Remove the aerator in the tip of the spray head and run hot and cold water to flush out any debris.*

INSTALLING WATER HEATERS

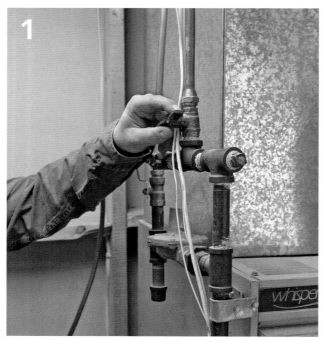

Shut off the gas supply at the stopcock installed in the gas line closest to the water heater. The handle of the stopcock should be perpendicular to the gas supply pipe. Also shut off the water supply.

Drain the water from the old heater by hooking a garden hose up to the sillcock drain and running it to a floor drain. If you don't have a floor drain, drain the water into buckets. For your personal safety, wait until the water heater has been shut off for a couple of hours before draining it.

Disconnect the gas supply from the water heater. To do so, loosen the flare fitting with two wrenches or pliers in a soft copper supply line or loosen the union fitting with two pipe wrenches for black pipe supply lines (inset).

Disconnect the vent pipe from the draft hood by withdrawing the sheet metal screws connecting the parts. Also remove vent pipes up to and including the elbow so you may inspect them for corrosion buildup and replace if needed.

Cut the water supply lines. Prior to cutting, shut off the cold water supply either at the stop valve near the heater or at the water meter. Inspect the shutoff valve. If it is not a ball-type valve in new condition, replace it with a ball valve.

Install a Relief Valve ▸

Prepare the new water heater for installation. Before you put the water heater in place, add a T & P (temperature and pressure) relief valve at the valve opening. Make sure to read the manufacturer's instructions and purchase the recommended valve type. Lubricate the threads and tighten the valve into the valve opening with a pipe wrench. *NOTE: The water heater shown in this sequence came with a T & P relief valve that's preinstalled.*

Remove the old water heater and dispose of it properly. Most trash collection companies will haul it away for $20 to $30. Don't simply leave it out at the curb unless you know that is allowed by your municipal waste collection department. A two-wheel truck or appliance dolly is a big help here. Water heaters usually weigh around 150 pounds.

Position the new unit in the installation area. If you have flooring you wish to protect from leaks, set the unit on a drip pan (available where water heater accessories are sold). The shallow pans feature a hose bib so you can run a drain line from the pan to a floor drain. If the water heater is not level, level it by shimming under the bottom with a metal or composite shim. Note that you'll need to shift the unit around a bit to have clearance for installing the water supply connectors (step 10).

(continued)

Attach a discharge tube to the T & P relief valve. You may use either copper pipe or CPVC drain pipe. Cut the tube so the free end is 6" above the floor (some locales may allow 3" above the floor). If you have floorcoverings you wish to protect, add a 90° elbow and a copper drain tube that leads from the discharge tube to a floor drain.

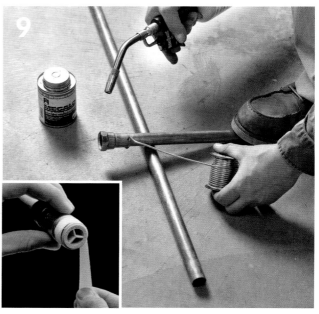

Fabricate water connectors from lengths of copper tubing, threaded copper adaptors, and plastic-lined galvanized threaded nipples. Plastic-lined nipples (inset) reduce the corrosion that can occur when you join two dissimilar metals. Size the connector assemblies so they will end up just short of the cut copper supply tubing when the connectors are inserted into the water heater ports.

Install the connectors in the cold water inlet port (make sure you use the blue-coded lined nipple) and the hot outlet port (red-coded nipple) on top of the water heater. Lubricate the nipple threads and tighten with channel-type pliers. Slip a copper tubing repair coupling over each connector and reposition the unit so the supply pipes and connector tops align.

Solder the connectors to the supply tubes with slip-fitting copper repair couplings. Be sure to clean and prime the parts first.

Reassemble the vent with a new elbow fitting (if your old one needed replacement). Cut the duct that drops down from the elbow so it will fit neatly over the top flange of the draft hood.

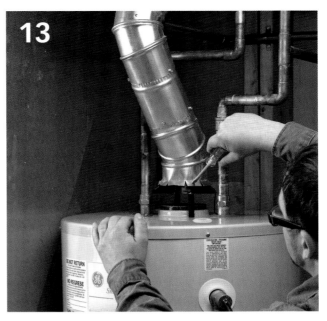

Follow the manufacturer's instructions for configuring the vent; this varies from model to model. Attach the vertical leg of the vent line to the draft hood with ⅜" sheet metal screws. Drive at least three screws into each joint.

Install the parts for the black pipe gas connector assembly. Use pipe dope to lubricate all joints. Attach a T-fitting to one end of a 3" nipple first and attach the other end of the nipple into the female-threaded regulator port. Attach a cap to another 6" nipple and then thread the other end into the bottom opening of the T-fitting to form a drip leg. Install a third nipple in the top opening of the T-fitting.

Connect the gas supply line to the open end of the gas connector. Use a union fitting for black gas pipe connections and a flare fitting for copper supply connections.

(continued)

16

Test the connections. Turn on the gas supply and test the gas connections with testing solution. Before turning on the water supply, make sure the tank drain valve is closed. Allow the tank to fill with water and then turn on a hot water faucet until water comes out (the water won't be hot yet, of course). Visually check all plumbing joints for leaks.

17

Light the pilot. This is usually a multistep process that varies among manufacturers, but all new water heaters will have pilot-lighting instructions printed on a label near the water heater controls. Adjust the water temperature setting.

TIP: Hooking Up Electric Water Heaters ▸

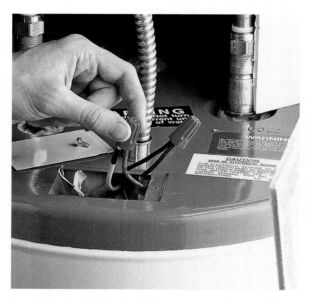

The fuel supply connection is the only part of installing an electric water heater that differs from installing a gas heater, except that electric heaters do not require a vent. The feeder wires (240 volts) are twisted together with mating wires in the access panel located at the top of the unit.

Temperature adjustments on electric water heaters are made by tightening or loosening a thermostat adjustment screw located near the heating element. Always shut off power to the unit before making adjustment. In this photo you can see how close the live terminals for the heating element are to the thermostat.

Problems	Repairs

No hot water, or not enough hot water.	1. Gas heater: Make sure gas is on, then relight pilot flame.
	   Electric heater: Make sure power is on, then reset thermostat.
	2. Flush water heater to remove sediment in tank.
	3. Insulate hot water pipes to reduce heat loss.
	4. Gas heater: Clean gas burner & replace thermocouple.
	   Electric heater: Replace heating element or thermostat.
	5. Raise temperature setting of thermostat.

Pressure-relief valve leaks.	1. Lower the temperature setting (photo, below). 2. Install a new pressure-relief valve. 3. Install a water hammer arrester.
Pilot flame will not stay lit.	Clean gas burner & replace the thermocouple.
Water heater leaks around base of tank.	Replace the water heater immediately.

Tips for Maintaining a Water Heater ▸

Flush the water heater once a year by draining several gallons of water from the tank. Flushing removes sediment buildup that causes corrosion and reduces heating efficiency.

Lower the temperature setting on thermostat to 120° F. Lower temperature setting reduces damage to tank caused by overheating and also reduces energy use.

HANGING PEGBOARD

Pegboard, also called perforated hardboard or perfboard, is one of the simplest and least expensive storage solutions for hanging tools and other lightweight objects. When mounted to the wall and outfitted with metal hooks, pegboard provides a convenient way to keep items from getting lost in the back of a drawer or the bottom of a tool chest. Pegboard also makes it easy to change the arrangement or collection of your wall-hung items, because you can reposition the metal hooks any way you like without measuring, drilling holes, or hammering nails into the wall. In fact, pegboard has served as a low-cost storage option for so long that there are a multitude of different hooks and brackets you can buy to accommodate nearly anything you want to hang. Any home center will carry both the pegboard and the hooks.

You need to install pegboard correctly to get the most value from it. If your garage walls have exposed studs, you can simply screw pegboard to the studs. The empty bays between the studs will provide the necessary clearance for inserting the hooks. On a finished wall, however, you'll need to install a framework of furring strips behind the pegboard to create the necessary clearance and provide some added stiffness. It's also a good idea to build a frame around your pegboard to give the project a neat, finished appearance.

If your garage tends to be damp, seal both faces of the pegboard with several coats of varnish or primer and exterior paint; otherwise it will absorb moisture and swell up or even delaminate.

▶ Tools + Materials ▸

Eye protection	Stud finder
Marker	Level
Tape measure	Drill
Circular saw	Pegboard panels
Straightedge	1 × 2 lumber
Miter saw	1" drywall screws
Caulk gun	Panel adhesive
Paint roller	Paint or varnish

Pegboard systems are classic storage solutions for garages and other utility areas. Outfitted with a variety of hangers, they offer flexibility and convenience when used to store hand tools and other small shop items.

Pegboard + Hanger Hardware Styles ▸

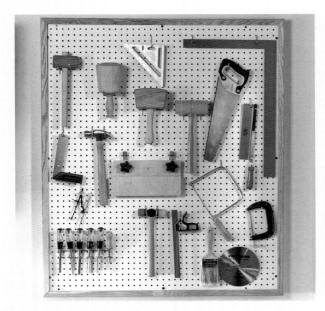

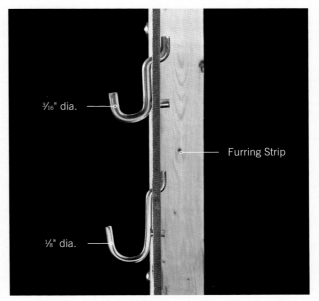

³⁄₁₆" dia.

Furring Strip

⅛" dia.

Hanger hardware comes in many shapes and sizes, from the basic J for hanging a single tool to double-prong hangers for hammers and even shelf standards. You can buy assorted hangers in kits or stock up on the type you're likely to use the most.

Two common thicknesses for pegboard hangers are ⅛"-dia. and ³⁄₁₆"-dia., both of which fit into standard pegboard hole configurations. The thicker the hanger, the more it can handle. Both types rely on the mechanical connection with the pegboard and can fail if the holes in the board become elongated. The pegboard must have furring strips on the back side to create a recess for the hangers.

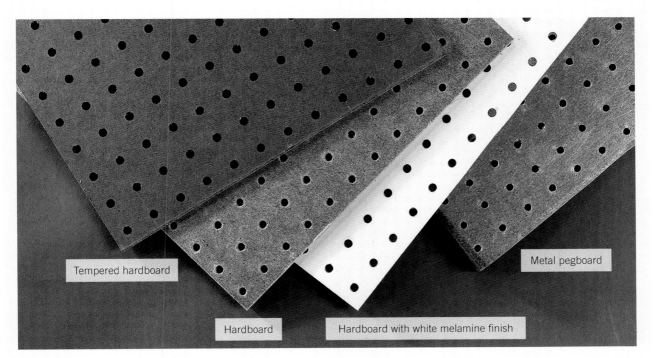

Tempered hardboard

Metal pegboard

Hardboard

Hardboard with white melamine finish

Pegboard is a single-purpose sheetgood material. It is used to create a wall surface with storage function (occasionally it may be used as a cabinet back where ventilation is desired). Although it comes in ⅛"-thick panels, avoid them in favor of ¼"-thick material. Most larger home centers carry it unfinished and in pre-finished white. Woodgrain and other decorative panels can be found, and you can also buy metal pegboard panels. The standard size holes are ¼"-dia. and spaced in a 1"-on-center grid.

HOW TO INSTALL A PEGBOARD STORAGE SYSTEM

Cut your pegboard panel to size if you are not installing a full sheet (most building centers sell 2 × 4' and 4 × 4' panels in addition to the standard 4 × 8'). If you are cutting with a circular saw, orient the panel face-up to prevent tearout on the higher-grade face. If cutting with a jigsaw, the good face of the panel should be down. If possible, plan your cuts so there is an even amount of distance from the holes to all edges.

Cut 1 × 2 furring strips to make a frame that is attached to the back side of the pegboard panel. The outside edges of the furring strips should be flush with the edges of the pegboard. Because they will be visible, cut the frame parts so the two side edge strips run the full height of the panel (36" here). Cut a couple of filler strips to fill in between the top and bottom rails.

Attach the furring strips to the back of the panel using 1" drywall screws and panel adhesive. Drive the screws through countersunk pilot holes in the panel face. Do not drive screws through the predrilled pegboard holes. Use intermediate furring strips to fill in between the top and bottom. These may be fastened with panel adhesive alone.

OPTION: Make a frame from picture frame molding and wrap it around the pegboard to conceal the edge grain and the furring strips. If you can't find picture frame molding with the correct dimensions, mill your own molding by cutting a ⅜"-wide by 1"-deep rabbet into one face of 1 × 2 stock.

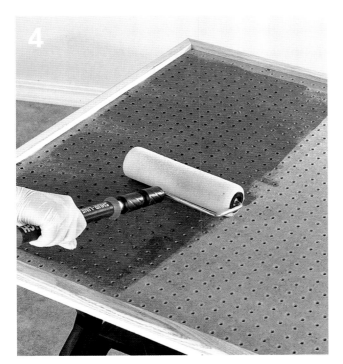

4

Paint or topcoat the pegboard. You can leave the pegboard unfinished, if you prefer, but a coat of paint or varnish protects the composite material from nicks and dings and hardens it around the hole openings so the holes are less likely to become elongated. A paint roller and short-nap sleeve make quick work of the job.

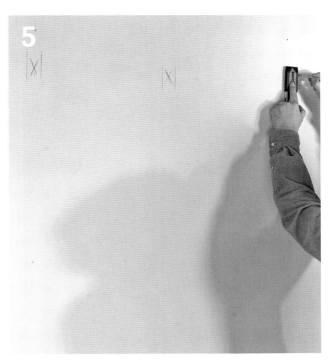

5

Locate and mark wall studs if your garage wall has a wall covering. Make sure the marks extend above and below the pegboard location so you can see them once the pegboard is positioned on the wall.

6

Tack the pegboard and frame to the wall in the desired location. Drive one 2½" screw partway through the top frame at the center of the pegboard. Place a long level on the top of the pegboard and adjust it to level using the screw as a pivot point.

7

Drive a drywall screw through the top and bottom frame rails at each wall stud location. Drill countersunk pilot holes first. Double-check for level after driving the first screw. Insert hangers as desired.

HOW TO INSTALL SLAT-WALL PANELS

Measure and mark the location of the wall panels. Use a level to mark lines across the stud faces for the starter strip to run under the top slat panel.

Install a 1 × 2 × 4 starter strip on the wall, checking carefully again to ensure it is level. Install the strip 1' below the top edge of the first panel in the wall.

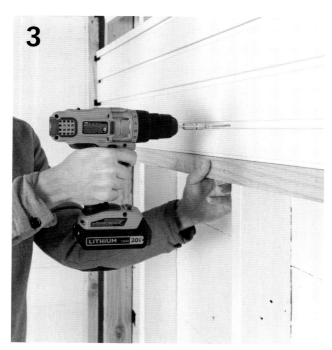

Install the first panel by sitting it on the starter guide and aligning it on the studs. Screw it to the wall with the supplied color-coordinated screws. For maximum support, use one screw per slat, per stud. *NOTE: If you're installing the panel on a finished wall, coat the back of the panel with construction adhesive before setting it in position.*

Snap the next panel into position underneath the first panel. Align the outside edges (there may be up to a ⅛" variation in panel width; the edge strips will conceal this). Double-check the panel to make sure it's level before fastening it to the wall with screws, as you did the top panel.

5

To accommodate wall outlets, switches, or other fixtures in the wall surface, measure and mark from the edge of the panel to the location of the outlet. Mark the outline of the opening on the face of the wall panel. Drill holes at the corners of the marked opening and cut it out with a jigsaw.

6

Unscrew the outlet receptacle or switch from the box frame. Install an outlet extender box, screwing it to the frame, then screw the receptacle or switch to the extender box. Install the wall panel over the receptacle and replace the outlet cover or switch plate.

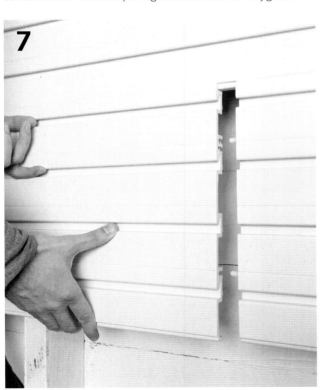

7

Add any additional wall panels to either side by inserting the supplied dowels into the slots on the back of the previous panel and pushing the panels together. Check for level as you work, and screw the new panels into the wall.

8

For larger obstructions, cut the panels as needed to fit around the obstruction. Measure and mark, and then cut the panels with a jigsaw.

(continued)

Clean newly installed panels with an all-purpose household cleaner. Install the edge caps, working from top to bottom on the right side, and bottom to top on the left.

HOW TO INSTALL SLAT-WALL CABINETS

Check all cabinet boxes for the correct sizes and to make sure that all the hardware has been included. The company that manufacturers the system shown here supplies cabinet bodies and their matching doors in separate boxes.

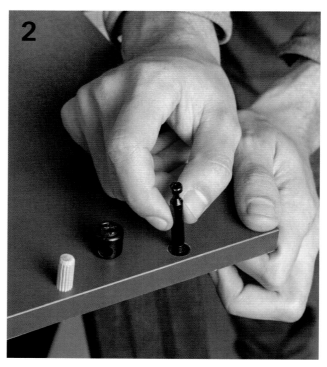

Set a cabinet bottom panel (the bottom and top are interchangeable with this system, as are the sides) on a flat work surface. Snug a dowel into each dowel hole. Separate the cam posts from the cam nuts and place the posts in the outside holes on each end of the panel.

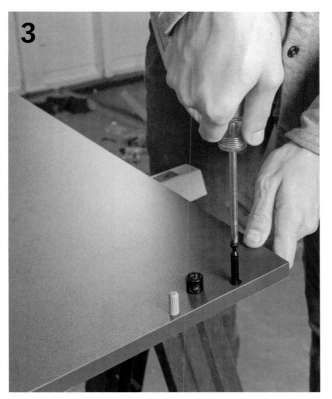

3

Use a screwdriver to hand-tighten the cam posts into the receiver holes. The post should still stick up far enough to accommodate the cam nut where it sits in the side-wall hole.

4

Push the cam nuts into the receiver holes in the one side wall. Make sure the line on the face of each nut is pointing vertically. Slide the wall down over the dowels and cam posts with the row of pin holes facing the inside of the cabinet (inset).

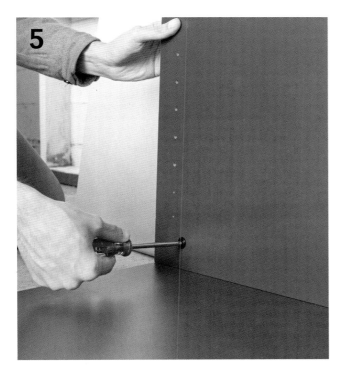

5

Use a screwdriver to turn the cam lock nuts to lock the side wall to the base. Repeat with the second side wall.

6

Align the cabinet spanner bar with the bolt holes in each side wall. Fasten the bar in place with the supplied Allen-head bolts. Repeat with the other spanner bar.

(continued)

Install dowels and the cam posts in the top of the side panel, and slide the top panel onto them. Lock the cam posts in place as you did on the bottom, by turning the cam nuts until tight.

Sit a shelf rear bracket into the recessed back edge of one shelf. Screw it into place with the wood screws provided. Repeat with the other shelves you'll be using in the cabinet.

Position each shelf at the level you prefer by levering it into the wall spanners for the shelf. Place pins in the corresponding side-wall panel pin holes at the front edge of the cabinet. Set the front of the shelf on the pins and check for level. Adjust as necessary, and repeat with the rest of the shelves.

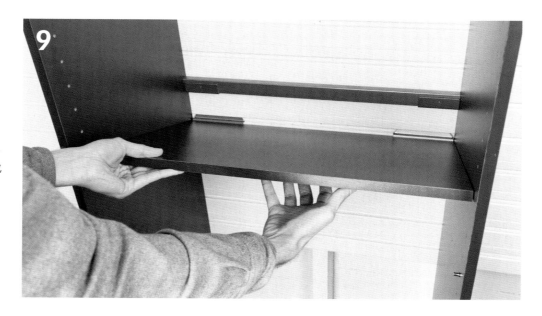

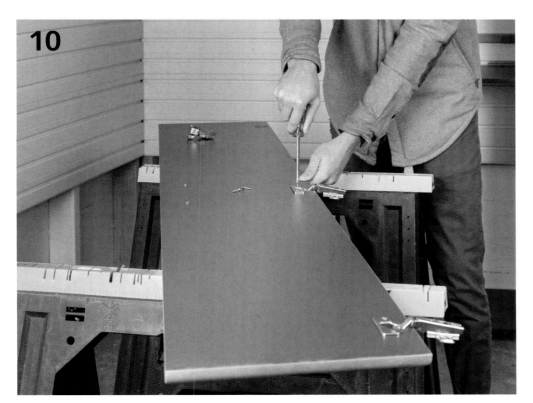

10

Screw the door hinges into the designated hinge holes in the doors (longer cabinets have hinges at top, bottom, and middle; smaller cabinets only have two hinges on each side).

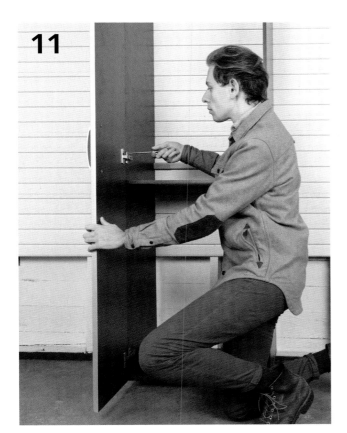

11

Sit one door in position with the round hinge projections secure into the door's receiver holes. Screw the hinges to the cabinet. Repeat with the opposite door.

12

Screw the door handles onto the cabinet doors. Adjust the position of the cabinets as needed—they can be easily slid in one direction or the other. Add other accessories, work surfaces, and specialty hooks as desired.

HOW TO INSTALL A GARAGE DOOR OPENER

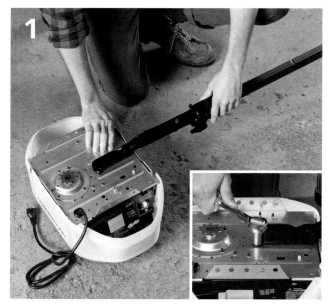

Start by aligning the rail pieces in proper order and securing them with the included braces and bolts. Screw the pulley bracket to the door end of the rail and slide the trolley onto the rail. Make sure the pulley and all rail pieces are properly aligned and that the trolley runs smoothly without hitting any hardware along the rail. Remove the two screws from the top of the opener, then attach the rail to the opener using these screws (inset).

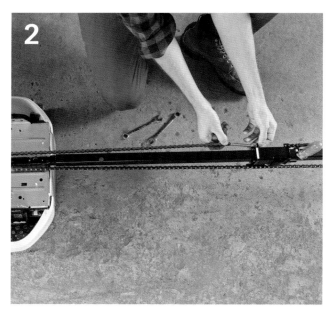

The drive chain/cable should be packaged in its own dispensing carton. Attach the cable loop to the front of the trolley using the included linking hardware. Wrap the cable around the pulley, then wrap the remaining chain around the drive sprocket on the opener. Finally, attach it to the other side of the trolley with linking hardware. Make sure the chain is not twisted, then attach the cover over the drive sprocket. Tighten the chain by adjusting the nuts on the trolley until the chain is ½" above the base of the rail.

To locate the header bracket, first extend a vertical line from the center of the door onto the wall above. Raise the door and note the highest point the door reaches. Measure from the floor to this point. Add 2" to this distance and mark a horizontal line on the front wall where it intersects the centerline. If there is no structural support behind the cross point, fasten 2× lumber across the framing. Then fasten the header bracket to the structural support with the included screws.

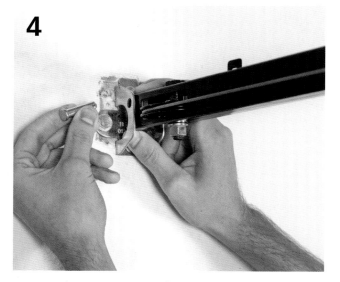

Support the opener on the floor with a board or box to prevent stress and twisting to the rail. Attach the rail pulley bracket to the header bracket above the door with the included clevis pin. Then place the opener on a stepladder so it is above the door tracks. Open the door and shim beneath the opener until the rail is 2" above the door.

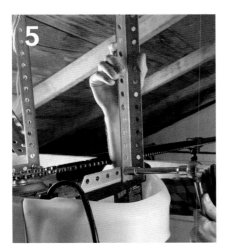

Hang the opener from the ceiling joists with the included hanging brackets and screws. Angle at least one of the hanging brackets to increase the stability of the unit while in operation. Attach the manual release cord and handle to the release arm of the trolley.

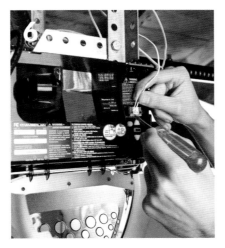

Strip ¼" of sheathing from the wall-console bell wire. Connect the wire to the screw terminals on the console, then attach it to the inside wall of the garage with the included screws. Run the wires up the wall and connect them to the proper terminals on the opener. Secure the wire to the wall with insulated staples, being careful not to pierce the wire. Install the light bulbs and lenses.

Install the sensor-eye mounting brackets at each side of the garage door, parallel to each other, about 4 to 6" from the floor. The sensor brackets can be attached to the door track, the wall, or the floor, depending upon your garage layout. See the manufacturer's directions for the best configuration for your garage.

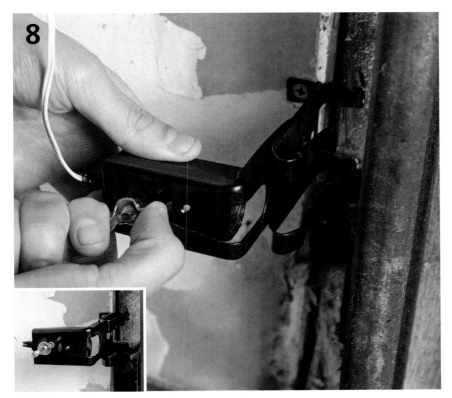

Attach the sensor eyes to the brackets with the included wing nuts but do not tighten the nuts completely. Make sure the path of the eyes is unobstructed by the door tracks. Run wires from both sensors to the opener unit and connect the wires to the proper terminals. Plug the opener into a grounded receptacle and adjust the sensors until the indicator light shows the correct eye alignment (inset), then tighten the wing nuts. Unplug the unit and attach the sensor wires to the walls with insulated staples.

Center the door bracket 2 to 4" below the top of the door. Drill holes and attach the bracket with the included carriage bolts. Connect the straight and curved arm sections with the included bolts. Attach the arm to the trolley and door bracket with the included latch pins. Plug the opener into a grounded receptacle and test the unit. See the manufacturer's directions for adjustment procedures.

VENT FANS

For most of us, a dream bathroom does not include foggy mirrors or unpleasant odors. Opening a window, if your bathroom is equipped with one, can help, but vent fans do the best job of clearing the air.

Most vent fans are installed in the center of the bathroom ceiling or over the toilet area. A fan installed over the tub or shower area must be GFCI protected and rated for use in wet areas. You can usually wire a fan with a light fixture into a main bathroom electrical circuit, but units with built-in heat lamps or blowers require separate circuits.

If the fan you choose doesn't come with a mounting kit, purchase one separately. A mounting kit should include a vent hose (duct), a vent tailpiece, and an exterior vent cover.

Venting instructions vary among manufacturers, but the most common options are attic venting and soffit venting. Attic venting routes fan ductwork into the attic and out through the roof. Always insulate ducting in this application to keep condensation from forming and running down into the motor. Carefully install flashing around the outside vent cover to prevent roof leaks.

Soffit venting involves routing the duct to a soffit (roof overhang) instead of through the roof. Check with the vent manufacturer for instructions for soffit venting.

To prevent moisture damage, always terminate the vent outside your home—never into your attic or basement.

You can install a vent fan while the framing is exposed or as a retrofit, as shown in this project.

Tools + Materials ▸

Eye protection
Flexible dryer vent duct
Screwdrivers
Jigsaw or drywall saw
Reciprocating saw
Voltage tester
Exhaust fan unit
Drywall screws
Drill

Hammer
Nails
Wire connectors
Dryer vent clamps
Vent cover
Drywall
4" hole saw
Rubberized work gloves

A combination light/vent fan is a great product in powder rooms and smaller baths that to do not generate excessive amounts of air moisture. In larger baths with tubs and showers, install a dedicated vent fan with a CFM rating that's at least 5 CFM higher than the total square footage of the bathroom (inset photo).

HOW TO REPLACE AN OVERHEAD LIGHT WITH A LIGHT/FAN

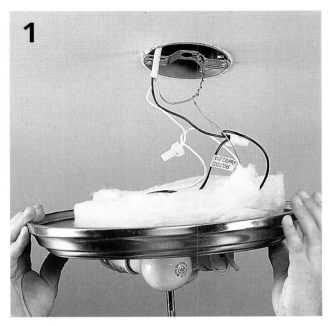

1

Shut off power to the ceiling light at the electrical service panel. Remove the globe and bulb from the overhead ceiling light, and then disconnect the mounting screws that hold the light fixture to the ceiling box.

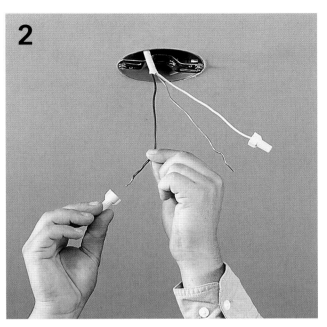

2

Test the wire connections with a voltage tester to make sure they are not live, and then disconnect the wires and remove the light fixture. Cap the wire ends.

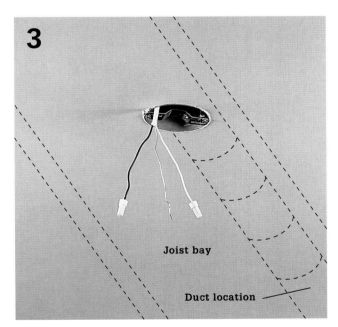

3

Joist bay

Duct location

Plan your exhaust pipe route. In most cases, this means determining the shortest distance between the fan and the outdoors. If the room is located at the top living level, venting through the roof is usually smartest. On lower levels and in basements, you'll need to go through an exterior wall. If you need to route through a wall in a room with a finished ceiling, choose a route that runs through a single ceiling joist bay.

4

Remove ceiling covering in the fan unit installation area and between the joists at the end of the run, next to the wall. You'll need at least 18" of access. If you are running rigid vent pipe or the joist bay is insulated, you'll need to remove ceiling material between the joists for the entire run. Make cuts on the centerlines of the joists.

(continued)

Insert flexible vent tubing into one of the ceiling openings and expand it so the free end reaches to the ceiling opening at the wall. A fish tape for running cable through walls can be a useful aid for extending the tubing.

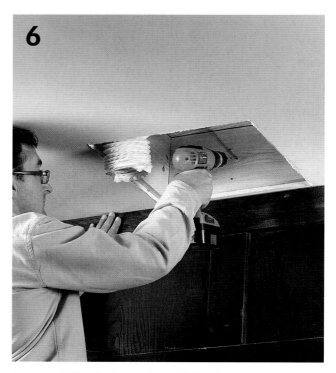

Draw a 4"-dia. circle on the wall framing at the end of the joist bay, marking the exit point for the duct. Choose a long, ¼"-dia. drill bit and drill a hole at the center of the circle. Drill all the way through the wall so the bit exits on the exterior side. This will mark your hole location outside.

On the exterior, draw a 4"-dia. circle centered on the exit point of the drill bit. Cut out the opening for the vent cover with a reciprocating saw or a 4" hole saw.

Insert the vent cover assembly into the opening, following the manufacturer's directions for fastening and sealing it to the house.

9

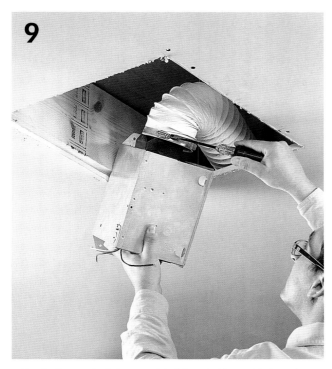

Attach the end of the vent tubing to the outlet on the vent cover unit and secure it with a large pipe clamp.

10

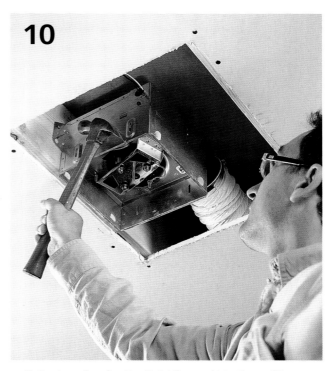

Nail the housing for the light/fan unit to the ceiling joist so the bottom edges of the housing are flush with the ceiling surface.

11

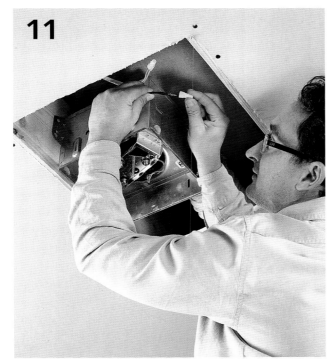

Make the wiring connections in the housing box according to the manufacturer's instructions. In just about every case you should be able to use the existing wires from the original light switch. Once you have connected the wires, restore the power and test the fan.

12

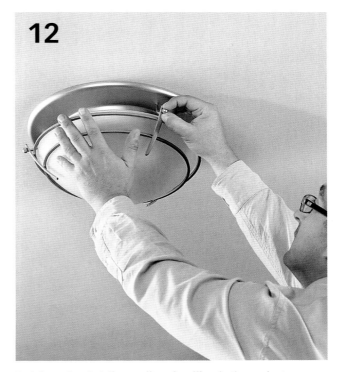

Patch and paint the wall and ceiling in the project area. Mount the light (the model we installed plugs into a receptacle in the fan box), grille, globe, and any other fixture parts.

GRAB BARS

EASY UPGRADES

Bathrooms are beautiful with their shiny ceramic tubs, showers, and floors, but add water and moisture to the mix and you've created the perfect conditions for a fall. The good news is that many falls in the bathroom can be avoided by installing grab bars at key locations.

Grab bars help family members steady themselves on slippery shower, tub, and other floor surfaces. Plus, they provide support for people transferring from a wheelchair or walker to the shower, tub, or toilet.

Grab bars come in a variety of colors, shapes, sizes, and textures. Choose a style with a 1¼- to 1½-inch diameter that fits comfortably between your thumb and fingers. Then properly install it 1½ inches from the wall with anchors that can support at least 250 pounds.

The easiest way to install grab bars is to screw them into wall studs or into blocking or backing attached to studs. Blocking is a good option if you are framing a new bathroom or have the wall surface removed during a major remodel (see Illustration A). Use 2 × 6 or 2 × 8 lumber to provide room for adjustments, and fasten the blocks to the framing with 16d nails. Note the locations of your blocking for future reference.

As an alternative, cover the entire wall with ¾-inch plywood backing secured with screws to the wall framing, so you can install grab bars virtually anywhere on the wall (see Illustration B).

Grab bars can be installed in areas without studs. For these installations, use specialized heavy-duty hollow-wall anchors designed to support at least 250 pounds.

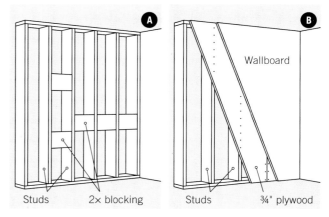

Blocking or backing is required for secure grab bars.
If you know where the grab bars will be located, add 2× blocking between studs (Illustration A). You also can cover the entire wall with ¾" plywood backing, which allows you to install grab bars virtually anywhere on the wall (illustration B).

Tools + Materials ›

Tape measure	Grab bar
Pencil	Hollow-wall anchors
Stud finder	#12 stainless-steel screws
Level	Silicone caulk
Drill	Eye protection
Masonry bit	Work gloves

Grab bars of different styles and configurations meet varied needs in any bathroom, and in different areas of the bathroom.

HOW TO INSTALL GRAB BARS

Locate the wall studs in the installation area using a stud finder. If the area is tiled, the stud finder may not detect studs, so try to locate the studs above the tile, if possible, then use a level to transfer the marks lower on the wall. Otherwise, you can drill small, exploratory holes through grout joints in the tile, then fill the holes with silicone caulk to seal them. Be careful not to drill into pipes.

Mark the grab-bar height at one stud location, then use a level to transfer the height mark to the stud that will receive the other end of the bar. Position the grab bar on the height marks so at least 2 of the 3 mounting holes are aligned with the stud centers. Mark the mounting-hole locations onto the wall.

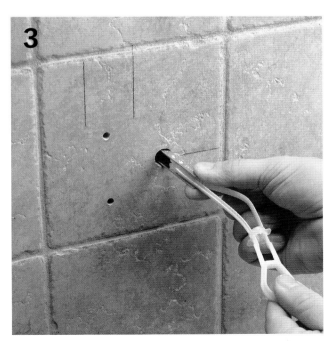

Drill pilot holes for the mounting screws. If you are drilling through tile, start with a small bit (about ⅛"), then redrill the hole with the larger bit. For screws that won't hit studs, drill holes for wall anchors, following the manufacturer's directions for sizing. Install anchors, if necessary.

Apply a continuous bead of silicone caulk to the back side of each bar end (inset). Secure the bar to the studs using #12 stainless-steel screws (the screws should penetrate the stud by at least 1"). Install a stainless-steel screw or bolt into the wall anchors. Test the bar to make sure it's secure.

BASEMENT STAIRWAY SHELVING

In many homes, the basement stairs offer two easy options for convenient and out-of-the-way storage. One utilizes the stud cavities along the stairwell wall. The other occupies that large yet awkward triangular area underneath the staircase. In both places, a simple lumber shelving system lets you take advantage of underused space without sacrificing valuable square footage.

Adding shelves along a stairwell wall couldn't be simpler. All it requires is notching a 2 × 6 shelf board to fit over the wall studs, then screwing the shelf in place. This gives you a 5½-inch-deep shelf space between the studs, plus a 2-inch-deep lip in front of each stud. Of course, the stairwell wall must be unfinished on one side for this type of shelving. If the stairwell wall isn't an option, perhaps you have an open wall in the basement or garage—any wall with exposed framing will work.

Utility shelves for the understairs space are made with a 2 × 4 support frame and plywood shelf surfaces. The stair structure itself provides support at one end of the shelves. Like the stud-wall shelves, you can set the understairs shelving at any height or spacing that you like. In the project shown on pages 420 to 421, the shelf system includes a low bottom shelf that's built with extra supports, good for keeping heavy items off of the basement floor.

Shelves along an open stairwell wall (left photo) can accommodate loads of smaller items. If your basement door is near the kitchen, these shelves are great for backup pantry storage. Shelves underneath the staircase (right photo) are ideal for basement workshop storage and for long pieces of lumber and other materials.

Tools + Materials ▶

For Stairway Shelves:
Work gloves
Eye protection
Level
Handsaw
Square
Wood chisel
Drill and countersink bit
2 × 6 lumber
3½" deck screws
Circular saw
Mallet

For Understairs Shelves:
Work gloves
Eye protection
Circular saw
Level
Drill and bits
Tape measure
2 × 4 pressure-treated lumber (for posts and struts)
2 × 4 standard lumber (for shelf supports)
2½" deck screws or coarse-thread wood screws
¾" AC (paint-grade on one side) plywood
2" coarse-thread drywall screws

HOW TO BUILD STAIRWAY WALL SHELVES

Mark the desired height for each shelf, then use a level to transfer the mark across the front edge of each stud. Measure from your level lines to mark the location of the next shelf up or down. The lines will represent the top face of the shelves.

Measure along each level line and cut the 2 × 6 shelf stock to length. Hold each shelf in place on its lines and mark the side edges of each stud for the notches. *TIP: If a stud is out of square to the wall plane, make the notch big enough so the shelf will fit straight on.*

Use a square to mark the notch depths at 3½". Make notch marks on both sides of the shelf. Cut the sides of the notches with a handsaw. Complete the notches by chiseling straight down from both sides of the board along the seat, or base, of the notch marks.

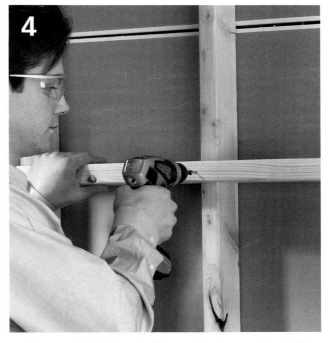

Position each shelf on its lines and make sure the shelf is level from front to back. Drill a pilot hole at the center of each stud location using a countersink bit. Fasten the shelf to each stud with a 3½" deck screw.

HOW TO BUILD UNDERSTAIRS BASEMENT SHELVES

EASY UPGRADES

Mark the locations of the two 2 × 4 posts onto the floor. The posts must be equidistant from the bottom end of the staircase. Cut each post a little longer than needed. Position the post plumb next to the floor mark, and trace along the stair stringer to mark the angled top cut for the post.

Cut the post ends with a circular saw or power miter saw. Set each post on its floor mark and fasten the top end to the bottom edge of the stair stringer with three 2½" deck screws or wood screws driven through pilot holes.

Mark the desired location of each shelf onto the stair stringers. Use a level—and a long, straight board as needed—to transfer the height marks to the inside faces of the posts.

For each shelf, measure and cut two 2 × 4 side supports to span from the outside edges of the posts to the back sides of the steps (or as far as practical). Also cut one 2 × 4 end support to span between the outside faces of the posts.

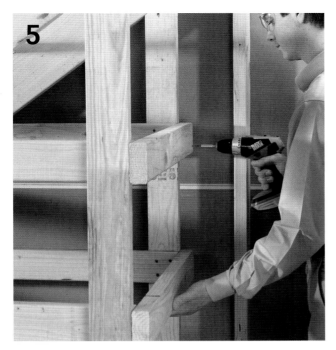

5

Fasten the side supports to the posts and stair stringers with four 2½" screws at each end. Fasten the end supports to the outside edges of the posts with two screws at each end. The end supports should be flush with the top edges of the side supports, with their ends flush with the outside faces of the posts.

OPTION: For long shelves that will hold heavy items, add midspan supports between the side supports. Reinforce a bottom shelf with 2 × 4 struts cut to fit between the side supports and the floor. *NOTE: Very heavy items should go on a reinforced bottom shelf, since stair structures aren't designed for significant extra weight loads.*

6

Cut the shelf panels to fit from ¾" plywood. The edges of the panels should be flush with the outside face of the side and end supports. Fasten the panels to the supports with 2" drywall screws.

VARIATION: If your staircase has a center stringer, notch the plywood shelf panels to fit around the stringer. Cut the sides of the notches with a circular saw or handsaw, and then make the seat cuts with a chisel to complete the notches.

SLIDE-OUT STORAGE

A base cabinet with slide-out trays or shelves is one of those great modern conveniences that has become standard in new kitchen design. Not only do slide-out trays make reaching stored items easier than with standard cabinet spaces—no more crouching and diving into the deep recesses of cavernous low shelves—they also store more items far more efficiently. With a few shallow trays, a standard base cabinet can hold dozens of food cans and still leave room for tall items like cereal boxes and bags of flour or even deep pots and countertop appliances.

To get the most from your new slide-out system, think carefully about how you will use each tray. Measure the items you're most likely to store together, and let the items dictate the spacing of the trays. Most standard base cabinets are suitable for trays. Wide cabinets (24 inches or wider) without a center partition (middle stile) are best in terms of space usage, but trays in narrow cabinets (18 inches wide) are just as handy. If you have a wide cabinet with a middle stile, you can add trays along one or both sides of the stile. For economy

and simplicity, the trays in this project are made with ¾-inch-thick plywood parts joined with glue and finish nails. If you prefer a more finished look (not that there's anything wrong with the look of nice plywood), you can use 1 × 4 hardwood stock for the tray sides and set a ⅜-inch-thick plywood bottom panel into dadoes milled into the side pieces. Another option is to assemble plywood tray pieces using pocket screws so the screw heads don't show on the front pieces of the trays.

Tools + Materials ▸

Circular saw with straightedge guide or tablesaw	1 × 2 hardwood stock
	¾" finish-grade plywood
	Wood glue
Drill	6d finish nails
Wood screws	Finish materials
Drawer slides (1 set per tray)	Tape measure
	Varnish or polyurethane
Hammer	Eye protection

Slide-out trays eliminate the everyday problem of hard-to-reach and hard-to-see spaces in standard base cabinets. Better still, you can install your trays to accommodate the stuff you use most often.

DRAWER SLIDES

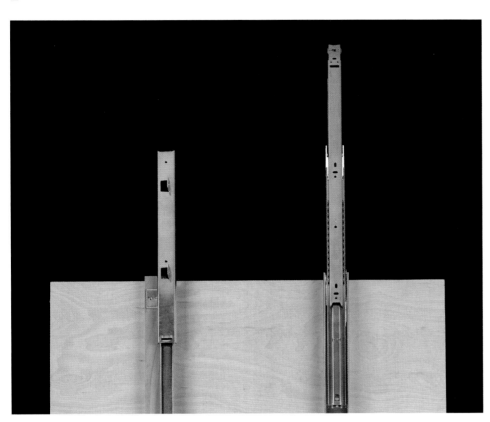

Drawer slides suitable for pullout shelves are commonly available in both standard (left) and full extension (right) styles. Standard slides are less expensive and good enough for most applications. They allow the tray to be pulled out most of the way. Full extension slides are a little pricier than standard slides but they allow the tray to be pulled completely out of the cabinet box for easy access to items in the back.

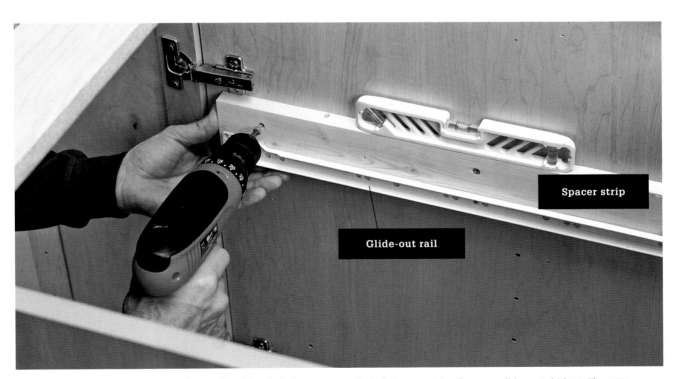

Spacers must be mounted to the wall cabinets before you can install drawer slides for your slide-out shelves. They are necessary for the drawers to clear the cabinet face frame and the door. For a ¾" spacer, a 1 × 3 or 1 × 4 works well. Paint or finish it to match the cabinet interior.

Spacer strip

Glide-out rail

HOW TO INSTALL SLIDE-OUT CABINET TRAYS

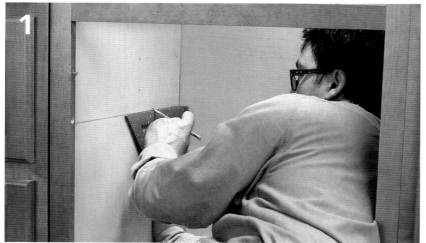

Lay out the tray positions, starting with the bottom tray. Check the drawer slides to see how much clearance you need for the bottom tray. Draw lines on the side panels of the cabinet to represent the bottom edges of the slide supports. Make sure the lines are level and are perpendicular to the cabinet front. Cut the slide supports to length from 1 × 2 hardwood stock (or any hardwood ripped to 1½" wide).

Mount the supports to the side panels of the cabinet with glue and screws driven through countersunk pilot holes. *NOTE: Depending on the overhang of the cabinet face frames, you may need thicker support stock to provide sufficient clearance for the trays and slide rails.*

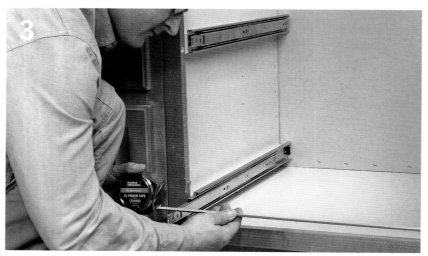

Install the drawer slides flush with the bottom edges of the slide supports using the provided screws. Assemble the two halves of each slide, and then measure between the drawer side pieces (rails) to find the exact width of each tray. Plan the depth of the trays based on the cabinet depth.

Cut the bottom piece for each tray from ¾" plywood 1½" smaller than the planned width and depth of the finished tray. Rip four ¾"-wide pieces for the sides, front, and back of each tray. Cut the side pieces to length, equal to the depth dimension of the bottom piece. Cut the front and back pieces 1½" longer than the width of the bottom.

Build the trays with glue and 6d finish nails or pneumatic brads. Fasten the sides flush with the bottom face and front and back edges of the bottom piece, and then add the front and back pieces. Sand any rough surfaces, and finish the trays with two or three coats of polyurethane or other durable varnish. If desired, you can stain the trays prior to finishing so they match your cabinets.

Partially mount the drawer slide rails to one of the trays, following the manufacturer's directions. Test-fit the tray in the cabinet and make any necessary adjustments before completely fastening the rails. Mount the slide rails on the remaining trays and install the trays to finish the job.

INSPECTING + REPAIRING A ROOF

A roof system is composed of several elements that work together to provide three basic, essential functions for your home: shelter, drainage, and ventilation. The roof covering and flashing are designed to shed water, directing it to gutters and downspouts. Air intake and outtake vents keep fresh air circulating below the roof sheathing, preventing moisture and heat buildup.

When your roof system develops problems that compromise its ability to protect your home—cracked shingles, incomplete ventilation, or damaged flashing—the damage quickly spreads to other parts of your house. Routine inspections are the best way to make sure the roof continues to do its job effectively.

Tools + Materials ▸

Tape measure	Replacement flashing
Wire brush	Replacement shingles
Aviation snips	Roofing cement
Trowel	Roofing nails
Flat pry bar	Double-headed nails
Hammer	Rubber-gasket nails
Utility knife	Chisel
Caulk gun	Eye protection
Plywood	Work gloves
Ladder	Fall-arrest harness

Ice dams above entryways pose a danger to everyone entering and leaving the house. To permanently solve ice damming problems, like the one shown here, improve roof ventilation to reduce attic temperatures.

Tips for Identifying Roofing Problems ▸

Ice dams occur when melting snow refreezes near the eaves, causing ice to back up under the shingles, where it melts onto the sheathing and seeps into the house.

Inspect both the interior and the exterior of the roof to spot problems. From inside the attic, check the rafters and sheathing for signs of water damage. Symptoms will appear in the form of streaking or discoloration. A moist or wet area also signals water damage.

EXTERIOR REPAIRS

SHINGLE MAINTENANCE TIPS

Buckled and cupped shingles are usually caused by moisture beneath the shingles. Loosened areas create an entry point for moisture and leave shingles vulnerable to wind damage.

Dirt and debris attract moisture and decay, which shorten a roof's life. To protect shingles, carefully wash the roof once a year, using a pressure washer. Pay particular attention to areas where moss and mildew may accumulate.

In damp climates, it's a good idea to nail a zinc strip along the center ridge of a roof, under the ridge caps. Minute quantities of zinc wash down the roof each time it rains, killing moss and mildew.

Overhanging tree limbs drop debris and provide shade that encourages moss and mildew. To reduce chances of decay, trim any limbs that overhang the roof.

HOW TO LOCATE + EVALUATE LEAKS

If you have an unfinished attic, examine the underside of your roof with a flashlight on a rainy day. If you find wetness, discoloration, or other signs of moisture, trace the trail up to where the water is making its entrance.

Water that flows toward a wall can be temporarily diverted to minimize damage. Nail a small block of wood in the path of the water, and place a bucket underneath to catch the drip. On a dry day, drive a nail through the underside of the roof decking to mark the hole.

If the leak is finding its way to a finished ceiling, take steps to minimize damage until the leak can be repaired. As soon as possible, reduce the accumulation of water behind a ceiling by poking a small hole in the wallboard or plaster and draining the water.

Once you mark the source of a leak from inside, measure from that spot to a point that will be visible and identifiable from outside the house, such as a chimney, vent pipe, or the peak of the roof. Get up on the roof and use that measurement to locate the leak.

HOW TO MAKE EMERGENCY REPAIRS

If your roof is severely damaged, the primary goal is to prevent additional damage until permanent repairs are made. Nail a sheet of plywood to the roof to serve as emergency cover to keep out the wind and water.

Cover the damaged area by nailing strips of lath around the edges of a plastic sheet or tarp. *TIP: For temporary repairs, use double-headed nails, which can be easily removed. Fill nail holes with roofing cement when the repair is complete.*

HOW TO MAKE SPOT REPAIRS WITH ROOFING CEMENT

To reattach a loose shingle, wipe down the felt paper and the underside of the shingle. Let each dry, then apply a liberal coat of roofing cement. Press the shingle down to seat it in the bed of cement.

Tack down buckled shingles by cleaning below the buckled area. Fill the area with roofing cement, then press the shingle into the cement. Patch cracks and splits in shingles with roofing cement.

Check the joints around flashing, which are common places for roof leaks to occur. Seal any gaps by cleaning out and replacing any failed roofing cement. *TIP: Heat softens the roof's surface, and cold makes it brittle. If needed, warm shingles slightly with a hair dryer to make them easier to work with and less likely to crack.*

HOW TO REPLACE ASPHALT SHINGLES

Pull out damaged shingles, starting with the uppermost shingle in the damaged area. Be careful not to damage surrounding shingles that still are in good condition.

Remove old nails in and above the repair area, using a flat pry bar. Patch damaged felt paper with roofing cement.

Install the replacement shingles, beginning with the lowest shingle in the repair area. Nail above the tab slots, using ⅞" or 1" roofing nails.

Install all but the top shingle with nails, then apply roofing cement to the underside of the top shingle, above the seal line.

Slip the last shingle into place, under the overlapping shingle. Lift the shingles immediately above the repair area, and nail the top replacement shingle.

HOW TO REPLACE WOOD SHAKES + SHINGLES

To age new shakes and shingles so they match existing ones, dissolve 1 pound of baking soda in 1 gallon of water. Brush the solution onto the shakes or shingles, then place them in direct sunlight for four to five hours. Rinse them thoroughly and let dry. Repeat this process until the color closely matches the originals.

Split the damaged shakes or shingles, using a hammer and chisel. Remove the pieces. Slide a hacksaw blade under the overlapping shingles and cut the nail heads. Pry out the remaining pieces of the shakes or shingles.

Gently pry up, but don't remove, the shakes or shingles above the repair area. Cut new pieces for the lowest course, leaving a ⅜" gap between pieces. Nail replacements in place with ring-shank siding nails. Fill in all but the top course in the repair area.

Cut the shakes or shingles for the top course. Because the top course can't be nailed, use roofing cement to fasten the pieces in place. Apply a coat of roofing cement where the shakes or shingles will sit, then slip them beneath the overlapping pieces. Press down to seat them in the roofing cement.

HOW TO PATCH VALLEY FLASHING

Measure the damaged area and mark an outline for the patch. Cut a patch wide enough to fit under shingles on both sides of the repair area, and tapered to a point at one end. Using a trowel or flat pry bar, carefully break the seal between the damaged flashing and surrounding shingles.

Scrub the damaged flashing with a wire brush, and wipe it clean. Apply a heavy bead of roofing cement to the back of the patch. Cut a slit in the old flashing. Insert the tapered end of the patch into the slit, and slip the side edges under the shingles. *TIP: Use the same material for your patch as the original flashing. When dissimilar materials are joined, corrosion accelerates.*

Rest the square end of the patch on top of the old flashing, and press it firmly to seal the roofing cement joint. Add roofing cement to the exposed seams. Using a trowel, feather out the cement to create a smooth path for water flow.

HOW TO REPLACE VENT FLASHING

Sleeve

Remove the shingles above and on the sides of the vent pipe. Remove the old vent flashing, using a flat pry bar. Apply a heavy, double bead of roofing cement along the bottom edge of the flange of the new flashing. Set the new flashing in place so it covers at least one course of shingles. Nail around the perimeter of the flange, using rubber-gasket nails.

Cut the shingles to fit around the neck of the flashing so they lie flat against the flange. Apply roofing cement to the shingle and flashing joints, and cover any exposed nail heads.

EXTERIOR REPAIRS

HOW TO REPLACE STEP FLASHING

Carefully bend up the counterflashing or the siding covering the damaged flashing. Cut any roofing cement seals, and pull back the shingles. Use a flat pry bar to remove the damaged flashing. *TIP: When replacing flashing around masonry, such as a chimney, use copper or galvanized steel. Lime from mortar can corrode aluminum.*

Cut the new flashing to fit and apply roofing cement to all unexposed edges. Slip the flashing in place, making sure it's overlapped by the flashing above and overlaps the flashing and shingle below.

Drive one roofing nail through the flashing, at the bottom corner, and into the roof deck. Do not fasten the flashing to the vertical roof element, such as the chimney.

Reposition the shingles and counterflashing, and seal all joints with roofing cement.

REPAIRING WOOD FASCIA + SOFFITS

Fascia and soffits add a finished look to your roof and promote a healthy roof system. A well-ventilated soffit system prevents moisture from building up under the roof and in the attic.

Most fascia and soffit problems can be corrected by cutting out sections of damaged material and replacing them. Joints between fascia boards are lock-nailed at rafter locations, so you should remove whole sections of fascia to make accurate bevel cuts for patches. Soffits can often be left in place for repairs.

Tools + Materials ▸

Circular saw
Jigsaw
Drill
Putty knife
Hammer
Flat pry bar
Nail set
Chisel
Caulk gun
Paintbrush
Ladder

Replacement materials
Nailing strips
2" and 2½" galvanized
    deck screws
4d galvanized casing nails
Acrylic caulk
Primer
Paint
Eye protection
Work gloves

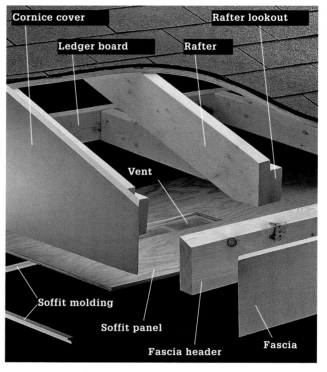

Cornice cover
Rafter lookout
Ledger board
Rafter
Vent
Soffit molding
Soffit panel
Fascia header
Fascia

Fascia and soffits close off the eaves area beneath the roof overhang. The fascia covers the ends of rafters and rafter lookouts, and provides a surface for attaching gutters. Soffits are protective panels that span the area between the fascia and the side of the house.

HOW TO REPAIR WOOD FASCIA

Remove gutters, shingle moldings, and any other items mounted on the fascia. Carefully pry off the damaged fascia board, using a pry bar. Remove the entire board and all old nails.

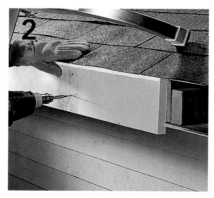

Set your circular saw for a 45° bevel, and cut off the damaged portion of the fascia board. Reattach the undamaged original fascia to the rafters or rafter lookouts, using 2" deck screws. Bevel-cut a patch board to replace the damaged section.

Rafter
Old
New

Set the patch board in place. Drill pilot holes through both fascia boards into the rafter. Drive nails in the holes to create a lock-nail joint (inset). Replace shingle moldings and trim pieces, using 4d casing nails. Set the nail heads. Prime and paint the new board.

HOW TO REPAIR WOOD PANEL SOFFITS

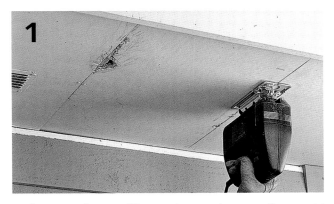

1

In the area where soffits are damaged, remove the support moldings that hold the soffits in place along the fascia and exterior wall. Drill entry holes, then use a jigsaw to cut out the damaged soffit area. *TIP: Cut soffits as close as possible to the rafters or rafter lookouts. Finish cuts with a chisel, if necessary.*

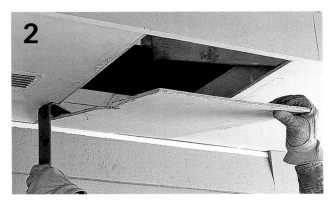

2

Remove the damaged soffit section, using a pry bar. Cut nailing strips the same length as the exposed area of the rafters, and fasten them to the rafters or rafter lookouts at the edges of the openings, using 2½" deck screws.

3

Using soffit material similar to the original panel, cut a replacement piece ⅛" smaller than the opening. If the new panel will be vented, cut the vent openings.

4

Attach the replacement panel to the nailing strips, using 2" deck screws. If you are not going to paint the entire soffit after the repair, prime and paint the replacement piece before installing it.

5

Reattach the soffit molding, using 4d casing nails. Set the nail heads.

6

Using siliconized acrylic caulk, fill all nail holes, screw holes, and gaps. Smooth out the caulk with a putty knife until the caulk is even with the surface. Prime and paint the soffit panels.

REPAIRING GUTTERS

Gutters perform the important task of channeling water away from your house. A good gutter system prevents damage to your siding, foundation, and landscaping, and it helps prevent water from leaking into your basement. When gutters fail, evaluate the type and extent of damage to select the best repair method. Clean your gutters and downspouts as often as necessary to keep the system working efficiently.

► Tools + Materials ►

Flat pry bar
Hacksaw
Caulk gun
Pop rivet gun
Drill
Hammer
Stiff-bristled brush
Putty knife
Steel wool
Aviation snips
Level
Paintbrush
Trowel
Garden hose
Chalk line
Ladder
Wood scraps
Replacement
    gutter materials
Siliconized
    acrylic caulk
Roofing cement
Metal flashing
Sheet-metal screws
    or pop rivets
Gutter hangers
Primer and paint
Gutter patching kit
Gutter guards
Eye protection
Work gloves

Use a trowel to clean leaves, twigs, and other debris out of the gutters before starting the repairs.

Keep gutters and downspouts clean so rain falling on the roof is directed well away from the foundation. Nearly all wet basement problems are caused by water collecting near the foundation, a situation that can frequently be traced to clogged and overflowing gutters and downspouts.

HOW TO UNCLOG GUTTERS

Flush clogged downspouts with water. Wrap a large rag around a garden hose and insert it in the downspout opening. Arrange the rag so it fills the opening, then turn on the water full force.

Check the slope of the gutters, using a level. Gutters should slope slightly toward the downspouts. Adjust the hangers, if necessary.

Place gutter guards over the gutters to prevent future clogs.

HOW TO REHANG SAGGING GUTTERS + PATCH LEAKS

For sagging gutters, snap a chalk line on the fascia that follows the correct slope. Remove hangers in and near the sag. Lift the gutter until it's flush with the chalk line. *TIP: A good slope for gutters is a ¼" drop every 10 ft. toward the downspouts.*

Reattach hangers every 24", and within 12" of seams. Use new hangers, if necessary. Avoid using the original nail holes. Fill small holes and seal minor leaks, using gutter caulk.

Use a gutter patching kit to make temporary repairs to a gutter with minor damage. Follow manufacturer's directions. For permanent repairs, see the following pages.

HOW TO REPAIR LEAKY JOINTS

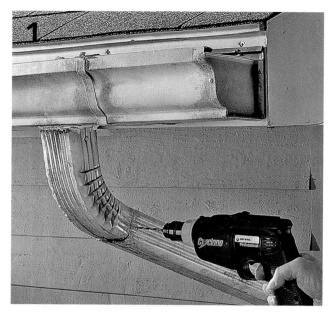

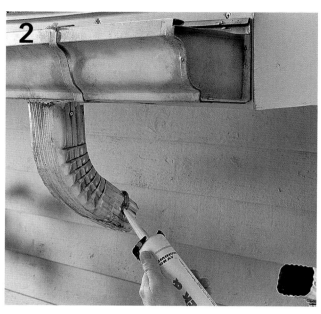

Drill out the rivets or unfasten the metal screws to disassemble the leaky joint. Scrub both parts of the joint with a stiff-bristled brush. Clean the damaged area with water, and allow to dry completely.

Apply caulk to the joining parts, then reassemble the joint. Secure the connection with pop rivets or sheet-metal screws.

HOW TO PATCH METAL GUTTERS

Clean the area around the damage with a stiff-bristled brush. Scrub it with steel wool or an abrasive pad to loosen residue, then rinse it with water.

Apply a ⅛"-thick layer of roofing cement evenly over the damage. Spread the roofing cement a few inches past the damaged area on all sides.

Cut and bend a piece of flashing to fit inside the gutter. Bed the patch in the roofing cement. Feather out the cement to reduce ridges so it won't cause significant damming. *TIP: To prevent corrosion, make sure the patch is the same type of metal as the gutter.*

HOW TO REPLACE A SECTION OF METAL GUTTER

Remove gutter hangers in and near the damaged area. Insert wood spacers in the gutter, near each hanger, before prying. *TIP: If the damaged area is more than 2 ft. long, replace the entire section with new material.*

Slip spacers between the gutter and fascia, near each end of the damaged area, so you won't damage the roof when cutting the gutter. Cut out the damaged section, using a hacksaw.

Cut a new gutter section at least 4" longer than the damaged section.

Clean the cut ends of the old gutter, using a wire brush. Caulk the ends, then center the gutter patch over the cutout area and press into the caulk.

Secure the gutter patch with pop rivets or sheet-metal screws. Use at least three fasteners at each joint. On the inside surfaces of the gutter, caulk over the heads of the fasteners.

Reinstall gutter hangers. If necessary, use new hangers, but don't use old holes. Prime and paint the patch to match the existing gutter.

REMOVING EXTERIOR SIDING

Although it's sometimes possible to install new siding over old if the old siding is solid and firmly attached to the house, it's often better to remove the siding, especially if it's damaged. Taking off the old siding allows you to start with a flat, smooth surface. And because the overall thickness of the siding will remain unchanged, you won't have to add extensions to your window and door jambs.

There's no "right" way to remove siding. Each type of siding material is installed differently, and consequently, they have different removal techniques. A couple of universal rules do apply, however. Start by removing trim that's placed over the siding, and work from the top down. Siding is usually installed from the bottom up, and working in the opposite direction makes removal much easier. Determine the best removal method for your project based on your type of siding.

Strip one side of the house at a time, then re-side that wall before ripping the siding off another section. This minimizes the amount of time your bare walls are exposed to the elements. Take care not to damage the sheathing. If you can't avoid tearing the housewrap, it can easily be replaced, but the sheathing is another story.

While the goal is to remove the siding quickly, it's also important to work safely. Take care when working around windows so the siding doesn't crack or break the glass. Invest the necessary time to protect the flowers and shrubs before starting the tear-off.

Renting a dumpster will expedite the cleanup process. It's much easier to dispose of the siding as soon as it's removed. When you're finished with your cleanup, use a release magnet to collect the nails on the ground.

Tools + Materials ▸

Cat's paw	Masonry-cutting blade
Flat pry bar	Masonry bit
Zip-lock tool	Aviation snips
Drill	Roofing shovel
Circular saw	Release magnet
Cold chisel	Eye protection
Hammer	Work gloves

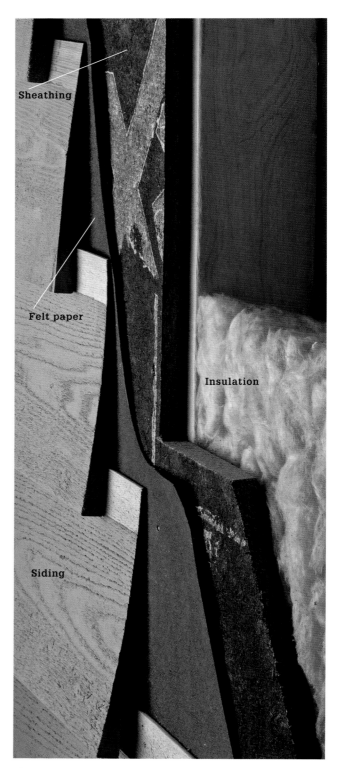

The exterior wall is composed of siding, housewrap or felt paper, and sheathing. Remove the siding without disturbing or damaging the sheathing.

Brick molding comes preattached to most wood-frame window and door units. To remove the molding, pry along the outside of the frame to avoid marring the exposed parts of the jambs and molding.

Lap siding is nailed at the top, then covered by the next course. Pry off the trim at the top of the wall to expose the nails in top row. Remove the nails using a cat's paw, and work your way down the wall.

Shakes and shingles are best removed with a roofing shovel. Use the shovel to pry the siding away from the wall. Once the siding is removed, use the shovel or a hammer to pull out remaining nails.

Board and batten siding is removed by prying off the battens from over the boards. Use a pry bar or cat's paw to remove the nails from the boards.

Siding shown cutaway for clarity

Vinyl siding has a locking channel that fits over the nailing strip of the underlying piece. To remove, use a zip-lock tool to separate the panels, and use a flat pry bar or hammer to remove the nails.

Building paper

Sheathing

Metal lath

Stucco

Stucco siding is difficult to remove. It's usually much easier to apply the new siding over the stucco than to remove it. If you're determined to take it off, use a cold chisel and hammer to break it into pieces, and aviation snips to cut the lath.

REPLACING WALL SHEATHING

After removing the old siding, inspect the sheathing to make sure it's still in good condition. If water penetrated behind the siding, there's a good chance the sheathing is warped, rotted, or otherwise damaged, and will need to be replaced. You'll only need to replace the section of sheathing that's damaged. Before cutting into the wall, make sure there are no wires, cables, or pipes under the sheathing.

Older homes typically have planks or plywood sheathing, while new homes may have a nonstructural sheathing. The replacement material doesn't have to be the same material as the original sheathing, but it does have to be the same thickness.

Tools + Materials ▶

Hammer	3" deck screws
Circular saw	2¼" deck screws
Tape measure	Drill
Chalk line	Eye and ear
Pry bar	protection
Sheathing	Work gloves
2 × 4	

Although the sheathing isn't visible, a smooth, solid sheathing installation is essential to a professional looking siding finish.

HOW TO REPLACE WALL SHEATHING

Snap chalk lines around the area of damaged sheathing, making sure the vertical lines are next to wall studs. Remove any nails or staples in your path. Set the depth of the circular saw blade to cut through the sheathing, but not cut the studs.

Pry off the damaged sheathing. Remove any remaining nails or staples in the studs. Measure the opening, subtract ⅛" from each side, then cut a piece of sheathing to size.

Align 2 × 4 nailing strips with the edges of the wall studs. Fasten the strips in place, using 3" deck screws.

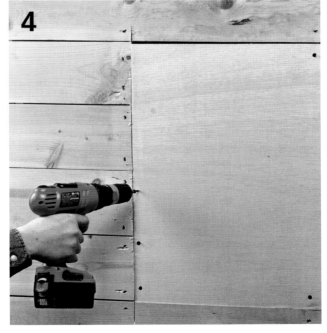

Place the new piece of sheathing in the opening, keeping a ⅛" gap on each side to allow for expansion. Attach the sheathing to the nailing strips and studs, using 2¼" deck screws driven every 12".

REPAIRING SIDING

Damage to siding is fairly common, but fortunately, it's also easy to fix. Small to medium holes, cracks, and rotted areas can be repaired with filler or by replacing the damaged sections with matching siding.

If you cannot find matching siding for repairs at building centers, check with salvage yards or siding contractors. When repairing aluminum or vinyl siding, contact the manufacturer or the contractor who installed the siding to help you locate matching materials and parts. If you're unable to find an exact match, remove a section of original siding from a less visible area of the house, such as the back of the garage, and use it for the patch. Cover the gap in the less visible area with a close matching siding, where the mismatch will be less noticeable.

Tools + Materials ▶

- Aviation snips
- Caulk gun
- Drill
- Flat pry bar
- Hammer
- Straightedge
- Tape measure
- Utility knife
- Zip-lock tool
- Chisel

- Trowel
- Screwdrivers
- Hacksaw
- Circular saw
- Jigsaw
- Keyhole saw
- Flat pry bar
- Nail set
- Stud finder
- Paintbrush

- Epoxy wood filler
- Epoxy glue
- Galvanized ring-shank siding nails
- Siliconized acrylic caulk
- Roofing cement
- Sheathing
- Trim

- Replacement siding, shakes, or shingles
- End caps
- Wood preservative
- Primer
- Paint or stain
- Metal sandpaper
- Eye and ear protection
- Work gloves

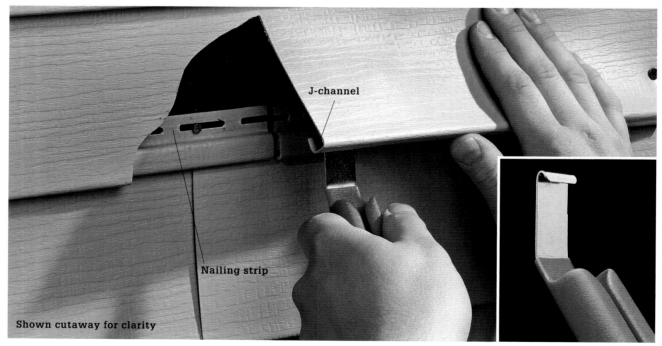

J-channel

Nailing strip

Shown cutaway for clarity

Vinyl and metal siding panels have a locking J-channel that fits over the bottom of the nailing strip on the underlying piece. Use a zip-lock tool (inset) to separate panels. Insert the tool at the seam nearest the repair area. Slide it over the J-channel, pulling outward slightly, to unlock the joint from the siding below.

HOW TO REPAIR VINYL SIDING

Starting at the seam nearest the damaged area, unlock interlocking joints, using a zip-lock tool. Insert spacers between the panels, then remove the fasteners in the damaged siding, using a flat pry bar. Cut out the damaged area, using aviation snips. Cut a replacement piece 4" longer than the open area, and trim 2" off the nailing strip from each end. Slide the piece into position.

Insert siding nails in the nailing strip, then position the end of a flat pry bar over each nail head. Drive the nails by tapping on the neck of the pry bar with a hammer. Place a scrap piece of wood between the pry bar and siding to avoid damaging the siding. Slip the locking channel on the overlapping piece over the nailing strip of the replacement piece. *TIP: If the damaged panel is near a corner, door, or window, replace the entire panel. This eliminates an extra seam.*

HOW TO PATCH ALUMINUM SIDING

Cut out the damaged area, using aviation snips. Leave an exposed area on top of the uppermost piece to act as a bonding surface. Cut a patch 4" larger than the repair area. Remove the nailing strip. Smooth the edges with metal sandpaper.

Nail the lower patch in place by driving siding nails through the nailing flange. Apply roofing cement to the back of the top piece, then press it into place, slipping the locking channel over the nailing strip of the underlying piece. Caulk the seams.

HOW TO REPLACE ALUMINUM END CAPS

Remove the damaged end cap. If necessary, pry the bottom loose, then cut along the top with a hacksaw blade. Starting at the bottom, attach the replacement end caps by driving siding nails through the nailing tabs and into the framing members.

Trim the nailing tabs off the top replacement cap. Apply roofing cement to its back. Slide the cap over the locking channels of the siding panels. Press the top cap securely in place.

HOW TO REPLACE BOARD + BATTEN SIDING

Remove the battens over the damaged boards. Pry out the damaged boards in their entirety. Inspect the underlying housewrap, and patch if necessary.

Cut replacement boards from the same type of lumber, allowing a ⅛" gap at the side seams. Prime or seal the edges and the back side of the replacement boards. Let them dry.

Nail the new boards in place, using ring-shank siding nails. Replace the battens and any other trim. Prime and paint or stain the new boards to blend with the surrounding siding.

HOW TO REPLACE WOOD SHAKES + SHINGLES

Split damaged shakes or shingles with a hammer and chisel, and remove them. Insert wood spacers under the shakes or shingles above the repair area, then slip a hacksaw blade under the top board to cut off any remaining nail heads.

Cut replacement shakes or shingles to fit, leaving a ⅛"- to ¼"-wide gap at each side. Coat all sides and edges with wood preservative. Slip the patch pieces under the siding above the repair area. Drive siding nails near the top of the exposed area on the patches. Cover nail heads with caulk. Remove the spacers.

HOW TO REPLACE LAP SIDING

If the damage is caused by water, locate and repair the leak or other source of the water damage.

Mark the area of siding that needs to be replaced. Make the cutout lines over the center of the framing members on each side of the repair area, staggering the cuts to offset the joints. *TIP: Use an electronic studfinder to locate framing members, or look for the nail heads.*

Insert spacers beneath the board above the repair area. Make entry cuts at the top of the cutting lines with a keyhole saw, then saw through the boards and remove them. Pry out any nails or cut off the nail heads, using a hacksaw blade. Patch or replace the sheathing and building paper, if necessary.

Measure and cut replacement boards to fit, leaving an expansion gap of ⅛" at each end. Use the old boards as templates to trace cutouts for fixtures and openings. Use a jigsaw to make the cutouts. Apply wood sealer or primer to the ends and backs of the boards. Let them dry.

Nail the new boards in place with siding nails, starting with the lowest board in the repair area. At each framing member, drive nails through the bottom of the new board and the top of the board below. *TIP: If you removed the bottom row of siding, nail a 1 × 2 starter strip along the bottom of the patch area.*

Fill expansion joints with caulk (use paintable, flexible exterior caulk for painted wood or tinted caulk for stained wood). Prime and paint or stain the replacement boards to match the surrounding siding.

REPAIRING EXTERIOR TRIM

EXTERIOR REPAIRS

Some exterior trim serves as decoration, like gingerbread and ornate cornice moldings. Other trim, such as brick molding and end caps, works with siding to seal your house from the elements. Damaged brick molding and corner boards should be patched with stock material similar to the original.

If you cannot find matching replacement parts for decorative trim at home improvement stores, check salvage shops or contact a custom millworker.

Repair delicate or ornamental trim molding in your workshop, whenever possible. You'll get better results than if you try repairing it while it's still attached.

Tools + Materials ▸

Hammer	Caulk
Chisel	10d galvanized casing nails
Circular saw	Galvanized ring-shank
Nail set	siding nails
Putty knife	Sandpaper
Utility knife	Primer
Paintbrush	Paint
Flat pry bar	Building paper
Caulk gun	Drip edge
Epoxy wood filler	Replacement trim
Epoxy glue	Eye protection
Panel adhesive	Work gloves

Tips for Repairing + Replacing Trim ▸

Reattach loose trim with new ring-shank siding nails driven near old nail locations. Fill old nail holes with paintable caulk, and touch up caulk and new nail heads with paint to match the surrounding surface.

Repair decorative trim molding with epoxy glue or wood filler. For major repairs, make your own replacement parts, or take the trim to a custom millwork shop.

HOW TO REPLACE BRICK MOLDING

Pry off old brick molding around windows and doors, using a flat pry bar. Remove any old drip edge. Inspect and repair the building paper.

Hold a replacement piece of brick molding, slightly longer than the original piece, across the opening. Mark cutting lines to fit the opening. Cut the replacement molding at the marks, matching any miter cuts.

Cut a 3"-wide piece of flashing to fit between the jambs, then bend it in half lengthwise to form the new drip edge (preformed drip edge is also available). Slip it between the siding and building paper, above the door or window. Do not nail the drip edge in place.

Test-fit the replacement piece of brick molding, then apply exterior-grade panel adhesive to the back side. Follow the manufacturer's directions for allowing the adhesive to set.

Nail the brick molding to the door header, using 10d galvanized casing nails. Lock-nail the miter joints, and set all nail heads. Seal joints, and cover nail holes with caulk. Prime and paint when the caulk dries.

IDENTIFYING EXTERIOR PAINT PROBLEMS

Two enemies work against painted surfaces—moisture and age. A simple leak or a failed vapor barrier inside the house can ruin even the finest paint job. If you notice signs of paint failure, such as blistering or peeling, take action to correct the problem right away. If the surface damage is discovered in time, you may be able to correct it with just a little bit of touch-up painting.

Evaluating the painted surfaces of your house can help you identify problems with siding, trim, roofs, and moisture barriers. The pictures on these two pages show the most common forms of paint failure, and how to fix them. Be sure to fix any moisture problems before repainting.

Evaluate exterior painted surfaces every year, starting with areas sheltered from the sun. Paint failure will appear first in areas that receive little or no direct sunlight and is a warning sign that similar problems are developing in neighboring areas.

COMMON FORMS OF PAINT FAILURE

Blistering appears as a bubbled surface. It results from poor preparation or hurried application of primer or paint. The blisters indicate trapped moisture is trying to force its way through the surface. To fix isolated spots, scrape and touch up. For widespread damage, remove paint down to bare wood, then apply primer and paint.

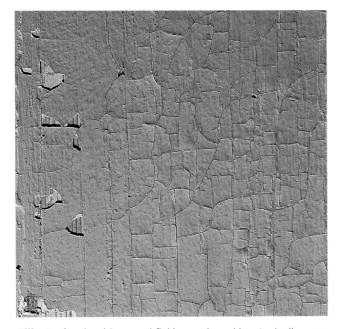

Alligatoring is widespread flaking and cracking, typically seen on surfaces that have many built-up paint layers. It can also be caused by inadequate surface preparation or by allowing too little drying time between coats of primer and paint. Remove the old paint, then prime and repaint.

Peeling occurs when paint falls away in large flakes. It's a sign of persistent moisture problems, generally from a leak or a failed vapor barrier. If the peeling is localized, scrape and sand the damaged areas, then touch up with primer and paint. If it's widespread, remove the old paint down to bare wood, then apply primer and paint.

Localized blistering and peeling indicates that moisture, usually from a leaky roof, gutter system, or interior pipe, is trapped under the paint. Find and eliminate the leak, then scrape, prime, and repaint the area.

Clearly defined blistering and peeling occurs when a humid room has an insufficient vapor barrier. If there's a clear line where an interior wall ends, remove the siding and replace the vapor barrier.

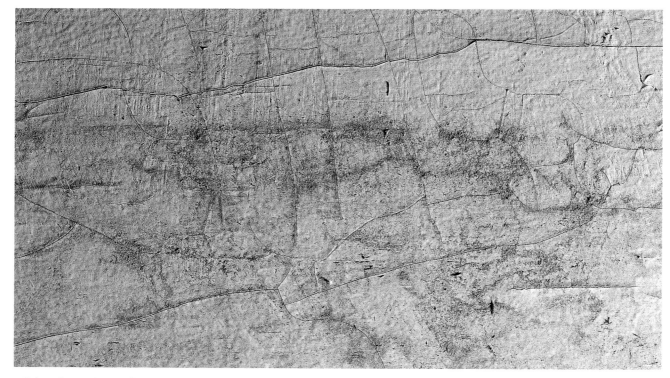

Mildew forms in cracks and in humid areas that receive little direct sunlight. Wash mildewed areas with a 1:1 solution of household chlorine bleach and water, or with trisodium phosphate (TSP).

Efflorescence occurs in masonry when minerals leech through the surface, forming a crystalline or powdery layer. Use a scrub brush and a muriatic acid solution to remove efflorescence before priming and painting.

Bleeding spots occur when nails in siding begin to rust. Remove the nails, sand out the rust, then drive in galvanized ring-shank nails. Apply metal primer, then paint to blend in with the siding.

Rust occurs when moisture penetrates paint on iron or steel. Remove the rust and loose paint with a drill and wire brush attachment, then prime and repaint.

PAINTING YOUR HOUSE

Schedule priming and painting tasks so that you can paint within two weeks of priming surfaces. If more than two weeks pass, wash the surface with soap and water before applying the next coat.

Check the weather forecast and keep an eye on the sky while you work. Damp weather or rain within two hours of application will ruin a paint job. Don't paint when the temperature is below 50°F or above 90°F. Avoid painting on windy days—it's dangerous to be on a ladder in high winds, and wind blows dirt onto the fresh paint.

Plan each day's work so you can follow the shade. Prepare, prime, and paint one face of the house at a time, and follow a logical painting order. Work from the top of the house down to the foundation, covering an entire section before you move the ladder or scaffolding.

Tools + Materials ›

Paintbrushes	House paint
Paint rollers	Trim paint
Sash brush	Cleanup materials
Scaffolding	Masking tape
Ladders	Eye protection
Primer	Work gloves

Paint in a logical order, starting from the top and working your way down. Cover as much surface as you can reach comfortably without moving your ladder or scaffolding. After the paint or primer dries, touch up any unpainted areas that were covered by the ladder or ladder stabilizer.

Tips for Selecting Brushes + Rollers ▸

Wall brushes, which are thick, square brushes 3" to 5" wide, are designed to carry a lot of paint and distribute it widely. *TIP: It's good to keep a variety of clean brushes on hand, including 2½", 3", and 4" flat brushes, 2" and 3" trim brushes, and tapered sash brushes.*

Trim and tapered sash brushes, which are 2" to 3" wide, are good for painting doors and trim, and for cutting-in small areas.

Paint rollers work best for quickly painting smooth surfaces. Use an 8" or 9" roller sleeve for broad surfaces.

Use a 3" roller to paint flat-surfaced trim, such as end caps and corner trim.

Tips for Applying Primer + Paint ▸

Use the right primer and paint for each job. Always read the manufacturer's recommendations. Different primers are formulated and labeled to be used for different materials, and interior or exterior applications.

Plan your painting sequence so you paint the walls, doors, and trim before painting stairs and porch floors. This prevents the need to touch up spills.

Tips for Loading + Distributing Paint ▸

Load your brush with the right amount of paint for the area you're covering. Use a full load of paint for broad areas, a moderate load for smaller areas and feathering strokes, and a light load when painting or working around trim.

Hold the brush at a 45° angle and apply just enough downward pressure to flex the bristles and squeeze the paint from the brush.

HOW TO USE A PAINTBRUSH

Load the brush with a full load of paint. Starting at one end of the surface, make a long, smooth stroke until the paint begins to feather out. *TIP: Paint color can vary from one can to the next. To avoid problems, pour all of your paint into one large container and mix it thoroughly. Pour the mixed paint back into the individual cans and seal them carefully. Stir each can before use.*

At the end of the stroke, lift the brush without leaving a definite ending point. If the paint appears uneven or contains heavy brush marks, smooth it out without overbrushing.

Reload the brush and make a stroke from the opposite direction, painting over the feathered end of the first stroke to create a smooth, even surface. If the junction of the two strokes is visible, rebrush with a light coat of paint. Feather out the starting point of the second stroke.

Tips for Using Paint Rollers ▸

Wet the roller nap, then squeeze out the excess water. Position a roller screen inside a five-gallon bucket. Dip the roller into the paint, then roll it back and forth across the roller screen. The roller sleeve should be full, but not dripping, when lifted from the bucket.

Doughnut-shaped rollers work well for painting the edges of lap siding and moldings.

Cone-shaped rollers work well for painting the joints between intersecting surfaces.

Tips for Cleaning Painting Tools ▸

Scrape paint from roller covers with the curved side of a cleaner tool.

Use a spinner tool to remove paint and solvent from brushes and roller covers.

Comb brushes with the spiked side of a cleaner tool to properly align bristles for drying.

HOW TO PAINT STUCCO WALLS

Using a large paintbrush, paint the foundation with anti-chalking masonry primer, and let it dry. Using concrete paint and a 4" brush, cut in the areas around basement windows and doors.

Apply concrete paint to broad surfaces with a paint roller and a ⅝"-nap sleeve. Use a 3" trim roller or a 3" paintbrush for trim.

HOW TO PAINT DOORS, WINDOWS + TRIM

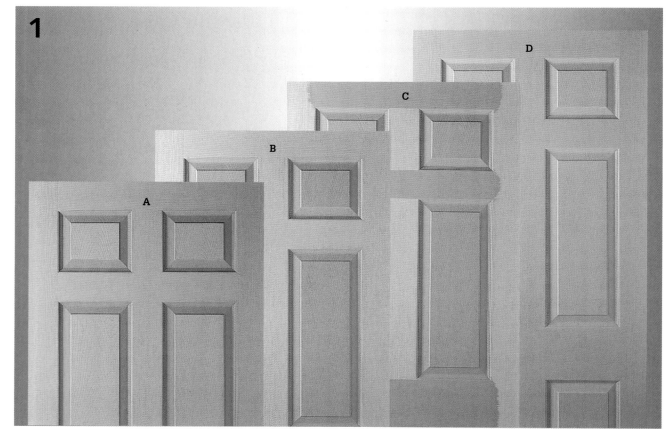

Using a sash brush, paint doors in this sequence: beveled edges of raised door panels (A), panel faces (B), horizontal rails (C), and vertical stiles (D).

For trim, use a trim brush or sash brush and a moderate load of paint to paint the inside edges of door and window jambs, casings, and brick molding. *TIP: Paint surfaces on the interior side of the door-stop to match the interior trim.*

Mask off the siding—if freshly painted, make sure it's completely dry first. Paint the outside edges of casings and brick molding. Work paint all the way into the corners created by the siding's profile.

Paint the faces of door jambs, casings, and brick molding, feathering fresh paint around the previously painted edges.

Paint wood door thresholds and porch floors with specially formulated enamel floor paint.

USING PAINT-SPRAYING EQUIPMENT

Spray equipment can make quick work of painting, but it still requires the same careful preparation work as traditional brush and roller methods. Part of that prep work involves using plastic to completely cover doors, windows, and other areas that you don't want painted, rather than just taping them off.

Spray equipment can be purchased or rented at hardware and home improvement stores. There are several types and sizes of spray equipment, including high-volume low-pressure (HVLP), airless, air-assisted airless, and electrostatic enhanced. They all work the same way—by atomizing paint and directing it to a work surface in a spray or fan pattern. For our project, we used an HVLP sprayer, which we recommend because it produces less overspray and more efficient paint application than other sprayers.

Be sure to read and follow all safety precautions for the spray equipment. Since the paint is under a lot of pressure, it can not only tear the skin, but it can inject toxins into the blood stream if used incorrectly. Wear the proper safety protection, such as safety glasses and a respirator, when spray painting the house.

As with other paint applications, pay close attention to the weather. Don't spray if rain is likely, and don't spray on windy days, since the wind can carry the paint particles away from the siding.

Tools + Materials ▸

Paint sprayer
Utility knife
Spray equipment
Paint
Paintbrushes
Respirator
Masking tape

Plastic
Cardboard
Cheesecloth
5-gallon bucket
Eye protection
Work gloves

Paint sprayers allow you to cover large areas of siding and trim in a short amount of time. They also make it easier to paint areas that are hard to reach with a brush or roller.

HOW TO PAINT USING A PAINT SPRAYER

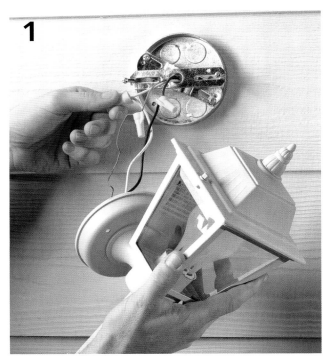

1

Remove outside light fixtures, window and door screens, and other detachable items that you don't want painted.

2

Cover doors, windows, and any other areas you don't want painted, using plastic and masking tape.

3

Strain the paint through cheesecloth to remove particles and debris. Mix the paint together in a 5-gallon bucket. Fill the sprayer container.

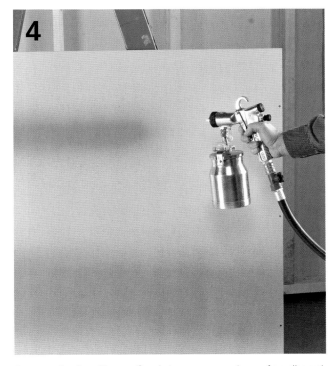

4

Spray a test pattern of paint on a scrap piece of cardboard. Adjust the pressure until you reach an even "fan" without any thick lines along the edge of the spray pattern.

5

Cut-in around doors and windows with the paint. Spray the paint along each side of the doors and windows, applying the paint evenly.

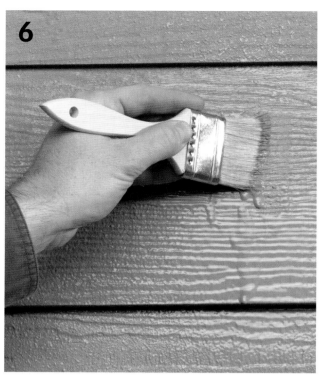

6

If you happen to spray an excessive amount of paint in an area and it starts to run, stop the sprayer. Use a paintbrush to spread out the paint and eliminate the runs.

7

Hold the spray gun perpendicular to the house, approximately 12" from the wall. Start painting near the top of the wall, close to a corner. Move your entire arm, rather than just the wrist, in a steady, side-to-side motion. Do not wave your arm in an arc. Start your arm movement, then start the gun.

8

Spray the paint in an even motion, being careful not to tilt the gun. As you sweep your arm back and forth, overlap each coat of paint by 20 to 30 percent, working your way down the wall. When stopping, release the trigger before discontinuing your motion.

HOW TO PAINT DOORS USING A PAINT SPRAYER

1

Remove the door by taking off the hinges. Remove all hardware from the door, such as handles and locks. If the door contains glass, you can either tape it off, or allow paint to get on the glass and then scrape it off with a razor after it's dry.

2

Prop up the door so it stands vertically. Starting at the top of the door, spray on the paint. As you make passes across the door, slightly go past the edges before sweeping back in the opposite direction. Wait until the paint is completely dry, then turn the door around and paint the other side.

STAINING SIDING

Stain lends color to wood siding, but because it is partially transparent, it also allows the natural beauty of the wood grain to show through. Water-based stains are applied with an acrylic or synthetic brush. Oil-based stains are usually applied with a natural-bristle brush.

Work in small sections at a time. Complete an entire length of board without stopping in the middle. Unlike paint, stain can darken or leave streaks if you go back over an area after it dries. Save the trim until the end, then stain it separately to get an even coverage.

Staining requires the same careful preparation work as painting. The surface must be clean and dry. Avoid working in direct sunlight so the stain doesn't dry too quickly. Check manufacturer's recommendations before staining. Some stains cannot be applied in temperatures below 50°F.

Tools + Materials ▶

Paintbrush or foam brush	Stain
Cloths	Eye protection
	Latex gloves

HOW TO STAIN LOG CABIN SIDING

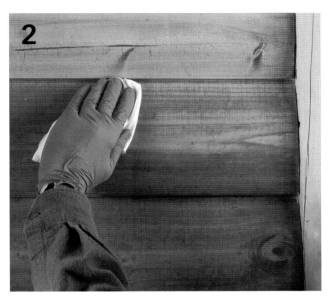

Load the brush with stain. Starting at a corner, move the brush across the siding with a long, smooth stroke. Cover the entire width of the log with stain, reloading the brush as needed, applying stain in the same direction. *TIP: Mix the stain thoroughly and often as it's being applied.*

Wipe away excess stain with a clean cloth. Keep applying stain until you reach the opposite corner or an edge. Once the top course is stained, go back to the corner and start on the next row of siding, using the same technique. If the run of siding is short, such as between windows, apply stain to two rows at a time. Stain remaining courses the same way.

HOW TO STAIN SHINGLE SIDING

Load the brush with stain. Starting at the top of a wall by a corner, apply stain to the shingles, using smooth, downward strokes. Wipe off excess stain with a cloth. Cover the face of the shingle and stain the bottom edge before moving on to the next one. Apply stain to one or two courses at a time, moving across the wall as you go. Never stop in the middle of a shingle. When you reach the opposite corner, start over on the next set of shingles. Stain remaining rows the same way.

Once all of the shingles are stained, apply stain to the trim. Move the brush in the same direction as the wood grain, then wipe away excess with a cloth.

REPAIRING STUCCO

EXTERIOR REPAIRS

Although stucco siding is very durable, it can be damaged, and over time it can crumble or crack. The directions given below work well for patching small areas less than 2 sq. ft. For more extensive damage, the repair is done in layers, as shown on the opposite page.

▶ Tools + Materials ▸

Caulk gun
Putty knife
Mason's trowel
Square-end trowel
Hammer
Whisk broom
Wire brush
Masonry chisel
Aviation snips
Scratching tool
Metal primer
Stucco patching
   compound

Stucco mix
Masonry paint
1½" roofing nails
15# building paper
Self-furring
   metal lath
Masonry caulk
Tint
Metal stop bead
Eye protection
Work gloves

Fill thin cracks in stucco walls with masonry caulk.
Overfill the crack with caulk, and feather until it's flush with the stucco. Allow the caulk to set, then paint it to match the stucco. Masonry caulk stays semiflexible, preventing further cracking.

HOW TO PATCH SMALL AREAS

Remove loose material from the repair area, using a wire brush. Use the brush to clean away rust from any exposed metal lath, then apply a coat of metal primer to the lath.

Apply premixed stucco repair compound to the repair area, slightly overfilling the hole, using a putty knife or trowel. Read manufacturer's directions, as drying times vary.

Smooth the repair with a putty knife or trowel, feathering the edges to blend into the surrounding surface. Use a whisk broom or trowel to duplicate the original texture. Let the patch dry for several days, then touch it up with masonry paint.

HOW TO REPAIR LARGE AREAS

Make a starter hole with a drill and masonry bit, then use a masonry chisel and hammer to chip away stucco in the repair area. *NOTE: Wear safety glasses and a particle mask or respirator when cutting stucco. Cut self-furring metal lath to size with aviation snips and attach it to the sheathing, using roofing nails. Overlap pieces by 2". If the patch extends to the base of the wall, attach a metal stop bead at the bottom.*

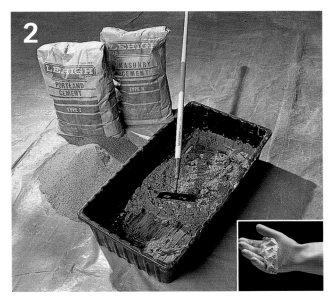

To mix your own stucco, combine three parts sand, two parts portland cement, and one part masonry cement. Add just enough water so the mixture holds its shape when squeezed (inset). Mix only as much as you can use in one hour. *TIP: Premixed stucco works well for small jobs, but for large ones, it's more economical to mix your own.*

Apply a ⅜"-thick layer of stucco directly to the metal lath. Push the stucco into the mesh until it fills the gap between the mesh and the sheathing. Score horizontal grooves into the wet surface, using a scratching tool. Let the stucco dry for two days, misting it with water every two to four hours.

Apply a second, smooth layer of stucco. Build up the stucco to within ¼" of the original surface. Let the patch dry for two days, misting every two to four hours.

Combine finish-coat stucco mix with just enough water for the mixture to hold its shape. Dampen the patch area, then apply the finish coat to match the original surface. Dampen the patch periodically for a week. Let it dry for several more days before painting.

REPAIRING CONCRETE

Concrete is one of the most durable building materials, but it still requires occasional repair and maintenance. Freezing and thawing, improper finishing techniques, a poor subbase, or lack of reinforcement all can cause problems with concrete. By addressing problems as soon as you discover them, you can prevent further damage that may be difficult or impossible to fix.

Concrete repairs fall into a wide range, from simple cleaning and sealing, to removing and replacing whole sections. Filling cracks and repairing surface damage are the most common concrete repairs.

Another effective repair is resurfacing—covering an old concrete surface with a layer of fresh concrete. It's a good solution to spalling, crazing, or popouts—minor problems that affect the appearance more than the structure. These problems often result from inadequate preparation or incorrect finishing techniques.

As with any kind of repair, the success of the project depends largely on good preparation and the use of the best repair products for the job. Specially formulated repair products are manufactured for just about every type of concrete repair. Be sure to read the product-use information before purchasing any products; some products need to be used in combination with others.

A good repair can outlast the rest of the structure in some cases, but if structural damage has occurred, repairing the concrete is only a temporary solution. By using the right products and techniques, however, you can make cosmetic repairs that improve the appearance of the surface and keep damage from becoming worse.

Probably the most important point to remember when repairing concrete is that curing makes repairs last longer. That means covering repaired surfaces with plastic sheeting and keeping them damp for at least a week. In dry, hot weather, lift the plastic occasionally, and mist with water.

Good repairs restore both the appearance and the function to failing concrete structures and surfaces. Careful work can produce a well-blended, successful repair like the one shown above.

CONCRETE REPAIR PRODUCTS

Concrete repair products include: vinyl-reinforced concrete patch (A) for filling holes, popouts, and larger cracks; hydraulic cement (B) for repairing foundations, retaining walls, and other damp areas; quick-setting cement (C) for repairing vertical surfaces and unusual shapes; anchoring cement (D) for setting hardware in concrete; concrete sealing products (E); masonry paint (F); concrete recoating product (G) for creating a fresh surface on old concrete; joint-filler caulk (H); pour-in crack sealer (I); concrete cleaner (J); concrete fortifier (K) to strengthen concrete; bonding adhesive (L) to prepare the repair area; and concrete sand mix (M) for general repairs and resurfacing.

▶ Tips for Disguising Repairs ▸

Add concrete pigment or liquid cement color to concrete patching compound to create a color that matches the original concrete. Experiment with different mixtures until you find a matching color. Samples should be dry to show the actual colors.

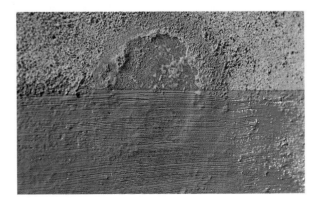

Use masonry paint to cover concrete repairs. Paint can be used on vertical or horizontal surfaces, but high-traffic surfaces will require more frequent touch-up or repainting.

IDENTIFYING PROBLEMS WITH CONCRETE

There are two general types of concrete failure: structural failure, usually resulting from outside forces like freezing water; and surface damage, most often caused by improper finishing techniques or concrete mixtures that do not have the right ratio of water to cement. Surface problems sometimes can be permanently repaired if the correct products and techniques are used. More significant damage can be patched for cosmetic purposes and to resist further damage, but the structure will eventually need to be replaced.

COMMON CONCRETE PROBLEMS

Sunken concrete is usually caused by erosion of the subbase. Some structures, like sidewalks, can be raised to repair the subbase, then relaid. A more common (and more reliable) solution is to hire a mudjacking contractor to raise the surface by injecting fresh concrete below the surface.

Frost heave is common in colder climates. Frozen ground forces concrete slabs upward, and sections of the slab can pop up. The best solution is to break off and remove the affected section or sections, repair the subbase, and pour new sections that are set off by isolation joints.

Moisture buildup occurs in concrete structures, like foundations and retaining walls, that are in constant ground contact. To identify the moisture source, tape a piece of foil to the wall. If moisture collects on the outer surface of the foil, the source likely is condensation, which can be corrected by installing a dehumidifier. If moisture is not visible on the foil, it is likely seeping through the wall. Consult a professional mason.

Staining can ruin the appearance of a concrete surface or structure. Stains can be removed with commercial-grade concrete cleaner or a variety of other chemicals. For protection against staining, seal masonry surfaces with clear sealant.

Widespread cracks all the way through the surface, and other forms of substantial damage, are very difficult to repair effectively. If the damage to the concrete is extensive, remove and replace the structure.

Isolated cracks occur on many concrete building projects. Fill small cracks with concrete caulk or crack-filler, and patch large cracks with vinyl-reinforced patching material.

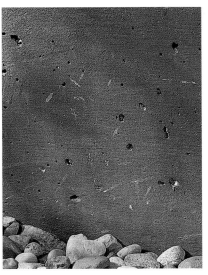

Popouts can be caused by freezing moisture or stress, but very often they occur because the concrete surface was improperly floated or cured, causing the aggregate near the surface of the concrete to loosen. A few scattered popouts do not require attention, but if they are very large or widespread, you can repair them as you would repair holes.

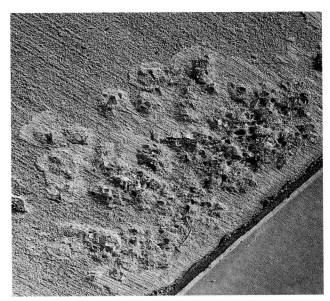

Spalling is surface deterioration of concrete. Spalling is caused by overfloating, which draws too much water to the surface, causing it to weaken and peel off over time. When spalling occurs, it is usually widespread, and the structure may need resurfacing.

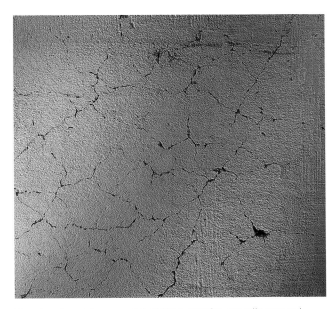

Crazing is widespread hairline cracks, usually caused by overfloating or too much portland cement in the concrete. Clean and seal the surface to help prevent further crazing. For a long-term solution, resurface.

PATCHING HOLES IN CONCRETE

Large and small holes are treated differently when repairing concrete. The best product for filling in smaller holes (less than ½" deep) is vinyl-reinforced concrete patcher, which is often sold in convenient quart or gallon containers of dry powder. Reinforced repair products should be applied only in layers that are ½" thick or less.

For deeper holes, use sand-mix concrete with an acrylic or latex fortifier, which can be applied in layers up to 2" thick. This material is sold in 60- or 80-pound bags of dry mix.

Patches in concrete will be more effective if you create clean, backward-angled cuts (page 11) around the damaged area, to create a stronger bond. For extensive cutting of damaged concrete, it's best to score the concrete first with a circular saw equipped with a masonry blade. Use a chisel and maul to complete the job.

(page 11)

Tools + Materials ▸

Trowels	Vegetable oil or
Drill and masonry-	commercial release
grinding disc	agent
Circular saw with	Hydraulic cement
masonry-cutting	Latex bonding agent
blade	Vinyl-reinforced
Masonry chisel	patching compound
Hand maul	Sand-mix concrete
Paintbrush	Concrete fortifier
Screed board	Plastic sheeting
Float	Floor scraper
Scrap lumber	Concrete primer
Vacuum	Paint roller
Hammer	Floor leveler
Eye and ear protection	Gauge rake or spreader
Work gloves	

Use hydraulic cement or quick-setting cement for repairing holes and chip-outs in vertical surfaces. Because they set up in just a few minutes, these products can be shaped to fill holes without the need for forms. If the structure is exposed constantly to moisture, use hydraulic cement.

HOW TO PATCH LARGE AREAS

Mark straight cutting lines around the damaged area, then cut with a circular saw equipped with a masonry-cutting blade. Set the foot of the saw so the cut bevels away from the damage at a 15° angle. Chisel out any remaining concrete within the repair area. *TIP: Set the foot of the saw on a thin board to protect it from the concrete.*

Tip ▶

You can enhance the appearance of repaired vertical surfaces by painting with waterproof concrete paint once the surface has cured for at least a week. Concrete paint is formulated to resist chalking and efflorescence.

Mix sand-mix concrete with concrete acrylic fortifier, and fill the damaged area slightly above the surrounding surface.

Smooth and feather the repair with a float until the repair is even with the surrounding surface. Re-create any surface finish, like brooming, used on the original surface. Cover the repair with plastic and protect from traffic for at least one week.

HOW TO CAULK GAPS AROUND MASONRY

Cracks between a concrete walk and foundation may result in seepage, leading to a wet basement. Repair cracks with caulk-type concrete patcher.

Caulk around the mud sill, the horizontal wooden plate where the house rests on the foundation. This area should be recaulked periodically to prevent heat loss.

HOW TO PATCH SMALL HOLES

Cut out around the damaged area with a masonry-grinding disc mounted on a portable drill (or use a hammer and stone chisel). The cuts should bevel about 15° away from the center of the damaged area. Chisel out any loose concrete within the repair area. Always wear gloves and eye protection.

Apply a thin layer of latex bonding agent. The adhesive will bond with the damaged surface and create a strong bonding surface for the patching compound. Wait until the latex bonding agent is tacky (no more than 30 minutes) before proceeding to the next step.

Fill the damaged area with vinyl-reinforced patching compound, applied in ¼ to ½" layers. Wait about 30 minutes between applications. Add layers of the mixture until the compound is packed to just above surface level. Feather the edges smooth, cover the repair with plastic, and protect from traffic for at least one week.

HOW TO PATCH CONCRETE FLOORS

Clean the floor with a vacuum, and remove any loose or flaking concrete with a masonry chisel and hammer. Mix a batch of vinyl floor patching compound following manufacturer's directions. Apply the compound using a smooth trowel, slightly overfilling the cavity. Smooth the patch flush with the surface.

After the compound has cured fully, use a floor scraper to scrape the patched areas smooth.

HOW TO APPLY FLOOR LEVELER

Remove any loose material and clean the concrete thoroughly; the surface must be free of dust, dirt, oils, and paint. Apply an even layer of concrete primer to the entire surface, using a long-nap paint roller. Let the primer dry completely.

Following the manufacturer's instructions, mix the floor leveler with water. The batch should be large enough to cover the entire floor area to the desired thickness (up to 1"). Pour the leveler over the floor.

Distribute the leveler evenly using a gauge rake or spreader. Work quickly: the leveler begins to harden in 15 minutes. You can use a trowel to feather the edges and create a smooth transition with an uncovered area. Let the leveler dry for 24 hours.

FILLING CRACKS IN CONCRETE

The materials and methods for repairing cracks in concrete depend on the location and size of the crack. For small cracks (less than ¼" wide), you can use gray-tinted concrete caulk for a quick fix. For more permanent solutions, use pourable crack filler or fortified patching cements. The patching cements are polymer compounds that increase the bonding properties and allow some flexibility. For larger cracks on horizontal surfaces, use fortified sand-mix concrete; for cracks on vertical surfaces, use hydraulic or quick-setting cement. Thorough preparation is essential for creating a good bonding surface.

Tools + Materials ▸

Wire brush
Drill and wire wheel
    attachment
Stone chisel
Hand maul
Paintbrush
Trowel
Latex bonding agent
Work gloves

Vinyl-reinforced
    patching compound
Concrete caulk
Fortified sand-mix
    concrete
Plastic sheeting
Pourable crack filler
Hydraulic or quick-
    setting cement

Use concrete repair caulk for quick-fix repairs to minor cracks. Although convenient, repair caulk should be viewed only as a short-term solution to improve appearance and help prevent further damage from water penetration.

Tips for Preparing Cracked Concrete for Repair ▸

Clean loose material from the crack using a wire brush or a portable drill with a wire wheel attachment. Loose material or debris left in the crack will result in a poor bond and an ineffective repair.

Chisel out the crack to create a backward-angled "keyhole" cut (wider at the base than at the surface), using a stone chisel and hammer. The angled cutout shape prevents the repair material from pushing out of the crack.

HOW TO REPAIR SMALL CRACKS

Prepare the crack for the repair (opposite page), then apply a thin layer of latex bonding agent to the entire repair area, using a paintbrush. The latex bonding agent helps keep the repair material from loosening or popping out of the crack.

Mix vinyl-reinforced patching compound, and trowel it into the crack. Feather the repair with a trowel, so it is even with the surrounding surface. Cover the surface with plastic and protect it from traffic for at least a week.

Variations for Repairing Large Cracks ▸

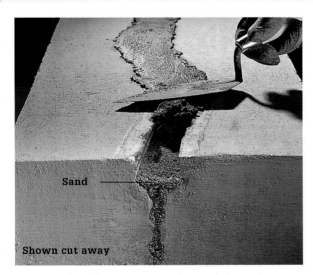

Sand

Shown cut away

Horizontal surfaces: Prepare the crack (opposite page), then pour sand into the crack to within ½" of the surface. Prepare sand-mix concrete, adding a concrete fortifier, then trowel the mixture into the crack. Feather until even with the surface, using a trowel.

Vertical surfaces: Prepare the crack (opposite page). Mix vinyl-reinforced concrete or hydraulic cement, then trowel a ¼"- to ½"-thick layer into the crack until the crack is slightly overfilled. Feather the material even with the surrounding surface, then let it dry. If the crack is over ½" deep, trowel in consecutive layers. Let each layer dry before applying another.

HOW TO SEAL CRACKS IN CONCRETE FOUNDATION WALLS

EXTERIOR REPAIRS

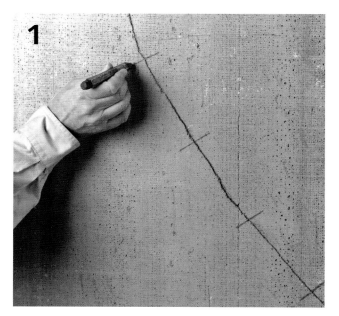

1

To determine if a foundation crack is stable, you need to monitor it over the course of several months, particularly over the fall and spring seasons. Draw marks across the crack at various points, noting the length as well as its width at the widest gaps. If the crack moves more than ⅟₁₆", consult a building engineer or foundation specialist.

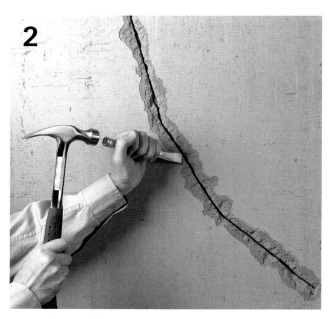

2

To repair a stable crack, use a chisel to cut a keyhole cut that's wider at the base then at the surface, and no more than ½" deep. Clean out the crack with a wire brush.

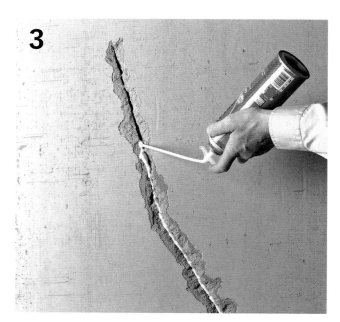

3

To help seal against moisture, fill the crack with expanding insulating foam, working from bottom to top.

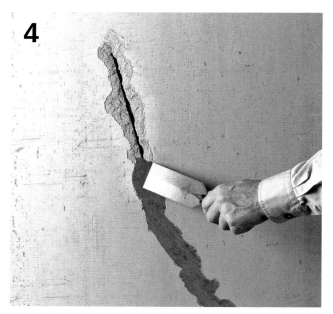

4

Mix hydraulic cement according to the manufacturer's instructions, then trowel it into the crack, working from the bottom to top. Apply cement in layers no more than ½" thick, until the patch is slightly higher than the surrounding area. Feather cement with the trowel until it's even with the surface and allow to dry thoroughly.

REPAIRING CONCRETE STEPS

Steps require more maintenance and repair than other concrete structures around the house because heavy use makes them more susceptible to damage. Horizontal surfaces on steps can be treated using the same products and techniques used on other masonry surfaces. For vertical surfaces, use quick-setting cement, and shape it to fit.

Tools + Materials ▸

Trowel
Wire brush
Paintbrush
Circular saw with
    masonry-cutting blade
Chisel
Float
Edger
Scrap lumber
Vegetable oil or
    commercial
    release agent
Latex bonding agent
Vinyl-reinforced
    patching
    compound
Quick-setting cement
Plastic sheeting
Tape
Heavy block
Eye protection
Work gloves

Isolated damage to step surfaces, like the deep popout being repaired above, can be fixed to renew your steps. If damage is extensive, you may need to replace the steps.

Damaged concrete steps are an unsightly and unsafe way to welcome visitors to your home. Repairing cracks as they develop not only keeps the steps in a safer and better looking condition, it prolongs their life.

HOW TO REPLACE A STEP CORNER

Retrieve the broken corner, then clean it and the mating surface with a wire brush. Apply latex bonding agent to both surfaces. If you do not have the broken piece, you can rebuild the corner with patching compound (below).

Spread a heavy layer of fortified patching compound on the surfaces to be joined, then press the broken piece into position. Lean a heavy brick or block against the repair until the patching compound sets (about 30 minutes). Cover the repair with plastic and protect it from traffic for at least one week.

HOW TO PATCH A STEP CORNER

Clean chipped concrete with a wire brush. Brush the patch area with latex bonding agent.

Mix patching compound with latex bonding agent, as directed by the manufacturer. Apply the mixture to the patch area, then smooth the surfaces and round the edges, as necessary, using a flexible knife or trowel.

Tape scrap lumber pieces around the patch as a form. Coat the insides with vegetable oil or commercial release agent so the patch won't adhere to the wood. Remove the wood when the patch is firm. Cover with plastic and protect from traffic for at least one week.

HOW TO PATCH STEP TREADS

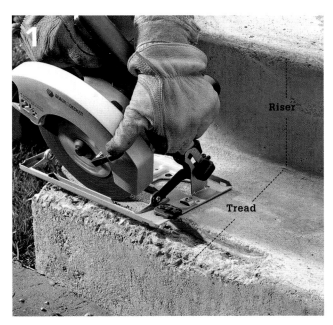

Make a cut in the stair tread just outside the damaged area, using a circular saw with a masonry-cutting blade. Make the cut so it angles toward the back of the step. Make a horizontal cut on the riser below the damaged area, then chisel out the area in between the two cuts.

Cut a form board the same height as the step riser. Coat one side of the board with vegetable oil or commercial release agent to prevent it from bonding with the repair, then press it against the riser of the damaged step, and brace it in position with heavy blocks. Make sure the top of the form is flush with the top of the step tread.

Apply latex bonding agent to the repair area with a clean paintbrush, wait until the bonding agent is tacky (no more than 30 minutes), then press a stiff mixture of quick-setting cement into the damaged area with a trowel.

Smooth the concrete with a float, and let it set for a few minutes. Round over the front edge of the nose with an edger. Use a trowel to slice off the sides of the patch, so it is flush with the side of the steps. Cover the repair with plastic and wait a week before allowing traffic on the repaired section.

MISCELLANEOUS CONCRETE REPAIRS

There are plenty of concrete problems you may encounter around your house that are not specifically addressed in many repair manuals. These miscellaneous repairs include such tasks as patching contoured objects that have been damaged and repairing masonry veneer around the foundation of your house. You can adapt basic techniques to make just about any type of concrete repair. Remember to dampen concrete surfaces before patching so that the moisture from concrete and other patching compounds is not absorbed into the existing surface. Be sure to follow the manufacturer's directions for the repair products you use.

Tools + Materials ▸

Putty knife	Eye protection
Trowel	Soft-bristle brush
Hand maul	Quick-setting cement
Chisel	Emery paper
Wire brush	Wire lath
Aviation snips	Masonry anchors
Drill	Concrete acrylic fortifier
Work gloves	Sand-mix concrete

Concrete slabs that slant toward the house can lead to foundation damage and a wet basement. Even a level slab near the foundation can cause problems. Consider asking a concrete contractor to fix it by mud-jacking, forcing wet concrete underneath the slab to lift the edge near the foundation.

HOW TO REPAIR SHAPED CONCRETE

Scrape all loose material and debris from the damaged area, then wipe down with water. Mix quick-setting cement and trowel it into the area. Work quickly—you only have a few minutes before concrete sets up.

Use the trowel or a putty knife to mold the concrete to follow the form of the object being repaired. Smooth the concrete as soon as it sets up. Buff with emery paper to smooth out any ridges after the repair dries.

HOW TO REPAIR MASONRY VENEER

Chip off the crumbled, loose, or deteriorated veneer from the wall, using a cold chisel and maul. Chisel away damaged veneer until you have only good, solid surface remaining. Use care to avoid damaging the wall behind the veneer. Clean the repair area with a wire brush.

Old metal lath

New metal lath

Clean up any metal lath in the repair area if it is in good condition. If not, cut it out with aviation snips. Add new lath where needed, using masonry anchors to hold it to the wall.

Mix fortified sand-mix concrete (or specialty concrete blends for wall repair), and trowel it over the lath until it is even with the surrounding surfaces.

Recreate the surface texture to match the surrounding area. For our project, we used a soft-bristled brush to stipple the surface. To blend in the repair, add pigment to the sand mixture or paint the repair area after it dries.

RESURFACING A CONCRETE WALKWAY

Concrete that has surface damage but is still structurally sound can be preserved by resurfacing—applying a thin layer of new concrete over the old surface. If the old surface has deep cracks or extensive damage, resurfacing will only solve the problem temporarily. Because new concrete will bond better if it is packed down, use a dry, stiff concrete mixture that can be compacted with a shovel.

Tools + Materials ▸

Shovel	Rubber mallet
Wood float	Level
Broom	Mortar bag
Circular saw	Stakes
Maul	2 × 4 lumber
Drill	Vegetable oil or commercial
Paintbrush	release agent
Paint roller and tray	4" drywall screws
Wheelbarrow	Sand-mix concrete
Screed board	Bonding adhesive
Groover	Plastic sheets
Edger	Brick pavers
Hose	Type N mortar
Bricklayer's trowel	Eye and ear protection
Jointer	Work gloves

Resurface concrete that has surface damage, such as spalling or popouts. Because the new surface will be thin (1" to 2"), use sand-mix concrete. If you are having ready-mix concrete delivered by a concrete contractor, make sure they do not use aggregate larger than ½" in the mixture.

HOW TO RESURFACE USING FRESH CONCRETE

Clean the surface thoroughly. If the surface is flaking or spalled, scrape it with a spade to dislodge as much loose concrete as you can, then sweep the surface clean.

Dig a 6"-wide trench around the surface on all sides to create room for 2 × 4 forms.

Stake 2 × 4 forms flush against the sides of the concrete slabs, 1" to 2" above the surface (make sure height is even). Drive stakes every 3 ft. and at every joint in forms. Mark control joint locations onto the outside of the forms directly above existing control joints. Coat the inside edges of the forms with vegetable oil or commercial release agent.

Apply a thin layer of bonding adhesive over the entire surface. Follow the directions on the bonding adhesive product carefully. Instructions for similar products may differ slightly.

Mix concrete, using sand-mix concrete. Make the mixture slightly stiffer (drier) than normal concrete. Spread the concrete, then press down on the concrete with a shovel or 2 × 4 to pack the mixture into the forms. Smooth the surface with a screed board.

Float the concrete with a wood float, then tool with an edger, and cut control joints in the original locations. Recreate any surface treatment, such as brooming, used on the original surface. Let the surface cure for one week, covered with plastic. Seal the concrete.

BUILDING CONCRETE STEPS

Designing steps requires some calculations and some trial and error. As long as the design meets safety guidelines, you can adjust elements such as the landing depth and the dimensions of the steps. Sketching your plan on paper will make the job easier.

Before demolishing your old steps, measure them to see if they meet safety guidelines. If so, you can use them as a reference for your new steps. If not, start from scratch so your new steps do not repeat any design errors.

For steps with more than two risers, you'll need to install a handrail. Ask a building inspector about other requirements.

Tools + Materials ▸

Tape measure	2 × 4 lumber
Sledge hammer	Steel rebar grid
Shovel	Wire
Drill	Bolsters
Reciprocating saw	Construction adhesive
Level	Compactible gravel
Mason's string	Fill material
Hand tamper	Exterior-grade
Mallet	¾" plywood
Concrete	2" deck screws
Concrete mixing tools	Isolation board
Screed board	#3 rebar
Jigsaw	Stakes
Clamps	Latex caulk
Ruler or	Vegetable oil
framing square	or commercial
Float	release agent
Step edger	Eye and ear protection
Broom	Work gloves

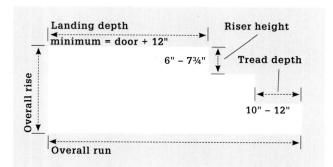

New concrete steps give a fresh, clean appearance to your house. And if your old steps are unstable, replacing them with concrete steps that have a non-skid surface will create a safer living environment.

HOW TO DESIGN STEPS

Attach a mason's string to the house foundation,
1" below the bottom of the door threshold. Drive a stake
where you want the base of the bottom step to fall. Attach the
other end of the string to the stake and use a line level to level
it. Measure the length of the string—this distance is the overall
depth, or run, of the steps.

**Measure down from the string to the bottom of the
stake** to determine the overall height, or rise, of the steps.
Divide the overall rise by the estimated number of steps. The
rise of each step should be between 6" and 8". For example, if
the overall rise is 21" and you plan to build three steps, the rise
of each step would be 7" (21 divided by 3), which falls within
the recommended safety range for riser height.

Measure the width of your door and add at least 12"; this
number is the minimum depth you should plan for the landing
area of the steps. The landing depth plus the depth of each
step should fit within the overall run of the steps. If necessary,
you can increase the overall run by moving the stake at
the planned base of the steps away from the house, or by
increasing the depth of the landing.

Sketch a detailed plan for the steps, keeping these
guidelines in mind: each step should be 10" to 12" deep, with
a riser height between 6" and 7¾", and the landing should be
at least 12" deeper than the swing radius (width) of your door.
Adjust the parts of the steps as needed, but stay within the
given ranges. Creating a final sketch will take time, but it is
worth doing carefully.

HOW TO BUILD CONCRETE STEPS

Remove or demolish existing steps; if the old steps are concrete, set aside the rubble to use as fill material for the new steps. Wear protective gear, including eye protection and gloves, when demolishing concrete.

Dig 12"-wide trenches to the required depth for footings. Locate the trenches perpendicular to the foundation, spaced so the footings will extend 3" beyond the outside edges of the steps. Install steel rebar grids for reinforcement. Affix isolation boards to the foundation wall inside each trench, using a few dabs of construction adhesive.

Mix the concrete and pour the footings. Level and smooth the concrete with a screed board. You do not need to float the surface afterwards.

When bleed water disappears, insert 12" sections of rebar 6" into the concrete, spaced at 12" intervals and centered side to side. Leave 1 ft. of clear space at each end.

Let the footings cure for two days, then excavate the area between them to 4" deep. Pour in a 5"-thick layer of compactible gravel subbase and tamp until it is level with the footings.

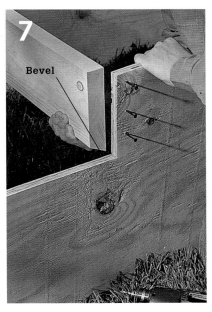

Transfer the measurements for the side forms from your working sketch onto ¾" exterior-grade plywood. Cut out the forms along the cutting lines, using a jigsaw. Save time by clamping two pieces of plywood together and cutting both side forms at the same time. Add a ⅛" per foot back-to-front slope to the landing part of the form.

Cut form boards for the risers to fit between the side forms. Bevel the bottom edges of the boards when cutting to create clearance for the float at the back edges of the steps. Attach the riser forms to the side forms with 2" deck screws.

Cut a 2 × 4 to make a center support for the riser forms. Use 2" deck screws to attach 2 × 4 cleats to the riser forms, then attach the support to the cleats. Check to make sure all corners are square.

Cut an isolation board and glue it to the house foundation at the back of the project area. Set the form onto the footings, flush against the isolation board. Add 2 × 4 bracing arms to the sides of the form, attaching them to cleats on the sides and to stakes driven into the ground.

(continued)

Fill the form with clean fill (broken concrete or rubble). Stack the fill carefully, keeping it 6" away from the sides, back, and top edges of the form. Shovel smaller fragments onto the pile to fill the void areas.

Lay pieces of #3 metal rebar on top of the fill at 12" intervals, and attach them to bolsters with wire to keep them from moving when the concrete is poured. Keep rebar at least 2" below the top of the forms. Mist the forms and the rubble with water.

Coat the forms with vegetable oil or a commercial release agent, then mist them with water so concrete won't stick to the forms. Mix concrete and pour steps one at a time, beginning at the bottom. Settle and smooth the concrete with a screed board. Press a piece of #3 rebar 1" down into the "nose" of each tread for reinforcement.

Float the steps, working the front edge of the float underneath the beveled edge at the bottom of each riser form.

14

Pour concrete into the forms for the remaining steps and the landing. Press rebar into the nose of each step. Keep an eye on the poured concrete as you work, and stop to float any concrete as soon as the bleed water disappears.

Shown cut away for clarity

OPTION: For railings with mounting plates that attach to sunken J-bolts, install the bolts before the concrete sets. Otherwise, choose railings with surface-mounted hardware (see step 16) that can be attached after the steps are completed.

15

Once the concrete sets, shape the steps and landing with a step edger. Float the surface. Sweep with a stiff-bristled broom for maximum traction.

16

Mounting plate

Remove the forms as soon as the surface is firm to the touch, usually within several hours. Smooth rough edges with a float. Add concrete to fill any holes. If forms are removed later, more patching may be required. Backfill the area around the base of the steps, and seal the concrete. Install a grippable hand railing that is securely anchored to the steps and the wall.

IDENTIFYING BRICK + BLOCK PROBLEMS

Inspect damaged brick and block structures closely before you begin any repair work. Accurately identifying the nature and cause of the damage is an important step before choosing the best solution for the problem and preventing the problems from recurring in the future.

Look for obvious clues, like overgrown tree roots, or damaged gutters that let water drain onto masonry surfaces. Also check the slope of the adjacent landscape; it may need to be regraded to direct water away from a brick or block wall. Water is the most common cause of problems, but major cracks that recur can be a sign of serious structural problems that should be examined by an engineer.

Repairs fail when the original source of the problem is not eliminated prior to making the repair. When a concrete patch separates, for example, it means that the opposing stresses causing the crack are still at work on the structure. Find and correct the cause (often a failing subbase or stress from water or freezing and thawing), then redo the repair.

TYPES OF BRICK + BLOCK PROBLEMS

Deteriorated mortar joints are common problems in brick and block structures—mortar is softer than most bricks or blocks and is more prone to damage. Deterioration is not always visible, so probe surrounding joints with a screwdriver to see if they are sound.

Major structural damage, like the damage to this brick porch, usually requires removal of the existing structure, improvements to the subbase, and reconstruction of the structure. Projects of this nature should only be attempted by professional masons.

Damage to concrete blocks often results from repeated freezing and thawing of moisture trapped in the wall or in the blocks themselves. Instead of replacing the whole block, chip out the face of the block and replace it with a concrete paver with the same dimensions as the face of the block.

Spalling occurs when freezing water or other forces cause enough directional pressure to fracture a brick. The best solution is to replace the entire brick while eliminating the source of the pressure, if possible. *TIP: Chip off a piece of the damaged brick to use as a color reference when looking for a replacement.*

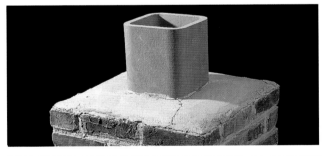

Damaged mortar caps on chimneys allow water into the flue area, where it can damage the chimney and even the roof or interior walls. Small-scale damage (top photo) can be patched with fire-rated silicone caulk. If damage is extensive (bottom photo), repair or replace the mortar cap.

Stains and discoloration can be caused by external sources or by minerals leeching to the surface from within the brick or block (called efflorescence). If the stain does not wash away easily with water, use a cleaning solution.

REPAIRING BRICK + BLOCK WALLS

The most common brick and block wall repair is tuck-pointing, the process of replacing failed mortar joints with fresh mortar. Tuck-pointing is a highly useful repair technique for any homeowner. It can be used to repair walls, chimneys, brick veneer, or any other structure where the bricks or blocks are bonded with mortar.

Minor cosmetic repairs can be attempted on any type of wall, from free-standing garden walls to block foundations. Filling minor cracks with caulk or repair compound, and patching popouts or chips are good examples of minor repairs. Consult a professional before attempting any major repairs, like replacing brick or blocks, or rebuilding a structure—especially if you are dealing with a load-bearing structure.

Basement walls are a frequent trouble area for homeowners. Constant moisture and stress created by ground contact can cause leaks, bowing, and paint failure. Small leaks and cracks can be patched with hydraulic cement. Masonry-based waterproofing products can be applied to give deteriorated walls a fresh appearance. Persistent moisture problems are most often caused by improper grading of soil around the foundation or a malfunctioning downspout and gutter system.

NOTE: The repairs shown in this section feature brick and block walls. The same techniques may be used for other brick and block structures.

Tools + Materials ▶

Raking tool	Drill and masonry-cutting disc and bit
Mortar hawk	
Tuck-pointer	Mortar
Jointing tool	Gravel
Bricklayer's hammer	Scrap of metal flashing
Mason's trowel	Concrete fortifier
Mason's or stone chisel	Replacement bricks or blocks
Pointing trowel	Eye and ear protection
Stiff-bristle brush	Work gloves

Make timely repairs to brick and block structures. Tuck-pointing deteriorated mortar joints is a common repair that, like other types of repair, improves the appearance of the structure or surface and helps prevent further damage.

EXTERIOR REPAIRS

HOW TO TUCK-POINT MORTAR JOINTS

Clean out loose or deteriorated mortar to a depth of ¼" to ¾". Use a mortar raking tool (top) first, then switch to a masonry chisel and a hammer (bottom) if the mortar is stubborn. Clear away all loose debris, and dampen the surface with water before applying fresh mortar.

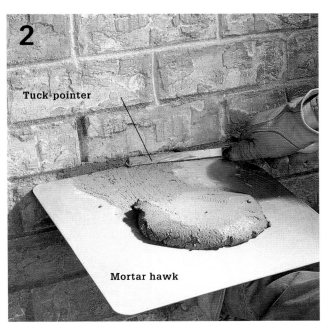

Mix the mortar, adding concrete fortifier; add tint if necessary. Load mortar onto a mortar hawk, then push it into the horizontal joints with a tuck-pointer. Apply mortar in ¼"-thick layers, and let each layer dry for 30 minutes before applying another. Fill the joints until the mortar is flush with the face of the brick or block.

Apply the first layer of mortar into the vertical joints by scooping mortar onto the back of a tuck-pointer, and pressing it into the joint. Work from the top downward.

After the final layer of mortar is applied, smooth the joints with a jointing tool that matches the profile of the old mortar joints. Tool the horizontal joints first. Let the mortar dry until it is crumbly, then brush off the excess mortar with a stiff-bristle brush.

HOW TO REPLACE A DAMAGED BRICK

Score the damaged brick so it will break apart more easily for removal: use a drill with a masonry-cutting disc to score lines along the surface of the brick and in the mortar joints surrounding the brick.

Use a mason's chisel and hammer to break apart the damaged brick along the scored lines. Rap sharply on the chisel with the hammer, being careful not to damage surrounding bricks. *TIP: Save fragments to use as a color reference when you shop for replacement bricks.*

Chisel out any remaining mortar in the cavity, then brush out debris with a stiff-bristle or wire brush to create a clean surface for the new mortar. Rinse the surface of the repair area with water.

Mix the mortar for the repair, adding concrete fortifier to the mixture, and tint if needed to match old mortar. Use a pointing trowel to apply a 1"-thick layer of mortar at the bottom and sides of the cavity.

Dampen the replacement brick slightly, then apply mortar to the ends and top of the brick. Fit the brick into the cavity and rap it with the handle of the trowel until the face is flush with the surrounding bricks. If needed, press additional mortar into the joints with a pointing trowel.

Scrape away excess mortar with a masonry trowel, then smooth the joints with a jointing tool that matches the profile of the surrounding mortar joints. Let the mortar set until crumbly, then brush the joints to remove excess mortar.

Tips for Removing + Replacing Several Bricks ▸

For walls with extensive damage, remove bricks from the top down, one row at a time, until the entire damaged area is removed. Replace bricks using the techniques shown above and in the section on building with brick and block. *Caution: Do not dismantle load-bearing brick structures like foundation walls—consult a professional mason for these repairs.*

For walls with internal damaged areas, remove only the damaged section, keeping the upper layers intact if they are in good condition. Do not remove more than four adjacent bricks in one area—if the damaged area is larger, it will require temporary support, which is a job for a professional mason.

HOW TO REFACE A DAMAGED CONCRETE BLOCK

Drill several holes into the face of the deteriorated block at the cores (hollow spots) of the block using a drill and masonry bit. Wear protective eye covering when drilling or breaking apart concrete.

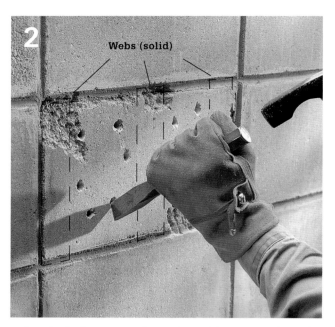

Using the holes as starting points, chip away the face of the block over the core areas, using a chisel and hammer. Be careful not to damage surrounding blocks and try to leave the block face intact in front of the solid web areas.

Use a stone chisel to carefully chip out a 2"-deep recess in the web areas. Mark and score cutting lines 2" back from the block face, then chisel away the block in the recess area. Avoid deepening the recess more than 2" because the remaining web sections provide a bonding surface for the concrete paver that will be installed to replace the face of the concrete block.

Mix mortar, then apply a 1"-thick layer to the sides and bottom of the opening, to the webs, and to the top edge and web locations on the paver (use an 8 × 16" paver to fit standard blocks). Press the paver into the cavity, flush with the surrounding blocks. Add mortar to the joints if needed, then prop a 2 × 4 against the paver until the mortar sets. Finish the joints with a jointing tool.

HOW TO REINFORCE A SECTION OF REFACED BLOCKS

Reinforce repair areas spanning two or more adjacent block faces. Start by drilling a few holes in a small area over a core in the block located directly above the repair area. Chip out the block face between the holes with a cold chisel.

Prepare a thin mortar mix made from 1 part gravel and 2 parts dry mortar, then add water. The mixture should be thin enough to pour easily, but not soupy. *NOTE: Adding small amounts of gravel increases the strength of the mortar and increases the yield of the batch.*

Pour the mortar/gravel mixture into the hole above the repair area, using a piece of metal flashing as a funnel. Continue mixing and filling the hole until it will not accept any more mortar. The mortar will dry to form a reinforcing column that is bonded to the backs of the pavers used to reface the blocks.

Patch the hole above the repair area by using a pointing trowel to fill the hole with plain mortar mix. Smooth the surface with the pointing trowel. When the mortar resists finger pressure, finish the joint below the patch with a jointing tool.

PAINTING BRICK + BLOCK

Check brick and block surfaces annually and remove stains or discoloration. Most problems are easy to correct if they are treated in a timely fashion. Regular maintenance will help brick and block structures remain attractive and durable for a long time. Refer to the information below for cleaning tips that address specific staining problems.

Painted brick and block structures can be spruced up by applying a fresh coat of paint. As with any other painting job, thorough surface preparation and a quality primer are critical to a successful outcome.

Many stains can be removed easily, using a commercial brick and block detergent, available at home centers, but remember:

- Always test cleaning solutions on a small inconspicuous part of the surface and evaluate the results.
- Some chemicals and their fumes may be harmful. Be sure to follow manufacturer's safety and use recommendations. Wear protective clothing.
- Soak the surface to be cleaned with water before you apply any solutions. This keeps solutions from soaking in too quickly. Rinse the surface thoroughly after cleaning to wash off any remaining cleaning solution.

Use a pressure washer to clean large brick and block structures. Pressure washers can be rented from most rental centers. Be sure to obtain detailed operating and safety instructions from the rental agent.

Solvent Solutions for Common Brick + Block Blemishes ›

- **Egg splatter:** Dissolve oxalic acid crystals in water, following manufacturer's instructions, in a nonmetallic container. Brush onto the surface.
- **Efflorescence:** Scrub surface with a stiff-bristled brush. Use a household cleaning solution for surfaces with heavy accumulation.
- **Iron stains:** Spray or brush a solution of oxalic acid crystals dissolved in water, following manufacturer's instructions. Apply directly to the stain.
- **Ivy:** Cut vines away from the surface (do not pull them off). Let remaining stems dry up, then scrub them off with a stiff-bristled brush and household cleaning solution.
- **Oil:** Apply a paste made of mineral spirits and an inert material like sawdust.
- **Paint stains:** Remove new paint with a solution of trisodium phosphate (TSP) and water, following manufacturer's mixing instructions. Old paint can usually be removed with heavy scrubbing or sandblasting.
- **Plant growth:** Use weed killer according to manufacturer's directions.
- **Smoke stains:** Scrub surface with household cleanser containing bleach, or use a mixture of ammonia and water.

Tips for Cleaning Brick + Block Surfaces ▸

Mix a paste made from cleaning solvents (chart, opposite page) and talcum or flour. Apply paste directly to stain, let it dry, then scrape it off with a vinyl or plastic scraper.

Use a nylon scraper or a thin block of wood to remove spilled mortar that has hardened. Avoid using metal scrapers, which can damage masonry surfaces.

Mask off windows, siding, decorative millwork, and other exposed nonmasonry surfaces before cleaning brick and block. Careful masking is essential if you are using harsh cleaning chemicals, such as muriatic acid.

Tips for Painting Masonry ▸

Clean mortar joints, using a drill with a wire wheel attachment before applying paint. Scrub off loose paint, dirt, mildew, and mineral deposits so the paint will bond better.

Apply masonry primer before repainting brick or block walls. Primer helps eliminate stains and prevent problems such as efflorescence.

REPAIRING STONEWORK

Damage to stonework is typically caused by frost heave, erosion or deterioration of mortar, or by stones that have worked out of place. Dry-stone walls are more susceptible to erosion and popping, while mortared walls develop cracks that admit water, which can freeze and cause further damage.

Inspect stone structures once a year for signs of damage and deterioration. Replacing a stone or repointing crumbling mortar now will save you work in the long run.

A leaning stone column or wall probably suffers from erosion or foundation problems, and can be dangerous if neglected. If you have the time, you can tear down and rebuild dry-laid structures, but mortared structures with excessive lean need professional help.

Stones in a wall can become dislodged due to soil settling, erosion, or seasonal freeze-thaw cycles. Make the necessary repairs before the problem migrates to other areas.

Tools + Materials ▸

Maul	Wood shims
Chisel	Trowels for mixing and pointing
Camera	Carpet-covered 2 × 4
Shovel	Chalk
Hand tamper	Compactible gravel
Level	Replacement stones
Batter gauge	Type M mortar
Stiff-bristle brush	Mortar tint
Mortar bag	Eye and ear protection
Masonry chisels	Work gloves

Tips for Replacing Popped Stones ▸

Return a popped stone to its original position. If other stones have settled in its place, drive shims between neighboring stones to make room for the popped stone. Be careful not to wedge too far.

Use a 2 × 4 covered with carpet to avoid damaging the stone when hammering it into place. After hammering, make sure a replacement stone hasn't damaged or dislodged the adjoining stones.

HOW TO REBUILD A DRY-STONE WALL SECTION

Before you start, study the wall and determine how much of it needs to be rebuilt. Plan to dismantle the wall in a "V" shape, centered on the damaged section. Number each stone and mark its orientation with chalk so you can rebuild it following the original design. *TIP: Photograph the wall, making sure the markings are visible.*

Capstones are often set in a mortar bed atop the last course of stone. You may need to chip out the mortar with a maul and chisel to remove the capstones. Remove the marked stones, taking care to check the overall stability of the wall as you work.

Rebuild the wall, one course at a time, using replacement stones only when necessary. Start each course at the ends and work toward the center. On thick walls, set the face stones first, then fill in the center with smaller stones. Check your work with a level, and use a batter gauge to maintain the batter of the wall. If your capstones were mortared, re-lay them in fresh mortar. Wash off the chalk with water and a stiff-bristle brush.

Tip ▶

If you're rebuilding because of erosion, dig a trench at least 6" deep under the damaged area, and fill it with compactible gravel. Tamp the gravel with a hand tamper. This will improve drainage and prevent water from washing soil out from beneath the wall.

Tips for Repairing Mortared Stone Walls ▸

Tint mortar for repair work so it blends with the existing mortar. Mix several samples of mortar, adding a different amount of tint to each, and allow them to dry thoroughly. Compare each sample to the old mortar, and choose the closest match.

Use a mortar bag to restore weathered and damaged mortar joints over an entire structure. Remove loose mortar (see below) and clean all surfaces with a stiff-bristle brush and water. Dampen the joints before tuck-pointing, and cover all of the joints, smoothing and brushing as necessary.

HOW TO REPOINT MORTAR JOINTS

Carefully rake out cracked and crumbling mortar, stopping when you reach solid mortar. Remove loose mortar and debris with a stiff-bristle brush. *TIP: Rake the joints with a chisel and maul, or make your own raking tool by placing an old screwdriver in a vice and bending the shaft about 45°.*

Mix type M mortar, then dampen the repair surfaces with clean water. Working from the top down, pack mortar into the crevices, using a pointing trowel. Smooth the mortar when it has set up enough to resist light finger pressure. Remove excess mortar with a stiff-bristle brush.

HOW TO REPLACE A STONE IN A MORTARED WALL

Remove the damaged stone by chiseling out the surrounding mortar, using a masonry chisel or a modified screwdriver (opposite page). Drive the chisel toward the damaged stone to avoid harming neighboring stones. Once the stone is out, chisel the surfaces inside the cavity as smooth as possible.

Brush out the cavity to remove loose mortar and debris. Test the surrounding mortar, and chisel or scrape out any mortar that isn't firmly bonded.

Dry-fit the replacement stone. The stone should be stable in the cavity and blend with the rest of the wall. You can mark the stone with chalk and cut it to fit, but excessive cutting will result in a conspicuous repair.

Mist the stone and cavity lightly, then apply type M mortar around the inside of the cavity, using a trowel. Butter all mating sides of the replacement stone. Insert the stone and wiggle it forcefully to remove any air pockets. Use a pointing trowel to pack the mortar solidly around the stone. Smooth the mortar when it has set up.

PRESSURE WASHING MASONRY

To clean the masonry and stonework surfaces around the outside of your home, there is nothing that works faster or more effectively than a pressure washer. A typical residential-grade unit can be as much as 50 times more powerful than a standard garden hose, while using up to 80% less water.

Pressure washing is quite simple: firmly grasp the spray wand with both hands, depress the trigger and move the nozzle across the surface to be cleaned. Although different surfaces require different spray patterns and pressure settings, it is not difficult to determine the appropriate cleaning approach for each project. The nozzle is adjustable—from a low-pressure, wide-fan spray for general cleaning and rinsing, to a narrow, intense stream for stubborn stains. But the easiest way to control the cleaning is to simply adjust the distance between the nozzle and the surface—move the nozzle back to reduce the pressure; move the nozzle closer to intensify it.

To successfully clean any masonry or stone surface using a pressure washer, follow these tips:

- When cleaning a new surface, start in an inconspicuous area, with a wide spray pattern and the nozzle 4- to 5-ft. from the surface. Move closer to the surface until the desired effect is achieved.

- Keep the nozzle in constant motion, spraying at a steady speed with long, even strokes to ensure consistent results.
- Maintain a consistent distance between the nozzle and the cleaning surface.
- When cleaning heavily soiled or stained surfaces, use cleaning detergents formulated for pressure washers. Always rinse the surface before applying the detergent. On vertical surfaces, apply detergent from bottom to top, and rinse from top to bottom. Always follow the detergent manufacturer's directions.
- After pressure washing, always seal the surface with an appropriate surface sealer (e.g., concrete sealer for cement driveways), following the product manufacturer's instructions.

Tools + Materials ▸

Pressure sprayer
Cleaning solution
Eye and ear protection
Work gloves

Pressure Washer Safety ▸

- Always wear eye protection.
- Do not wear open-toed shoes.
- Make sure the unit is on a stable surface and the cleaning area has adequate slopes and drainage to prevent puddles.
- Assume a solid stance, and firmly grasp the spray gun with both hands to avoid injury if the gun kicks back.
- Always keep the high-pressure hose connected to both the pump and the spray gun while the system is pressurized.
- Never aim the nozzle at people or animals—the high-pressure stream of water can cause serious injury.

Tips for Pressure Washing Masonry ▸

Even steady path

Always keep the nozzle in motion, spraying at a steady speed and using long, even strokes. Take multiple passes over heavily soiled areas. Take care not to dwell on one spot for too long, especially when using narrow, high-pressure spray patterns.

Hold the spray wand so that the nozzle distributes the spray pattern across the surface evenly. Holding the nozzle at too low an angle can cause an uneven spray pattern, resulting in "zebra striping." Also, maintain a consistent distance between the nozzle and the cleaning surface to ensure consistent results and help flush dirt and debris from the area.

Work in identifiable sections, such as the area between the expansion joints in concrete. If there is a slope, work downhill to promote drainage and help flush away dirt and debris. Wet entire surface to prevent streaking.

To prevent streaks on vertical surfaces, always begin pressure washing or applying cleaning detergent at the bottom of the surface, then work upward. When rinsing, start at the top and work downward—gravity will help the clean water flush away dirt, debris, and detergent residue.

REPAIRING AN ASPHALT DRIVEWAY

The two most popular hard surface driveway materials are asphalt and concrete. Both are used, almost interchangeably, throughout the country in cold and hot climates. But there are some basic differences. Concrete generally costs more to install and asphalt generally costs more to maintain as the years go by. And, concrete doesn't always perform well in cold areas. It's susceptible to damage from the freeze-and-thaw cycle and it can be damaged by exposure to road salt. Asphalt, on the other hand, doesn't always perform well in hot climates. It absorbs a lot of heat from the sun and tends to stay soft during very hot periods. And, of course, when the surface is soft, it can wear more quickly.

A typical asphalt driveway is formed by pouring and compressing a layer of hot asphalt over a subbase of compacted gravel.

Tools + Materials ▸

Driveway cleaner or detergent
Brushes
Work gloves

Eye protection
Cold chisel
Hammer
Vacuum

Asphalt patching compound
Trowel
Asphalt crack filler
Caulk gun

Driveway sealer
Squeegee brush

HOW TO REPAIR AN ASPHALT DRIVEWAY

Carefully inspect the asphalt surface for any oil and grease stains. Then remove them with driveway cleaner or household detergent. Scrub the cleaner into the surface with a soft brush and rinse the area clean with a garden hose. Repeat until the stain is gone. If using driveway cleaner, wear the recommended safety equipment.

Once the stains are removed, thoroughly rinse the entire driveway with a garden hose and nozzle. The goal is to wash away any debris and to remove the dust and dirt from the surface cracks.

EXTERIOR REPAIRS

Repair the small cracks first. Chip out any loose debris with a cold chisel and hammer. Then clean out all debris with a wire brush. Remove all the dust with a shop vacuum. A crevice tool on the end of the hose will do the best job.

Place asphalt patching compound in the holes with a small trowel. Overfill the hole so the patch material is about ½" higher than the surrounding asphalt surface.

Compact the patch material with a small piece of 2 × 4. Tamp the board up and down with your hand, or strike the board with a hammer. Keep working until you can't compress the patch any more.

Finish the patch by covering it with a piece of 2 × 6 and striking it with a hammer or mallet. Work back and forth across the board to smooth out the entire patch and make it flush to the surrounding surface.

(continued)

On narrower patches, the compound can be smoothed with a small trowel. Just move the tool across the surrounding surface and then over the patch. This should flatten the patch. Finish up by compressing the compound by pushing it down with the trowel.

Prepare larger potholes by undercutting the edges with a cold chisel and a hammer. Then, remove all the debris and fill the hole with cold-patch asphalt mix. Working directly from the bag or bucket, fill the hole about 1 in. higher than the surrounding surface. Then compact it with a 2 × 4, as before.

One great way to compress cold-patch asphalt is to cover the patch with a piece of plywood. Then, drive your car onto the plywood and stop when one tire is centered on the panel. Wait a few minutes, then move the car back and forth a few times.

Once the hole patching is done, fill the routine cracks (less than ¼" wide) with asphalt crack filler. This material comes in a caulk tube, which makes it very easy to apply. Just clean the crack with a wire brush and a vacuum, then squeeze the filler into the crack.

After the crack filler has cured for about 10 or 15 minutes, smooth it out with a putty knife as you force the filler down into the crack. If this creates small depressions, fill these with a second application of filler.

Driveway sealer should always be mixed thoroughly before use. Take a 2× stir stick that's about 30 in. long and stir the sealer until it has a uniform consistency. Pour out enough to cover a strip across the driveway that's about 3-ft. or 4-ft. wide.

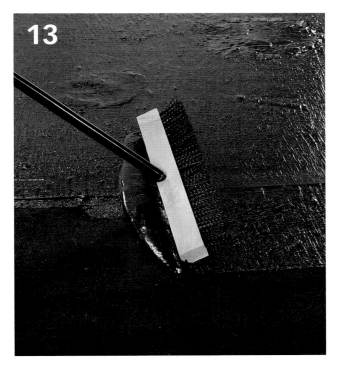

Spread the sealer with the squeegee side of the application brush. Try to keep this coat as uniform as possible. Work the sealer into the small cracks and pull it gently over the big patches.

Flip the squeegee over to the brush side and smooth out the lap marks and other irregularities that were left from the application coat. Work at right angles to the first pass.

MAINTAINING A WOOD DECK

Inspect your deck at least once a year, more often if the weather over any given season is especially severe. Replace loose or rusting hardware or fasteners as soon as you detect them to prevent future problems. Apply a new coat of sealant as necessary, according to the requirements of the type of wood or other material used in your deck.

Carefully inspect the deck surface, railings, and structure for signs of damage. Replace or reinforce damaged wood as soon as possible. Replace damaged composite decking if it is split or otherwise compromised.

Restore an older, weathered deck to its original wood color and luster with a deck-brightening product. Brighteners are available at most hardware stores and home centers.

NOTE: Even the sharpest DIYer cannot spot many signs that a deck has developed dangerous structural issues. Especially if your deck is more than ten years old, hire a professional deck inspector to examine it.

Inspect the entire deck, including underneath. Look for signs of rot, damage, or wear. Probe suspect areas with a screwdriver or awl to determine the extent of any rot. Apply a sealant or new finish regularly, as required for the wood in your deck.

Tools + Materials ▸

Flashlight	Putty knife	Eye protection	Deck brightener
Awl or screwdriver	Scrub brush	Pressure sprayer	Work gloves
Screwgun	Rubber gloves	2½" deck screws	

MAINTAINING AN OLDER DECK

1

Use an awl or screwdriver to check the deck for soft, rotted wood. Replace or reinforce damaged wood.

2

Clean debris from cracks between decking boards with a putty knife. Debris traps moisture and can cause wood to rot.

3

Drive new fasteners to secure loose decking to joists. If using the old nail or screw holes, new fasteners should be slightly longer than the originals.

HOW TO RENEW A DECK

Mix deck cleaning solution as directed by the manufacturer. Apply the solution with a pressure sprayer and let it set for 10 minutes.

Scrub the deck thoroughly with a stiff scrub brush. Wear rubber gloves and eye protection.

Rinse the deck with clear water. If necessary, apply a second coat of cleaner to extremely dirty or stained areas. Rinse and let dry. Apply a fresh coat of waterproofing sealer or stain.

EXTERIOR REPAIRS

Power Washing ▸

An alternative to hand scrubbing a deck, power washing can be an economical way to clean and prepare even a large deck for sealant in the space of a few hours. Inexpensive home power washers don't always have enough power to completely strip the accumulated coating of dirt and debris off a deck. Instead, rent a gas-powered unit from a local rental center. Use a medium number 2 or 3 nozzle and hold the jet of water about 4 to 6" off the surface of the wood. You can easily clean to the bare wood with one slow pass. Apply a sealant/protectant as soon as the wood dries. Do not use too much water pressure, however, as that may damage the wood.

REPAIRING A DECK

Replace or reinforce damaged deck wood as soon as possible. Wood rot can spread and weaken solid wood.

After replacing or reinforcing the rotted wood, clean the entire deck and apply a fresh coat of clear sealer-preservative or staining sealer. Apply a fresh coat of finish each year to prevent future water damage. If you need to repair more than a few small areas, it is probably time to replace the entire deck.

Be aware that if your deck is older, newer building codes may require more substantial support or loadbearing members or different styles of hangers or post hardware. If it is time to update or even replace your deck, start by consulting the local building department to learn about the best materials, methods, and practices for your area.

Tools + Materials ▶

Cat's paw	Ratchet wrench
Flat pry bar	Sealer-preservative
Screwgun	or staining sealer
Awl or screwdriver	Galvanized nails (6d, 10d)
Hammer	Deck lumber
Chisel	Baking soda
Eye protection	Corrosion-resistant
Pressure washer	deck screws
Circular saw	⅝" masonry anchor
Scrub brush	⅜" lag screw
Paintbrush	Rubber gloves
Hydraulic jack	Bucket
Drill or hammer drill	Concrete block
⅝" masonry bit	Scrap plywood
Level	

HOW TO REPAIR DAMAGED DECKING + JOISTS

Remove nails or screws from the damaged decking board if you can. Remove the damaged board.

Inspect the underlying joists for signs of rotted wood. Joists with discolored, soft areas should be repaired and reinforced.

Use a mallet and chisel to remove any rotted portions of the joist.

Apply a sealer-preservative to the damaged joist. Let it dry, then apply a second coat of sealer. Cut a reinforcing joist (sister joist) from pressure-treated lumber. *NOTE: Consult local building codes; they may dictate using larger lumber to support the joist, or replacing the existing hanging hardware for newer technology.*

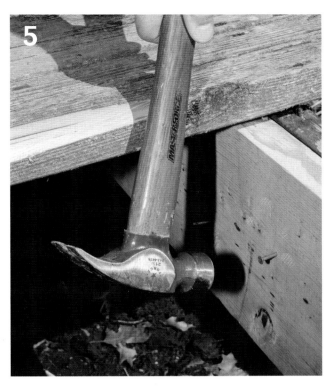

Position the sister joist tightly against the damaged joist, and fasten it in place with 10d nails or screws driven every 2'.

Joist hanger location

Attach the sister joist to the ledger and the header joist. Cut replacement decking boards from matching lumber using a metal joist hanger. You may tack the joist in place with a nail prior to installing the hangers.

If the existing decking is gray, "weather" the new decking by scrubbing it with a solution made from 1 cup baking soda and 1 gallon of warm water. Rinse and let dry.

(continued)

Apply a coat of sealer-preservative or staining sealer to all sides of the new decking boards.

Position the new boards and fasten them to the joists with galvanized deck screws. Make sure the space between boards matches that of the existing decking.

HOW TO REPLACE A POST ON A LOW DECK

Build a support using plywood scraps, a concrete block and a hydraulic jack. Place plywood between the head of the jack and the beam. Apply just enough pressure to lift the beam slightly. *NOTE: Because of code revisions, you may be required to replace old posts with larger lumber. Check with your local building department.*

Remove any nails or screws holding the damaged post to the post anchor or anchor pad and to the beam. Remove the damaged post and anchor pad or post anchor. Clean the concrete pier of any debris.

If an anchor pad was previously used, use a drill and ⅜" masonry bit to drill a hole in the concrete pier. Insert a ⅜" masonry anchor. If the post was held in place by a metal post anchor, you may be able to use the existing hole.

Position a galvanized post anchor on the pier block, and thread a ⅜" lag screw with washer through the hole in the anchor and into the masonry anchor. Tighten the screw with a ratchet wrench.

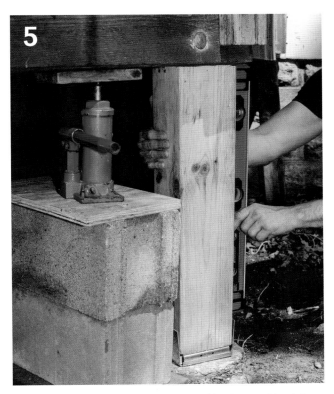

Cut a new post from pressure-treated lumber, and treat the cut ends with sealer-preservative. Position the post and make sure it is plumb.

Attach the bottom of the post to the post anchor using the recommended fasteners. Attach the post to the beam by redriving the lag screws, using a ratchet wrench. Release the pressure on the jack and remove the temporary support.

HOW TO REPAIR POPPED DECKING NAILS

The cure for most popped nails is simply to remove the nail. Use a nail extractor, cat's paw, or a claw hammer, using a scrap of wood or other protective surface to limit damage to the deck surface. Once the nail is removed, drive a 3" galvanized deck screw down through the nail hole.

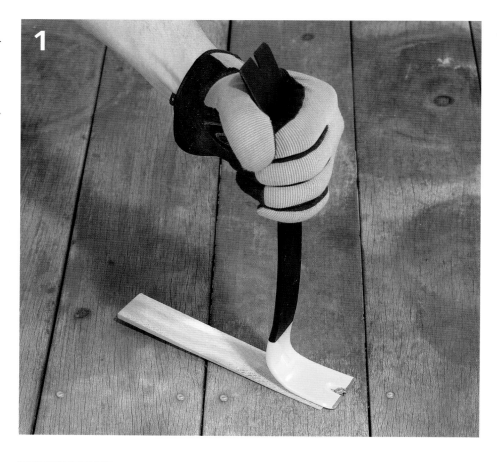

Where a nail has come loose from the joist below, but the head is still securely buried in the board, digging the popped nail out would damage the board. Instead, drive a 3" galvanized deck screw right next to the nail, so that the screw head overlaps the nail head.

HOW TO REFACE A ROTTED DECK EDGE

Measure the deck overhang from the joist outward.
Decide how far back you want to cut the edge of the deck
(usually about ½" to ¾" less than the measurement from
the joist).

Transfer that measurement to the two end boards on the
deck. Drive nails into the boards and snap a chalk line between
them to create the cut line.

Use a circular saw to cut along the chalk line. Depending
on how much you've cut off and what type of material
the decking is, you may need to seal the ends with a
waterproof protectant/sealant.

Cut a cedar, redwood, or pressure treated 1 × 2 to length
to cover the edges. Scarf any joints that are necessary along
the edging. Use 2½" galvanized deck screws to fasten the 2 × 2
in place. As an alternative, you can stain the 2 × 2 edging in a
contrasting shade from the deck, and seal it before fastening
to the edge.

CLEANING VINYL + COMPOSITE DECKING

Vinyl, recycled plastic, aluminum, and composite decking may be easier to maintain and is often more durable than solid wood, but these materials aren't completely exempt from a bit of cosmetic cleanup now and again. Non-wood decking will get dirty and stained in the course of normal use, and you'll need to use different cleaning products, depending on the type of stain. Although it may be tempting to pull out the pressure washer and give your deck a good going over, pressure washers can harm some types of synthetic decking and may even void your deck warranty (check with the manufacturer of your particular decking). A little elbow grease and the right cleaners are often a better approach. Here are suggestions for cleaning various types of stains and marks from vinyl, plastic, or composite decking. Be sure to wear safety glasses and protective gloves when working with strong chemicals.

Dirt & tree sap: Remove ordinary residue from foot traffic, bird droppings, or tree sap with household dish soap diluted with water. Mix a strong concentration in a bucket, scrub the stains, and rinse with clean water.

Fastener, leaf, or tannin: Steel fasteners, tree leaves, or resin stains from cedar or redwood can leave dark tannin stains on composite decking. To remove these, spray on a deck brightener/cleaner product that contains oxalic or phosphoric acid, then flush the surface with lots of fresh water.

Oil & grease: Oil and grease spots from barbecuing or tanning lotions should be cleaned immediately, before they dry. Use a household degreaser (such as an orange citrus cleaner), Simple Green, or ammonia and a scrub brush to remove the stain. Follow with soapy water and thorough rinsing.

Mold & mildew: Use a mildew and stain remover formulated specifically for use on composites or PVC decking to kill off mold and mildew growth. A good preventive measure is to scrub and wash your deck at least once a season, especially in shady or damp areas where mold and mildew are likely to grow.

Berry & wine: Use a dilute solution of household bleach and water to spot-clean wine or berry stains from decking (only after checking manufacturer's recommendations to ensure the solution won't damage the decking). Depending on the depth of the stain, you may not be able to remove it entirely, but generally these stains will fade over time.

Crayon & marker: If you have young kids, sooner or later crayon or marker stains are inevitable. The trick to removing them is using the correct solvent. Mineral spirits will remove crayon wax, and soapy water cleans up water-based marker stains. Use denatured alcohol (available at home centers) to remove dye-based, permanent markers.

HOW TO STOP DECK SWAY

Measure 24" down from where the post meets the beam. Clearly mark that point on the post.

Measure 24" from one edge of the post out along the beam. Mark that point on the beam. Repeat on the other side of the beam. Measure from the mark on the beam to the mark on the post. Add 4" for the total length of the brace.

Hold the brace in place between the mark on the post and the mark on the beam, so that the marks intersect the brace on center. Mark the brace for the angled end cuts, using the underside of the beam and edge of the post as straightedges.

TOP: Use a miter saw to make the angled end cuts. Place the brace in position and drill top and bottom pilot holes (two at each location), and then screw the brace to the post and beam using 6" lag screws.

BOTTOM: Fasten the brace to the underlying deck joists by drilling pilot holes through the post and into the brace and securing again with carriage bolts.

HOW TO STIFFEN A SPONGY DECK

1

Measure the space between joists. Use this measurement to cut blocking from pressure treated lumber the same size as the joists. Snap a chalkline down the center of the joists' span. A more permanent (but much more expensive and difficult) solution is to add new intermediate joists.

2

Tap the blocking in place, positioning blocks in an alternating pattern with one block to the left and one to the right of the chalk line.

3

Screw through the joists into the end of the blocks on each side using 3" galvanized decking screws.

METRIC CONVERSIONS

Metric Conversions

TO CONVERT:	TO:	MULTIPLY BY:
Inches	Millimeters	25.4
Inches	Centimeters	2.54
Feet	Meters	0.305
Yards	Meters	0.914
Square inches	Square centimeters	6.45
Square feet	Square meters	0.093
Square yards	Square meters	0.836
Ounces	Milliliters	30.0
Pints (U.S.)	Liters	0.473 (Imp. 0.568)
Quarts (U.S.)	Liters	0.946 (Imp. 1.136)
Gallons (U.S.)	Liters	3.785 (Imp. 4.546)
Ounces	Grams	28.4
Pounds	Kilograms	0.454

TO CONVERT:	TO:	MULTIPLY BY:
Millimeters	Inches	0.039
Centimeters	Inches	0.394
Meters	Feet	3.28
Meters	Yards	1.09
Square centimeters	Square inches	0.155
Square meters	Square feet	10.8
Square meters	Square yards	1.2
Milliliters	Ounces	.033
Liters	Pints (U.S.)	2.114 (Imp. 1.76)
Liters	Quarts (U.S.)	1.057 (Imp. 0.88)
Liters	Gallons (U.S.)	0.264 (Imp. 0.22)
Grams	Ounces	0.035
Kilograms	Pounds	2.2

Converting Temperatures

Convert degrees Fahrenheit (F) to degrees Celsius (C) by following this simple formula: Subtract 32 from the Fahrenheit temperature reading. Then, multiply that number by $\frac{5}{9}$. For example, 77°F − 32 = 45. 45 × $\frac{5}{9}$ = 25°C.

To convert degrees Celsius to degrees Fahrenheit, multiply the Celsius temperature reading by $\frac{9}{5}$. Then, add 32. For example, 25°C × $\frac{9}{5}$ = 45. 45 + 32 = 77°F.

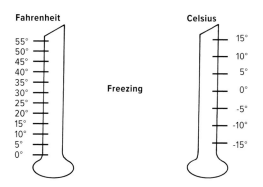

Metric Plywood Panels

Metric plywood panels are commonly available in two sizes: 1,200 mm × 2,400 mm and 1,220 mm × 2,400 mm, which is roughly equivalent to a 4 × 8-ft. sheet. Standard and Select sheathing panels come in standard thicknesses, while Sanded grade panels are available in special thicknesses.

STANDARD SHEATHING GRADE		SANDED GRADE	
7.5 mm	($\frac{5}{16}$ in.)	6 mm	($\frac{4}{17}$ in.)
9.5 mm	($\frac{3}{8}$ in.)	8 mm	($\frac{5}{16}$ in.)
12.5 mm	($\frac{1}{2}$ in.)	11 mm	($\frac{7}{16}$ in.)
15.5 mm	($\frac{5}{8}$ in.)	14 mm	($\frac{9}{16}$ in.)
18.5 mm	($\frac{3}{4}$ in.)	17 mm	($\frac{2}{3}$ in.)
20.5 mm	($\frac{13}{16}$ in.)	19 mm	($\frac{3}{4}$ in.)
22.5 mm	($\frac{7}{8}$ in.)	21 mm	($\frac{13}{16}$ in.)
25.5 mm	(1 in.)	24 mm	($\frac{15}{16}$ in.)

Lumber Dimensions

NOMINAL — U.S.	ACTUAL — U.S. (IN INCHES)	METRIC
1 × 2	$\frac{3}{4}$ × $1\frac{1}{2}$	19 × 38 mm
1 × 3	$\frac{3}{4}$ × $2\frac{1}{2}$	19 × 64 mm
1 × 4	$\frac{3}{4}$ × $3\frac{1}{2}$	19 × 89 mm
1 × 5	$\frac{3}{4}$ × $4\frac{1}{2}$	19 × 114 mm
1 × 6	$\frac{3}{4}$ × $5\frac{1}{2}$	19 × 140 mm
1 × 7	$\frac{3}{4}$ × $6\frac{1}{4}$	19 × 159 mm
1 × 8	$\frac{3}{4}$ × $7\frac{1}{4}$	19 × 184 mm
1 × 10	$\frac{3}{4}$ × $9\frac{1}{4}$	19 × 235 mm
1 × 12	$\frac{3}{4}$ × $11\frac{1}{4}$	19 × 286 mm
$1\frac{1}{4}$ × 4	1 × $3\frac{1}{2}$	25 × 89 mm
$1\frac{1}{4}$ × 6	1 × $5\frac{1}{2}$	25 × 140 mm
$1\frac{1}{4}$ × 8	1 × $7\frac{1}{4}$	25 × 184 mm
$1\frac{1}{4}$ × 10	1 × $9\frac{1}{4}$	25 × 235 mm
$1\frac{1}{4}$ × 12	1 × $11\frac{1}{4}$	25 × 286 mm
$1\frac{1}{2}$ × 4	$1\frac{1}{4}$ × $3\frac{1}{2}$	32 × 89 mm
$1\frac{1}{2}$ × 6	$1\frac{1}{4}$ × $5\frac{1}{2}$	32 × 140 mm
$1\frac{1}{2}$ × 8	$1\frac{1}{4}$ × $7\frac{1}{4}$	32 × 184 mm
$1\frac{1}{2}$ × 10	$1\frac{1}{4}$ × $9\frac{1}{4}$	32 × 235 mm
$1\frac{1}{2}$ × 12	$1\frac{1}{4}$ × $11\frac{1}{4}$	32 × 286 mm
2 × 4	$1\frac{1}{2}$ × $3\frac{1}{2}$	38 × 89 mm
2 × 6	$1\frac{1}{2}$ × $5\frac{1}{2}$	38 × 140 mm
2 × 8	$1\frac{1}{2}$ × $7\frac{1}{4}$	38 × 184 mm
2 × 10	$1\frac{1}{2}$ × $9\frac{1}{4}$	38 × 235 mm
2 × 12	$1\frac{1}{2}$ × $11\frac{1}{4}$	38 × 286 mm
3 × 6	$2\frac{1}{2}$ × $5\frac{1}{2}$	64 × 140 mm
4 × 4	$3\frac{1}{2}$ × $3\frac{1}{2}$	89 × 89 mm
4 × 6	$3\frac{1}{2}$ × $5\frac{1}{2}$	89 × 140 mm

Liquid Measurement Equivalents

1 Pint	= 16 Fluid Ounces	= 2 Cups
1 Quart	= 32 Fluid Ounces	= 2 Pints
1 Gallon	= 128 Fluid Ounces	= 4 Quarts

RESOURCES

TOOLS, MATERIALS + GEAR
Black & Decker (US), Inc.
www.blackanddecker.com

OUTDOOR PLAY + ENTERTAINMENT
CedarWorks
www.cedarworks.com

Consumer Product Safety Commission
www.cpsc.gov

Detailed Play Systems
www.detailedplay.com

GameTime
www.gametime.com

Gorilla Playsets
gorillaplaysets.com

National Program for Playground Safety
www.playgroundsafety.org

Playgrounds & Playground Equipment
www.playstarinc.com

RubberScapes
www.rubberscapes.net

Safe Kids
www.safekids.org

Surface America
www.surfaceamerica.com

Swing Kingdom
www.swingkingdom.com

Swingsetmall.com
www.swingsetmall.com

SHEDS + OUTDOOR STRUCTURES
Arrow Storage Products
www.arrowsheds.com

Asphalt Roofing Manufacturers Association
www.asphaltroofing.org

Best Barns
www.bettersheds.com

Cedarshed Industries
www.cedarshed.com

Finley Products, Inc.
www.2x4basics.com

Jamaica Cottage Shop
www.jamaicacottageshop.com

Outdoor Living Today
www.outdoorlivingtoday.com

Reeds Ferry Small Buildings, Inc.
www.reedsferry.com

Simpson Strong-Tie Co.
www.strongtie.com

Summerwood Products
www.summerwood.com

Suncast Homeplace Collection
www.suncast.com/homeplacecollection

Tuff Shed
www.tuffshed.com

WALKWAYS, PATIOS + DECKS
American Society of Landscape Architects
www.asla.org

AZEK Building Products
www.azek.com

Belgard Hardscapes
www.belgard.com

The Brick Industry Association
www.gobrick.com

Common Ground Alliance
www.call811.com

Portland Cement Association
www.cement.org

Quikrete
www.quikrete.com

WALLS + CEILINGS
Fypon Ltd.
Urethane Millwork
www.fypon.com

Masking Paper and 3M Hand-Masker
www.3m.com

The Steel Network, Inc.
Curved Steel Track
www.steelnetwork.com

STONE WALLS + FENCES
The Masonry Society
www.masonrysociety.org

National Concrete Masonry Association
www.ncma.org

Southern Pine Council
www.southernpine.com

WINDOWS + DOORS
Access One, Inc
www.lifewaymobility.com

Andersen Windows, Inc.
www.andersenwindows.com

The Bilco Company
www.bilco.com

Designer Doors
www.cambek.com

JELD-WEN, Inc.
www.jeld-wen.com

Kolbe Windows & Doors
www.kolbewindows.com

Kwikset Corporation
www.kwikset.com

Larson Manufacturing
www.larsondoors.com

Marvin Windows and Doors
www.marvin.com

Milgard Windows
www.milgard.com

Roto Frank of America
roto-frank.com/us

Simpson Door Company
www.simpsondoor.com

VELUX America, Inc.
www.velux-america.com

Wheatbelt, Inc.
www.rollupshutter.com

INDEX